CW00621370

About the author

Catriona Bass is a Tibet specialist who has taught in China (at Hubei University in Wuhan) and in the Tibet Autonomous Region (TAR). In the 1980s, she worked for the Lhasa City Government Education Department and the TAR Academy of Social Sciences. Now based in Oxford, she works as a consultant specializing in Tibetan affairs. She has addressed the European Parliament and the United Nations on educational development in the TAR. She is the author of *Inside the Treasure House: A Time in Tibet* (Victor Gollancz, 1990) and contributed to *Tibet, a Collection of Essays* (Reidar Verlag, Germany, 1992).

Tibet Information Network

The Tibet Information Network (TIN) is an independent news and research service that collects and distributes information on what is happening in Tibet. Set up in 1987 and based in London, TIN monitors social, economic, political, environmental and human rights conditions in Tibet and then publishes the information in the form of e-mailed or faxed news updates, briefing papers and analytical reports, details of which are carried on the pages of TIN's own Website. Its information comes from a variety of sources inside and outside Tibet as well as from interviews with Tibetan refugees and the monitoring of established Chinese and international sources, including radio and television broadcasts and printed material.

Addresses for the Tibet Information Network:

TIN UK: City Cloisters, 188–196 Old Street, London EC1V 9FR, UK

Tel: (+44) 171 814 9011
Fax: (+44) 171 814 9015
e-mail: tin@tibetinfo.net

TIN USA: PO Box 2270, Jackson, WY83001, USA

Tel: (+1) 307 733 4670
Fax: (+1) 307 739 2501
e-mail: tinusa@wyoming.com

http://www.tibetinfo.net

The Tibet Information Network Trust is registered as a charity in the UK (No. 1057648) and as a non-profit organisation in the USA (Federal IRS number 94-3192461).

Education in Tibet
Policy and Practice since 1950

Catriona Bass

Tibet Information Network
LONDON

Zed Books
LONDON AND NEW YORK

Education in Tibet: Policy and Practice since 1950 was first published by Zed Books Ltd, 7 Cynthia Street, London N1 9JF, UK and Room 400, 175 Fifth Avenue, New York, NY 10010, USA in 1998 in association with Tibet Information Network, City Cloisters, 188–196 Old Street, London EC1V 9FR.

Distributed exclusively in the USA by St Martin's Press, Inc., 175 Fifth Avenue, New York, NY 10010, USA.

Cover designed by Andrew Corbett
Set in Monotype Dante by Ewan Smith
Printed and bound in the United Kingdom
by Biddles Ltd, Guildford and King's Lynn

A catalogue record for this book is available from the British Library

ISBN 1 85649 673 2 cased
ISBN 1 85649 674 0 limp

Library of Congress Cataloging-in-Publication Data
Bass, Catriona.
    Education in Tibet: policy and practice since 1950 /
Catriona Bass.
        p.   cm.
    Includes bibliographical references and index.
    ISBN 1-85649-673-2. — ISBN 1-85649-674-0 (pbk.)
    1. Education and state—China—Tibet. 2. Education–
–China—Tibet. 3. Education and state—China. 4. Education–
–China—Tibet. 5. Tibetans—Education—China.   I. Title.
LC94.C5837   1998
379.414–dc21   98–36349
                                                  CIP

Contents

Tables, Boxes, Figures and Maps

Tables

Boxes

Figures

Maps

Acknowledgements

In writing this book, the work of a number of scholars and educationalists has been of great benefit and guidance. Some of the most important work comes from inside the TAR and China; the greatest debt of gratitude is therefore owed to those authors. However, for reasons of security, in some instances the title of a research paper or government document has not been cited, in order to protect the author. In other cases the author has not been cited even if the material is publicly available in China. This is because when material is considered controversial, publicity in the West is likely to jeopardize its author's position in China. For similar reasons, some of the interviews are not given full titles.

I am grateful to the Barrow Cadbury Trust for the grant it made to TIN while this project was in progress. I am also grateful to Professor Keith Lewin for making available to me his report for UNESCO on *Implementing Basic Education in China*, and to Hugh Richardson for his comments on education in Tibet before 1950. I would like to thank Robbie Barnett, John Bray, Jim Lixian and Tsering Shakya for their advice on the manuscript, Ann Carr and Victoria Conner for assistance with the maps, tables and graphs and Louise Fournier for general advice and support while the project was in progress. I am grateful to Susie Barker and Harley Evans for taking the author photograph. Finally, I would like to thank the Barrow Cadbury Trust for funding several education projects for Tibetan and Chinese students over the past ten years.

Preface

China has the largest student body in the world with over 188 million students in school. Tibetans in the Tibet Autonomous Region (TAR) make up around 260,000 of this body, only 0.1 per cent. However, the nature of their history over the last forty-six years, continuing scrutiny by the Dalai Lama's government-in-exile in India and the particular interest of the West have led the Chinese government to focus more public attention on the education of Tibetans in the TAR than on other so-called minority nationalities in China.

This makes the researcher's task both easier and more difficult. It is easier because the positive developments in Tibetan education are well documented and easily accessible. However, because of the political debate over Tibetan independence, and because education in the 1990s has come to be viewed as a battleground in that debate, critical discussion of the education system is politically sensitive in the TAR, to a far greater extent than in other parts of China. This is particularly the case when the discussion involves foreign parties. No detailed field research by foreign educationalists has been permitted in the TAR.[1] Furthermore, research documents and government planning documents, particularly relating to culturally specific education – the kind of material that is available to foreign educationalists studying other parts of China – are classified documents in the TAR.

This book is therefore a preliminary study; it is the first full-length account of education in the TAR published outside China. While it does not present a theoretical treatise or an over-arching conceptual theme, it aims to provide a description of developments in education since 1950 and an analysis of education policy and implementation. At the same time, it is designed as a handbook for those with a more practical need to understand the education system and administrative structure at each level of education. Every chapter contains basic facts about different aspects of the system with translations from Chinese and Tibetan of important terminology. The Appendices include salient policy documents as well as a transcript of an important Lhasa TV debate.

The primary research for the book is based on extensive interviews carried out over the past twelve years with Tibetans, Han Chinese and westerners who have worked in the region. Further analysis of policy and implementation has been based on a number of unpublished government documents as well as on published and unpublished statistical data; it has also been informed by the author's personal experience of working in the 1980s as a teacher at Hubei University in Wuhan, and subsequently for the Lhasa City Government Education Department and the Tibetan Academy of Social Sciences. The book provides a survey of recent literature on education in the TAR by Tibetan and Chinese educationalists and officials. The text includes extensive extracts from the research of Tibetan and Chinese scholars. There are two reasons for this: the first is that little of this research has been published outside China; the second is to give readers an idea of the extent of the debate over education that is taking place inside the TAR and China. This is particularly important with regard to the TAR since China's monolithic political system often makes outsiders unaware that considerable debate (albeit within certain parameters) does occur within the confines of Chinese society.

The TAR (*Xizang Zizhiqu*) was set up by the Chinese government in 1965 and covers the area of Tibet, west of the Yangtse River, which was previously under the jurisdiction of the Dalai Lama's government, and is often referred to as central Tibet in English. After 1949, other Tibetan-inhabited areas were incorporated in the neighbouring Chinese provinces of Qinghai, Gansu, Sichuan and Yunnan. Where Tibetan communities were said to have 'compact inhabitancy' in these provinces they were designated autonomous Tibetan prefectures. There are significant differences between the TAR and these autonomous Tibetan prefectures in both education policy and its implementation with regard to Tibetans. Where information is available we make references to and comparisons with these areas; however, a detailed analysis of educational provision for Tibetans outside the TAR is beyond the scope of this study.

The main purpose of this book is to look at the development of education in the TAR within the framework of education in China as a whole. Its aim is to provide a context for people approaching the subject from two directions: for those concerned primarily with Tibet and for those coming from the perspective of the education system in China. At present, discussion in the West of education in Tibet tends to be restricted to a recitation of the shortcomings of the system – poor provision, underfunding, low enrolment and discrimination against Tibetans – with little explanation of the background to these problems. This book, by comparing conditions found in the TAR with developments in the rest of China and (where information is available) against other provinces with Tibetan populations, aims to give a sense of where conditions are unique to the TAR and where they are the result of education strategies affecting the whole of China. The intention is, thereby, to provide a broader basis upon which the achievements and failings of the system can be discussed. This book also seeks to present a case study (albeit with a broad brush) of a so-called 'minority' nationality area of China to which few Western educationalists have had access. It is thus also intended for those who are familiar with the trends in education in China as a whole but who may lack a detailed knowledge of how these trends affect China's extremities. Its second aim, therefore, is to fill in a corner of the vast picture that is the education system in China.

Note on names

Names are given in the English phonetic spelling of Tibetan names where appropriate, with Chinese pinyin spelling in brackets.

Note

1. A number of foreign sociologists, agriculturalists and historians have been able to undertake limited fieldwork in the TAR in recent years, and foreign educationalists have been permitted to work in Tibetan prefectures of other provinces where the political situation is deemed to be more stable.

Abbreviations

China	area now comprising the People's Republic of China
CCP	Chinese Communist Party
CPPCC	Chinese People's Political Consultative Conference
FBIS	Foreign Broadcast Information Service
NGO	non-governmental organization
NPC	National People's Congress
PCART	Preparatory Committee for the Establishment of the Autonomous Region of Tibet
SWB	Summary of World Broadcasts
TAR	Tibet Autonomous Region
TIN	Tibet Information Network

Introduction

Around the seventh century, a formal system of religious education began to be developed in Tibet. It started as a private system with individual religious teachers giving instruction to small groups, often travelling from place to place followed by their disciples. Later, around 860CE, the first monasteries were established and an institutionalized form of religious education was introduced for the first time. The private system of religious tutelage continued alongside the monastic system. It was particularly important for the training of girls, who might join a nunnery after their formal education had finished at the age of sixteen, or who might simply remain with their gurus, following them as they gave teachings throughout Tibet. By 1694CE, around 26 per cent of Tibetan males and 13 per cent of the total population were living in Tibet's monasteries. By no means all of them, however, were scholars or 'readers' (*pecawa*) as they were known in Tibetan.[1] Most were manual labourers servicing the needs of the monastic community who, typically, were educated to the extent that they were able to read or chant their prayer books.[2]

Outside the monasteries, the Tibetan government ran only two schools in Tibet, both of which were in Lhasa. One was the *Tse Laptra* for training boys who were to become ecclesiastical officials in the government, the other was a school run by the *Tsikhang* (the Finance Office) where the children of the aristocracy were taught accounting, calligraphy, law and etiquette for entry into government service.[3] Apart from these two government schools, secular education was based on a private tutorial system established by the traditional elite for the education of their children. Wealthy landowners or traders would make arrangements with religious or lay scholars to educate their sons and daughters in basic literacy and numeracy. Some families would gather a number of children together, sometimes educating the children of their servants, and, in the towns of Lhasa, Shigatse and Gyantse, small schools were established on this basis.[4] The teachers often came from the families of junior civil servants, in which the tradition of teaching had been passed down from generation to generation. They did not receive a fixed salary but the students' parents would offer various gifts according to their means and the students themselves would perform domestic duties in return for tuition.[5] By the 1930s, some wealthier Tibetans were inviting teachers from abroad to educate their children; others sent their children to British public schools established by the Raj at the hill stations of Darjeeling and Kalimpong in India.

At the beginning of the twentieth century, the Tibetan government itself, under the Thirteenth Dalai Lama, made a number of short-lived attempts to develop a modern secular education system in Tibet. In 1912, the Thirteenth Dalai sent four boys from Tibetan aristocratic families to be educated at Rugby School in England. The experiment did not prove a great success and no more Tibetan children went to Britain for schooling, primarily because their parents were reluctant to send them so far away.[6] Thus, a few years later, a British educationalist, Frank Ladlow, was invited by the Tibetan government to establish a school in Gyantse, based on the English public school system. The school opened in December 1923 but ran for only three years.[7] A similar government school project, set up by a Mr Parker in Lhasa in 1944, ran for a mere six months before it too was closed.[8] From the outset, these foreign secular establishments had faced considerable opposition from traditional conservative groups among the clergy and aristocracy. It was believed that the schools would be vehicles for introducing Western ideas into Tibet, and would undermine Tibet's cultural and religious traditions. One of the popular sayings current in the capital at the time, ran: 'In the holy city of Lhasa there is an unholy school.'

This was the situation in 1950 when the Chinese People's Liberation Army entered Tibet with the declared aim of 'liberating the Tibetan masses', reunifying Tibet with the motherland, and introducing modernity into Tibetan society. Official Chinese sources estimate the illiteracy rate to have been 90 per cent in 1951.[9] While this can only be a guess, at best, secular education was undoubtedly the preserve of the Tibetan elite. In 1951, the new Chinese government signed a treaty with the Tibetan government known as the 'Agreement of the Central People's Government and the Local Government of Tibet on Measures for the Peaceful Liberation of Tibet'.[10] This treaty included a pledge to develop education in Tibet 'step by step in accordance with actual conditions'.[11]

Compared with achievements in education in China as a whole over the past fifty years, the development of a modern education system in the TAR has been slow. According to official statistics, illiteracy and semi-illiteracy still stand at 60 per cent; the enrolment rate in junior secondary school is 12.5 per cent;[12] enrolment in primary schools is 67 per cent but is lower than 10 per cent in some rural prefectures.[13] It is the background to these official statistics that this book sets out to explore.[14]

Since the communist government came to power in China, the direction of education and priorities in funding have changed, often abruptly, with the shifts in the political climate. Broadly speaking, the focus of education development has swung between one strategy that makes quality in education a priority and another strategy that puts emphasis on quantity, i.e. meeting the mass educational needs of workers and peasants. The 'quality' strategy emphasizes academic and technical education, while the 'quantity' strategy prioritizes ideological, revolutionary training. Thus the two types of education came to be known as 'red' and 'expert' – qualities which would, in an ideal world, be combined but which, in fact, have been more or less in conflict over the past fifty years. In the so-called 'minority' nationality areas of China, such as the TAR, the conflict between these two strategies has played a direct role in education. Here, however, there is an additional strategy that has shaped the development of education. Education for 'minority' nationalities has the primary political goal of instilling a sense of com-mitment to the unity of China – the 'ancestral land' (*zuguo*) – and encouraging patriotism towards it.[15]

Chapters 1–4 trace the development of education in China and the TAR from 1950 to 1998, charting the changes in direction from the 'quality' strategy promoted in the early 1950s, the early 1960s, and again in the 1980s, to the 'quantity' strategy promoted during the Great Leap Forward (1958–59) and the Cultural Revolution decade (1966–76). The extent to which these strategies affected educational developments in the TAR is discussed, alongside the specific impact of the 1959 Lhasa Uprising against Chinese rule, the flight of the Dalai Lama to India, and the Cultural Revolution in the TAR when all aspects of Tibetan culture in the curriculum came under attack, including the Tibetan language.

The end of the Cultural Revolution marked a return to 'quality'-oriented educational policies which were aimed at promoting the rapid economic development of China but which included renewed recogni-tion of the diverse cultural needs of China's different nationalities. In the TAR, plans were drawn up to implement Tibetan medium education for Tibetans and to devise a curriculum that was more relevant to their lives. At the same time, the return to a 'quality'-oriented education policy in China set up a series of priorities in the funding of education, where urban education took precedence over rural education, the train-ing of the educational elite took precedence over mass education, and higher education took precedence over primary education. Furthermore, new plans for the economy made investment in the more developed eastern regions of China a priority over rural western provinces; the economic development of the TAR was scheduled for the mid-1990s.

By the end of the 1980s it had become clear that the rapid change to a market economy and the decentralization of education funding had wrought havoc on the education system, leading Deng Xiaoping to say in 1989: 'The greatest mistake we made in the last ten years was in education.' There has been much debate in China over what Deng Xiaoping meant by the great mistake. Some took it to be a reflection on the problems of the provision of education.[16] It was also widely taken to mean that education in the previous ten years had failed to produce loyal citizens: that 'bourgeois liberalism' in education was responsible for the nationalist unrest in non-Han Chinese regions such as the TAR, and the pro-democracy campaigns in Central China. After the re-emergence of pro-independence demonstrations in the TAR in the late 1980s, the primary political role of 'minority' education was reasserted. The consequence of this was that the concessions made in the early 1980s to Tibetan language education and to a culturally relevant curriculum were partially eroded. At the same time, the renewed emphasis on the notion of the unity of nationalities (*minzu tuanjie*) resulted in the abandonment of some of the preferential policies designed to increase the enrolment of Tibetans in secondary and higher education, on the grounds that they caused tension between nationalities.

The second part of this book provides detailed analysis of each level of education. Chapters 5 to 10 trace the impact of economic and ideological educational policies on primary, secondary and tertiary education in the TAR since 1980. These chapters focus on issues such as funding, quality of provision, enrolment, drop-out, the curriculum, the medium of instruction and the conditions for Tibetan children in education. Chapter 11 provides a discussion of teachers and teaching in the TAR, with particular reference to the problems of recruitment and high turnover of staff, and to the deterioration in teaching quality, which occurred towards the end of the 1980s. In this chapter, the efforts made by the TAR government to improve teacher training in the 1990s are also discussed, including the particular problem of training teachers to teach in Tibetan.

One of the most controversial issues in education in the TAR is the medium of instruction in schools. Since the first constitution of the PRC, the 1949 Common Programme, the language rights of all China's nationalities have been enshrined in Chinese law. However, because language is so closely connected with national identity it has borne the brunt of attacks against non-Han Chinese culture during 'leftist' periods in China's history over the last five decades. In the early 1980s, the Chinese government made attempts to reinstate Tibetan as the official language of the TAR. Given that the majority of the population in the TAR does not speak Chinese, the use of Tibetan was deemed to be important not just for the preservation of Tibetan culture but for economic development and for the dissemination of government policy and information. However, despite the law and government directives on the use of 'minority' languages, the implementation of the Tibetan language policy has been relatively unsuccessful. In 1991, at the Conference on Tibetan Language Teaching, TAR Deputy Party Secretary Tenzin described the implementation of the Tibetan language policy as 'not working and at a stalemate'.[17]

The final chapter provides a discussion of the controversy surrounding the medium of instruction in schools in the TAR, which began after the 1984 Second Tibet Work Forum (Second Forum) with the introduction of Tibetan medium instruction at primary level for Tibetan children. Policy documents drawn up at this time included the gradual extension of Tibetan medium teaching for Tibetans into secondary education. However, these were never implemented and all secondary education continues to be taught in Chinese. This dislocation between primary and secondary education lies at the centre of the present debate over Tibetan language education. In this chapter, the views of the two groups that have emerged over the issue are examined, as are the various practical steps each side has taken to find a resolution. One group advocates the importance of further developing Tibetan as the language of education and commerce including the extension of Tibetan medium education up to tertiary level; the other group argues for increasing the teaching of Chinese at primary level.[18] The views of the first group, which has included Tibetan officials such as TAR Party Secretary Wu Jinghua, the late Tenth Panchen Lama, Hu Yaobang, Yin Fatang, Li Peng, Ngapo Ngawang Jigme, Dorje Tsering, Dorje Tseten, and Tenzin, acquired dominance in the mid-1980s. Proponents of the second strategy include TAR Party Secretary Chen Kuiyuan and Executive Deputy Party Secretary Ragdi. In the political climate of the 1990s, in which the Chinese government's response to Tibetan nationalism has led to a gradual de-emphasis of Tibetan language and culture in education, the views of this second faction came to dominate the TAR government's education policy.

Notes

1. Melvyn Goldstein, *A History of Modern Tibet, 1913–1951, The Demise of the Lamaist State* (University of California Press, 1989), p. 21.

2. Goldstein cites the example of Mey College in Sera Monastery, outside Lhasa, where 29 per cent of the monks were 'readers'. Ibid., p. 24.

3. Charles Bell, *The People of Tibet* (Oxford University Press, 1968), p. 205.

4. Ibid., pp. 201–2. See also the Chinese educationalist Yang Wanli. He states that before 1951 there were '100 private schools, household schools and old-style government-run schools in the region, with 3,000 students'. Yang Wanli, '*Xizang Kecheng Jiaocai Yanjiu De Teshuxing Jiqi Duice*' (The Countermeasure and Particularity of Research on Teaching Materials), *Xizang Yanjiu* (Tibet Studies), Vol. 58, No. 1, 1996.

5. Interview with Tibetan historian, August 1996; see also Bell, *The People of Tibet*, pp. 201–2.

6. See Tsering Shakya, 'Making of the Great Game Players: Tibetan Students in Britain between 1913–1917', *Tibetan Review*, Vol. 21, No. 1, 1986.

7. Alex McKay, *Tibet and the British Raj: The Frontier Cadre, 1904–1947* (Curzon Press, 1997), pp. 115–18.

8. Alastair Lamb, *Tibet, China & India 1914–1950: A History of Imperial Diplomacy* (Roxford Books, 1989), pp. 336–7.

9. See: *Tibet: From 1951 to 1991* (New Star Publisher, Beijing, 1991), p. 85.

10. The Tibetan government later said that the treaty had been signed under duress. For further details on the Seventeen-Point Agreement see: Tsering Shakya, 'The Genesis of the Sino-Tibetan Agreement of 1951', in Per Kvaerne (ed.), *Tibetan Studies. Proceedings of the 6th International Conference of Tibetan Studies, Fagernes, Norway* (Institute of Comparative Research in Human Culture, Oslo, 1994), pp. 739–54.

11. 'Agreement of the Central People's Government and the Local Government of Tibet on Measures for the Peaceful Liberation of Tibet', *Xinhua*, 27 May 1951.

12. 'Outline of the TAR's Five-Year Plan for Economic and Social Development and Its Long-term Target for 2010, Approved by the Fourth Session of the Sixth Regional People's Congress on 24th May 1996', *Xizang Ribao* (Tibet Daily), 7 June 1996, pp. 1–4 (TAR 9th Five-Year Plan, 1996); 'Outline of the TAR Child Development Programme for the 1990s', *Xizang Ribao* (Tibet Daily), 11 November 1996, p. 2 (TAR Child Development Programme); 1990 TAR Statistical Yearbook.

13. Pama Namgyal, '*Xianjieduan Xizang Zongjiao de Diwei He Zuoyong*' (Lamaism in the Tibet Autonomous Region), *Xizang Yanjiu* (Tibet Studies) No. 1, 1989; trans. in J. Seymour and Eugen Werli (eds), *Chinese Sociology & Anthropology, A Journal of Translations*, Spring 1994, p. 70.

14. The accuracy of official statistics in China is sometimes questioned as having a tendency to exaggerate achievements; those compiled during the Cultural Revolution are considered to be particularly unreliable. Official

statistics have been used quite extensively in this text, with caution, but in the belief that they indicate general trends and do not underestimate achievements.

15. Bernhard Dilger, 'The Education of Minorities', *Comparative Education*, Vol. 20, No. 1, 1984, p. 156.

16. See Dalu Yin, 'Reforming Chinese Education: Context, Structure and Attitudes in 1980s', *Compare*, Vol. 23, No. 2, 1993, p. 124; see also Samuel Wang, 'Teaching Patriotism in China', *China Strategic Review*, Vol. 1, No. 3, 1997.

17. Tenzin (TAR Deputy Party Secretary), 'Report of Speech to First Regional Conference on Tibetan Language Teaching', 16–21 July 1991, *Xizang Ribao* (Tibet Daily), 23 July 1991.

18. See TAR Deputy Party Secretary Tenzin, Speech to Meeting of TAR Guiding Committee on Spoken and Written Tibetan, 16 March 1993, in Duojie Caidan (Dorje Tseten) *Xizang Jiaoyu* (Education in Tibet) (China Tibetology Publishers, Beijing, 1991); Chen Kuiyuan, 'Speech on Literature and Art', *Xizang Ribao* (Tibet Daily), 11 July 1997; 'Raidi and Gyaltsen Norbu Summarize Third Tibet Work Forum Conclusions', *Xizang Ribao* (Tibet Daily), 2 August 1994 [SWB 21/8/94].

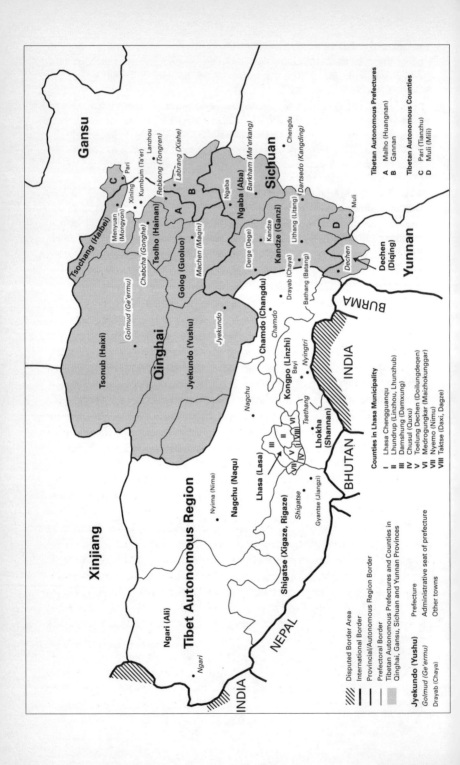

CHAPTER I

Background

Educating China's 'minority' nationalities

China has fifty-five recognized nationalities in addition to the majority Han Chinese. Some of these nationalities have fewer than 2,000 members, others have several million. The Chinese government refers to the non-Han nationalities as *shaoshu minzu*, 'minority nationalities' or simply 'minorities'. When looking at statistical data on an area such as the TAR, this terminology can be confusing since Tibetans, for example, are referred to as *shaoshu minzu* even although they form the majority of the population. The issue has become politically sensitive in recent years, with the result that the term 'nationalities' is now sometimes officially used as being less offensive, hence *Minzu Xueyuan* (Nationalities Institute).[1] Similarly, westerners tend to refer to the Han as simply Chinese. This is not tolerated by the Chinese government since they claim that all the nationalities that make up the People's Republic of China are Chinese (*Zhonghua minzu*); that is, Tibetans, Mongolians, Uigurs, Han and so on are all Chinese. In this book, for the sake of clarity, since it includes official statistical tables, I have chosen to use the terms Tibetan (Tib: *Purik*, Ch: *Zangzu*) and Han Chinese (Tib: *Gemi*, Ch: *Hanzu*).

In total, the 'minority' nationalities of China are about 80 million people, or 8 per cent of the whole population, and in the areas where these nationalities were said to have 'compact inhabitancy as an ethnic group',[2] the Chinese government established five so-called autonomous regions: Guangxi Zhuang Autonomous Region, Inner Mongolia Autonomous Region, Ningxia Hui Autonomous Region, Tibet Autonomous Region and Xinjiang Uigur Autonomous Region. In addition, there are thirty-one autonomous prefectures and sixty-nine autonomous counties throughout China.

The education of the non-Han Chinese nationalities has generally been of greater significance than their numbers would suggest. The reasons for this are both political and economic. Between 50 and 60 per cent of China's territory is occupied by non-Han nationalities (the TAR alone accounts for around 13 per cent),[3] much of this territory is in sensitive border regions, and several nationalities have kinsmen in neighbouring countries. Furthermore, most of the areas inhabited by non-Han Chinese nationalities are rich in minerals and contain a large proportion of China's forest and grasslands.[4] Describing the TAR in 1980, the Minister of Nationalities Affairs, Yang Jingren, wrote:

> On the one hand, it is high, cold, lacks oxygen, and living and working conditions are hard. More importantly, however, it covers an extensive area with wide grasslands, rich forests and water resources; there are many important underground minerals. It can be called a big treasure land of the motherland ... From a long-term point of view, Tibet has a huge potential and big prospects for development. It will make a very important contribution to the socialist construction of the motherland once it is developed.[5]

For China's stability and prosperity, therefore, it is vitally important that all its nationalities identify with China. This has always been stated as the major political reason for promoting 'minority education'. From the outset, the policy for 'minority education' (*minzu jiaoyu*) differed from the education policy for Han Chinese which is termed 'regular education' (*zhenggui jiaoyu*). While Han Chinese were to be educated to provide technical personnel for economic development, the overriding goal of education for 'minority' nationalities was to encourage political allegiance towards China and enhance stability in border areas; this principle still underpins China's education policy in the TAR.[6] In a paper on the curriculum in the TAR in 1996, Yang Wanli wrote: 'The curriculum for both higher and basic education must depend on whether it can guarantee the unity and territorial integrity of the country; the curriculum is directly connected with the question of the "stability" of the whole country.'[7]

Nevertheless, despite the Chinese government's commitment to 'minority education' in principle, educational levels among the non-Han Chinese nationalities of China are in fact lower than for the population as a whole.[8] Table 1.1 shows that while educational levels are higher than the national level among 'minority' nationalities in the Inner Mongolia Autonomous Region, in the other four autonomous regions they are significantly lower. In the TAR, educational levels are lower than in any region in China. In 1990, of the TAR's Tibetan and other non-Han nationalities,[9] 21.92 per cent had received primary education, compared with the national figure for non-Han nationalities of 43.47 per cent. Furthermore, the higher the educational level, the greater the discrepancy between the TAR and China as a whole. In

Table 1.1 Educational attainment of the non-Han Chinese population in the five autonomous regions and in the whole of China compared with the total population, 1990 (percentages)

Educational attainment	Total	Non-Han Chinese					
	China	China	TAR	Inner Mongolia	Guangxi	Ningxia	Xinjiang
University degree	0.63	0.42	0.09	0.80	0.19	0.28	0.54
Technical university degree	0.97	0.64	0.25	1.31	0.43	0.58	0.62
Senior secondary (vocational)	1.72	1.62	1.02	2.83	1.35	1.10	2.25
Senior secondary (general)	7.30	5.16	0.47	9.97	5.17	3.33	4.87
Junior secondary	26.44	18.80	2.96	26.06	19.49	13.97	16.21
Primary	44.63	43.47	21.92	41.17	52.96	32.98	51.94
Illiterate/semi-illiterate	18.31	29.86	73.27	17.86	20.41	47.75	23.56
Illiterate/semi-illiterate (women)		39.20	84.22	21.92	30.03	61.40	25.65

Sources: Specialized Plan for the TAR Territory, 1993 (Internal government document); Tabulation on China's Minority Nationalities (1990 Population Census), May 1994.

1990, 2.96 per cent of Tibetans and other non-Han nationalities in the TAR had received junior secondary school education compared with 18.8 per cent of the non-Han population of China, and 26.44 per cent of the total population of China. At the tertiary level, the figures show an even greater discrepancy: by 1990, only 0.09 per cent of Tibetans and other non-Han nationalities in the TAR had received a university education. This compares with 0.42 per cent of all non-Han Chinese nationalities in China, and 0.63 per cent of the whole population.

The low educational levels in the TAR are due to a combination of historical, political, geographical and economic factors. [10] As mentioned earlier, when the Communists came to power in 1949, the Tibetan government was providing education mainly through the monasteries unlike, for example, China's Korean population which, having no dominant religious preference, had developed a substantial secular educational infrastructure. [11] Since Tibetan monasteries were seen by the Chinese government as one of the greatest obstacles to modernization, as well as being the bastions of 'feudal' power, education had to be shifted to secular educational establishments of which there were very few. Geographically, the TAR is one of the most inaccessible regions in China; much of the land is mountainous and has an extremely low population density. Such factors increase the cost of education in the region and have consequently contributed to its slow development. But by far the most significant factor in the low levels of education is economic. [12] The non-Han nationalities in China whose educational levels equal or exceed those of the Han Chinese population live in areas where there is a well-developed industrial infrastructure and where there is relatively high investment in education. [13] The economy of the TAR is less developed than in any region in China, and investment in education has been correspondingly low over the last fifty years.

Education and the economy in China

China is today one of the world's biggest producers; it has one of the largest current account surpluses, and its foreign reserves are exceeded in Asia only by Taiwan and Japan. In 1993, Southern China recorded annual growth rates of around 25 per cent. [14] However, although China is a giant in terms of GNP, in terms of GNP per capita its vast population puts it among the twenty-four poorest countries in the world: in 1992, its per capita GNP was $380. [15] In this context, therefore, providing education for its 1.2 billion people is a monumental task. Although considerable advances have been made since the 1950s, with the enrolment rate in primary education increasing from 49 per

Figure 1.1 Education expenditure in China as a percentage of GDP,
1978–94 (*Source*: 1995 China Statistical Yearbook)

cent to 98 per cent,[16] China still ranks 101st of 120 countries in the
number of university students per 10,000 inhabitants; there are estim-
ated to be 20 million children waiting to enter primary schools every
year, and over 4 million school drop-outs. [17]

Historically, investment in education in China has been low, and
today it is still low even by the standards of developing countries. Most
countries allocate around 5 per cent of GDP to education.[18] In 1992,
according to statistics presented in UNESCO's *World Education Indicators*,
of the 153 countries tabulated, China came 145th, allocating 2 per cent
of its GNP to education.[19] This percentage is less than recommended
by reports commissioned in recent years by the Chinese government.[20]
In 1993, the 'Programme for China's Educational Reform and Development', issued by the Central Committee and the State Council, directed
that the state funding of education should represent 4 per cent of GDP
towards the end of the century.[21] Other Chinese educationalists argue
that if the percentage of education expenditure does not rise to 6 per
cent or 7 per cent of GDP, education will not be able to fulfil its
strategic objectives of promoting economic development by the end of
the century.[22] However, China, unlike most countries around the world,
has chosen not to enshrine in law the percentage of GDP that should
be spent on education.[23] Despite the plans outlined in the 1993 'Programme for China's Educational Reform and Development', which
includes the statement that 'we should ensure stable sources and the
growth of funds for education through legislation', the 1995 Education

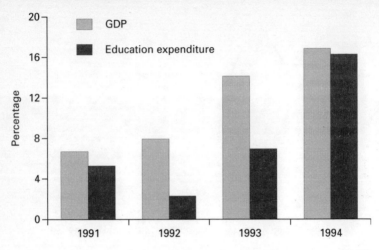

Figure 1.2 Growth of education expenditure in China compared with growth of GDP, 1991–94 (*Source*: 1995 China Statistical Yearbook)

Law is unspecific about education funding, stating only that funding should be 'gradually increased', the amount being stipulated by the State Council.[24] In reality, investment in education has never even come close to the target ratios. In fact, the percentage of GDP invested in education has been declining in recent years, falling from 2.69 per cent in 1986 to 2.18 per cent in 1994 (see Figure 1.1).

Until 1978, the poor funding of education was due in part to policies that undervalued the importance of education for economic development. Mao believed that for the 'socialist reconstruction' of China emphasis should be placed on the development of heavy industry and agriculture. Education was seen as a form of social consumption the economic benefits of which were not recognized.[25] Indeed, until the implementation of the 1995 Education Law, the costs of education were included in the figure for cultural expenditure in government budgets at every level, with no separate figure being given for education.[26]

In the 1980s, with the development of the market economy and the 'open-door' policy, Chinese economists and educators began lobbying for increased education funding in a way that reflected a belief in the principles of human capital theory.[27] Two strategies for educational development emerged: the first proposed that the annual growth rate in educational investment should equal the economic growth rate, the second suggested that the growth in education investment should exceed the economic growth rate, making education 'the engine for growth'.[28] The latter strategy had particular significance for undeveloped regions like the TAR, which were to be incorporated only in the second stage of China's economic development plan scheduled for the late 1990s. It was argued by some Chinese educationalists that if educational investment did not increase at a faster rate than GDP in these regions where educational levels were so low, there would not be sufficient 'human capital' to develop the economy. This would result in a 'vicious circle' of low educational levels leading to poor economic development leading on to lower educational levels.[29] Of the two strategies put forward in the 1980s, it was the second, which allowed education investment to grow faster than GDP, that was endorsed by China's legislators. In 1985, the idea of education as 'the engine for growth' was enshrined in the 'Decision of the CCP Central Committee on the Reform of China's Educational Structure';[30] ten years later, the same principle became part of the 1995 Education Law.[31]

However, the growth in educational investment has not kept pace with the growth of China's GDP, despite this legislation (see Figure 1.2), and, as shown in Figure 1.1, the percentage of GDP invested in education in China has decreased in recent years. The decline is partly due to the fact that under the 1985 legislation the funding of education was devolved from the central government to regional governments and from government to non-government sources. Educational provision has therefore become increasingly dependent on the economies of individual regions and this has meant that, in practice, educational development still follows economic development. Fei Xiaotong, a vice-chairman of the National People's Congress (NPC) Standing Committee, reported to the Eighth NPC Standing Committee in October 1996 that 'regulations in the Education Law concerning the guarantees for investment in education have not been fully implemented'. He added that although the Education Law states that the percentage of GDP for education expenditure should 'rise gradually' and should grow faster than the growth of fiscal revenues, the reverse has in fact been the case.[32]

Education and the economy in the TAR

For regions like the TAR, which has a high level of illiteracy and a very small GDP, the debate over investment in education has particular significance. In 1992 the per capita GDP of the TAR was $178, half the national per capita GDP; although it had reached $238 by 1994, this was still only just over half the national figure.[33] Thus, linking the rate of education investment to GDP is unlikely to provide sufficient funding to make education 'the engine for growth'. Between 1990 and 1994,

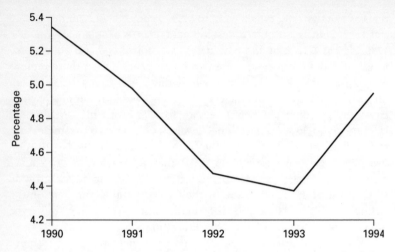

Figure 1.3 Education expenditure in the TAR as a percentage of GDP, 1990–94 (*Source*: 1995 TAR Statistical Yearbook)

the TAR government in fact spent a higher percentage of its GDP on education than the central government, and throughout the period the percentage remained above the 4 per cent recommended by the State Education Commission report (see Figure 1.3). Furthermore, although educational expenditure fell in 1992, in the following two years it increased at a faster rate than GDP (see Figure 1.4). However, while these figures indicate positive trends in education funding in the last few years, they are of course based on very low starting figures. Perhaps a more accurate indication of the priority given to education funding in the TAR can be seen in the ratio of government spending on education to total government spending. Here, we find that education receives a lower percentage of total government expenditure in the TAR than in China as a whole; and furthermore the percentage has declined through the 1990s (see Figure 1.5).

Given the backward state of the TAR's economy, the main thrust of the education debate has been whether the development of education should precede or succeed economic development. Until the 1980s, the view that education should follow economic development dominated state planning in the TAR.[34] However, in recent years, this view has been challenged by a number of educationalists, economists and government leaders. They describe the strategy of investing in the economy first and in education later as short-sighted, as putting short-term financial gains above the long-term development of the economy.[35] One Tibetan government official describes the issue thus:

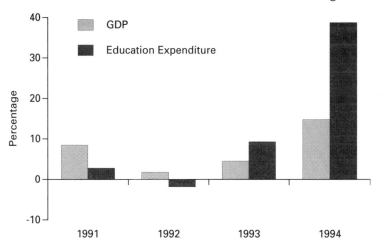

Figure 1.4 Growth of education expenditure in the TAR compared with growth of GDP, 1991–94 (*Source*: 1995 TAR Statistical Yearbook)

We are used to the old saying: 'the area is poor and short of funds, so we can only increase educational funding by developing the economy first.' It is exactly this way of talking that caused the problems. Let us think seriously. Doesn't this mean that in solving the relationship between the economy and education some people have been short-sighted and only see present interests? We have claimed that 'if you don't work, you can't survive; if we don't have agriculture, then there's no stability; if there's no commerce then we can't be well-off.' From now on we should add 'if there's no education, then there's no prosperity.' If we implement this in our work thoroughly, then there's hope that our nationality will make great economic progress.[36]

By the 1990s, the principle of developing education alongside, rather than after, the economy was endorsed by a number of senior government officials in the TAR. At the Fifth TAR Conference on Education in 1994, the TAR government chairman, Gyaltsen Norbu, described future development in the region in terms of 'continuing to give strategic priority to educational development and doing well the work of expanding education as we promote the economy'. In describing the connection between the economy and education, Gyaltsen Norbu emphasized the importance of investment in education, quoting Deng Xiaoping as saying: 'a locality or department that pays attention to economic growth at the expense of educational endeavours will fail to focus on its major work. Any leaders who neglect education undertakings are short-sighted and inexperienced. Such leaders will not be able to lead the work of turning China into a modern country.'[37]

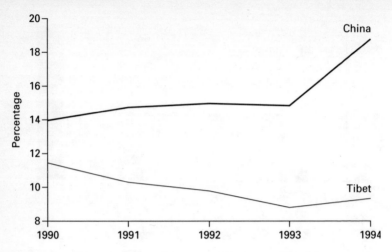

Figure 1.5 Education expenditure as a percentage of total government expenditure in China and the TAR, 1990–94 (*Sources*: 1995 China Statistical Yearbook; 1995 TAR Statistical Yearbook)

It appears, therefore, that the importance for economic development of adequate investment in education has been recognized in principle in the TAR, although there is little evidence of the notion of 'education as the engine for growth' being adopted. In practice, however, education is still seriously underfunded. Part of the reason for this is that the culture of undervaluing education still persists among many officials. In 1994, Chen Kuiyuan, the General Secretary of the TAR Communist Party said:

> A serious problem is that some leading cadres are not concerned about work for schools ... The task for educational development is not a special job of education departments but the entire Party's job. There will be no healthy development in education if Party committees and governments at all levels do not attach importance to and support the task.[38]

In the next section we look at how, historically, the political culture has affected the direction and extent of education funding in China, and we trace the impact of the changing political climate on education funding in the TAR.

Education and politics

Over the past forty-five years, the pattern of educational funding in China has, more dramatically than in most other places, been bound up with the political swings that have affected the country. Not only does the political climate have an impact on educational funding in general, but political shifts alter priorities within the educational budget, and even affect the administrative structure of funding. At different times in the past decades, depending largely on the political struggles within the Chinese Communist Party, the goal of education development has alternated between emphasizing the provision of basic socialist education for all citizens, and focusing on the training of skilled experts. The two strategies, which came to be known as 'quantity' versus 'quality' or egalitarian versus hierarchical, were identified with different political leaders in China. Liu Shaoqi and Deng Xiaoping, who were influential in educational policy-making from the mid-1950s to the early 1960s, were proponents of the 'quality' argument, believing in the importance of academic learning and the training of the best students in order to accelerate economic development. Mao Zedong, by contrast, promoted mass education and the moulding of China's youth through ideological education to create 'the socialist constructors' of China. [39]

While each strategy has in practice contained elements of the other, the conflict between the two has produced some dramatic reversals in education planning during the past fifty years. As mentioned above, the 'quality' strategy was dominant in the early 1950s and early 1960s. The 'quantity' strategy promoted by Mao was introduced at the time of the Great Leap Forward and again, more systematically, during the Cultural Revolution decade 1966–76.[40] Mao described the ideal graduate as 'red and expert'; however, in reality, the all-consuming nature of ideological education in the 1970s allowed little academic learning. In 1977, when Deng Xiaoping was rehabilitated and made Vice Premier in Charge of Education, education policy reverted to emphasizing quality over quantity. The importance of education for economic development was again underlined, and technical and higher education became priorities. At the same time, the political content of the curriculum was reduced, textbooks were rewritten to remove a substantial amount of ideology and political study classes became less important. From the mid-1980s, educational development took a more pragmatic and less political direction. However, with the crushing of the student democracy movement in 1989, ideological conflict returned: hard-line conservatives, or 'leftists' as they are known in China, regained power in Beijing, and although the 'quality' argument in educational development has continued into the 1990s, ideology has crept back into the curriculum.

Education development in the TAR has been directly affected by the political shifts that have occurred in China over the past forty years. In addition, it has been further affected by the specific ideological nature of 'minority' education, as mentioned above. Local political conflicts have also played a role in formulating education policy in the region.

In theory, the TAR should have benefited most when the 'quantity' strategy dominated Chinese politics. Since educational levels in the region were universally low, a strategy that focused on the extension of basic education, rather than on improving existing educational establishments at higher levels, should have been more advantageous. In practice, this has been true only to a certain extent since the egalitarian strategy propounded by Mao, although it promoted the extension of basic education, was highly politicized. Where the 'quality' strategy had recognized the distinctions between China's nationalities, and thus, for example, the importance of using Tibetan language and culture for successful educational development, Mao's 'quantity' strategy included the interpretation of national characteristics in terms of 'class struggle'. Anything that could be labelled 'nationality' became the focus of attack on the grounds that ethnic characteristics emphasized differences between nationalities and created tension between them which was contrary to the concept of communism. During the Cultural Revolution, when the 'quantity' strategy became dominant, all concessions to culturally specific education for China's nationalities were abolished; the political nature of education during this period meant that it consisted almost entirely of launching attacks on the traditional Tibetan culture, the prime target being the Tibetan language. Furthermore, although on paper it appears that primary and secondary enrolment increased at a phenomenal rate during the Cultural Revolution, and that the widespread construction of new schools took place, doubt has since been cast on the extent to which the development of mass education as presented in Chinese statistics for that period reflects real improvements on the ground.[41]

As mentioned earlier, during the 1980s, education policy in China returned to emphasizing quality over quantity. With education strategies focused on enabling China to compete internationally in economic and technological terms, higher education and education in urban areas became the main funding priority. Provision of basic education in poor rural areas like TAR was, to a certain extent, overlooked. In 1994, the Minister of the State Education Commission, Zhu Kaixuan, told the National People's Congress: 'The current accelerated shift from a planned economy to a socialist market economy has posed many new problems regarding educational reform and development, and brought to light some glaring difficulties ... The main problems and difficulties we currently encounter are in primary education, especially primary education in the countryside.'[42] In the TAR, around one-third of school-age children could not afford to go to school by the end of 1993, according to the TAR government chairman, Gyaltsen Norbu.[43]

Although the extent of education provision declined during the mid-1980s, the pragmatic nature of education policy allowed for the promotion of education that was more relevant to the cultural needs of Tibetans and, in particular, it allowed the development of Tibetan medium education for Tibetans. The rewriting of textbooks in the TAR not only included the removal of a certain amount of ideology but also the insertion of more information specifically about Tibetan culture. As in the rest of China, political study and the class background of students became less important for educational advancement.[44] Furthermore, the educational policies promulgated in the early 1980s outlined strategies designed to increase the proportion of Tibetans in the student population of the TAR.

However, ideological conflict returned to the TAR earlier than to the rest of China. Pro-independence demonstrations in Lhasa in 1987 sparked off a new period of increased political control in society, which fed into education planning. By the end of the 1980s, 'leftist' conservatives had regained power in Lhasa. In 1988, TAR Party Secretary Wu Jinghua, who was widely perceived as a liberal, was replaced after his failure to control the resurgence of nationalist unrest. In education, the pendulum swung back to promote ideological education over academic education. At the Fifth TAR Conference on Education in 1994, the TAR Party Secretary, Chen Kuiyuan, announced that ideological goals should once again take precedence over the academic goals of education:

> The success of our education does not lie in the number of diplomas issued to graduates from universities, colleges, polytechnic schools, and secondary schools. It lies, in the final analysis, in whether our graduating students are opposed to or turn their hearts to the Dalai clique and in whether they are loyal to or do not care about our great motherland and the great socialist cause. This is the most salient and the most important criterion for assessing right and wrong, and the contributions and mistakes of our educational work in Tibet. To successfully solve the problem, we must improve political and ideological work in schools.[45]

In the 1990s, although the designation of the TAR as a 'special economic zone' and the subsequent growth of the TAR economy has meant increased funding for education, conservatives in the TAR Communist Party have increasingly linked Tibetan culture to Tibetan nationalism. This has resulted in the undermining of a culturally distinct education for Tibetans. Textbooks have again been rewritten to reintroduce greater political content, and specifically to emphasize the inalienable unity of Tibet and China.[46] Furthermore, plans to introduce Tibetan medium education at secondary level were abandoned in 1996. This development has caused considerable concern in some quarters since low educational achievement in the TAR is believed to be connected with the lack of mother-tongue tuition.[47]

Summary

It is clear that the education of the non-Han nationalities in China has generally been of greater significance than their numbers would suggest. Many of these nationalities, including Tibetans, inhabit the sensitive border regions of China in areas that are rich in minerals or fertile for agriculture. The TAR is a border region that is both fertile and filled with largely untapped mineral resources. Indeed, its riches have acquired it the Chinese name of *Xizang* (the Western Treasure House). Because of the TAR's economic and strategic importance, it has always been crucial for the Chinese government that Tibetans in the region should clearly identify with China. Education became the vehicle through which this identification and patriotism was to be instilled.

During the last fifty years, this strategic priority has been a defining influence on development of education in the TAR. Consequently, the direction of educational development has not only shifted with the rest of China as policy swung between the 'quality' strategy and the 'quantity' strategy, it has also been altered according to the perceived security needs of China.

China as a whole has achieved considerable educational advances in the last fifty years, despite a history of underfunding. In the TAR, due to a combination of historical, political, geographical and economic factors, educational levels are lower than in any region or province in China. In the 1980s, debate over the relationship between education and GDP in China led to the promulgation of policies that would make investment in education grow faster than GDP. In practice, however, because the same reforms devolved funding from the central government to regional and provincial governments, education development still largely follows economic development. This is particularly true of the TAR where the backward economy meant that the debate over whether education development should precede or succeed the development of the economy was particularly significant. By the 1990s, the importance of developing education alongside the economy was endorsed at the highest levels of government.

Although education all over China is subject to the swing of the political pendulum, in the TAR the priority of educating Tibetans to be patriotic, and the politicization of the Tibetan language in recent years, mean that educational development in the region is particularly susceptible to political interference. In the next chapter we look in detail at how the political climate has affected the development of different types of education since 1950.

Notes

1. Yenming Zhang, *Effects of Policy Changes on College Enrolment of Minority Students in China, 1949–1989*, Doctoral Thesis (Harvard University, 1991), p. 10.

2. The 1954 Constitution of the People's Republic of China.

3. Hu Yaobang, 'Tibetan leaders set six requirements for Tibet', *Xinhua*, 30 May 1980.

4. Bernhard Dilger, 'The Education of Minorities', *Comparative Education*, Vol. 20, No. 1, 1984, p. 156.

5. Yang Jingren, *'Jianjue Guanche Zhongyang Zhishi Zuo Hao Xizang Gongzuo'* (On the Correct Implementation of the Central Committee's Directive and Carrying Out Work for Tibet Well), *Hongqi* (Red Flag), No. 15, 1980, pp. 2–8.

6. See Yang Jingren, 'Tasks of Nationality Work in the New Socialist Period' (1979), cited in Yenming Zhang, *Effects of Policy Changes*.

7. Yang Wanli, *'Xizang Kecheng Jiaocai Yanjiu De Teshuxing Jiqi Duice'* (The Countermeasure and Particularity of Research on Teaching Materials), *Xizang Yanjiu* (Tibet Studies), Vol. 58, No. 1, 1996.

8. See also Lei Yongsheng, *'Xiandaihua Jiaoyu Fazhan Yu Xizang Jiaoyu Gaige'* (The Development of Modern Education and the Reform of Tibetan Education), *Xizang Yanjiu* (Tibet Studies), Vol. 58, No. 1, 1996.

9. Of the total number of non-Han Chinese nationalities in the TAR, 99.1 per cent are Tibetan (1990 Census figures), *Encyclopaedia of Chinese Counties*, Vol.: South-West China (China Social Publishing House, 1993).

10. See Yang Jingren, 'On the Correct Implementation of the Central Committee's Directive', pp. 2–8.

11. Educational levels among Koreans in China are among the highest in the country. Chae Jin Lee, *China's Korean Minority* (Westview Press, Boulder, CO, 1986), p. 142.

12. For an assessment of the TAR's economic problems see Wang Xiaoqiang and Bai Nanfeng, *The Poverty of Plenty*, trans. Angela Knox (Macmillan, London, 1991).

13. Chae Jin Lee, *China's Korean Minority*, p. 142.

14. Yat Ming Leung, 'The People's Republic of China', in *Education and Development in East Asia* (Garland Press, London, 1995), p. 211.

15. UNESCO *World Education Indicators* (World Education Report, Oxford, 1995).

16. 1995 China Statistical Yearbook.

17. Yat Ming Leung, *Education and Development in East Asia*, p. 204; see also Simon X. B. Zhao and Christopher S. P. Tong, 'Spatial Disparity in China's Educational Development: An Assessment from the Perspective of Economic Growth', *China Information*, Vol. XI, No. 4, Spring 1997.

18. See Zhao and Tong, 'Spatial Disparity in China's Educational Development', p. 21; see also M. Bastid, 'Chinese Educational Policies in the 1980s and Economic Development', *China Quarterly*, No. 6, 1984, pp. 189–219; C. Y. Kong, 'It is Imperative to Strengthen China's Higher Education', *Ming Pao*, 29 September 1995.

19. UNESCO, *World Education Indicators*; China's Statistical Yearbook put investment in education in 1992 at 2.3 per cent of GDP (see Table 1.1).

20. See Yat Ming Leung, 'The People's Republic of China', p. 218.

21. 'Programme for China's Educational Reform and Development', *Xinhua*, 25 February 1993 [SWB 5/3/93].

22. See Yat Ming Leung, 'The People's Republic of China'.

23. Zhao and Tong, 'Spatial Disparity in China's Educational Development', p. 21.

24. See 'Programme for China's Educational Reform and Development', and 'Education Law', 18 March 1995, *Xinhua*, 20 March 1995 [SWB 29/3/95].

25. Jin Lin, *Education in Post-Mao China* (Praeger, London, 1993), p. 93.

26. The 1995 Education Law stipulated that provinces should eventually list education expenditures as an independent unit in their fiscal budgets.

27. Yat Ming Leung, 'The People's Republic of China', p. 218.

28. See Teng Xing, '*Wo Guo Shaoshu Minzu Diqu Jiaoyu Zhengti Gaige Guanjian*' (The Essence of Overall Educational Reform in China's Minority Regions), *Qiu Shi*, No. 7, April 1989, pp. 19–24.

29. Ibid.

30. CCP Central Committee, 'Decision of the CCP Central Committee on the Reform of China's Educational Structure' (Foreign Languages Press, Beijing, 1985).

31. Article 55 of the Education Law states: 'The growth of educational funds to be appropriated by people's governments at various levels should be higher than the growth of regular revenues. The average educational expenditure per student should be gradually increased, and it is also necessary to guarantee that wages for teachers and the average expenses per student are gradually increased.'

32. Report by Fei Xiaotong, vice-chairman of Eighth National People's Congress Standing Committee, to the Committee's 22nd Session, *Xinhua*, 26 October 1996 [SWB 28/10/96].

33. 1995 China Statistical Yearbook.

34. Internal Party discussion paper, 1995.

35. Television debate on education, Lhasa TV, 30 July 1988 (see Appendix 6 for transcript); see also Xiang Xiao Li and Zhang Qing; internal Party discussion paper, 1995; Paper on Education Development among Tibetans, by Tibetan scholar, 1995.

36. Internal Party discussion paper, 1995.

37. Gyaltsen Norbu, speech to Fifth TAR Conference on Education, 26 October 1994 [FBIS 18/11/94].

38. Chen Kuiyuan, Secretary of TAR Regional CCP Committee, Speech to Fifth TAR Conference on Education, 26 October 1994, *Xizang Ribao* (Tibet Daily), 28 October 1994 [FBIS 15/11/94].

39. Dalu Yin, 'Reforming Chinese Education: Context, Structure and Attitudes in the 1980s', *Compare*, Vol. 23, No. 2, 1993.

40. Suzanne Pepper, 'Chinese Education After Mao: Two Steps Forward, Two Steps Back and Begin Again?' *China Quarterly*, No. 81, 1980, p. 3.

41. See Dilger, 'Education of Minorities'; see also Keith M. Lewin, Xu Hui, Angela Little and Zheng Jiwei, *Educational Innovation in China* (Longman, Harlow, 1994), p. 35.

42. Zhu Kaixuan, 'Report to Fourth Session of Eighth National People's Congress Standing Committee on Educational Work', *Xinhua*, 28 October 1993 [SWB 10/11/93].

43. Gyaltsen Norbu, *Xinhua*, 5 June 1994 [SWB 8/6/96].

44. See Dilger, 'Education of Minorities'; see also Catriona Bass, *Inside the Treasure House: A Time in Tibet* (Gollancz, London, 1990), pp. 70–1.

45. Chen Kuiyuan, Speech to Fifth TAR Conference on Education, 26 October 1994.

46. Interview with Tibetan educationalist, 7 August 1996.

47. See TAR Deputy Party Secretary Tenzin, 'Speech to Meeting of TAR Guiding Committee on Spoken and Written Tibetan', 16 March 1993, published in *Dakpo* (The Owner), No. 2, 1993, pp. 13–18; see also Phunstok Tsering, TAR CPPCC, Eleventh Bulletin of the Second Plenary Session, May 1994; Teng Xing, 'The Essence of Overall Educational Reform'; Internal Party discussion paper, 1995; Duojie Caidan (Dorje Tseten), *Xizang Jiaoyu* (Education in Tibet) (China Tibetology Publishers, Beijing, 1991).

CHAPTER 2

Red or Expert: Shifting Priorities in Education, 1949–78

'Democratic Revolution', 'Socialist Reconstruction' and 'Socialist Transformation' in China, 1949–65

In 1949, the Communists came to power in China, having achieved what they termed the 'new democratic revolution'. The 'democratic revolution' was said to have had three goals: the expulsion of imperialism, the overthrow of feudalism and the toppling of bureaucratic capitalism. Once in power, the new government's first plan was to boost the Chinese economy, which had been dragged down by years of conflict and war. They termed this objective 'socialist reconstruction', and it was to be followed by 'socialist transformation'. Targets were set to bring China up to the standards of the industrialized world. Over the next few years education was made to serve directly the needs of the economy: to produce large numbers of skilled technical and scientific personnel. Government funding of education was largely concentrated in urban areas, and on higher education. The 'quality' or hierarchical strategy, as propounded by Deng Xiaoping and Liu Shaoqi and discussed in Chapter 1 above, essentially dominated education planning.

However, Mao Zedong, who had been advocating the need for mass education in rural areas since 1927, had already begun to encourage the development of community-funded schools known as *minban* (*mangtsuk lobchung* in Tibetan). These schools were to be set up by individual communes or villages and were intended to cater directly to the needs of the local community. In his 'Investigations of the Peasant Movement in Hunan', Mao had expressed the need for a rural-based education system as a counter to China's existing urban-oriented system which he saw as serving the educational needs only of the elite.[1] The first community schools were established between 1950 and 1951; the system expanded slowly until 1955, when it was undermined by renewed emphasis on the state-sponsored school system.[2] In 1957, when the collectivization of agriculture was intensified and rural industrialization began, the argument for raising the educational level of the peasants began to gain increased support. At this time the 'quantity' or egalitarian strategy, propounded by Mao, gained new momentum. In rural areas, the number of community schools began to increase, and with the Great Leap Forward the principle of 'walking on two legs' (*liangtiao tui zou lu*) was adopted. This strategy encouraged the simultaneous development of community and state-funded primary schools (known as *gongban* in Chinese and *shungtsuk lobchung* in Tibetan).[3] The Great Leap Forward, during which Mao set China the economic goal of catching up with the industrialized world in twelve years, was also intended to speed up the educational revolution. A goal was set to make university education universal within fifteen years. Like the apparent achievements in agriculture and industry, the number of tertiary institutions was said to have increased from 229 in 1957 to 791 in 1958.[4] The enrolment rate in primary education is reported to have increased from 54 per cent in 1955 to 80 per cent in 1958.[5]

In the early 1960s, with the failure of the Great Leap Forward, when famine and economic collapse struck China, another shift in policy took place. Mao was blamed for these crises, and his education strategies similarly came under attack. Education policy swung back towards improving the quality of the existing, principally urban and academic, educational infrastructure rather than to extending basic education further into rural areas. As part of this renewed 'quality' strategy, Liu Shaoqi announced the dual-track system (*liang zhong jiaoyu zhidu*) which was to divide secondary education into general secondary schools and work-study schools. The general secondary schools were to take the brightest students who would study full-time; the less able students were to enrol in the work-study schools where they would study for only half the day and labour for the other half.[6] The work-study schools were intended to play a particularly important role in education development among non-Han nationalities.[7] Furthermore, the return to the 'quality' strategy in the 1960s brought with it the promotion of key schools (*zhongdian xuexiao*). The key-school system was designed to concentrate financial and human resources in schools which already had a well-developed educational infrastructure. The schools were given priority in terms of funding, provision of equipment and capital investment, and they were encouraged to recruit the best teachers and students. The system was said to be necessary in order to train personnel as rapidly as possible. The idea was to concentrate the scarce resources in a few key centres where they were capable of producing maximum returns in the shortest time.

The 'minority' nationality education policy and Tibet, 1950–65

From the start, the Chinese government set different priorities for the education of Han Chinese and for the so-called 'minority' nationalities. In September 1951, the First National Conference on Minority Education took place in Beijing. The conclusions of the conference made it clear that the main task of education in 'minority' nationality areas was to be the political training of cadres for government administration.[8] This contrasts with the education policy for Han Chinese regions, which emphasized the training of 'large numbers of technical personnel in order to meet the needs of the country's industrialization', as discussed above.[9] The reason for this difference in focus was that the Chinese government had yet to win over the peoples of these areas, and education provided the means by which this was to be achieved. In the case of Tibet, the Dalai Lama's government still retained certain powers in the early 1950s; therefore, educating Tibetan cadres to have patriotic sentiments towards China was considered to be a crucial stage in the process of 'democratic revolution'. Cadres educated by the new Chinese government were to provide the link between the government and non-Han Chinese peoples, to help mobilize them for 'socialist construction'.[10] In June 1951, an article in the *People's Daily* (*Renmin Ribao*) explained the rationale behind the education of 'minority' nationality cadres: 'It is natural that the members of any nationality will have respect for the cadres of their nationality. "Minority" nationalities ... have often expressed the view that although Han cadres are very likeable, they still cannot completely understand the situation and problems of the minorities.'[11]

At the First National Conference on Minority Nationality Education, the Education Minister, Ma Xulun, outlined education priorities for 'minority' nationality areas, which included the following provisions:

1. Political education programmes must foster a spirit of equality, unity, fraternity and co-operation among the nationalities, including preserving minority cultures, and enhancing patriotism and support for the People's Government.
2. Education must be scientific, popular and reflect the characteristics of the nationalities, including being appropriate to their development.
3. The curriculum must be modified to meet local conditions.
4. Indigenous languages should be used in primary and secondary schools.
5. The People's Government at different levels must make educational appropriations to minority areas according to general guidelines.[12]

The training of teachers was also emphasized at this conference, and the lack of 'minority' nationality teachers and teaching materials was recognized as being the most urgent issue. This led to the 'Tentative Plan for Training Teachers from Minority Nationalities' which was discussed and approved by the conference and issued by the Chinese government in September 1951.[13] In 1954, the Constitution of the People's Republic of China gave guarantees of support to 'minority' nationality regions for educational progress. The Second National Conference on Minority Education in 1956 reaffirmed these principles.

As far as Tibet was concerned, China made somewhat vague promises about educational development. The 'Seventeen-Point Agreement', signed between the Tibetan and Chinese governments in 1951, states that: 'the spoken and written language and the school education of the Tibetan nationality shall be developed step by step in accordance with the actual conditions in Tibet.'[14] Initially, it was decided that Tibet was not ready for 'socialist transformation', which was taking place in the rest of China, as the 'democratic revolution' had yet to be achieved. Indeed, during the 1950s, the Chinese government forged an alliance with the Tibetan government, with the result that the monasteries retained their privileges and continued to be the main educational institutions.[15] The Chinese government planned to reform from the top, so as to avoid appearing too revolutionary. Some children of the aristocracy were sent to China for further education while others continued to travel to India to be educated in the Indian public school system. Nevertheless, *Tse Laptra*, the Tibetan government school that educated members of the clergy to become government officials, was closed down in 1952.[16]

Tibet was considered to be two steps behind the rest of China in carrying out the new reforms. In Central China, during the First Five-Year Plan (1953–57), 'socialist construction' was already taking place, while in other 'minority' nationality regions 'democratic reform', or 'land reform' as it was also known, was under way. 'Democratic reform' and 'land reform' were the terms used to describe the system of redistributing land, considered part of the process of abolishing 'the old feudal slavery system'.[17] By 1958, 'socialist transformation' in Xinjiang and Inner Mongolia was already being synchronized with Central China in the establishment of communes.[18] In central Tibet, with tension rising between Tibetans and Han Chinese cadres, Mao promised that 'democratic reform' could be postponed even to the Third Five-Year Plan (1963–67). However, in 1959, Tibetans rebelled against the Chinese government in a revolt that became known as the Lhasa Uprising. In the crushing of the uprising, the Dalai Lama escaped to India and the

Tibetan government was dissolved. Tibet was immediately brought in line with the rest of China: 'land reform' was carried out with the confiscation and redistribution of aristocratic and monastic estates. All the monasteries ceased to function, many of them were destroyed and the monks evicted, or arrested and imprisoned.[19] In 1965, central Tibet was renamed the Tibet Autonomous Region; it was the last of the five autonomous regions to be established. Only then did collectivization begin, a decade later than in China.

In education, while the 'quality' or 'expert' educational strategy was being implemented in schools and universities throughout Central China, the specific goals of 'minority education' were being pursued in the TAR. Liu Shaoqi and Deng Xiaoping, unlike Mao, adopted a gradual-ist approach to 'minority' education. In Tibet, the traditional elite were the initial recipients of the new education. Instruction was in the Tibetan medium and religious education was tolerated. As mentioned above, selected Tibetans from wealthy families were taken to China to be educated as cadres and teachers. In 1951, 600 Tibetans were sent to the Central Institute for Nationalities in Beijing and the Southwest Institute for Nationalities in Chengdu, Sichuan Province, for political training.[20] In 1952, the Chinese government set up its first state primary school in Lhasa, the Lhasa Primary School. Teachers were selected from both Tibetan and Chinese personnel; the first contingent of teachers included ten Tibetan monk officials, seven Tibetan government officials, ten teachers from Tibetan society, and twenty teachers sent from Central China. Three hundred students were admitted in the first year, enrolment rising to 1,000 by 1956. The curriculum was taught entirely in Tibetan and included subjects such as Party policy, science, Tibetan literature, mathematics, general knowledge, music, art, physical education, history and geography. Initially, the curriculum included religious instruction as well but this was stopped in 1956.[21] By 1958, there were only thirteen state primary schools for the whole of central Tibet, enrolling 2,600 pupils, many of whom were the children of the former Tibetan elite.

The first secondary school established by the Chinese government in Tibet was the Lhasa Secondary School, which was founded in 1956, offering three years of the standard six-year secondary course.[22] By 1957, when the other four autonomous regions had institutes of higher education, Tibet still remained without one. Instead, another secondary level school, the Tibet State School, was set up 'to train more cadres for social construction'.[23] However, this school was not in Tibet itself; it was situated outside the city of Xian at a place called Xianyang, in Shaanxi Province. In the first year of the school's existence, 3,688 students were enrolled. Two years later, in 1959, most of these students were sent back to Tibet to participate in the suppression of the Lhasa Uprising. The school did not recover its initial number of students before it was closed by the Cultural Revolution.[24] Box 2.1 gives a glimpse of the life of Tashi Tsering, a young Tibetan in the school in 1964, a year before it was upgraded to a university.

The 1959 Lhasa Uprising and the escape of the Dalai Lama into India came at a time when China was caught up in the excesses of the Great Leap Forward. Abandoning the gradualist approach to 'minority education' fostered by Liu Shaoqi and Deng Xiaoping, Mao launched a full attack on all forms of traditional 'minority' nationality culture in education. In Tibet the 'egalitarian' or 'quantity' education strategy, which he was promoting throughout China during this period, led to a reinterpretation of Tibetan culture in terms of the 'class struggle'. The focus of education was described as being to fight against 'old customs', which were now associated with the ruling class. Tibetan language came under attack in the so-called 'new high tide of enthusiasm for learning Han'.[25] At the same time, central Tibet joined in the China-wide drive to expand education into rural areas as fast as possible. In line with the goals of the 'quantity' strategy, primary education policy in central Tibet suddenly veered towards the establishment of community schools, which were supposed to give priority to educating the children of peasants and nomads. In November 1959, the Preparatory Committee for the Establishment of the Autonomous Region of Tibet (PCART), issued a new directive to 'concentrate on community schools which would be supplemented by state schools'. The Tibetan educationalist and government official Dorje Tseten describes community schools at this time as 'flourishing all over Tibet like bamboo shoots sprouting up after the spring rains'. By 1961, there were said to be 1,496 community schools, including travelling schools in nomadic areas. Fifty-two thousand pupils, between the ages of six and twenty, were said to have been enrolled. Teachers were drawn from members of the community, and the community provided the teachers' wages and the schools' running costs. Teachers and pupils were also said to collect yak dung and medicinal herbs to supplement the schools' income.

By the early 1960s, however, it had become clear that local communities had been unable to meet the demands made on them both in terms of providing teachers and in funding these local schools. In 1962, the proponents of the 'quality' strategy gained power once more in Beijing. Officials in Tibet were told to abandon the development of community schools and focus on improving the quality of state-run primary schools, as in the rest of China. In February of that year, a

Box 2.1 Life in Tibet state school, Xianyang, Shaanxi Province, 1964

There were about 2,500 students at the university, almost all Tibetans. My unit, the Department of Education, numbered about five hundred, most of whom were the children of poor peasant families. We did many things together, but of course when we studied we were divided into smaller classes. Mine met on the third floor of the building where the Department of Education was housed. It contained forty Tibetan students in all, about half of them from the Chamdo area, near the border with China in Eastern Tibet. They were more literate in Chinese than the rest of us. The other half were mostly from the Tsang area, much closer to my own village, and we were more literate in Tibetan. Everyone in my group was, I found, fairly well prepared compared to many of the other students, some of whom were nearly or completely illiterate. Whatever our background or state of preparation, however, our mission was clear enough. We were there to be trained as teachers and then sent back to Tibet to teach others.

Our days followed a strict routine. The school's sense of discipline and order was like the army's, and in fact I learned that many of the teachers had come from the military before being assigned to the school. On a typical day, we woke up early, washed in a common washroom, and then participated in group exercises. We had three meals a day at the school canteen. Breakfast followed the exercise period, and going to classes followed that ... Once we were assigned to a class, the students belonging to that class stayed in one room and different teachers came to lecture us at various times. There were teachers who taught Tibetan for those students who needed help learning to read and write their own language. Then we also had to learn Chinese. (It was so important that we learn Chinese quickly that some students – I was one of them – were given private tutors to help speed up the learning process.) There were four classes in the morning from eight to twelve and then we broke for lunch. In the summer we were allowed to rest after lunch until one-thirty, after which we went back to the classroom again, usually for political lessons. This went on until it was near time for dinner.

Source: The Struggle for Modern Tibet, The Autobiography of Tashi Tsering *(M. E. Sharpe, New York, 1997) p. 94.*

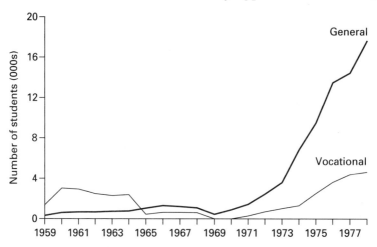

Figure 2.1 Enrolment in vocational and general secondary education in the TAR, 1959–87 (*Sources*: 1995 TAR Statistical Yearbook; 1989 TAR Statistical Yearbook)

meeting of the CCP Tibet Working Committee stipulated that all community schools failing to meet appropriate standards should be shut down; 196 schools were closed immediately.

While the political imperatives of 'minority education' continued, the early 1960s saw a return to the gradualist approach, favoured by Liu Shaoqi and Deng Xiaoping, that allowed for elements of a distinctive Tibetan system to emerge in the curriculum once again. In 1960, the Tibet Educational Materials Translation and Editing Committee was set up under PCART to compile and translate textbooks for community schools in the region. The committee was directed to use the Han Chinese textbooks as models, but to include stories and characters from Tibetan literature as well as real Tibetan figures.[26]

In secondary education (once more in line with the national 'quality' strategy) a dual-track system was established with vocational or work-study schools a high priority. In 1961, over 80 per cent of secondary-school pupils were channelled into central Tibet's only vocational secondary school (see Figure 2.1). Furthermore, even though educational levels in the TAR were extremely low, the prevailing national educational policy was followed in giving priority to the development of higher education. In 1965, the TAR got its first institute of higher education. This was, in fact, the Tibet State School in Xianyang, which had been upgraded to university level and renamed the TAR Nationalities Institute. As Figure 2.2 shows, between 1965 and 1969 there was a larger

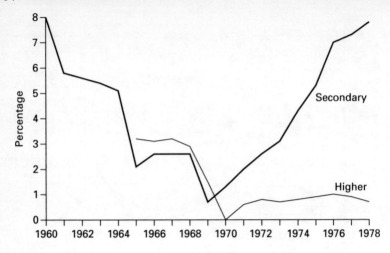

Figure 2.2 Enrolment in secondary and higher education in the TAR as a percentage of total enrolment, 1960–78 (*Sources*: 1995 TAR Statistical Yearbook; 1989 TAR Statistical Yearbook)

proportion of students in higher education than in secondary education. It is, however, hard to imagine that the education provided at TAR Nationalities Institute was of university level if, as indicated in Box 2.1, some of the students studying at the university were illiterate.

The Cultural Revolution in China, 1966–76

By the mid-1960s, Mao Zedong was still lacking support within the CCP and thus, in 1966, in an attempt to thwart his opponents, he called on the people to launch the Cultural Revolution in China. In education, all policies connected with the 'quality' strategy were immediately overturned. All forms of elitist education came under attack: the notion of key schools was discarded; work-study schools were described as discriminating against the children of the lower classes and were abolished. Distinctive education for China's non-Han nationalities, with its concessions to traditional cultures and mother-tongue instruction, was also termed as elitist and abandoned. Furthermore, the goal of trying to achieve international standards in education was no longer seen as realistic or desirable; mass education at primary and secondary level became the main funding priority.[27] 'Red', 'quantity' or 'egalitarian' educational policies dominated government planning. In 1966, schools throughout China closed. Institutions of higher education, being one of the main targets of the anti-elitist revolution, remained closed for at least five years, and the university entrance examination was reinstated only eleven years later, in October 1977. Class background rather than academic ability became the criterion for educational advancement. Children from intellectual families were sent to work on the land as manual labourers, while the education of children from 'worker-peasant-soldier' families became the priority. From 1972, when the universities reopened, only students from these classes were allowed to enrol.

Primary schools reopened after two or three years, around 1969, although it was only a year later that mass education was reintroduced on a more systematic basis. From 1970, emphasis was placed on achieving universal primary school education, and expanding secondary education as fast as possible. Enrolment in primary education was said to have risen from 85 per cent in 1965 to 96 per cent in 1975.[28] The increase in enrolment in rural areas was achieved through the renewed expansion of community schools, which were financed and staffed from the resources available at the commune and production brigade levels, with some state aid to pay teachers' salaries. The original idea behind the development of community-run schools had been to provide an education for rural children that was not based on an alien urban curriculum, although during the Cultural Revolution education con-sisted almost entirely of learning Mao Zedong's quotations. Another reason for the development of community schools was that research in China had shown that the cost, in time and money, associated with boarding school or travelling some distance to school were major factors in the low enrolment and high drop-out rates in rural areas.[29] Secondary education also expanded during the Cultural Revolution decade. This was made possible largely through the addition of junior secondary classes to the village primary schools. The length of primary schooling was reduced and two-year secondary school classes were added.[30]

Experts are divided on the extent to which the expansion in primary and secondary education, which appears in the statistics during the 1970s, represents an improvement in mass education during that decade. Pressure to achieve the quantitative goals set by the Chinese leadership was often extreme, and this is believed to have led local officials to exaggerate achievements in school construction and enrolment. It is now generally agreed that the statistics presented during the Cultural Revolution are unreliable, but they are still believed by scholars to provide an indication of general trends.[31] In China today, the accepted view is that many schools that were allegedly built during the Cultural Revolution existed only on paper, that there were few facilities or textbooks and that teachers were simply recruited from members of the production teams. The Cultural Revolution is now denounced as having been a total disaster for education. This is largely true; on the other hand, there is a tendency among some officials to overstate the case, i.e. to blame today's problems in education entirely on the Cultural Revolution, particularly in regions such as the TAR where educational provision is still poor.

The Cultural Revolution in the TAR, 1966–76

In the TAR, as in the rest of China, the years from 1966 to 1970 wreaked havoc on society and education. In 1966 all schools closed; Tibetan and Chinese students formed themselves into Red Guard brigades and set about following Mao's command to attack the 'Four Olds': old thoughts, old customs, old habits and old culture. Chinese students travelled to the TAR, and a few Tibetan students travelled to other parts of China, to engage in what was called 'revolutionary learning'. School buildings were taken over by Red Guard students who organized the writing of revolutionary slogans, putting up posters in public places and planning 'struggle sessions' in which suspected counter-revolutionaries were denounced. All aspects of traditional Tibetan culture came under attack: monasteries were destroyed, monks were beaten and imprisoned as were members of the aristocracy; even traditional hairstyles and dress were banned. Red Guard students would go from house to house demanding that families hand over their statues of deities, religious paintings (*thangka*), items of clothing, jewellery, etc. They would hang around the centre of Lhasa with knives ready to cut the hair of any Tibetan who continued to wear it in long plaits.

As mentioned above, provisions for distinctive 'minority' education were particularly attacked. Nationality institutes all over China were closed down. When universities reopened in 1971 only two of China's ten nationalities institutes still existed.[32] In the TAR, concessions to the specific needs of Tibetans were denounced as 'revisionist'. In particular, the gradualist approach of adapting economic development and education to the special conditions in the TAR, which had prevailed throughout the 1950s and again in the early 1960s, was termed 'revisionist'.[33] Tibetan medium instruction and a Tibet-centred curriculum were abandoned. In 1974, according to the report of a regional meeting on education in the TAR, textbooks were rewritten for all levels of education. The report stated: 'the teaching materials for colleges, secondary schools and primary schools are being revised, and the reactionary ideas on education peddled by Confucius, Liu Shaoqi and Lin Biao are being liquidated.'[34] Furthermore, the administrative structure of schools was

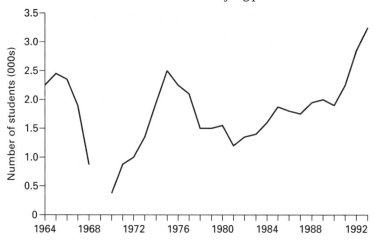

Figure 2.3 Enrolment in higher education in the TAR, 1965–94 (*Sources:* 1995 TAR Statistical Yearbook; 1989 TAR Statistical Yearbook)

altered to ensure that 'poor and lower-middle peasants' were in charge of running schools.[35] Teachers came under particular attack during the 1974 TAR education meeting, when delegates to the conference resolved to lower their status. According to a report on Lhasa Radio on 16 December: 'The delegates also criticized and repudiated "the teacher's absolute authority". Many educational workers and revolutionary teachers expressed their resolve to further wipe out the pernicious influence of the "teacher's absolute authority" and establish a new proletarian teacher–student relationship.'[36]

As far as secondary education was concerned, the two-track system of general secondary schools and vocational work-study schools was termed elitist, and abolished. Figure 2.1 shows the dramatic drop in enrolment in vocational secondary education in the TAR after 1965. However, as in other parts of China, higher education was the most seriously affected by the Cultural Revolution. Mao's plan to make primary education available to all citizens was carried out at the expense of university education. The TAR Nationalities Institute was to enrol no new students for five years after 1966, and was closed completely between 1969 and 1971.[37] When it opened again in 1971, the university entrance examination had been abolished and enrolment depended on class background: only students from the families of workers, peasants or soldiers were eligible for admission. As Figure 2.3 shows, the enrol-ment figures began rising quite dramatically from 1972 when political reliability was the only enrolment requirement. Enrolment reached its

---

Box 2.2 Class struggle at TAR Teachers' College, 1976

A struggle to beat back the Right deviationist wind of reversing pre-vious verdicts is developing in depth in the TAR Teachers' College ... The broad masses of revolutionary teachers and students of the TAR Teachers' College have actively participated in this struggle. Various departments and teachers' groups in the college held debates and criticism meetings and fought tit-for-tat against the revisionist line that dominated education during the 17 years preceding the cultural revolution ... This college has put up more than 700 big-character posters, and held over 10 debate and criticism meetings. The broad masses of revolutionary teachers and students have regarded Marxism-Leninism-Mao Zedong thought as the basis in conducting debates.

They held that during the 17 years preceding the cultural revolution, the revisionist line had dominated education, and the bourgeoisie exercised the dictatorship over the proletariat. Tibet was no exception. The claim that 'Tibet is different owing to special circumstances', is a fallacy. Only by realizing that the revisionist line had dominated education during the 17 years preceding the cultural revolution, will it be possible for us to see that the main danger in educational circles today remains revisionism ...

In the course of the great debate on the educational revolution, the members of the Party's core group of the TAR Teachers' College stood in the vanguard of the struggle. They ran study classes of various types to study Chairman Mao's teaching, 'Class struggle is the key link and everything else hinges on it', and to study his instructions on educational revolution.

Source: Lhasa Radio, 'Struggle Against Revisionists in TAR Teachers' College', 1100 gmt, 4 March 1976 [SWB 9/3/76].

---

highest point in 1977, and then, with the reintroduction of the entrance examination, it declined by almost a half.

In 1975, the TAR Teachers' College was established in Lhasa.[38] At the opening ceremony Tian Bao, Deputy Secretary of the TAR Party Committee, announced: 'students should be selected from among workers and peasants with practical experience, and they should return to production after a few years of study.' The 'major topic' of the new college was to be class struggle, and the curriculum was to focus on the 'ideological transformation' of the students.[39] One hundred uni-

Figure 2.4 Enrolment in primary education in the TAR, 1960–94 (*Sources:* 1995 TAR Statistical Yearbook; 1989 TAR Statistical Yearbook)

versity teachers were said to have been sent from Shanghai to set up the college which was to have three departments: Politics and Language; Mathematics and Physics; Culture and Physical Education. Between them these departments ran seven courses: Politics, Tibetan Language, Mathematics, Physics, Chemistry, Fine Art, Music and Physical Education.[40]

Box 2.2 provides a glimpse of life in TAR Teachers' College a year after its foundation. It gives an indication of the lengths to which students and teachers apparently went to achieve the revolutionary goals set for it.

As far as primary education is concerned, enrolment figures for the TAR show a dramatic increase between 1972 and 1978. In fact, the TAR Statistical Yearbooks suggest that primary enrolments were higher in 1978 than at any time since then (see Figure 2.4). The increase in enrolments in rural areas was once again achieved through the widespread expansion of community schools. National targets urged local officials to provide a primary school for every production brigade, as well as a junior secondary school. However, it is difficult to tell the extent to which this actually happened. The chronic shortage of teachers, which was acknowledged before the Cultural Revolution, must cast doubt on the teaching in the new schools, even if new schools were constructed. According to Israel Epstein: 'It was pointed out that

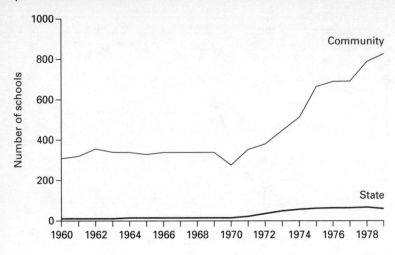

Figure 2.5 State and community primary schools in Lhasa Municipality, 1960–79 (*Source*: Lhasa in Progress 1952–84)

in some cases, because of the continuing burden, schools that had begun well had later fallen off or even gone out of commission.'[41]

Figure 2.5 shows the apparent rapid growth of primary schools in the Lhasa Municipality in the 1970s, and the particular growth of community schools.[42] Even if some of these schools barely functioned, the rationale behind the development of community schools – to cut down the costs of boarding or travel by building a greater quantity of smaller schools – had particular significance for the TAR. Since much of the region is remote and sparsely populated, an increase in the number of schools would undoubtedly have a positive effect on enrolment. As we will see in Chapter 6, the reversal of this policy in the 1980s led to a decline in enrolment and widespread drop-out. In Box 2.3 below, we find a description of life in one of these community schools in the late 1970s.

On paper, secondary education also expanded in the TAR during the Cultural Revolution decade. By 1978 there were said to be eighty-eight secondary schools in the region and just over 22,000 students (see Figure 2.6). As in the rest of China, the expansion of secondary education was made possible largely through the addition of junior secondary classes to the village primary schools.[43] The curriculum was based essentially on vocational skills and politics, with a stripped-down academic curriculum which included basic Tibetan, Chinese and physical education. Box 2.4 gives an indication of what life was like in Lhasa's No. 1

Figure 2.6 Enrolment in secondary education in the TAR, 1960–94 (*Sources*: 1995 TAR Statistical Yearbook; 1989 TAR Statistical Yearbook)

Secondary School in 1976, when Mao's 'red' and 'quantity' educational strategy was still dominant.

Summary

Between 1949 and 1978, educational policy in China swung between two strategies that came to be known as 'red' and 'expert', 'egalitarian' and 'hierarchical', or 'quantity' and 'quality'. The changes in strategy, which were often abrupt, reflected the power struggles at the centre of Chinese politics between Mao Zedong, who promoted mass education with a strong ideological content (red), and Liu Shaoqi and Deng Xiaoping, who promoted technical, academic education (expert). Educational development in central Tibet, which was to become the TAR in 1965, was driven by these political conflicts at the centre. Community schools were hurriedly established in central Tibet in 1959, during Mao's Great Leap Forward campaign. Many of them were then abruptly closed in the early 1960s following directives from Central China by proponents of the 'quality' strategy. It appears that, at times, the implementation of these different strategies in Tibet was a question of paying lip-service to the correct political line since they often bore little relation to the realities of educational development in the region. This can be seen particularly in the drive to promote higher education in the mid-1960s. The upgrading of Tibet State School, from a secondary to

Box 2.3 Red Flag People's Commune School, 1978

The commune has one primary school with one teacher and about 70 students. The school has five grades and schooling lasts for five years. Our first teacher was Tsering Dhondup but he was dismissed due to his unsatisfactory class background, and replaced by a young man of about twenty, named Tsering. He was not well educated and could not teach well as he had only been to our commune school and had 6 months teacher's training after that.

Children above 16 are not allowed to remain in the commune school and those below 16 cannot get work-points if they want to work. So these children have to attend the school, even if the education is unsatisfactory. Another incentive is that all school children get five work-points whenever there is work organized by the schools.

The school has a six-hour working day during which songs, arithmetic, dances and Tibetan would be taught along with some manual work. On Sundays the children work within their brigade. During spring and autumn the school is closed and the children have to store grain, repair roads, cut grass and manure the fields. On completing the fifth class the students work in their own brigades.

The teachers' salary is deducted from the work-points of all the members of the commune and the parents have also to pay for the expenses incurred at school (books, pens etc.) The Chinese send children for higher education only if they have a sound class background. Above the primary level Chinese predominates increasingly. About 90 per cent of the children are not sent for further education. The few who go to China for higher education do so on the basis of class background and not on merit.

There is a meeting once in every week where the children engage in criticism and self-criticism. The Chinese emphasize that the essence of education is to develop a love for hard labour and humble style of living. The children are asked to report any anti-Chinese remark or act they see. They are also made to cultivate a garden and kill flies, birds, rats and dogs. The Chinese lecture them constantly about the prosperity and happiness brought by the Chinese liberation and condemn the old society where the 'crimes committed by the three big serf owners cannot fit in the sky'.

Source: Dhondub Choedon, Life in the Red Flag People's Commune (Information Office of H.H. the Dalai Lama, 1978), pp. 22–3.

Box 2.4 A Lhasa secondary school at the end of
the Cultural Revolution, 1976

Lhasa's No. 1 Secondary School ... had 1,400 students ... Over nine-tenths were from labouring-class families. Students were both Tibetan and Han, about half and half (since this school was directly under the autonomous region, it served also the children of in-coming cadres). Instruction was in both tongues, depending on the students. For the Han, Tibetan was taught as a second language, we were told.

There was a very heavy emphasis on labour. Besides going to communes and factories for a period, the students reclaimed land for grain and vegetable farms and worked in a school factory making cement and reinforced concrete products. Their chalk workshop produced not only for themselves but for Lhasa's educational goods market. All this, we were informed, had made the school self-supporting; it no longer took a cent from the state.

Many subjects besides were learned not in the classroom or laboratory but in workshop or field. Each class, in each grade, concentrated on one or more practical specialities, as follows:

Junior 1: Barley and wheat cultivation; pig raising; making fermented fodder.

Junior 2: Agricultural meteorology and simple soil analysis; hot house vegetable growing; preparation and application of compost and other fertilizers; chalk manufacture.

Junior 3: Farm machinery; farm accounting; elementary veterinary work; methane gas installation and use.

Senior 1: Farm machinery; farm electricity; 'barefoot' medicine; household and farm use of solar energy; observation and prediction of earthquakes (frequent in Tibet).

Senior 2: Irrigation; building construction; intermediate veterinary training; rural broadcasting.

The overall curriculum, reduced from six years to five, had also been stripped down to a few headings: politics, Han language, Tibetan language, mathematics, basic industrial and agricultural knowledge, and athletics. We found few students indoors. Part of the campus had become a yard for concrete and cement work (slabs for bridges, telegraph poles etc.). Mixers churned. Hammers clanged. In a nearby section, students were catching and castrating pigs as their veterinary practice. In the vegetable garden other students were using an old tractor. Off-

> season, we were told, they took it apart, put it together again and practised repairs.
>
> Most textbooks had been replaced by teaching notes and mimeographed sheets. Some of this seemed a refreshing departure from too much academicism. Some was an exaggeration, in part stemming from the 'model' set up in the Chaoyang Agricultural College in Northeast China under the 'Gang of Four'.
>
> Source: Israel Epstein, Tibet Transformed (New World Press, Beijing, 1983), p. 343.

a tertiary institution, appears to have been no more than a change of name since few, if any, of the students were of university standard; indeed, some were illiterate.

Events of this period also demonstrate that while these China-wide shifts in educational policy directly affected educational development in Tibet, specific strategies connected with China's 'minority education' policy (minzu jiaoyu) had a further bearing on the development of education in the region, although these strategies were also affected by the 'red' and 'expert' dichotomy. In the early 1950s, when the Dalai Lama was still in Tibet and the 'expert' or 'quality' strategy was dominant, the Chinese government took a gradualist approach to educational development in the region. It began by providing further education for the traditional elite, which was not only strategically important in terms of winning over the Tibetan people, it also coincided with the goals of the 'quality' strategy, since these students were from educated families and had been to school already. In the first schools set up by the Chinese communist government, religious instruction was permitted as well as Tibetan medium instruction. The ascendancy of Mao's 'red', 'egalitarian' or 'quantity' strategy coincided with the Lhasa Uprising in 1959 and the flight of the Dalai Lama to India. The coincidence of these two events – revolt by Tibetans and revolutionary policies from Beijing – led to the reinterpretation of Tibetan culture and language as being unpatriotic and ultimately elitist. In the early 1960s the policy was reversed when Mao's influence waned briefly. In 1966, when the Cultural Revolution engulfed China, the policies connected with developing a distinctive Tibetan education system in the TAR were rejected. In China, anything that could be considered elitist in education was attacked. In the TAR, this included all manifestations of Tibetan culture in the curriculum.

With the end of the Cultural Revolution, the 'quality' strategy under

Deng Xiaoping once more took hold in China and has continued up to the present day. The next chapter deals with how the priorities connected with this strategy have affected educational developments in the TAR during the past two decades; it also describes the renewed importance given to the specific strategic role of 'minority education' in the TAR after the resurgence of nationalist unrest at the end of the 1980s.

Notes

1. Mao Zedong, 'Investigations of the Peasant Movement in Hunan' (1927), cited in Keith M. Lewin, Xu Hui, Angela Little, Zheng Jiwei, *Educational Innovation in China* (Longman, Harlow, 1994), p. 34.

2. Ibid., p. 36.

3. Ibid.

4. Yenming Zhang, *Effects of Policy Changes on College Enrolment of Minority Students in China, 1949–1989*, Doctoral Thesis (Harvard University, 1991), p. 97.

5. Lewin et al., *Educational Innovation in China*, p. 7.

6. Suzanne Pepper, 'Chinese Education After Mao: Two Steps Forward, Two Steps Back and Begin Again?', *China Quarterly*, No. 81, 1980, p. 7.

7. Bernhard Dilger, 'The Education of Minorities', *Comparative Education*, Vol. 20, No. 1, 1984, p. 158.

8. Yenming Zhang, *Effects of Policy Changes*, p. 43.

9. Ma Xulun, Report on the First National Conference on Nationality Education, 23 November 1951, cited in ibid.

10. Ibid., p. 45.

11. *Renmin Ribao*, 14 June 1951, cited in Dilger, 'The Education of Minorities'.

12. 'Shaoshu Minzu Jiaoyu', 'Minority Nationality Education', in *Jianyu Nianjian 1985–86* (Education Yearbook of China), cited in Gerard Postiglione, 'Implications of Modernization for the Education of China's Minorities', in Ruth Hayhoe (ed.), *Education and Modernization – The Chinese Experience* (Pergamon Press, London, 1992).

13. Yenming Zhang, *Effects of Policy Changes*, p. 49.

14. Clause 9, 'Agreement of the Central People's Government and the Local Government of Tibet on Measures for the Peaceful Liberation of Tibet', *New China News Agency*, 27 May 1951.

15. Yang Jingren, *'Jianjue Guanche Zhongyang Zhishi Zuo Hao Xizang Gongzuo'* (On the Correct Implementation of the Central Committee's Directive and Carrying Out Work for Tibet Well), *Hongqi* (Red Flag), No. 15, 1980, pp. 2–8.

16. Ibid.

17. Yenming Zhang, *Effects of Policy Changes*, p. 73.

18. Ibid., p. 101.

19. The Panchen Lama's 1962 petition to Mao Zedong provides considerable detail on the repercussions of 'land reform' in Tibet. See *A Poisoned Arrow, The Secret Report of the Tenth Panchen Lama* (Tibet Information Network, London, 1997).

20. Yenming Zhang, *Effects of Policy Changes*, p. 87.

21. Duojie Caidan (Dorje Tseten), *Xizang Jiaoyu* (Education in Tibet) (China Tibetology Publishers, Beijing, 1991) (Dorje Tseten was one of the first deputy headmasters of Lhasa Primary School).

22. Israel Epstein, *Tibet Transformed* (New World Press, Beijing, 1983), p. 342.

23. Editorial, *People's Daily*, 22 April 1956, p. 1, cited in Yenming Zhang, *Effects of Policy Changes*, p. 86.

24. Yenming Zhang, *Effects of Policy Changes*, p. 166.

25. *Minzu Tuanjie* (Unity of Nationalities), No. 4, 1958, pp. 7–8. Cited in Dilger, 'The Education of Minorities', p. 158; see also Duojie Caidan (Dorje Tseten), *Education in Tibet*, p. 36.

26. Duojie Caidan (Dorje Tseten), *Education in Tibet*.

27. Pepper, 'Chinese Education After Mao', p. 7.

28. 1995 China Statistical Yeabook.

29. Pepper, 'Chinese Education After Mao', p. 7.

30. Ibid.

31. Ibid.; Lewin et al., *Educational Innovation in China*, p. 35.

32. Yenming Zhang, *Effects of Policy Changes*.

33. Lhasa Radio, 'Struggle Against Revisionists in TAR Teachers' College', 1100 gmt, 4 March 1976 [SWB 9/3/76].

34. Lhasa Radio, 'Report of Regional Meeting on Educational Work', 1100 gmt, 10 December 1974 [SWB 13/12/74].

35. Ibid.

36. Lhasa Radio, 'Tibet Education Conference', 1100 gmt, 27 December 1974 [SWB 17/1/75].

37. 1988 TAR Statistical Yearbook; see also Yenming Zhang, *Effects of Policy Changes*, p. 131.

38. TAR Teachers' College was upgraded to university status in 1985 and was renamed Tibet University.

39. Lhasa Radio, 'Report of a Ceremony in Lhasa on 16th July to Mark the Foundation of the TAR Teachers' College', 1100 gmt, 17 July 1975 [SWB 23/7/75].

40. *Introduction of Institutions of Higher Education in China* (Beijing Educational Science Press, 1982), p. 624.

41. Epstein, *Tibet Transformed*, p. 351.

42. Lhasa Municipality has the same administrative status and function as a prefecture of which there are six in the TAR: Lhasa Municipality, Chamdo (*Qamdo* or *Changdu*) Prefecture, Lhokha (*Shannan*) Prefecture, Ngari (*Ali*) Prefecture, Kongpo (*Linzhi*) Prefecture, Nagchu (*Naqu*) Prefecture and Shigatse (*Xigaze* or *Rigaze*) Prefecture.

43. Pepper, 'Chinese Education After Mao', p. 7.

CHAPTER 3

Socialist Modernization, 1978–97

The Four Modernizations: return of quality over quantity

After the death of Mao, the policies of the previous decade were declared by the new leaders to have been an unmitigated disaster. In 1977, Deng Xiaoping was rehabilitated and elected Vice Premier in Charge of Education. In December 1978, the Third Plenary Session of the Eleventh Central Committee of the CCP was convened. This meeting is now regarded as a historic turning point which terminated Mao Zedong's 'class struggle' and shifted the focus of the CCP's attention to economic construction and, in the words of Deng Xiaoping, 'socialist modernization with Chinese characteristics'.[1] In 1978, in a speech to the National Conference on Science, Deng Xiaoping said: 'We must eliminate for good the pernicious influence of the Gang of Four and take up the major task of producing as quickly as possible experts in science and technology who are up to the highest international standards.'[2] The following month at the National Conference on Education he reiterated the need to eliminate the 'absurdities spread by the Gang', adding that the first task was to 'improve the quality of education and raise the level of teaching in the sciences'.[3]

The 'egalitarian' strategy of the Cultural Revolution was severely criticized. The expansion of community schools during the 1970s was described as putting undue financial burdens on the people. As far as secondary education was concerned, the policies of the Cultural Revolution were held responsible for having 'spread financial resources very thinly, and aggravated the shortage of qualified teachers'.[4] In short, the 'quantity' strategy was blamed for having expanded the provision of education to the extent that the system had broken down altogether. Furthermore, in its 'unitary approach' to secondary education (i.e. in the abandoning of vocational and specialized secondary education) the strategy was said to have failed to meet the demands of economic development. But the new leadership reserved its greatest criticism for the policy towards higher education. The higher education system had been so disrupted by the Cultural Revolution that it was calculated that China had been deprived of 1.5 million potential graduates between 1965 and 1979.[5]

The new leadership declared China to be decades behind developed countries in science, technology and education. Finding an efficient way to modernize China became a national priority. The Four Modernizations programme (the modernization of industry, agriculture, science-technology and defence) was implemented to address this need and, consequently, the rapid training of high-level and specialized personnel became the priority. The new leaders still maintained a commitment to basic education, but not at the expense of urban, higher and specialized education. The imbalance between rural and urban provision was recognized, but it was no longer the priority; it would be rectified in time with the eventual development of the rural economy. The development of the national economy became paramount.

The Four Modernizations programme was planned in a way that could be described as capitalizing on existing assets. Investment would be focused on areas where it would produce maximum returns in the shortest time. Since the coastal provinces in Eastern China already had an established economic infrastructure, it was decided that the first stage of reform would concentrate investment in these areas. The underdeveloped, rural and mountainous regions to the west, which include the TAR, would form part of a second stage of economic development scheduled for the end of the 1990s.[6]

If we look at the development of education in China since 1978, we can see that a similar strategy for investment has been adopted. On the basis of cost-effectiveness, in order to produce maximum skilled manpower in the shortest time, investment has been greatest in areas where there is already a well-established educational infrastructure. This has marked a full-scale return to the 'quality', or 'hierarchical', strategy in education. 'The Ninth Five-Year Plan and Long-Term Targets for Education in China to the Year 2010', published in 1996, provides the following detailed directive about the need to promote 'quality' in education over 'quantity':

> It is imperative to correctly comprehend and handle the dialectical relationship between quantity and quality, between speed and efficiency and adhere to a developmental policy unifying scale and speed of development, on the one hand, and quality and efficiency on the other hand ... In view of prevalent tendencies of placing emphasis on speed at the cost of efficiency, it is imperative to give high priority to the quality and efficiency of educational provision so that the pattern of educational development will shift

from one emphasizing scale and speed to one placing greater emphasis on quality and efficiency. The choice of developmental strategies and the determination of speed of development should be made in the light of these considerations, and efforts should be made to attain an optimal allocation of educational resources through a proper combination of educational planning and market mechanisms.[7]

The result of this drive for quality – of giving emphasis to improving the best rather than the worst – is that certain priorities have emerged in education funding. These can be described as follows:

• developed provinces over less developed provinces
• urban education over rural education
• elite education over mass education
• higher education over basic education

In the following chapters we look at these priorities in detail, discussing each with regard to a particular aspect or level of the education system in the TAR and China.

Another development connected with the promotion of improved quality in education was the start of a process of drafting legislation relating to education. Until 1978, the Chinese government had relied entirely on administrative decrees and Party directives to guide and administer education.[8] However, during the drive to improve the quality of education, moves were made towards drawing up legislation for education. In 1983, the 'Provisional Regulations on Basic Requirements for Universalizing Primary Education' were adopted. In 1985, after wide consultation and the preparation of eleven drafts,[9] a more extensive policy document emerged: 'The Decision of the CCP Central Committee on the Reform of China's Educational Structure' (the 1985 'CCP Decision on Education'). It was this document, adopted on 27 May 1985, which provided the legal framework for adapting education development to the demands of the economy. The 'CCP Decision on Education' addressed several main issues:

• the introduction of nine-year compulsory education
• the promotion of vocational and technical education
• the reform of enrolment, job assignment and financial control in higher education
• the improvement in teaching quality and the expansion of teaching staff
• the reduction of Party involvement in the daily management of schools
• the diversification of sources of funding for education

Over the next ten years, these provisions were extended and adapted to produce a number of education laws. In 1986, the Law on Compulsory Education was adopted; this was followed in 1993 by the 'Programme for China's Educational Reform and Development', as well as the Law on Teachers. On 18 March 1995 the Education Law of the People's Republic of China was adopted by the Third Session of the National People's Congress; this was the first comprehensive education law in China's history.[10] According to the Chinese press, the drafting process of this law had taken ten years and had included extensive research in China and abroad, as well as five national discussion meetings. It was followed in 1996 by the Law on Vocational Education.

Changes in China's 'minority' nationality education policy

The rejection of the 'leftist' policies of the Cultural Revolution and the return to the 'quality'-oriented strategy of the early 1960s brought renewed recognition of the diverse needs of China's different nationalities. In March 1978, the State Nationalities Affairs Commission was re-established; Yang Jingren, who was of Hui nationality, became the minister-in-charge. In the same year, there were several regional conferences on 'minority education', followed, in May 1979, by the first conference of the State Nationalities Affairs Commission in Tianjin. The conference outlined the shift in the government's 'nationality work' from emphasizing politics to focusing on economic and educational development.[11] Nevertheless, Yang Jingren made it clear that the 'task of nationality work' was still to 'maintain social stability in border areas', as well as to train cadres for socialist modernization.[12] In 1981, there were three further national conferences, the most important being the National Conference on Education for 'Minority' Nationalities, which took place in Beijing.

As a result of these conferences a number of new measures were adopted. These included:

1. The establishment of a Department of Minority Education under the State Ministry of Education with corresponding departments or appointments at provincial, prefectural and county level.
2. New legislation allowing national minority areas to develop their own education programmes, including kinds of schools, curriculum content and the language of instruction.
3. The use of special funds for minority education: a portion of the annual budget for minority areas could be used for education.
4. The establishment of boarding schools and grants for students in pastoral areas.

5. The encouragement of 'minority' nationality languages, culture and traditions.
6. Co-operation between 'minority' nationality areas and inland provinces for the development of education.[13]

On 4 December 1982, the Fifth National People's Congress adopted the Fifth Constitution of the People's Republic of China. The constitution gave several guarantees for the education of non-Han Chinese nationalities. Article 119 stated that autonomous regions should have autonomy in the administration of education and should protect their cultural heritage in order 'vigorously to develop their cultures'. Article 121 allowed 'minority' nationalities to employ the written and spoken language in common use. Article 122 guaranteed that the state would provide financial, material and technical assistance to the 'minority' nationalities in order to accelerate economic and cultural development.[14] The Law of the PRC on Regional Autonomy, 1984, also included the right of 'minority' nationalities to conduct their affairs in their own languages, and to 'independently develop education for nationalities ... in order to train specialized personnel of "minority" nationalities'.[15] Eleven years later, the option for non-Han Chinese nationalities to provide teaching in their own languages became part of the 1995 Education Law. Article 12 of the law states that 'schools and other educational institutions primarily for "minority" nationalities may use the spoken or written language in common use among the ethnic group or in the locality as the language of instruction'.[16]

Education reforms in the TAR: the 1980s

The First Tibet Work Forum   In April 1980, the First Tibet Work Forum (First Forum) was held in Beijing to draw up plans for the development of the economy and education in the region. Following the meeting, the General Secretary of the Chinese Communist Party, Hu Yaobang, led a working group to the TAR, which included the head of the State Commission for Nationalities Affairs, Yang Jingren. The aim of the visit was to report to regional government officials on the decisions reached at the conference and to make an inspection tour. Hu Yaobang criticized local TAR officials for being slow to reject the policies of the Cultural Revolution, and outlined six major 'requirements' that needed to be addressed. These were intended to improve 'existing conditions', and Hu Yaobang set target dates by which these improvements were to be achieved.[17]

Of the 'six requirements' perhaps the most important for education was the renewed recognition of the TAR's 'special conditions'. Hu

Yaobang stated: 'anything that is not suited to Tibet's conditions should be rejected or modified.' The TAR government was to 'lay down laws, rules and regulations according to its special characteristics to protect the right of national autonomy and its special national interests'. The 'six requirements' also included the provision that state funds to the TAR should be increased, and should be used for what was termed the 'one development and two improvements', that is, the development of the economy and the improvement of living standards and education. In education, Hu Yaobang announced that, once again, Tibet's special characteristics should be taken into consideration, and that provided 'the socialist orientation is upheld, vigorous efforts should be made to revive Tibetan culture, education and science'.

One of the most important points made at the First Forum was the decision to transfer Han Chinese cadres out of the TAR and to train Tibetans to take their place.[18] Furthermore, those Han Chinese who remained in the TAR would henceforth be required to learn Tibetan.[19]

Yang Jingren remained in the TAR for two months, after which he wrote a report on conditions in the region and further directives on the implementation of the decisions of the First Forum. These included emphasis on the development of primary and secondary education, on training non-Han nationalities in the TAR, on scientific education, the use of Tibetan as the first language in education and public life, and the state funding of education.[20] His report was published in the journal *Hongqi* (Red Flag), the main ideological journal for the Chinese Communist Party. (An extract from the report regarding the 'special conditions' of the TAR and its rights to autonomy can be found in Appendix 4.)

It is clear from Yang Jingren's report and others written at the time, that the education of Tibetans in the TAR was in a parlous state. Yang's report contained the following observation: 'A typical situation in the TAR is that at the beginning of the school year the enrolment rate is high, about 70–80 per cent. In the second half of the year it drops to 40–50 per cent; by the second year the enrolment rate is about 30 per cent; by graduation only about 12 pupils are left.'[21]

Another report, written by the Tibetan university lecturer Tashi Tsering, mentions the disproportionate number of Han Chinese students in the education system in the TAR at that time. In one Lhasa secondary school, 55 per cent of the students were Han Chinese. According to his figures, in 1979, out of the TAR's quota of 600 students sent to institutes of higher education in Central China, only 10 per cent were Tibetan.[22] At the TAR Nationalities Institute there were only fifty-four Tibetan students out of a total of 175.[23]

Yang Jingren blamed poverty for the low educational levels in Tibet, which he said was due partly to historical factors but 'mainly to the destruction wrought by Lin Biao and the Gang of Four, as well as our shortcomings and mistakes in carrying out policy'. For this reason, he said, education in the TAR could be developed only with the help of the state.[24]

The Second Forum, in 1984, built on the plans outlined in the First Forum. Tibetan medium primary education was implemented for Tibetan children in all primary schools in the TAR.[25] As part of the state support promised at the First Forum for education, teachers were sent from other provinces in China to work in the TAR, and secondary school Tibetan students were sent to be educated in Central China. In 1987, a major policy document on the use of the Tibetan language in the TAR was drawn up by the TAR People's Congress at the instigation of the Tenth Panchen Lama and Ngapo Ngawang Jigme, a senior Tibetan official in China's CPPCC Standing Committee. The 'Provisions on the Study, Use and Development of Spoken and Written Tibetan (for trial implementation)' ('Provisions on the Use of Tibetan') was a detailed document that set out procedures for implementing Tibetan-language policy in education and public life. The regulations allowed the use of both Tibetan and Chinese, but Tibetan was to be the first language.[26] It also outlined a strategy for extending Tibetan medium instruction into secondary education.

Central government support for education in the TAR: the 'intellectual aid' scheme The pledge of increased state support to the TAR that was made at both the First and Second Forum included the incorporation of the TAR into the co-operation programme between non-Han nationality areas and Central China, adopted at the National Conference on 'Minority' Nationalities (see above). The educational part of this programme, known as the 'intellectual aid scheme',[27] has had considerable impact on educational development in the TAR over the last seventeen years. The scheme has three components:

1. Sending selected Tibetan children for secondary education to Central China.
2. Sending teachers from other provinces in China to work in schools and colleges in the TAR on two- to eight-year contracts.
3. The creation of links between certain schools and colleges in the TAR and similar institutions in China in order to improve teaching standards and school management.[28]

The scheme was designed to be the most efficient and cost-effective way to raise educational levels among Tibetans, in order to provide skilled manpower for the development of the Tibetan economy. Urban areas are the major beneficiaries of the scheme, although the 'Tibetan schools in China' programme was to select 60 per cent of its students from rural areas.[29] In the early 1980s, the short-term cost benefits of the 'intellectual aid' scheme were clear. The TAR had an acute lack of qualified Tibetan personnel. Furthermore, the difficult terrain and low numbers of pupils in rural areas made unit costs higher in the TAR than in other provinces in China.

Nevertheless, the programme has a number of side effects which are likely to have a negative impact on the long-term success of educational development in the TAR itself, as well as having implications for the development of Tibetan language and culture. Although the programme is substantially funded by the central government and by other provincial governments, the TAR government provides a proportion of the budget for the programme, and this includes costs for the construction of schools outside the TAR. This inevitably reduces the resources available for education in the region itself. The programme of sending teachers to Tibet, although it answers an urgent need for qualified teaching staff, also leads to a high turnover of staff in schools as Chinese teachers are entitled to extended home leave and some have relatively short-term contracts. Furthermore, since these teachers do not speak Tibetan (many of them are unable to speak even standard Chinese, *putonghua*), additional learning difficulties are created for Tibetan students.

It now appears that the 'intellectual aid' scheme, which was presented as an interim measure in 1980, has become a permanent feature of educational development for Tibetans. In 1996, provisions for education set out in the Ninth Five-Year Plan for the TAR indicated that the scheme would be a priority for the future, at least for the next fifteen years.[30] The scheme is discussed in greater detail in Chapter 7.

Patriotic education and the political role of 'minority' nationality education in the TAR: 1990s

By the beginning of the 1990s, the mood of compromise towards Tibetans and their traditional culture, which had emerged in the 1980s to compensate for the devastation of the Cultural Revolution, had evaporated. In the TAR, the autumn of 1987 saw the re-emergence of nationalist unrest which grew over the next ten years to reach levels not seen since the 1950s; nationalist movements were reappearing in other parts of China, and 1989 saw the crushing of the democracy movement in Beijing. By the beginning of the 1990s, the Chinese government needed to find a way of rallying the country behind it. With Marxist-Leninist ideology having lost much of its power, the government sought a cohesive ideology that would legitimize the CCP authority, and unite the Party and country.[31]

Patriotism became the dogma for the 1990s, which was to be instilled in China's citizens through a series of Patriotic Education Campaigns. Of course, patriotism has always been used in conjunction with other political doctrines in education, particularly in 'minority' education, but this was the first time that the Chinese government had made patriotism the primary ideology to legitimize its power throughout China.[32] Patriotic education campaigns took place throughout the 1990s; in the TAR there were major campaigns in 1990, 1994 and 1997. Although the campaigns were directed at all generations, young people were particularly targeted and thus schools became the main fora for patriotic education.[33] In 1993, the 'Programme for China's Educational Reform and Development' outlined the direction that education should take to the end of the century. The following year, the 'Guidelines for Patriotic Education' provided a handbook on the development of patriotic education in schools. The goals of patriotic education were defined as being: (1) to rejuvenate China's national spirit; (2) to strengthen the unity of nationalities (*minzu tuanjie*); (3) to reconstruct a sense of national esteem; and (4) to build a broad coalition under the Communist Party.

National unity and territorial integrity formed a major part of the re-education campaign. The government created an atmosphere of crisis in which hostile forces surrounding China were portrayed as being bent on either removing part of China's territory (Tibet) or preventing China from getting it back (Hong Kong and Taiwan). China's fight against 'external hostile forces' and for 'reunification' were important components of the patriotic education curriculum set out in the 'Guidelines for Patriotic Education'.

The use of patriotism by the Chinese government as a legitimizing ideology had two major repercussions on education in the TAR during the 1990s. First, the interpretation of Tibetan nationalism as being a plot by 'external hostile forces' headed by the Dalai Lama to split the motherland led to the reassertion of the primary political role of 'minority education' (*minzu jiaoyu*) to ensure stability. Secondly, the renewed emphasis on ethnic unity and amalgamation (*ronghe*), and on the Central Committee directive to use 'the guiding spirit of close connection with the Interior',[34] led to the reinterpretation of the notion of a separate Tibetan education system, giving priority to the education of Tibetans, as unpatriotic. Slogans of the 1980s such as 'Putting more

Tibetans in the Saddle' were replaced in the 1990s with calls for Tibetans to 'Greet people from outside our region with broad-minded hospitality'. Government officials, resorting to Engel's theories of social evolution (in the light of which the CCP describe Han Chinese culture as more advanced than 'minority' culture)[35] exhort Tibetans to 'allow other people to make money while we [Tibetans] make progress'.[36]

In 1994, the programme of educating Tibetan children in Central China was altered to include Han Chinese children resident in the TAR.[37] During the 1990s, the proportion of Tibetans in secondary and higher education has been declining. Furthermore, the policies of the 1980s that gave greater scope for including aspects of Tibetan culture in the school curriculum have been overtaken by the strategies of the patriotic education campaign in the TAR, which has focused on the 'backwardness' of Tibetan culture, including the language and religion, in comparison with Han Chinese culture. In recent years, it has also focused on attacking the Dalai Lama, portraying him as 'attempting to split the motherland under the guise of religion'.[38]

The Third Tibet Work Forum (Third Forum), which took place in Beijing from the 20 to 23 July 1994, stressed that stability was essential for reform: 'Tibet's stability is a prerequisite for guaranteeing the sustained development of various undertakings and gradually raising the people's living standards there. Without stability, we cannot establish anything.'[39] The Fifth TAR Conference on Education, which followed the Third Forum, discussed what this meant in terms of education, re-emphasizing that allegiance to China was the overriding goal of education in the TAR.[40] Chen Kuiyuan, TAR Party Secretary, told delegates: 'the success of our education does not lie in the number of diplomas issued … It lies, in the final analysis, in whether our graduating students are opposed to or turn their hearts to the Dalai clique and in whether they are loyal to or do not care about our great motherland and the great socialist cause.'[41] In a Lhasa Radio broadcast the following month, he explained more fully the rationale behind this policy:

> The essence of educational work is to cultivate qualified constructors and successors for the socialist cause, and this is the sole basic mission of minority nationality education … Currently, there is a practice that merely stresses education in science and culture and overlooks moral education. A man who merely receives education is certainly not a constructor and successor for the socialist cause. He may advocate socialism, but it is also likely that he opposes socialism. He may safeguard the unification of the motherland and national unity, but it is also possible that he will disrupt national unity and engage in activities to split the motherland. The broad masses of comrades on the educational front should have a clear understanding of this fact.[42]

The primary curriculum was defined as being fundamental to implementing the policies of the Third Forum and the Fifth TAR Conference on Education.[43] In his paper on curriculum in 1996, Yang Wanli explained the importance of the primary curriculum in fulfilling the political role of education in the TAR: 'The curriculum for both higher and basic education must depend on whether it can guarantee the unity and territorial integrity of the country; the curriculum is directly connected with the question of "stability" of the whole country.'[44]

Following the Third Forum, the TAR CCP set up the TAR Curriculum Co-ordination Leading Group in order to carry out curriculum reform to reflect the new priorities of patriotic education.[45] The curriculum has a different emphasis in rural areas and urban areas. In urban areas it focuses on teaching students about the benefits of economic reform and the socialist market system. It aims to encourage them 'to voluntarily commit themselves to reforms, opening up and Tibet's economic development'.[46] However, in rural areas where the population has yet to taste the benefits of economic reform, teachers of patriotic education have been instructed to focus on contrasting life in Tibet before 1950 with the TAR today, by using family archives, genealogical records, village histories.[47] During the 1994 patriotic education campaign, educators were directed to encourage patriotism by: 'The method of recalling past suffering and considering the source of present happiness, and comparing the old society and the new society, [and by this] we should let the young generation acquire an understanding of the dark serf system and see the true colours of the Dalai clique.'[48]

Since 1994, the patriotic education programme has been firmly integrated into the education system. Flag-raising and lowering, singing the national anthem, making speeches on patriotism, and staging patriotic performances are some of the ways in which political education is carried out in schools.[49] In 1997, Tibet University became a particular focus of the patriotic education programme. A three-month campaign was launched on the campus, from April to June; it included a study of the theories of Marx and Lenin, including their theories on nationality and religion; and a series of lectures and discussions on 'special topics'. According to a Lhasa Radio broadcast on 14 April, the campaign was designed to 'rid the Dalai's influence in the spiritual area', in order 'to build spiritual civilization in Tibet … and to improve [students'] understanding and enhance consciousness of safeguarding the unification of the motherland and ethnic unity'.[50]

The renewed emphasis on the primary political role of 'minority education' in the last ten years has had a number of repercussions on

---

Box 3.1 Patriotic education: test paper from a Lhasa
secondary school, 1990

*Question 3. How can Tibet become a powerful and wealthy nation?
Through:*

*i. Continuation of the leadership of the Communist Party, of the
Reform and Open Door Policy, and advancing in harmony between the
nationalities.*

ii. Independence.

Part Two: Easy Answers

*1. The 40 years of peaceful liberation of Tibet have meant the 40
years of development in society and in the overall situation. It has also
meant 40 years of development in social production and people have
begun to own their own homes. What is your opinion about this?*

*4. Since the end of last year, 66.6 per cent (a total of 37,000) of
school staff are members of the minority nationality of the Autonomous
Region. Also more than half of skilled workers are from minority
nationality groups. Many people from other parts of the country come
to help and support nationality areas, particularly those who are being
trained as skilled workers. What is your opinion of these facts?*

*6. Since 1987 there have been many riots in Lhasa, including riots
by monks. What is your new opinion of the principle behind these
demonstrations and their damaging nature?*

*8. Relations between the Yuan dynasty and the Sakya sect in Tibet
were strengthened and Tibet became a real member and an inseparable
part of the motherland, which is an unchangeable fact of historical
development. How do you see these [developments]?*

*10. Do you believe in religion? What are the common religious
festivals or activities?*

*11. Do you consider that the Dalai Lama is a religious leader or a
political leader? Give your reasons.*

*12. What particular area are you interested in: international affairs
and internal affairs or Tibetan affairs?*

---

life in schools in the TAR. The extent of the patriotic education campaigns has led to a significant erosion of time available for other subjects: during the 1990 campaign, half a day per week was devoted to
political study in every school in Lhasa.[51] The political imperative of
fostering patriotism towards China has resulted in Tibetan and Chinese

children being taught to denigrate traditional Tibetan culture. Furthermore, the seriousness of the campaign has meant that children who do not display patriotic tendencies have been arrested and imprisoned.[52] A circular from a secondary school in Lhasa sent on 3 January 1989 to officials and parents about the continuation of political study during the holidays, told parents: 'If anyone is found to have done anything against the rules, no matter for what reason, they will be expelled. In serious cases they will be reported to the Public Security Department for punishment. All parents of students must co-operate with their unit and with the school in order to educate their children.' Between 1989 and 1994, there have sixty-four known arrests of children under the age of eighteen in the TAR.[53] In December 1989, five schoolchildren from No. 1 Secondary School were arrested and imprisoned for displaying pro-independence posters in their school and making copies of the banned Tibetan national flag.[54] Box 3.1 gives an indication of the sort of questions Tibetan children have to answer in patriotic education. It is an extract from a test paper from a Lhasa secondary school.

Summary

After the death of Mao, the Four Modernizations programme was adopted, in order to modernize China efficiently. Modernization was planned in such a way as to capitalize on existing assets. In education, a similar strategy was adopted, with a full-scale return to the 'quality', or 'hierarchical', strategy. As a part of this strategy, moves were made to draft legislation by which education was to be guided and administered.

Meanwhile, there was a renewed recognition of the diverse needs of China's different nationalities. Departments of Minority Education were established at each level of government, and legislation was passed allowing minority areas to develop their own education programmes. The Fifth Constitution, adopted in 1982, gave several guarantees relating to autonomy of minority nationalities as regards education. In the TAR, the First Tibet Work Forum, which was convened in 1980, drew up a set of guidelines for the development of the region that included the renewed recognition of the TAR's 'distinctive character', and the transfer of Han Chinese personnel out of the region. Furthermore, the TAR was incorporated into the 'intellectual aid scheme', which included sending teachers from Central China to the TAR and Tibetan children to Central China for secondary education. In 1985, Tibetan medium education was introduced into all primary schools for Tibetans in the TAR, and in 1987 the 'Provisions on the Use of Tibetan' outlined a strategy for extending Tibetan medium instruction into secondary schools.

However, the situation changed once more in the early 1990s. With the resurgence of nationalist unrest in the TAR and in other parts of China over the subsequent ten years, the authorities needed to find a cohesive ideology that would legitimize CCP authority and unite the Party and country. A series of Patriotic Education Campaigns resulted; in the TAR there were major campaigns in 1990, 1994 and 1997, during which special emphasis was placed on national unity and territorial integrity. The results for education in the TAR were twofold: first, the use of patriotism as a legitimizing ideology resulted in 'minority education' once more having the primarily political role of ensuring stability. Second, the renewed emphasis on ethnic unity led to the idea that a Tibetan education system, prioritizing the education of Tibetans, was unpatriotic. Following the Third Forum in 1994, curricular reform was carried out to reflect the new priorities of patriotic education.

Notes

1. CCP Central Party Committee, 'Communiqué of the Third Party plenary Session of the Eleventh Central Committee of the CCP', 22 December 1978, *Beijing Review*, No. 52, 29 December 1978.

2. Deng Xiaoping, 'Speech to the Opening Ceremony of National Conference on Science', 18 March 1978, in Deng Xiaoping, *Speeches and Writings* (Pergamon Press, London, 1984).

3. Ibid.

4. *Xinhua*, 17 August 1979.

5. Yat Ming Leung, 'The People's Republic of China', in *Education and Development in East Asia* (Garland Press, London, 1995).

6. Teng Xing, '*Wo Guo Shaoshu Minzu Diqu Jiaoyu Zhengti Gaige Guanjian*' (The Essence of Overall Educational Reform in China's Minority Regions), *Qui Shi*, No. 7, April 1989, pp. 19–24.

7. State Education Commission of the PRC, 'Five-Year Plan for Educational Development Toward the Year 2010' [sic], Beijing, 1996.

8. Huang Wei, 'Authoritative Comments on China's Education Law', *Beijing Review*, 22–28 May 1995, p. 12.

9. Y. M. Leung, *China's Education System in Crisis: Can Structural Reform Help?* (University of Hong Kong, Dept of Professional Studies in Education, mimeo, 1986, cited in Keith M. Lewin, Xu Hui, Angela Little and Zheng Jiwei, *Educational Innovation in China* (Longman, Harlow, 1994), p. 7.

10. Huang Wei, 'Authoritative Comments', p. 12.

11. Zhang Ru, 'The Starting Point of Nationality Work', *Unity of Nationalities*, No. 1, 1979, pp. 14–17.

12. Yang Jingren, 'Tasks of Nationality Work in the New Socialist Period',

cited in Yenming Zhang, *Effects of Policy Changes on College Enrolment of Minority Students in China, 1949–1989*, Doctoral Thesis (Harvard University, 1991), p. 173.

13. Gerard Postiglione, 'Implications of Modernization for the Education of China's Minorities', in R. Hayhoe (ed.), *Education and Modernization – The Chinese Experience* (Pergamon Press, London, 1992), p. 315.

14. Constitution of People's Republic of China (Foreign Languages Press, Beijing, 1987), pp. 70–1.

15. 'Law on Regional Autonomy for "Minority" Nationalities of the People's Republic of China', 1984, article 37.

16. Education Law, 1995, article 12.

17. Hu Yaobang, 'Report to TAR Regional Party Committee Cadres', Lhasa Radio, 1430 gmt, 30 May 1980 [SWB 4/6/80].

18. Yang Jingren, *'Jianjue Guanche Zhongyang Zhishi Zuo Hao Xizang Gongzuo'* (On the Correct Implementation of the Central Committee's Directive and Carrying Out Work for Tibet Well), *Hongqi* (Red Flag), No. 15, 1980, pp. 2–8; Wang Yao, 'Hu Yaobang's Visit to Tibet, May 22–23 1980', in Robert Barnett and Shirin Akiner (eds), *Resistance and Reform in Tibet* (Hurst and Co., London, 1994), p. 288.

19. Wang Yao, 'Hu Yaobang's Visit to Tibet'.

20. Yang Jingren, 'On the Correct Implementation of the Central Committee's Directive', p. 99.

21. Ibid., pp. 2–8.

22. Melvyn Goldstein, William Siebenschuh and Tashi Tsering, *The Struggle for Modern Tibet, The Autobiography of Tashi Tsering* (M. E. Sharpe, New York, 1997), p. 188.

23. Introduction of Tibet Institute of Nationalities, cited in Yenming Zhang, *Effects of Policy Changes*, p. 193.

24. Yang Jingren, 'On the Correct Implementation of the Central Committee's Directive', pp. 2–8.

25. 'Summary Report of Second Work Forum', cited in Duojie Caidan (Dorje Tseten), *Xizang Jiaoyu* (Education in Tibet) (China Tibetology Publishers, Beijing, 1991).

26. 'Provisions on the Study, Use and Development of Spoken and Written Tibetan (for trial implementation)', cited in Luo Qun, *The Tibetan People's Right of Autonomy* (New Star Publishers, Beijing, 1991).

27. Dai Yannian, 'Helping Tibet Train Its People', *Beijing Review*, Vol. 30, No. 42, 19 October 1987, p. 4.

28. Tibet University, the TAR Institute of Agriculture and Animal Husbandry, and the TAR Nationalities Institute are run with the assistance of nine Chinese institutions of higher education including the Beijing Institute of Economics. Nine of Tibet's vocational secondary schools, including the schools of animal husbandry, finance, and art, are being run with the assistance of Chinese educational institutions in the ministries and commissions under the State Council. Seven provinces and cities have links with general secondary schools in Lhasa, Shigatse, Ngari and Chamdo. See Dai Yannian, 'Helping Tibet Train Its People'.

29. *Xinhua*, 31 July 1994 [SWB 2/8/94].

30. 'Outline of the TAR's Five-Year Plan for Economic and Social Development and Its Long-term Target for 2010, Approved by the Fourth Session of the Sixth Regional People's Congress on 24 May 1996', *Xizang Ribao* (Tibet Daily), 7 June 1996, pp. 1–4 (TAR Ninth Five-Year Plan, 1996).

31. Samuel Wang, 'Teaching Patriotism in China', *China Strategic Review*, Vol. 1, No. 3, 1997.

32. Ibid.

33. *Renmin Ribao* (People's Daily), 15 September 1994.

34. See Yang Wanli, '*Xizang Kecheng Jiaocai Yanjiu De Teshuxing Jiqi Duice*' (The Countermeasure and Particularity of Research on Teaching Materials), *Xizang Yanjin* (Tibet Studies), Vol. 58, No. 1, 1996.

35. See Yang Jingren, 'On the Correct Implementation of the Central Committee's Directive'.

36. Tibet TV, 26 November 1997.

37. 'Raidi and Gyaltsen Norbu Summarize Third Tibet Work Forum Conclusions', *Xizang Ribao* (Tibet DaiLy), 2 August 1994 [SWB 21/8/94].

38. Tibet Radio, 14 April 1997.

39. See 'Raidi and Gyaltsen Norbu Summarize Third Tibet Work Forum Conclusions'.

40. See Chen Kuiyuan, 'Speech on Education in Tibet', Fifth Regional Meeting on Education in the TAR, 26 October 1994, *Xizang Ribao* (Tibet Daily), 28 October 1994.

41. Ibid.

42. 'Chen Kuiyuan in Qamdo Says Prosperity Will Drive Out Religion', Tibet People's Broadcasting Station, Lhasa, 28 November 1994 [SWB 5/12/94].

43. Yang Wanli, 'The Countermeasure and Particularity of Research on Teaching Materials'.

44. Ibid.

45. Ibid.

46. *Renmin Ribao* (People's Daily), 1 October 1994.

47. Ibid.

48. Document No. 5 of the Sixth Enlarged Plenary Session of the Standing Committee of the Fourth Congress of the TAR Branch of the CCP, 5 September 1994.

49. TAR CCP, 'Circular on Patriotic Education', *Xizang Ribao* (Tibet Daily), 22 December 1994.

50. Lhasa Radio, 14 April 1997.

51. *Lasa Wanbao* (Lhasa Evening News), 21 August 1990.

52. Lhasa Radio, 8 December 1989.

53. TIN Prisoners Database.

54. Lhasa Radio, 8 December 1989.

CHAPTER 4

Economic Reform: Regional Disparity in Education Provision

Funding: diversification of sources

The last two chapters have examined the extent to which educational development in the TAR has been bound up with the political struggles in China during the last fifty years. This chapter looks at the role of the economy in the development of education in the region. More specifically, it looks at the effect on educational development of China's transition from a centrally planned economy to a market economy, and at how educational development has become dependent on the economic development of individual provinces or regions.

Of all the issues addressed in the 1985 'CCP Decision on Education', the diversification of educational funding has had the greatest impact on regional disparity in education provision in the last decade. Indeed, the reform of education funding was probably the most significant of all the financial reforms instituted in China in the early 1980s. The reform was essentially realized on two levels. It involved the devolution of central government funding to local government, and the diffusion of government sources of funding to non-government sources. Local governments were to take over financial responsibility for developing basic education from the central government. They were required not only to allocate 'a proper percentage of their reserve funds' to education, but also to raise revenue in a variety of ways. These included charging education surtaxes; eliciting donations from organizations and individuals; encouraging state-owned enterprises, public organizations and individuals to run schools; charging certain fees to students.

The effect of these financial reforms has been to render school finance almost totally reliant on the local economy. In 1991, of the total funding for education, 88.03 per cent was raised at the provincial and sub-provincial level; and, of that, 37.97 per cent came from non-government sources.[1] Certain provisions were made in the 1985 'CCP Decision on Education' about the funding of education in underdeveloped areas and in areas inhabited by 'minority' nationalities. These provisions included an allocation for education in the annual central government budget for 'minority' nationality areas. Other central government funding programmes such as the subsidy for economically underdeveloped areas and the funding for frontier construction included an education component, for the first time. (In Qinghai, Guizhou and Yunnan, it was stipulated that 25 to 30 per cent of the subsidy for underdeveloped areas could be used for 'minority education'.)[2] The proportion of state assistance to 'minority' nationality areas was not defined in the 1985 'CCP Decision on Education', nor the proportion that was to come from the central government; the 1993 'Programme for China's Educational Reform and Development' made further recommendations for funding in 'minority' nationality areas. However, despite the policy ambitions of the government, according to some educationalists and government officials, the amount of funding for 'minority' nationality areas has not been enough to be effective.[3] In May 1996, Zhu Kaixuan, Minister of the State Education Commission, announced that 'insufficient investment' was 'the key obstacle' to spreading compulsory education in the underdeveloped areas of China.[4]

Before the reforms, all revenues from regional and provincial governments were submitted to the central government which redistributed them throughout the country. After the 1985 'CCP Decision on Education', however, local governments were allowed to retain most of their revenues to spend on local expenditures, and education was the main expenditure.[5] But, although local governments now controlled education expenditure, the central government still gave direction as to how it should be allocated. The new process came to be described by the catchphrase 'the central government hosts the banquet – the local governments foot the bill'.[6]

The consequences of these financial reforms were dramatic. From 1985, education investment was directly dependent on the local economy – on the economic performance of the individual region, province, county or even village. At the regional or provincial level, the reforms not only meant that provinces with richer economies could allocate more to education from the start, but the government's strategy of investing in these provinces first – granting them tax exemptions, cheap industrial land and making substantial government investment in their infrastructure – meant that the disparity between these provinces and the underdeveloped regions, in terms of revenue available for education, grew sharply over the subsequent ten years (see Map 4.1). Shenzhen, for example, which was designated a 'special economic zone' in 1979, developed in ten years from a small agricultural county into a modern industrial city. In 1990, it had the highest per capita GNP in China: 6,963 yuan.[7] The TAR, which was a low priority for investment since its economic development was only planned for the 1990s, inevitably had, and still has, fewer resources at its disposal for educational development. In 1990, the GNP per capita in the TAR was 1,270 yuan.[8] In 1995, one Tibetan government official wrote a paper in which he discussed the dangers of neglecting investment in areas such as the TAR in favour of the developed coastal regions:

> Tibetan areas must depend on the investment of the state to develop themselves. In recent years Tibet developed quite quickly. This was due to the favoured policies and investments of the central government. Why did the coastal areas develop so quickly? Apart from their favourable natural conditions, this was due to substantial government investment and favourable policies. So, if the Tibetan areas want to develop, they also need State investment.
>
> If there is a continuation of the present economic strategy of focusing construction and investment on coastal regions and in central China, and making Tibetan areas depend on their support for economic development, then the economic gap between Tibetan areas and other parts of the county will widen. This means that the current inequitable situation, where Tibetan areas supply raw materials and primary products to coastal regions and central China at very low prices and then have to buy back from them the manufactured goods at very high prices, will continue and the State will have to support Tibetan areas for ever. This violates the principle of making all nationalities equal in a socialist society, on the basis of developing and thriving together.
>
> Secondly, if the 'minority' nationalities are not able to improve their backward economy and education, or obtain material guarantees, then the so-called autonomy system of being masters of their own affairs won't be able to come into effect, in spite of the State delegating to the nationalities the right and authority to administer their own affairs. And then the historically-inherited problem of inequality between the nationalities will become more conspicuous. In this way there will be more misunderstanding between the nationalities and this will provoke national conflicts. Therefore, in order to develop the economy and education in Tibetan areas, it is vitally important that the State practices more favourable policies and invests more in these areas.[9]

In 1992, the TAR was made a 'special economic zone'; tax concessions were given to the region as well as low land-use fees to encourage investment from other parts of China and abroad.[10] Expenditure on education shows a significant increase after this date, as does enrolment at all levels. According to official statistics, between 1991 and 1996, educational expenditure of local governments below provincial level in

GDP per capita below 1,500 yuan
GDP per capita between 1,500 and 2,500 yuan
GDP per capita between 2,500 and 3,500 yuan
GDP per capita between 3,500 and 4,500 yuan
GDP per capita between 4,500 and 5,500 yuan

1. GDP per capita = 8,240 yuan
2. GDP per capita = 6,075 yuan
3. GDP per capita = 11,700 yuan

Map 4.1 Per capita income by province in China, 1993 (*Source*: 1995 China Statistical Yearbook)

the TAR increased by 60 per cent over the preceding five years.[11] In 1994, state appropriation per student appears to have been almost double that in China as a whole, although this increase is likely to reflect higher unit costs rather than better facilities.[12] However, despite the growth of GDP in the 1990s and the growth in education expenditure, the economic and educational gap is widening between rural western regions such as the TAR and the developed coastal provinces. At its most extreme, the economic gap is such that in 1993, the per capita GDP for Shanghai was 11,700 yuan compared with 1,642 yuan for the TAR (see Map 4.1).[13]

Nine-year compulsory education: regional disparity in implementation

The provision of nine-year compulsory education was a key point of the 1985 'CCP Decision on Education', the guidelines of which were enshrined in the Law on Compulsory Education the following year. The 'CCP Decision on Education' outlined plans for the gradual introduction of six years of primary education and three years of junior secondary education which eventually would be compulsory for all children in China. The implementation of compulsory education was to follow the same regional strategy as economic development: (1) cities and economically developed areas in coastal provinces and some parts of the interior would universalize compulsory education by 1990; (2) economically semi-developed townships and villages would universalize compulsory education by 1995; (3) economically underdeveloped areas would, as economic development permitted, take a variety of measures to spread elementary education in varying degrees.

No time limit was given for the universalization of compulsory education in underdeveloped areas, which include the TAR. Despite the arguments put forward to make education 'the engine for growth', the 'CCP Decision on Education', the 'Programme for China's Educational Reform and Development' and the 1986 Law on Compulsory Education all stipulated that compulsory education should be implemented gradually, region by region, 'in accordance with the degree of economic and cultural development in their own localities'.[14] Indeed the Programme for China's Educational Reform and Development made it clear that economically developed areas were to 'take the lead in having their educational levels reaching those of medium developed countries by the end of the 1990s'.[15] All these documents nevertheless indicated that state support would be given to regions inhabited by 'minority' nationalities 'by providing them with teachers and funds'.[16]

In the TAR, the Compulsory Education Programme was not introduced until 1994. A directive issued by the TAR Education Commission in May 1993 indicated that it would be introduced initially on an experimental basis in ten counties. The length of compulsory education outlined in the directive was as follows:

- four years in pastoral areas
- six years in agricultural areas
- nine years in major cities and towns[17]

By 1996, according to the TAR Regional Education Commission, only Chushul (*Quxu*) county in Lhasa Municipality, which in 1995 had been awarded the status of a model county, and the Chengguan district of Lhasa city had achieved six-year compulsory education for all its children.[18] Chushul is an agricultural area, but Lhasa is the TAR's largest city, and should, according to the above guidelines, be providing nine years of compulsory education to all its children. The 1993 directive

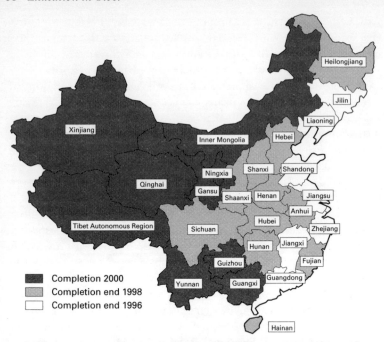

Map 4.2 Implementation of compulsory education by region in China (*Source*: Data from *China Daily*, 8 May 1996)

had allowed a grace period for postponing school attendance to the age of nine in remote pastoral parts of the TAR. By 1996, the length of compulsory education for all pastoral areas had been reduced from four years to three.[19]

It was not only in the TAR that the implementation of compulsory education was lagging behind projected targets. In 1995, the targets were reset for the whole of China, as is shown in Map 4.2; in July of that year, the Chinese government announced that it would cost 22 billion yuan ($2.7 billion) to make nine-year compulsory education available to 85 per cent of the population of China by the year 2000.[20] Funding was to come from three sources: the Central Compulsory Education Fund for Poverty-Stricken Areas, regional Compulsory Education funds, and from the World Bank.[21] In 1996, a five-year, 10 billion yuan ($1.2 billion) programme was launched with central government funding, and new dates were set for the universalization of compulsory education. It was the largest single expenditure of central government money on education since 1949.[22] However, priority in investment was again given to the more developed provinces. Over half of it, 5.3 billion yuan ($0.64 billion) was spent in the first year on eastern provinces.[23] This, in fact, ran counter to pledges that Zhu Kaixuan, the State Education Commission (SEC) Minister, had made in 1995. At a meeting in November 1995 on compulsory education in nine underdeveloped provinces and autonomous regions – Inner Mongolia, Yunnan, Guizhou, the TAR, Guangxi, Gansu, Qinghai, Ningxia and Xinjiang – he announced that 'the SEC and the Ministry of Finance will use most of the special funds for popularizing compulsory education allocated by the central government in [these] nine provinces and autonomous regions'.[24]

Summary

The education funding reforms were the most significant of all the financial reforms carried out during China's transition to a market economy in the 1980s. These reforms were set out in the 1985 'CCP Decision on Education'. Local governments were to take over the financing of education from the central government; and government funding of education was to be dramatically reduced overall. Although non-Han nationality areas, such as the TAR, continued to receive some funding from the central government, it was regarded as being too little to be effective.[25]

Although the TAR economy has grown in the 1990s, there is still a considerable disparity between levels of development in the region and more developed parts of China. This is largely due to the economic policies of the 1980s, which made the more developed eastern provinces of China the main focus of economic development. Economic underdevelopment and a lack of resources have inevitably had an impact on the levels of investment in education in the TAR. The statistics suggest that investment in education has increased significantly during the 1990s. Nevertheless, the continuing tendency to give priority to investment in the more developed provinces of China, even for basic education, is leading to a widening gap in educational levels between the TAR and eastern parts of China.

The following chapters consider each level of education in detail, assessing the impact of the post-Cultural Revolution reforms on development, and discussing the issues of urban versus rural education, elite versus mass education and higher versus basic education.

Notes

1. State Education Commission and Shanghai Institute of Human Resources Development, 'Annual Development Report of China's Educational Finance,

1992', cited in Cheng Kai-Ming, 'The Changing Legitimacy in a Decentralizing System: The State and Education Development in China', *International Journal of Educational Development*, Vol. 14, 1994, pp. 265–9.

2. Wang Tiezhi, 'Zhongguo Shaoshu Minzu Xinquang', in *Jiaoyu Jianxun*, No. 4, 1987, cited in Gerard Postiglione, 'Implications of Modernization for the Education of China's Minorities', in R. Hayhoe (ed.), *Education and Modernization – The Chinese Experience* (Pergamon Press, London, 1992), p. 315.

3. Teng Xing, '*Wo Guo Shaoshu Minzu Diqu Jiaoyu Zhengti Gaige Guanjian*' (The Essence of Overall Educational Reform in China's Minority Regions), *Qiu Shi*, No. 7, April 1989, pp. 19–24.

4. Zhu Kaixuan, Minister of the State Education Commission, announcing the introduction of a 10 billion yuan programme to introduce compulsory education in poor regions. Reported in *China Daily*, 8 May 1996.

5. Cheng Kai-Ming, 'Changing Legitimacy in a Decentralizing System', pp. 265–9.

6. Ibid.

7. Yat Ming Leung, 'The People's Republic of China', in *Education and Development in East Asia* (Garland Press, London, 1995), p. 240.

8. 1995 TAR Statistical Yearbook.

9. Internal Party discussion paper, 1995.

10. *China Daily*, 11 May 1992.

11. Gyaltsen Norbu, 'Text of Work Report on the TAR Ninth Five-Year Plan, 1996', delivered at the Fourth Session of the Sixth Regional People's Congress on 15 May 1996, *Xizang Ribao* (Tibet Daily), 5 June 1996 [FBIS 9/7/96].

12. Figures calculated from 1995 China Statistical Yearbook, and 1995 TAR Statistical Yearbook.

13. 1995 China Statistical Yearbook; 1995 TAR Statistical Yearbook.

14. Law on Compulsory Education of the People's Republic of China (Adopted at the Fourth Session of the Sixth National People's Congress, Promulgated by Order No. 38 of the President of the People's Republic of China on 12 April 1986, and Effective as of 1 July 1986) (Foreign Languages Press, Beijing, 1987); 'Programme for China's Educational Reform and Development', 1993.

15. Ibid.

16. Law on Compulsory Education of the People's Republic of China, 1986.

17. *Xinhua*, 16 December 1993 [SWB 21/12/93].

18. *Xinhua*, 3 January 1996.

19. 'Outline of the TAR's Five-Year Plan for Economic and Social Development and Its Long-term Target for 2010, Approved by the Fourth Session of the Sixth Regional People's Congress on 24th May 1996', *Xizang Ribao* (Tibet Daily), 7 June 1996, pp. 1–4 (TAR Ninth Five-Year Plan, 1996).

20. Report from Conference on World Bank-backed projects in Xining, quoted in *Xinhua*, 7 July 1995 [SWB 10/7/95].

21. Ibid.

22. *China Daily*, 8 May 1996.

23. Ibid.

24. *Xinhua*, 19 November 1995.

25. Teng Xing, 'The Essence of Overall Educational Reform', pp. 19–24; see also Postiglione, 'Implications of Modernization', p. 315; Zhu Kaixuan, Minister of the State Education Commission, announcing the introduction of a 10 billion yuan programme to introduce compulsory education in poor regions. Reported in *China Daily*, 8 May 1996.

CHAPTER 5

Primary Education

The 'consolidation' of primary schools, 1978–84

After the end of the Cultural Revolution, the all-out drive to bring China up to the economic level of Western industrialized countries and the campaigns by the new leadership against 'egalitarianism and the indiscriminate transfer of resources'[1] led to what was termed the 'consolidation' of primary schooling.

In January 1979, the Central Committee issued the 'Regulations on the Work of the Rural People's Communes'. These regulations, among other things, stipulated that non-productive expenditures for production teams should be reduced. This meant that personnel engaged in 'non-productive' work – and this included teachers – should be returned to production.[2] As a result, all over China, schools were closed or merged in the name of efficiency and improving quality. New regulations also provided that rural secondary schools and most primary schools should gradually be taken over by the state and that community primary teachers should be made to sit a qualifying exam.[3] In the TAR, this policy began to be implemented only in the mid-1990s.[4] Many community schools did indeed close after 1978 but in most cases they were not replaced by state-run institutions. The reasons were largely financial. As has been noted in other parts of China, the priority attached to universalizing basic education in principle has not been matched by patterns of resource allocation.[5]

In 1980, the directive ordering the return of 'non-productive' personnel to the production line was followed by de-collectivization. This had a further dramatic effect on rural schools. Until the disbanding of the communes, the collectives had essentially provided for the schools in the area. Rural teachers received grain and some salary each month from the collective team, which meant that teaching had been a popular job in rural areas. However, after 1980, the collectively-owned land was distributed among commune members for cultivation; individual households were no longer obliged to supply the teacher with food.[6] In the

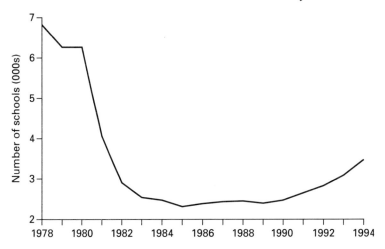

Figure 5.1 Primary schools in the TAR, 1978–94 (*Source*: 1995 TAR Statistical Yearbook)

TAR, from 1 July 1980, provision of state funds for teachers' salaries was transferred back to county education bureaux from individual production brigades.[7] However, the education finance reforms of the 1980s, which made funding reliant on local revenues, meant that in the TAR, as in many other parts of China, county governments' education budgets were largely insufficient to provide for teachers' needs.[8] In 1996, the State Education Commission issued a circular in which it stated that, in some areas of China, teachers' salaries were often months or even years late.[9]

Figure 5.1 shows the dramatic reduction in primary schools in the TAR in the early 1980s through closure and merging. The number of primary schools declined by 70 per cent between 1978 and 1985; enrolment dropped by 55 per cent over the same period.[10] The steepest decline occurred between 1980 and 1982 when the statistics suggest that over 50 per cent of schools were closed. The 1980–82 decline may be partly attributed to more accurate statistics following Hu Yaobang's criticism in 1980 of TAR officials for being slow in rejecting the policies of the Cultural Revolution;[11] during his visit to the TAR, Hu Yaobang urged officials to follow Deng Xiaoping's slogan of the period, 'Seek Truth from Facts' (*Shi Shi Qiu Shi*). At the same time, he called on officials to begin disbanding the communes, and this led to the closure of large numbers of commune schools.

In the TAR, primary school closures were most significant in rural areas where education is almost entirely provided by community

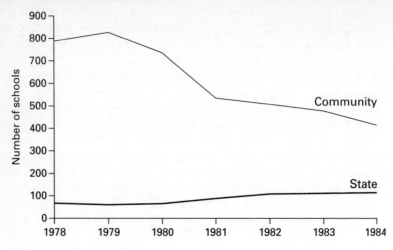

Figure 5.2 State and community primary schools in Lhasa Municipality, 1978–84 (*Source: Lhasa in Progress 1952–1984*)

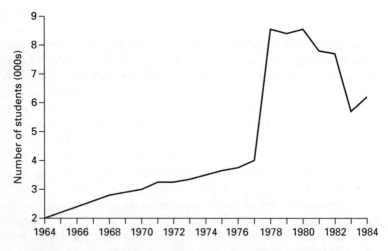

Figure 5.3 Enrolment in primary schools in Lhasa Municipality, 1964–84 (*Source*: Cheng Guan Qu (City District of Lhasa) National Economic Statistical Data 1985)

schools. Since the rural population comprises over 83 per cent of the total population,[12] changes in the situation of community schools inevitably have a dramatic and widespread effect on the development of education in the whole of the TAR. School closures were carried out in the name of increased efficiency. The egalitarian priorities of the 1970s, when every village or production brigade was instructed to establish a primary school, resulted in a large number of very small schools which meant that unit costs were high. Nevertheless, such policies had been justified by earlier research in China which had shown that long distances and boarding were significant factors in low enrolment and high drop-out rates.[13] In rural and nomadic areas of the TAR, the closure of community schools was to make a significant contribution to declining enrolment and increasing drop-out rates by the end of the 1980s.

Figure 5.2 demonstrates the effects of 'consolidation' in the Lhasa Municipality between 1978 and 1984. The number of community primary schools dropped by almost half, from 788 to 414, and enrolment declined by 63.7 per cent. At the same time, the number of state primary schools increased from 67 to 114 and enrolment in state primary schools increased by 16.8 per cent. In total, however, there was a 62 per cent reduction in the number of primary schools and a 31 per cent decline in primary enrolment in the Lhasa Municipality between 1978 and 1984 (see Figure 5.3).

Enrolment in primary education

Accurate enrolment figures are extremely difficult to calculate. Most educationalists writing on China note the haphazard nature of monitoring.[14] In the TAR, some counties collect data only from selected schools since there are not the resources available to establish monitoring and assessment systems in all schools; this inevitably has an effect on the accuracy of aggregate statistics.[15] Furthermore, since enrolment was made one of the main indicators of progress in the educational reforms of the 1980s, there is believed to be a general tendency to inflate figures. There are also problems in the way the figures are calculated. Enrolment rates are reached by calculating the total number of children in school as a percentage of the primary school-age population. However, since the number of children in school includes children who have repeated classes or attended school late and may be over the age of twelve and who would not, therefore, be included in the calculation of the school-age population, the enrolment rate is artificially increased. Indeed, in urban areas, tables often present enrolment rates of over 100 per cent. The calculation of enrolment rates is further flawed by the fact that the calculation of the school-age population does not include certain physically disabled children.[16] In some cases it also does not include children who have been born to parents who already have one child, i.e. whose parents have not followed the government's birth control regulations.[17] A second child is usually not registered, and therefore does not exist in

Table 5.1 Changes in primary school-age population and primary enrolment in the TAR, 1982–89

	1982	1989	Percentage change
Population: 7–11 years	222,999	250,801	+12.5
Enrolment	141,587	124,976	-11.7
Enrolment rate of primary school-age children	78%	50%	

Sources: 1988, 1990 and 1995 TAR Statistical Yearbooks.

terms of population calculation. Consequently, the total population of school-age children is likely to be higher than the total given in statistical tables, and the enrolment rate therefore lower.

Throughout China, primary enrolment declined in the 1980s. This is partly explained by the decline in the age cohort of seven- to eleven-year-olds due to increasing success in the implementation of the 'one child' policy from the early 1980s.[18] However, Tibetans, like other 'minority' nationalities, were exempt from the 'one child' policy in the 1980s. In urban areas, state-employed Tibetan couples were permitted to have two children and non-state workers were permitted to have three. Rural families were also permitted to have three children and there were officially no restrictions on rural families in remote areas.[19] Although Tibetans were often pressurized into restricting the number of children they had, particularly state workers in urban areas,[20] the population of seven- to eleven-year-olds increased between 1982 and 1989, as Table 5.1 shows.

In 1982, the cohort of seven- to eleven-year-olds in the TAR was 222,999 and by 1989 it had risen to 250,801. This represents an increase of 12.5 per cent and yet, over the same period, enrolment declined by 11.7 per cent. Thus it is clear that while in China as a whole the decline in enrolment in primary schools may be partly explained by the introduction of the 'one child' policy, this cannot be said of the TAR. This is confirmed by the fact that enrolment rates for primary school-age children also declined over the period, from 78 per cent in 1982 to 50 per cent in 1989.

The enrolment figures began to rise again by the 1990s when we also see greater investment in education. By 1994, there were 232,976 children in primary education. However, according to the statistics, enrolment still had not regained the levels of 1980, when over 240,000 were in primary education. In the next sections we look in detail at the causes of low enrolment in primary education and why rural areas are particularly affected.

Urban versus rural provision in the TAR

At the Fifth TAR Conference on Education in 1994, TAR government chairman Gyaltsen Norbu acknowledged the disparity in education provision between different regions of the TAR. The fault, he implied, lay with the local authorities:

> We should also be aware that educational reform and development in our region are still not fully meeting the needs of the new situation and tasks. Localities differ in their understanding of the strategic importance of giving priority to expanding education. Each locality carries out its educational policy in its own way and some localities are far from achieving the expected goal.[21]

The disparity in the provision of education between different areas in the TAR may reflect the levels of commitment of different prefectural governments but it also follows very clearly the rural/urban divide. In a paper for *Tibet Studies* in 1996, the Chinese educationalist Yang Wanli compares educational provision in Lhasa Municipality with Ngari Prefecture, which he describes as covering a quarter of the whole of the TAR.[22] Lhasa Municipality had 538 primary schools compared with 44 in Ngari. Ngari had only one general secondary school and no vocational schools. In 1994, only 249 students graduated from primary school, 67 from junior secondary school and 20 from senior secondary school.[23] The disparity in educational provision is reflected in the enrolment rates in different prefectures. Figure 5.4 gives a comparison of enrolment rates in the prefectures of the TAR in 1988 and 1989.[24]

As Figure 5.4 shows, in 1988 and 1989, the enrolment rate of seven-to eleven-year-olds for the whole of the TAR was 55.7 per cent and 53.1 per cent respectively. However, in Lhasa Municipality in 1989 the enrolment rate was 69.11 per cent, while in Ngari (*Ali*) and Nagchu (*Naqu*) enrolment was just over 17 per cent. Figure 5.4 also shows the extent to which each of the prefectures is urbanized, and this can be seen to correspond roughly to the level of educational development. The only prefecture which does not fit this pattern is Lhokha (*Shannan*) where the urban population makes up only 7 per cent of the total and yet the enrolment rate was over 62 per cent in 1989. This can perhaps be explained by its proximity to Lhasa. In none of the prefectures did the growth of enrolment between 1988 and 1989 match the growth in the age cohort.[25]

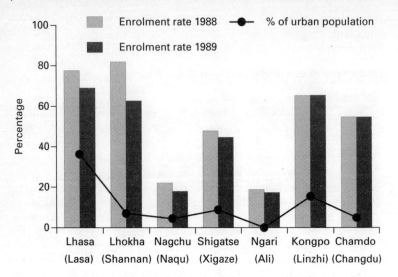

Figure 5.4 Primary enrolment rates and percentage of urban population in
TAR prefectures, 1988 and 1989 (*Sources*: 1990 TAR Statistical
Yearbook; 1989 TAR Statistical Yearbook; 1990 Census, published
in *Tibet Daily*, 23 November 1990)

Drop-out from primary education

The problem of drop-out from primary school is again more serious
in rural areas, although it is not clear what the real situation is anywhere. The Tibetan media and TAR government documents suggest
that the primary school drop-out rate is high in the TAR,[26] and yet the
available statistics indicate relatively low drop-out rates, as is shown in
Figure 5.5. At the Fifth TAR Conference on Education, in November
1994, Chen Kuiyuan, the TAR Party Secretary, told delegates:

> School-age children's attendance at primary school is low and their drop-
> out rate is high. As a result, the number of illiterates remains large ...
>
> Although we have set up many schools, the teaching level of various
> schools at all levels is poor, as is the quality of their graduates. If the
> situation continues we will not be able to solve the basic problems of having
> leading cadres and professional personnel at all levels. Backward education
> will directly restrict the TAR's progress towards economic and social
> modernisation.[31]

Figure 5.5 presents the drop-out rates for individual prefectures in
the TAR in 1988 and 1989. In four of the seven prefectures, drop-out
increased in 1989. Furthermore, like the pattern of enrolment, drop-

out is higher in prefectures with a low urban population; thus the drop-out rate for Lhasa in 1989 was 2.9 per cent while the drop-out rate for Ngari and Nagchu were 19.4 per cent and 13.4 per cent respectively.

Several speculative explanations can be offered for the discrepancy between the apparently low drop-out rates given in the statistics and official statements about high drop-out. The practice of calculating statistics from a small selection of schools probably distorts the real picture; another possible factor is that students who fail to attend school do not necessarily become de-registered within the year so they may be counted as present when they have long since stopped attending. Seasonal absenteeism is particularly high in rural areas in the TAR where children's labour is needed by their families at particular times of year. In 1993, in an article in the *Chamdo Daily*, two journalists described the problem of drop-out in some counties in Chamdo Prefecture:

> One thing that inevitably has to be acknowledged is that there has certainly been an exhibition of commitment in education at all levels, yielding con-crete results. For example, in the most densely populated county of Chamdo the number of children enrolling in schools, remaining in them and getting promoted from one class to the next has become the highest in all of Chamdo Prefecture. But in some other areas, the situation has remained the same as before: 'hot in the beginning, lukewarm in the middle and cold in the end.' Efforts are underway to halt this trend at all levels as a manner of taking a step forward.[28]

Probably the most likely explanation for the apparently low drop-out rates, however, is that many children in rural areas are unable to attend school at all, and many of those to whom schools are available may receive one to three years' education at most. Therefore, drop-out figures become less relevant as an indication of educational success than they are in areas with higher enrolment rates. Table 5.2 shows the number of classes in each grade of primary school for state and community schools in the TAR in 1994. It can be seen that the number of classes in community schools drops by 20 per cent after grade one, and by a further 39 per cent after grade two, and a further 73 per cent after grade three. Indeed, only forty pupils graduated from community schools in that year. Statistics for the period 1980–94, presented in Table 5.3, show the number of children in the TAR who enrolled in the first year of primary school compared with the number who graduated six years later. It would appear from these figures that, during this period, an average of 30 per cent of children enrolling in primary schools in the TAR received six years of education and graduated.

In 1992, in recognition of the problem of drop-out, the TAR branch

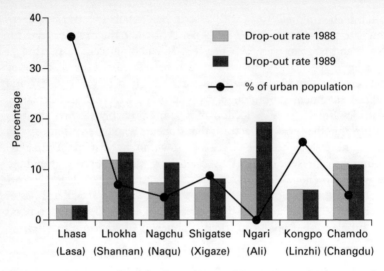

Figure 5.5 Primary school drop-out rates and percentage of urban population by prefecture in the TAR, 1988–89 (*Sources*: 1990 TAR Statistical Yearbook; 1989 TAR Statistical Yearbook; 1990 Census figures)

of the 'Hope Project' was launched. The 'Hope Project' had been set up in 1989 by the China Children's Foundation to help drop-outs in poor rural areas in China to return to school. In the TAR, the project, which is funded by charitable donations, planned to build twenty-two primary schools by 1995. By June 1994, according to official reports, eight schools and two classes had been built and seven other schools were under construction; 2,000 drop-outs had returned to school.[29]

What is interesting about the 'Hope Project' in the TAR is that it acknowledges the failure for rural areas of the quality-oriented 'consolidation' policies of the 1980s. It recognizes that the closure of a large number of rural primary schools instead of increasing efficiency led directly to low enrolment and high drop-out. In January 1994, a government report for *Xinhua* outlined the difference between the way the 'Hope Project' was being implemented in the TAR and the way it was implemented in other parts of China:

> To properly use the money, Tibet has not copied other provinces in carrying out the project. Officials found that it is the huge area and limited number of schools that result in school drop-outs. From some remote pastoral areas, it takes three days on horseback to reach a school. For education to penetrate into every corner of the broad plateau, the region has put its focus on building more schools although this consumes more money and energy.[30]

Table 5.2 Number of classes in each grade of primary school and number of students enrolling and graduating in state and community schools in the TAR, 1994

Run by:	No. of schools	Number of classes							Repeat class	Students enrolling	Students graduating
		Grade One	Grade Two	Grade Three	Grade Four	Grade Five	Grade Six				
Education Department	1,185	1,305	1,030	751	494	418	349	2	27,382	10,837
Communities	1,866	1,947	1,577	962	252	4	0	0	24,612	40
Other Departments	39	34	37	34	29	34	29	3	746	566
Total	3,090	3,286	2,644	1,747	775	456	378	5	52,740	11,443

Note: Yang Wanli cites these figures as relsating to 1994 although according to the 1995 TAR Statistical Yearbook the figures he gives for schools and students relate to 1993.

Source: Yang Wanli, 'The Countermeasure and Particularity of Research on Teaching Materials', *Xizang Yanjiu* (Tibet Studies), Vol. 58, No. 1, 1996.

Table 5.3 Number of students enrolling in and graduating from primary school in the TAR, 1980–94

Year	80–86	81–87	82–88	83–89	84–90	85–91	86–92	87–93	88–94
Enrolement	61,312	38,106	25,572	30,736	43,746	25,282	30,333	32,057	37,657
Graduation	11,724	13,167	7,467	7,483	9,314	8,607	12,403	11,443	12,594
Percentage graduating	19.1	34.6	29.2	24.3	21.3	34.0	40.9	35.7	33.4

Sources: 1995 TAR Statistical Yearbook; 1988 Statistical Yearbook.

According to research undertaken by one Tibetan official, the most efficient way to reduce drop-out in rural areas would be to increase the number of boarding schools. In his view the scattered population and the hazardous mountain terrain, which mean that children have a long and difficult journey to school, are the main factors in low enrolment and high drop-out in rural areas:

> Normally the Tibetan areas are big, with a small population. Transportation is not convenient. Most of the students live far away from their schools and they have difficulties travelling to school along mountain tracks. These are the objective reasons for the low enrolment of school-age children. Further-more, because student numbers in the schools are not stable, and the proportion of students entering schools of a higher grade is small, it has been difficult to open new schools. At present there are some schools in Tibetan areas which are boarding schools, where the students' results and the proportion of students entering schools of higher grade are better than other schools. Practice has proved them to be successful, so if we run boarding schools it accords with the practical situation in Tibetan areas and enlarges the ratio of school-age children's enrolment. This is a good ex-periment: to develop basic education we should enlarge the scale of the boarding school system.[31]

Illiteracy[32]

Considerable progress has been made in the reduction of illiteracy in China as a whole in recent years. By 1995, the illiteracy rate in China had fallen to less than 7 per cent.[33] However, illiteracy figures show the same urban/rural divide as enrolment and drop-out. In June 1996, Chinese Premier Li Peng told participants at a conference on education held by the State Education Commission that in rural areas all over China illiteracy was rising.[34] In the TAR, illiteracy rates for the whole region are also said to have fallen in recent years. In 1988, the official figure for illiteracy was 73 per cent, and by 1994 it had dropped to 40 per cent, although if one takes semi-illiteracy into account we see an increase. Illiteracy and semi-illiteracy was 53 per cent in 1990; by 1995 it had risen to 60 per cent (see Table 5.4). Furthermore, as in China as a whole, aggregate statistics for the TAR mask the situation in rural areas. The 1990 Census figures presented in Table 5.4 show that while illiteracy for the TAR stood at 44 per cent, illiteracy in rural areas was 70 per cent.

At the Third TAR Regional Conference on Education in 1987, illiteracy was cited as one of the major problems to be tackled. The problem of illiteracy includes semi-literacy, or lapsed literacy, which is

Table 5.4 Illiteracy in the population of the TAR between the ages of fifteen and forty, 1988–95 (%)

	1988	1990	1991	1993	1994	1995
Total illiteracy						
Urban and rural population	73	44	44	44	40	
Rural population		70				
Illiteracy and semi-illiteracy		53				60
Lhasa population		34				
Total non-Han population		73				
Total female non-Han population		84				

Sources: 1988: State Education Commission in *Children and Women of China – A Unicef Situation Analysis* (Beijing 1989). 1990: Tabulation on China's National Minorities (1990 Population Census), May 1994; Communiqué Details Census Results of the Population Survey of City of Lhasa in 1990 by the Lhasa Municipal Bureau of Statistics; *Lasa Wanbao* (Lhasa Evening Paper) (Chinese-language version) 24 November 1990; *The Change in Education in Tibet* (pamphlet distributed at UN by PRC) (New Star Publishers, Beijing 1992); Specialized Plan for the TAR Territory (internal government document). 1991: *Tibet from 1950–1991*, compiled by China's *Tibet and Beijing Review* (New Star Publishers, Beijing, 1992). 1993: *Xinhua* 18 March 1994, figures for the TAR academic year 1993–94. 1994: *Tibet Special – Beijing Review* 7–13 August 1995. 1995: TAR Ninth Five-Year Plan, 1996.

particularly high in the TAR. Lapsed literacy is common in areas where significant numbers of children have dropped-out of school, or in areas where Tibetans are a small minority and therefore attend Chinese medium primary schools, for example in parts of Qinghai and Sichuan. The major problem for children attending Chinese schools is that once they return to their own communities they do not use, and therefore eventually are unable to use, Chinese, which is the only language they have learned to read and write.[35]

Following the 1987 Regional Conference on Education and the announcement of the 1988 State Council's Guidelines on the Eradication of Illiteracy, a literacy programme was launched on an experimental basis in rural areas of the TAR. The programme involved nine counties in the Lhasa, Shigatse and Kongpo prefectures. Other prefectures also set up literacy programmes, some of them with basic vocational training in agricultural skills. According to a TAR Education Commission report, 8,000 people acquired literacy in the TAR between 1988 and 1990; of these, 7,000 had been part of the experimental programme.[36]

Box 5.1 A report on the 1990 experimental literacy
programme in Nedong county

*At present Nedong county has 113 evening literacy schools running 169
classes with 3505 students. These students make up over 76 per cent of
the county's 45 per cent illiterates and semi-illiterates. Out of a total
population of 34,154 in the county, 14,567 are young people between
the ages of fifteen and forty. So far a total of 8,928 young people have
gained literacy. 1,093 are still illiterate.*

*As regards the curriculum, it is pragmatic and consistent with the
local situation and needs. The programme includes cultural classes,
scientific and technical skills, Party policies and laws, short courses
etc. 123 vocational training sessions have been held, with over 4,366
trainees. To popularize the understanding of law, introductory courses
were held. In 1989 alone, 3 introductory sessions to the legal system
were run with 283 people.*

*The literacy programme in Nedong county has been successful
mainly due to the following reasons:*

1. *Identification of the nature and importance of the literacy programme by all the relevant leaders and the people.*
2. *Priority accorded by xiang (township) Party leaders, government
   leaders and various departments.*
3. *The people's natural interest and motivation.*
4. *Curriculum relevant to the practical aspects of life.*

*What Nedong county has achieved can also be achieved by other
counties by taking their good example and experience but adjusting it
to local situations and needs.*

Source: *Literacy Section, TAR Education Commission, reported in
Xizang Ribao (Tibet Daily), 23 October 1990.*

According to the report, the success of such literacy programmes
depends primarily on the commitment of officials and the programme's
relevance to people's lives. Box 5.1 gives a description of this experimental programme and how it was carried out in one county in the
Lhasa Municipality.

Since the mid-1990s there has been a drive to improve rates of adult
literacy through classes for fifteen- to forty-year-olds in township (*xiang*)
centres in the TAR. The classes are particularly aimed at teenage

illiterates or lapsed literates of which there is a large percentage.[37] In 1996 new targets were set for the eradication of literacy in the TAR. These were:

- The rate of illiteracy and semi-illiteracy to be brought down to 40 per cent by the year 2000.
- Illiteracy to be eliminated among young and middle-aged people in the cities and economically developed areas by the year 2000.
- Illiteracy to be basically eliminated among all young and middle-aged people by the year 2010.[38]

In general, however, despite the proclaimed targets for the eradication of illiteracy, county governments do not have the funding to implement literacy classes. In 1995, the average county government education budget was around 2 million yuan ($235,000) depending on the size of the population.[39] This sum has to cover all education costs. In order to set up projects such as adult literacy, county governments are instructed to save money from their existing budgets. This means that teachers, who are usually from the local primary school, receive little or no pay for the classes that they are supposed to teach in the evenings. Furthermore, in villages where there is no electricity, there are often not the funds to provide kerosene for lamps. Consequently, the campaigns are often of limited success.[40] In 1990, the literacy section of the TAR Education Commission published an article in the *Tibet Daily* which complained about a lack of commitment and co-ordination in the eradication of illiteracy in the TAR:

> The relevant departments should strengthen their support and involvement in the literacy movement. Certain fundamental policy decisions need to be made and arrangements made for their legal enforcement. So far, we lack a dependable and suitable system for eradicating illiteracy in our region. Furthermore, we do not have a coherent policy of eradicating illiteracy. At present, responsibility for adult literacy is left entirely to the Education Commission instead of it being considered an important social issue, with equal responsibility being taken by the various government bureaux and relevant departments. There is a lack of guidance, supervision and evaluation of these programmes. Therefore many problems of raising literacy levels remain. For example, there is no regulation specifying who should take responsibility for the literacy campaign at the different levels of county government. There are no funds specified for literacy programmes in each county. Thus although the Education Commission has had to increase its budget for the development of literacy, a lot more needs to be done to strengthen educational facilities and to carry out the literacy programme.[41]

Low enrolment and high drop-out in rural schools: a review of contributory factors

During the 1980s and early 1990s, the economy of rural areas in the TAR was unable to provide schooling for a large percentage of its population. In 1990, 17 per cent of the rural primary school-age population were enrolled in primary school education, although the average for the whole region was 67 per cent.[42] According to a report by the Tibetan scholar Pama Namgyal, in 1994 in Nagchu Prefecture only 10 per cent of school-age children were in school. Even here there was regional variation with 12 per cent enrolment rate in counties with the highest enrolment, but between 0 and 3 per cent in the counties and townships with the lowest enrolment.[43]

In the debate over the causes of low enrolment and high drop-out among non-Han nationalities, and particularly in rural areas, parents are apportioned much of the blame in the Chinese press and academic research papers. This view is often echoed by Western educationalists. Parents are seen to deprive their children of an education either for economic reasons or for religious reasons: 'Education was already played down in these cultures where parents were more proud to have their sons joining the temples than enrolling in schools'[44]; 'The reasons for the drop in enrolment have not been researched but doubtless relate to the overall socio-economic conditions and historical attitudes and beliefs among minority groups.'[45] Parents are simultaneously criticized for wanting to keep their children in the fields, and for wanting an education that will enable their children to get out of the fields and find work in urban areas.[46]

Box 5.2 A school teacher talks about the problems of enrolment and drop-out in his village, in a Tibetan county in Gansu province, where people's livelihood was severely affected by the blizzards of winter 1995–96

The situation in our village is really very bad; and when I look around I can see that the future is going to be very bleak for us, because we don't have cattle, most of our cattle have died; and then our people don't have education, so the future generation is really going to have a difficult time.

Those families whose cattle have died will have to work as labourers for people who have cattle or more money, or they will have to go to the mountains to look for yartsagunpu. It is a kind of herb for making a

---

Chinese medicine; it's a very important ingredient. Actually the Chinese use it as an aphrodisiac. There's no restriction on harvesting yartsagunpu. But you can pick only for three months a year so there is a lot of competition because so many people have nothing left. So now you get very little …

My township (xiang) has a population of 5,018. There is one primary school with 14 students. The school cannot take more students because there are no facilities. There is only one building and two teachers, neither of whom are qualified, so the school cannot enrol more than that number of children. The school is financed by taxes from the people. It gets no grant from the government.

There are very few literate people in the township. Most children cannot go to school, although some people go to the monasteries where they learn to read and write in Tibetan. Only people who are settled near the school can go to school; most of the nomads, because they are so far from the school, cannot send their children to school.

If you want to send your child to school you have to apply to the township education office, the leader will contact the school and ask them how many children there are in the school at that time, and if the school says, for example: 'we can take three more children', and there are more applicants than that then the leaders will select only three.

The school should provide six years of schooling, but hardly anyone stays that long. The buildings are not good and the facilities are very bad and there is a lot of wind; it is very cold; the children have to sit on the floor. Also, if people can send their children to school, it is usually not before the age of eight, so if they study for six years by the time they finish primary school they will be fifteen, which means they will be too old to go to secondary school at the county level …

No one from my village has ever got into secondary school … You have to sit exams to get into secondary school and you have to compete with children who have been living in the town, and with children of Chinese and Tibetan officials, or rich Tibetans who have had much better primary school education. So rural children stand no chance against them. They don't get in, so there is no motivation at primary school.

One lama has a plan to open a school next to the monastery. The school would have religious as well as secular education for the people. But I don't think it will materialize because there is no money to do it. It is just a plan.

Source: *Interview with Tibetan school teacher, September 1996.*

Box 5.3 Palden Gyal: a primary school career through a key primary school in Huangnan Tibetan Prefecture, Qinghai province

I began primary school at the age of six in 1975. The primary school was in my village, Jangcha. The village is 8km from Rongwo, the county headquarters of Tongren and the government headquarters of Huangnan Prefecture. My village was on the main road between Tongren (Tongrin) county and Zekog (Zeku) county. The village school was a state primary school, gongban, and it was a key school. It had six classrooms, two of which were well built and in a good condition. Three of the classrooms were built by local people in Tibetan style, they were darker and of not such good quality. The classrooms were well furnished with desks and chairs.

The school had five grades and one pre-school class. There were six full-time teachers, one for each class. The teachers were government teachers who came from outside the village; they all lived in the school. They were all Tibetans, but they could speak Chinese as well. They had all been sent from Huangnan Teacher Training school. This is a specialized secondary-level teacher training school. Several of the teachers were very young, only fifteen years old.

All the children at the school came from the village, there were no boarders from nomadic areas in the school. In my class there were about sixteen students, six of whom were girls. I was among the youngest; some children were as old as eight or nine. Several of these had repeated a year because they were unable to keep up with the other children in the higher class; others started school late for family reasons.

We had five lessons per day, three in the morning and two in the afternoon. We started at 9.30 a.m. and went home for lunch. We studied Tibetan, mathematics, music, sport and in the final year we studied Chinese. In some primary schools in Qinghai they started learning Chinese in the first year, and in other schools they didn't study Chinese at all. All the teaching was in Tibetan. The stories in the Tibetan and Chinese textbooks were about Chinese Communist heroes. There was one about a Chinese soldier during the Vietnam war who was told to blow up a bridge and being unable to find anyone to lay the bomb, stood with it himself under the bridge and blew himself up. From the second year in the Tibetan textbooks we read Mao Zedong's speeches on the importance of education. Our music classes consisted mainly of singing Chinese revolutionary songs. Sometimes we were taught them in Tibetan, and sometimes in Chinese, which had been translated into Tibetan; we learned them by heart but we had no idea what they were about. On Wednesdays the whole afternoon was spent doing sport with the whole school, either climbing a mountain or playing basket ball.

Several pupils in the school had to repeat a year because they couldn't keep up. And pupils began dropping out of school in the fourth and fifth years to help their families. One dropped out from my class. He was the oldest student in the class, he dropped out in the fourth year because he had already repeated a class and he was already thirteen. His name was Tsenther, but we called him amnyi, *Grandpa.*

All tuition at the school was free; we did not receive any grants. For the first two years our textbooks and exercise books were free as well, but in 1978 we started having to pay for textbooks, as well as paying for pens, pencils and notebooks. We had to pay 5 mao per book; we usually used two every year. It was a huge sum of money to us. My mother said we couldn't afford to pay, but eventually my father gave me the money. Then the next year a lama came to our village and my mother gave him 5 yuan, so I felt very angry.

At the end of every year we had exams, pupils who failed the exams had to repeat the year. In July 1980 I sat the secondary school entrance exam with my class-mates to enter Tongren Minority Nationalities Secondary School in Rongwo. The exam was in Tibetan and we had to pass three subjects: maths, Tibetan and Chinese. Tongren 'Minority' Nationalities Secondary school was a key school so it was quite difficult to get into. But my primary school was the best in the county. Out of fifteen pupils who took the exam from my class twelve passed, including all the girls.

Source: *Interview with Palden Gyal, 20 October 1996.*

This section looks at these claims and sets them against other factors. Behind the public propaganda, lack of funding is acknowledged to be the principal reason for low enrolment; this is examined in the next chapter. Other reasons for low enrolment include lack of schools, poor conditions and facilities in schools, restrictive enrolment criteria, rising costs for parents, an irrelevant curriculum, and poor teaching quality. However, before we go on to examine these different problems, let us take a look at the experience of primary education in two different regions at different historical periods. Box 5.2 gives an illustration of the extreme poverty of some rural areas inhabited by Tibetans and the problems of providing even basic education in such places. Box 5.3 gives a glimpse inside a state primary school in a more affluent road-side village in Qinghai province in the late 1970s.

Conditions in rural schools The conditions described in Box 5.2 were common in many schools throughout rural China and the TAR in the 1980s. According to a national survey in 1987, school buildings totalling 45 million square metres were unsafe; 50–60 per cent of schools' routine expenditure was spent on repairing dangerous classrooms. Furthermore, less than 10 per cent of all primary and secondary schools had all the scientific equipment required by the curricula.[47]

Newspaper reports in the Tibetan press and reports of government meetings indicate a widespread lack of facilities, including textbooks and desks, as well as insufficient classrooms, many of which are in poor condition or structurally unsound. In Chamdo Prefecture in 1993, 20 per cent of all school buildings were declared to be unsafe.[48]

By the mid-1990s the enormity of the problem in the TAR was becoming clear, and efforts were being made to contain the situation. In 1994, according to a broadcast on Lhasa Radio, the TAR government spent 60 million yuan on capital construction, prefectural governments spent 11.26 million yuan and county governments spent 7.11 million yuan. This money was said to have gone towards renovating and expanding 358 primary schools, and establishing 331 new primary schools.[49] In May 1996, in his work report to the Sixth Regional People's Congress, Gyaltsen Norbu, chairman of the TAR government, announced that in the previous five years 300,000 square metres of school buildings had been rebuilt.[50]

Box 5.4 provides an example of conditions found in some counties in Chamdo in 1993; it illustrates the extent to which poor provision is a major contributory factor in low educational levels in some areas.

Rural education: high cost, low gain It seems likely that the socio-economic reason for drop-out cited by government officials is not necessarily a simple question of rural families needing their children's labour. In may involve a series of pragmatic decisions connected with the relevance and quality of the education provided and the extent to which it will facilitate social advancement, against the cost in terms of expenses and loss of production. Dalu Yin writes: 'education is sup-ported to the extent that it will lead to "a leap over the village gate", (*tiaochu nongmen*). Since most rural education will not do this, students and their parents feel that schooling offers little. Bearing the cost of a sub-standard education makes no sense to them.'[51]

Box 5.4 Conditions in rural schools in Chamdo Prefecture in 1993

On 20th April this year [1993] officials from the TAR Education and Science Committee and the Chamdo Prefecture Sports and Education Committee inspected a primary school in Kyithang township (xiang) Dragyab county (xian; Tib: dzong). They observed that on a single wooden bench six students sat huddled together. There were no chairs. There is no reason to see anything wrong in finding out whether in such circumstances students can learn anything at all ...

There is no school that is not beset with various problems. It is there for everyone to see. One only has to step out of one's office and take a look at the situation in any one of them. In some schools, one sees mechanically operated printing equipment which has been used since the old days, still in use, bearing scars of repair works done by carpenters. In some counties, more than 20 per cent of the Community Primary school classes are still held in the teachers' homes, for almost the entire year. In some of the schools, deserted buildings still remain in a state of disrepair, and empty.

... When the monsoon comes one cannot help but endure the downpour outside and the dripping inside. According to statistics compiled by the Sports and Education Department for the whole of Chamdo Prefecture, the percentage of school buildings in a perilous state still stands at 20 per cent. Although since 1987 the TAR People's Government has made education a higher priority, because of many historical reasons and, especially, due to very obvious financial short-ages at the township and village levels in educational matters, expen-diture on education is still inadequate. It has always been impossible to tackle all the problems at the same time.

Source: *Xiang Xiaoli and Zhang Qing, 'Courage of Conviction Con-sists in Tackling the Reality of the Situation Today with a Clear Vision for the Future',* Chamdo Daily, *15 July 1993.*

As far as the education of rural Tibetans is concerned, one Tibetan official argues against the trend that blames parents' attitudes for not sending their children to school. In his view, it is essentially poverty which prevents parents from enrolling their children in primary education:

In the Tibetan areas there are many reasons for the low enrolment rate, but the most important reason is economic, due to poverty. This is the root cause of education in Tibetan areas falling into dire straits.

Especially on the cold plateau, if one wants to send children to school, one must at least let the children have clothes to wear and food to eat. However, those peasants and nomads who were struggling to get necessary food and clothing, who didn't have enough money to buy their monthly salt and tea, and who couldn't even afford a needle and thread, how could they be able to send their children to school? To speak from the heart, what parents would want to prevent their children from being educated, from understanding science or having a bright future? Who would like their children to be illiterate? Aren't the trials and sufferings that the parents themselves endured, as a result of being uneducated, more than enough? Isn't it just because of poverty that they couldn't do anything about it? After all, at least we cannot let 45 per cent of school-age children be illiterate. If we don't take remedial measures, then the vicious circle of poverty causing ignorance, and ignorance bringing poverty will continue to exist in the Tibetan areas for a long time.

The present gap of economy and education will be more prominent, so I ask the Party and the State to give free education in primary and lower secondary schools in Tibetan areas, and let the emancipated serfs who have been liberated politically also be liberated and stand up in the field of culture and education.[52]

Tuition is free for compulsory education, and a certain percentage of Tibetan children receive grants.[53] However, many children, even those with grants, are unable to meet the full cost of primary education.[54] Furthermore, in the TAR, the economic viability of education in rural areas has yet to been proven. For the most part, the nomads and subsistence farmers still use the traditional farming methods which have served them for centuries, and, since the curriculum in primary schools still pays scant attention to rural agriculture (despite official directives), education in rural areas contributes little to families' lives or livelihood.[55] Children who have been sent to school eventually return to their families in rural or pastoral areas, having sacrificed family labour for long periods, for little reward.[56]

Relevance of curriculum Since the Cultural Revolution, primary curriculum policy has been the subject of considerable discussion in China. On the one hand there have been calls by Chinese educators and economists to adapt the curriculum in rural areas to the needs of the rural economy and to make it more relevant to the lives of rural children, and, on the other hand, there have been moves to increase or decrease the ideological content of the curriculum, depending on

Box 5.5 'Like thousands of people trying to cross a single log bridge' – Vice Premier Li Lanqing describes China's education system

At present the textbooks used in the countryside are more or less the same as those used in the cities. Consequently, when students graduate after nine years of study, they do not know a trade. Parents therefore are not eager to send their children to school if the students are not motivated. Rural cadres in the countryside also raise the question: 'What is the point of going to school?' If one knows how to read and write but has no skill, it is possible for him to degenerate into semi-literacy after a certain period of time ... Li Lanqing hopes that the educational circle can overcome a chronic and stubborn disease that has existed for many years, that is, operating primary and secondary school education as education for preparing students to take entrance examinations for schools at a higher level. He said: 'Nowadays, a large number of primary and secondary school students want to enter universities, just like thousands upon thousands of people crossing a single-log bridge. The students' workload at school is especially heavy, with each course trying to add more. It is actually difficult for students to develop morally, intellectually, and physically in an all-round way. My heart aches when I see children wearing glasses in many schools. One of the main causes is malpractice brought about by the irrational education structure.'

Source: *Xu Hong, 'An Interview with Vice-Premier Li Lanqing: Vocational Education Can Invigorate the Country', Tzu Ching (Hong Kong), No. 10, 5 October 1994 [SWB 14/11/94].*

whether liberals or hardliners have control in the Chinese government.

The 1985 'CCP Decision on Education' cited the curriculum as one of the major problems in the education system. It described textbooks as outdated, teaching methods as stereotyped and the range of subjects covered as very limited. These problems were reiterated in the 1993 'Programme for China's Educational Reform and Development'. Indeed, this policy document stipulated that local authorities should be encouraged to compile teaching materials that are suitable for children in rural areas. Nevertheless, for several reasons, the curriculum is still far from meeting China's rural children's needs. First, despite government publicity about the importance of vocational education, Chinese culture still ranks academic education as first rate, and vocational education as second rate.[57] Consequently, the education system is still oriented towards academic, textbook-based learning. Furthermore, the drive to improve the quality of education since the Cultural Revolution has lead to a situation where schools are judged in terms of examination pass rates and the number of students who get into higher levels of general secondary schools and higher education institutions. In a paper for *Tibetan Studies*, in 1996, Lei Yongsheng explains how the notion of quality in education has become distorted:

> What is good quality education? In reality, this is not at all a new subject but is a return to a correct and scientific educational ideology ... With good quality education students should obtain an all-round and healthy maturity and become the builders and successors of socialism. However, in China there has been a long period of all kinds of complex historical and social factors and as a result of these we have deviated in various degrees from the ideas of comprehensive development contained in the Party's educational policies. By simply equating good quality education with examination success, the result has been a loss for education ... We should not be one-sided and only be concerned with the numbers of students graduating into higher schools and view examinations as the sole criteria for evaluating students. Instead we must actively promote 'quality education', increase the overall quality of students and so create 'miracles' in school education, and students who can make a major contribution to the development of society.[58]

Furthermore, despite the disparity in educational provision between rural and urban areas and despite government directives to increase vocational education in rural areas, rural schools are judged by the same academic benchmark of success. The result of this, according to many educationalists and officials, is that primary education in rural areas and particularly in non-Han areas bears little relationship to children's lives.[59] Textbooks often present alien social and economic conditions, and therefore what the students learn at school does not allow them to contribute to the traditional economy or society.[60] This in turn is seen to be a major factor in low enrolment and high dropout. The Chinese educationalist Yang Wanli notes in his discussion of the curriculum in the TAR:

> The more backward the area [of the TAR], the more students are unable to study, or are only able to study up to the third year of primary school. Furthermore, in those three years, apart from a little simple mathematics, a few Chinese characters and a little simple Tibetan, what students learn about such matters as ideology, how to earn a living, Tibetan economy and society, is almost nothing. This means that the knowledge gained by the students is

either useless, or they do not know how to use it to make a living, which seriously dampens students' enthusiasm for study.[61]

The issue of the relevance of the curriculum in rural areas, and particularly the introduction of vocational skills into primary education, has been made public at the highest levels of the Chinese government in recent years.[62] In October 1996, on an inspection tour of Qinghai, Vice-Premier Li Lanqing said:

> We must vigorously promote educational reform. Primary education should be reformed to put less emphasis on passing examinations and more on the quality of education. Primary education in agricultural and minority nationality areas should be carried out in the light of local conditions in a practical and realistic manner ... In agricultural areas training in agricultural skills should be incorporated into the curriculum so that in addition to general knowledge, schools will teach crop farming and livestock breeding knowledge and train more badly needed agricultural personnel.[63]

But as Li Peng acknowledged in 1996, the main problem in introducing vocational training into primary schools is that there are not enough teachers skilled in vocational education to satisfy demand even at secondary level.[64]

PRIMARY CURRICULUM IN THE TAR   In addition to the problems of the suitability of the primary curriculum, which are faced by rural communities all over China, in the TAR the availability of Tibetan medium education, including the provision of textbooks in Tibetan, and the appropriateness of the curriculum also have a bearing on the perceived relevance of education to Tibetan children's lives, and consequently on enrolment rates.

The issue of Tibetan medium education is discussed in detail in Chapter 12. Here it is noted that the availability of classes taught in Tibetan appears to be a significant factor in enrolment among Tibetans in rural areas. In 1985, education reforms in the TAR ensured that primary education for Tibetans would be in the Tibetan medium. However, in areas where there is a high concentration of Chinese children, particularly in the Tibetan-inhabited prefectures of Qinghai, Gansu and Sichuan provinces, primary education is still largely conducted in Chinese. In a paper for *Xizang Yanjiu* in 1996, Yang Chunjing describes a situation in Gansu province where students dropped out of one school because the tuition was in Chinese instead of in Tibetan:

> In a school in a Tibetan area of Zhuo ni county, Tibetan was not used for teaching. This created a language barrier in all subjects so that the students

couldn't understand what was being taught. Consequently the parents lost confidence in the school and all but 150 of the students dropped out of the school. Subsequently, out of necessity, the curriculum was revised, and Tibetan was used in teaching wherever possible, increasing the students' ability to learn and their confidence. The curriculum was therefore welcomed by the students and parents with the result that the number of pupils quickly rose to 290.

Another school in a Tibetan area served over 100 large households but, because it neglected Tibetan teaching, the curriculum did not receive popular support. When the school was inspected, only 8 pupils were found to be attending. The other 40 pupils, come rain or snow, were going to school in another county over 10 kms away, because the school in the other county laid stress on Tibetan language education; it was well organised and had comparatively high teaching quality.

... At the Third Session of the Gansu province 10th National People's Congress, 20 per cent of the proposals made at the meeting were requests to begin Tibetan language classes and develop nationality education. At the same time, basic level cadres, farmers and herdsmen made a special trip to see the Party Secretary, Provincial head and the Education Department head to discuss nationality education, and to request that sufficient Tibetan language teachers be provided.[65]

In the 1990s, the teaching of mathematics, even in Tibetan medium primary schools, was hampered by an inadequate supply of textbooks in Tibetan; in Tibetan primary schools in Lhasa, mathematics was taught using Chinese textbooks.[66] In 1996 the Lhasa Education Bureau made attempts to address the problem by printing 10,000 copies of a translation from Chinese of four mathematics workbooks for primary grades 1–4. They were sold at 1 yuan, which was below cost price, to all county education bureaux in Lhasa Municipality for distribution to rural and urban primary schools. They were sold at market price (5 yuan) to education bureaux in other prefectures in the TAR. Money from the sale of the books was to be used to support the translation and printing of other materials in Tibetan.[67] However, while the fact that the textbooks were in Tibetan improved their accessibility for Tibetan children, these books were translations of Chinese primary school textbooks and had not been written specifically for Tibetans. Indeed, even the mathematical terminology used was not the traditional Tibetan terminology but direct translations of the Chinese terms.[68]

Beyond the use of the Tibetan language, the cultural relevance of education taught in schools is believed by several educationalists in China to be a significant factor in enrolment. One Tibetan educationalist writes:

An educational system has been established in Tibetan areas that is almost wholly based on Han culture and way of thinking. Because Han culture is believed to be the most advanced culture, and Han look down on other cultures, 'minority' nationalities are forced to learn Chinese and completely unrelated courses. For example, Tibetans have many trees but they always teach how to plant rice, etc. Chinese history is taught, Han dynasty, Sui dynasty etc, but they do not allow Tibetan history to be taught. Thus there is a big gap between the nationality people's character and the courses they are being taught. What they are reading in books and what they experience in life is completely unrelated. Thus their mental ability actually regresses. This creates a situation where people have an education but can't use it. For example in 1985 in X Commune in Amdo only 1.5 per cent of school-age children were in school. Many children stopped going to school and went to the monasteries. They think this 'school' is meaningful.[69]

Another Tibetan scholar takes the argument beyond the issue of enrolment and drop-out to suggest that a nationality's knowledge of its own culture has a direct bearing on empowerment and its ability to act autonomously:

It is important for us to know about our own national history, religion, culture, geography and customs. If a minority nationality cadre doesn't know, or just knows a bit of his own national history, origins, customs, habits and social development, then it is just like him not even knowing about his own family history and situation, and then of course one cannot become the master of one's own affairs. These days there are a number of Tibetan cadres who don't even have much knowledge of our basic history; they have no knowledge about the Empire of the Early Kings of Tibet, Sakya Kingdom, the Kashag Government, about Songtsen Gampo and Pandita Kunga Gyaltsen, etc.

Of course, there are some objective reasons for it. Although we have plenty of Tibetan history books most of the Tibetan cadres now don't know the Tibetan written language, and on the other hand, the history taught in our schools from primary and secondary schools up to college and university is the 'History of China', and its main content is about Han nationality history, and apart from a few wars, the history of other nationalities is not mentioned.[70]

In the early 1980s, the issue of mother-tongue education for 'minority' nationalities, as well as the revival of China's different cultures, were being discussed at the highest level of government in China. In the TAR, after the First and Second Tibet Work Fora, less publicity was given to ideology and to the role of education in national security. As mentioned above, the First Forum emphasized that education should be developed to encourage the revival of Tibetan culture (provided socialist orientation was maintained). Following this principle, the 'Five Provinces and Region Jointly Published Teaching Materials' Committee (*Wu Sheng Qu Tongbian Jiaocai*) was established in 1982 to co-ordinate the development of textbooks for the TAR and the four other provinces with Tibetan populations.[71] The notion behind the establishment of the *Wu Sheng Qu* was not only to translate textbooks from Chinese into Tibetan but to develop textbooks for Tibetan children that were culturally more relevant. In the TAR itself, the Teaching Materials Translation and Compilation Bureau, which had been set up in 1960, was also re-established under the TAR Education Commission.

Box 5.6 contains an example of a story from the primary school Tibetan textbook for grade 4, published in 1994. The book contains a lesson on the Potala Palace, a practical writing lesson on composing a note to the teacher about being absent, and lessons in Tibetan calligraphy. The first lesson of the book is a story about Lenin.

However, although in principle the TAR government continues to express a commitment to the cultural relevance of the curriculum, several factors have affected the development of Tibetan education in recent years. Although in the early 1980s less publicity was given to ideology and to the role of education in national security, by the end of the decade its overriding importance was again being stressed.[72] What this has meant, in effect, is that with economic development and stability reasserted as the main goals of education, efforts to develop an education system that is sympathetic to Tibetan culture have been undermined. By the late 1980s, traditional Tibetan culture with its dominant Buddhist traditions was being described as both a hindrance to economic development and a threat to security. Yang Wanli writes in his paper on the Tibetan curriculum:

> Religion is a restricting factor in Tibetan economic development, since there are numerous scientific techniques which cannot be broadly applied because they offend religious regulations. If a mountain has a mountain spirit, then reclaiming and cultivating or excavating minerals are not permitted on it; if a lake is a holy lake then building or moving earth are not possible. In herding areas pests run rampant for long periods seriously damaging the grasslands but many among the masses won't adopt positive vermin extermination policies because they hold to the doctrines of Buddhism; in agricultural areas many pests that damage crop growth go without effective control for long periods because the masses are bound by the fetters of religious belief. Moreover, many among the masses will offer up the harvest won from a year of bitter toil to the monastery without a thought.[73]

Since the resurgence of nationalist unrest in 1987, connections have been made between the traditional culture, particularly Tibetan

Box 5.6 The Potala Palace: primary school text

The term Potala is a Sanskrit word. In Tibetan, it is called Riwo Druzin. To the south-west of the motherland, in the centre of Tibet, lies Lhasa city. It looks magnificent against the landscape resembling a reclining elephant. In the middle of Lhasa there is a hill called Marpo Ri on which a Tibetan king named Lhatho Thori Nyentsen once lived in the fourth century. Not long after the 33rd king of Tibet, Songtsen Gampo, was enthroned at the age of thirteen, he left his palace – Jampa Migyur Ling – and moved to Marpo Ri. In the seventh century, the fifteen-year-old Tibetan king, Songtsen Gampo, built the White Palace on the hill which is now 1,300 years old. In later years, another 999 rooms were built, based on the foundations of the White Palace. There were 1000 rooms including the king's room on the top. The palace was surrounded by iron walls which were built at the same time …

The Fifth Dalai Lama, having taken on great political responsibilities rebuilt the White Palace in 1645. From that time onwards, the Potala became a holy site. In 1690, Desi Sangyay Gyatso built the Ser Dung Zam Ling Gyan Chalk after the Fifth Dalai Lama died. And at the same time he expanded the Red Palace, rebuilding it in a very grand style to the magnificent size that it is today. It is thirteen storeys high and rises 110 feet into the sky. The Potala Palace covers an area of about 130 thousand square feet. Its expansion had three great features: it became 1. very stable and refined, withstanding any form of earthquake, storm or strong winds; 2. high and magnificent and wonderful to look at; 3. a unique artistic achievement of the people.

The Potala is altogether a beautiful and extraordinary work. Its architecture, carvings and paintings all show the hard work and bravery of the Tibetan people. It is the greatest embodiment of the unique Tibetan ideas and thoughts.

Explanations:
Lhatho Thori Nyentsen is the 27th king of Tibet
A century is a hundred years

Source: Primary School Tibetan Language Book Seven *(Tibetan People's Publishing House, 1994).*

Buddhism, and nationalist separatism. The primary goal of education for Tibetans has been reasserted as being 'to guarantee the unity and territorial integrity of China'.[74] This, in effect, has set up a conflict of interests in curriculum development. As described in Chapter 3, from 1990, a series of 'patriotic' education campaigns were introduced, which were developed and extended after the Third Forum in 1994.

Since then, attempts to make education more relevant to Tibetan culture, and efforts to teach Tibetan children about their own history, have been hampered by the overriding demand that Tibetan children are taught to appreciate what China has brought to Tibet by making negative comparisons with Tibetan culture and society before 1950. Indeed, in the 1990s, textbooks have frequently been rewritten, sometimes within one academic year, to conform with political imperatives to stress 'the unity of the Motherland' and the importance of Chinese culture.[75] Apart from the denigration of Tibetan culture, which is the result of these political demands on education, the practice also increases delays in the publication of material and is felt to add considerably to teachers' workload, since they frequently have to prepare new texts.[76] By 1996, China's Ninth Five-Year Plan included the stipulation that 'measures should be taken to ensure the publication and distribution of textbooks published in minority languages', but despite comments made by China's leaders about the necessity of making primary education relevant to rural children's lives and needs, the plan states that 'most [textbooks in minority nationality languages] are translated from the Han Chinese version'.

Another hindrance to the development of Tibetan language education is that, although primary school and junior secondary school textbooks continue to be compiled and translated by the *Wu Sheng Qu* committee as well as the TAR Teaching Materials Translation and Compilation Bureau, such organizations have little control over publication and distribution.[77] According to Dorje Tseten, by 1991 the *Wu Sheng Qu* had compiled a complete set of Tibetan textbooks for primary and junior secondary school;[78] however, several reports note the chronic shortage in the number of textbooks published.[79] Publication is carried out by the Tibetan People's Publishing House (*Xizang Renmin Chuban She*), printing is done by the TAR Xinhua Press and the TAR Military Region Press, and the books are distributed by the TAR Xinhua Bookshop. The result of the involvement of these organizations is that the teaching materials bureaux have little say in editorial decisions.[80] Furthermore, the lack of co-ordination between the different organizations and the lack of overall supervision of publication lead to a situation where the TAR has been ranked the lowest in China in the quality of its

Table 5.5 Percentage of new educational material not reaching schools on time

1993	1994		1995	
Autumn	Autumn	Spring	Autumn	Spring
34	36	40	41	23

Source: Yang Wanli, 'The Countermeasure and Particularity of Research on Teaching Materials'.

educational books. In 1995, print quality, design, paper-cutting and book jackets were all said to have noticeable defects according to national standards.[81]

Another problem connected with the publication of Tibetan educational books is that there are long delays in the printing and distribution of a substantial percentage of the material. The delays are partly attributed to the number of organizations involved in the process and to the lack of co-ordination between them, and partly to the fact that, for the Tibetan People's Publishing House, Tibetan educational publications are a low priority, unless the books are connected with political education.[82]

Table 5.5 gives an indication of the percentage of teaching material that did not reach schools before the start of term in the TAR between 1993 and 1995. The longest delay in this period was five months during which students were without textbooks for some classes.[83]

The TAR is the only region or province in China that does not have an educational publisher.[84] Of the two publishers in the region, one – the Tibetan Classics Publishing House (*Zang Wen Gu Ji Chu Ban She*) – exists solely for the publication of Tibetan classics. The other is the Tibetan People's Publishing House (*Xizang Chuban She*) which has responsibility for publishing educational material. However, its major responsibility, since it was founded in 1971, has been the publication of political texts such as Marxist-Leninist ideological theory, the works of Mao, reading materials for propaganda departments in the TAR, as well as for documents and directives issued by the local Party Committee and the TAR government.[85] In the educational field, its publications have been focused on Party history and political theory for popular consumption, as well as reading materials for political education in schools. Although the Tibetan People's Publishing House also has responsibility for school textbooks, the priority given to its political work has meant that little attention has been paid to this area.[86] Yang

Wanli discusses the problem in his paper on curriculum development in the TAR:

> In recent years, the Tibetan People's Publishing House has not had the energy to publish popular reading materials in literature and art, science and technology. Nor have they had the will to publish children's books that are pleasing to the broad mass of Tibetan people, relevant to their everyday lives and which provide moral instruction at the same time as giving pleasure. Theoretically, publishing houses in regions that are backward in science and technology should have a greater responsibility for publishing scientific material but, in fact, because the Tibetan People's Publishing House manages the publication both of its own political works and of educational materials, and because it gives priority to the political publications, the publication of scientific and cultural works for general consumption by the broad masses is neglected.[87]

In his conclusion, Yang Wanli, who in 1996 was deputy director of the Secondary School Teaching Centre of the People's Educational Publishing House in Beijing (*Renmin Jiaoyu Chuban She*) and had been seconded to the TAR Teaching Materials Translation and Compilation Bureau, recommended that an educational publisher be established in the TAR immediately. He suggested that it be set up under the auspices of the TAR Teaching Materials Translation and Compilation Bureau so that curriculum research, textbook compilation and translation as well as editorial and publishing decisions could be planned and co-ordinated more efficiently. At the same time, he suggested that a new publishing house would stimulate competition and therefore perhaps encourage the Tibetan People's Publishing House to greater efforts with regard to educational publishing. This would undoubtedly be beneficial for the quality and efficiency of publications in the TAR. However, in the current political climate, with the new drive for 'close connections with the interior [Central China]',[88] efforts by some educationalists and officials to develop a curriculum that is both relevant to Tibetan children and allows them to take pride in their cultural distinctiveness are likely to continue to provoke conflict.

Religion and education With the more liberal religious policy of the 1980s, the practice of sending children to monasteries began to take hold once again in the TAR. However, in recent years the practice has been increasingly portrayed in the official media as an example of the primitive influence of religion on the minds of Tibetans. Tibetan Buddhism is presented as being a major cause of educational and economic backwardness in the TAR. Indeed, the Chinese government has never officially recognized the educational function of the monasteries in

Tibet.[89] Furthermore, since the resurgence of nationalist unrest in 1987, in which monks and nuns have played a leading role, the monasteries have been the focus of increasingly negative government propaganda. The campaign against the monasteries has involved giving publicity to the view that religious traditions are responsible for making Tibetans resistant to modern education. This became the focus of the Fifth TAR Conference on Education in 1994, since when there has been a new trend in the official media of linking poor educational levels with Tibetan Buddhism. The trend has included frequent comparisons between the number of monks in the TAR and the number of school students. In 1996, *Tibet Daily* reported: 'there are over 46,000 nuns and monks outnumbering secondary school students throughout the region.' The article went on to state that Tibetans spent more money on building monasteries than on building schools.[90]

There is no doubt that the re-emergence of religion into public life in the 1980s has had an effect on enrolment in secular schools in the TAR. However, the reasons for this are certainly more complicated than the media make it appear. A more detailed analysis of the phenomenon of enrolment in monasteries suggests that it is not always resistance to modern education on the part of parents but in many cases it is a rational response to the educational options available to their children.

As several educationalists point out, the monasteries are the traditional centres of education in Tibet; in the past, apart from providing religious education, they were also responsible for teaching literacy.[91] What is less frequently acknowledged, however, is that in the 1980s, with the closure of primary schools throughout the TAR, the newly re-established monasteries once again played an important role in the spread of literacy and basic education. In fact, sending children to the monasteries was often the only means that parents had of providing their children with any education. Furthermore, even when there were schools in the area, the monasteries often proved to be a better choice, not simply in cultural terms, but in educational and economic terms as well. Most monks, certainly older ones, have a higher command of both written and spoken Tibetan and are generally better educated than many community school teachers; in some areas they are the only teachers available.[92] The basic literacy and numeracy provided in the monasteries, even today, have the advantage of being in Tibetan, being culturally more relevant, and are often cheaper than in the schools.

In 1996, Yang Wanli wrote: 'the challenge to school education from religion and monastic education cannot be ignored.' Yang holds the view that Buddhism represents an obstacle to the spread of modern education. However, he acknowledges the monasteries' role in the

---

Box 5.7 Sending children to monasteries: a religious leader's view

In the 1980s, there was a great rush to send children to monasteries. There were several reasons for this. Firstly, all religious activity had been suppressed for so long that there was a great desire among Tibetans, particularly in rural areas, to rebuild monasteries: every village and rural community wanted its own monastery once more. Offering children to the local monastery to help with the reconstruction was part of this process. Secondly, the economic situation in rural areas was very bad and so many parents sent their children to monasteries in order to secure their livelihood. They knew that they would be fed and looked after there, when often the parents didn't have the means to provide for them at home. The third reason for sending children to the monasteries in the 1980s was that in some rural areas, there were no schools and therefore the monasteries provided children with their only education.

Now the situation has changed. In Kham[93], fewer people are sending their children to monasteries. This is largely because, in Kham at least, the economic situation has improved. Rural Tibetans have diversified their income; there is now more opportunity to trade, to get jobs in cities, to engage in business. This means that families need a larger work force – one child to look after the livestock, one to sell their produce in the city and so on. Nowadays, few families can spare a child to send to the monasteries.

Source: *Interview with a senior Tibetan religious leader, 17 February 1997.*

---

spread of literacy and goes on to say that the poor state of secular education in the TAR, even in the 1990s, is at least part of the reason why many parents send their children to monasteries.[94] This view is reiterated by the Tibetan religious leader interviewed in Box 5.7 above. Another scholar, Pama Namgyal, writes:

> The reason the people would rather let their children become lamas than go to school is many-sided, the chief ones being a lack of teachers, poor school conditions, and a low quality of education. Some pupils are still studying the Tibetan alphabet after three to five years of school. Parents are therefore not very interested in schools.[95]

By contrast, it appears that when suitable secular education is provided, young Tibetans studying in monasteries do sometimes transfer to secular schools. In one case in the Ngaba (*Aba*) Tibetan and Qiang Autonomous Prefecture in Sichuan province, several monks left the local monastery to pursue a secular education when a Tibetan medium secondary school was built in the area.[96]

There is another aspect to the monasteries' role in education (at least in the 1980s) which receives scant publicity. Indeed, the propaganda drive against the monasteries in recent years masks what appears to be a division between liberals and hardliners among government officials over the extent to which the religious community can contribute to education. In some areas, the monasteries' role has gone far beyond providing teaching for young monks. In the 1980s, officials in some Tibetan regions engaged monks from local monasteries to work in primary and secondary schools, and to run adult literacy classes.[97] In Gannan Tibetan Autonomous Prefecture in Gansu province, for example, 150 monks were employed in local schools to make up for a lack of teachers qualified to teach in Tibetan.[98] In Ngaba Tibetan and Qiang Autonomous Prefecture in Sichuan province, there has also been cautious co-operation between the monasteries and schools, according to one report.[99] In the TAR itself, it appears that there have been few if any links between state schools and monasteries, although some community schools have used monks as teachers.[100]

However, the link between schools and monasteries has always been fragile and is threatened by the changing political climate. Writing in 1996, on the situation in Ngaba Tibetan and Qiang Autonomous Prefecture, Janet Upton made the following observation:

> As educators attempt to negotiate the relationship between their institutions and local monasteries, they must be cautious. If they are viewed as having ties that are too close, they may be putting themselves and their schools in jeopardy. The boundary between religion and politics in Tibetan communities, both in the past and today, is not an easy one to draw. Because of the political tensions that are associated with religious practice in the contemporary Tibetan context, educators must be extremely careful. They are constantly in danger of being accused of 'splitism' (*fenlie zhuyi*) – a desire to break up China, which in the Tibetan context usually refers to supporting, directly or indirectly, Tibetan independence. As advocates of the revitalisation of Tibetan culture, these individuals run the risk of being accused of 'local nationality chauvinism' (*difang minzu zhuyi*) should the political tides turn, and the tides need not turn far for such accusations to surface.[101]

In the TAR itself, given its predominant Tibetan population and its position along the length of China's south-west border, the educational function of the monasteries has always been more sensitive an issue than in Tibetan areas of other provinces. Since 1987, the political tension in the TAR has made the role of religious figures as educators increasingly untenable.

Summary

A national policy of improving efficiency and quality in education and the economy throughout the 1980s and early 1990s led to a situation where funding and expertise were focused on provinces and regions in China that were deemed to be able to produce the best results. Increasingly, the notion of quality in education came to be associated with examination success and the number of students graduating to higher levels of education. This led, in spite of government directives, to the neglect of education in rural areas, and to the development of an exam-oriented curriculum.

In the TAR we see a sharp decline in primary enrolment up to the mid-1980s, and then an improvement into the mid-1990s. Nevertheless, by 1994 the primary enrolment rate was 66.6 per cent, still 11.4 per cent lower than the enrolment rate in 1982, and this figure disguises the situation in some rural areas where enrolment is between zero and 10 per cent.[102] Furthermore, this figure represents only the percentage of children receiving some primary education; many will receive one to three years at most.

The causes of low enrolment appear to be a combination of financial and cultural factors. In the TAR, unlike in other parts of China, declining enrolment in the 1980s was not connected with a declining birth rate. The practical problems of inadequate provision of education and the poor quality of the education that is provided are acknowledged by government officials and educators. The cultural questions connected with the medium of instruction and the relevance of curriculum and the greater appeal of monastic education are more complicated. In theory, mother-tongue education and a curriculum that is relevant to children's lives are, in Chinese law, deemed to be important factors in increasing enrolment. However, in recent years, perceived notions of security have undermined the development of more culturally relevant education for Tibetans. There is no doubt that many parents prefer to send their children to the monasteries rather than to schools. Indeed, the monasteries played a significant role in the spread of literacy in the Tibetan-inhabited areas of China during the 1980s. However, this role is not publicly acknowledged; in fact, the monasteries are portrayed as being obstacles to the spread of education in the TAR.

Official statistics and basic facts

Table 5.6 Types of primary school and terminology in Tibetan, Chinese and English

English	Tibetan	Chinese	No. of schools
State school (Integrated school)	Shungtsuk lobchung (Chatsang lobchung)	Gongban (Wangquan xiaoxue)	1,185
Community school (Preliminary)	Mangtsuk lobchung (Ngondrol lobchung)	Minban (Chuji xiaoxue)	1,866

Note: In 1995, the terms state school and community school were replaced with 'preliminary' schools for primary schools with fewer than 6 grades and 'integrated' schools for those providing the full 6 years of primary education; the words in brackets refer to the post-1995 titles.

Source: Figures are for 1993, taken from Yang Wanli, 'The Countermeasure and Particularity of Research on Teaching Materials'

Table 5.7 Number of primary schools, students, teachers and number of students per teacher in the TAR, 1994

	Total	Urban	County town	Rural	Tibetans etc.
Schools	3,477	29	159	3,289	
Students	232,976	18,695	40,346	173,935	226,349
Teachers	11,514	1,076	2,808	7,630	
Students:teacher	20.2	17.4	14.4	22.8	

Source: *China's Ethnic Statistical Yearbook* (Ethnic Publishing House, Beijing, 1995)

Table 5.8 Length of primary school education and primary curriculum

Urban 6 years	County towns 3–5 years	Rural 1–3 years
Ideology/morality	Ideology/morality	Ideology/morality
Mathematics	Mathematics	Mathematics
Tibetan	Tibetan	Tibetan
Chinese	(Chinese)	
Singing	(Singing)	

Table 5.9 Primary enrolment rates in the TAR and China, 1980–94 (%)

	China	TAR
1980	93.4	–
1981	–	76
1982	–	78
1983	–	42.1
1984	95.3	46.4
1985	96	46
1986	96.4	50
1987	97.2	48.4
1988	97.2	55.7
1989	97.4	53.1
1990	97.8	67.4
1991	97.8	45.6
1992	97.2	52.4
1993	97.7	58.9
1994	98.4	66.6

Source: 1995 China Statistical Yearbook; 1995 TAR Statistical Yearbook

Notes

1. These referred to the policies of the Cultural Revolution.
2. Suzanne Pepper, 'Chinese Education After Mao: Two Steps Forward, Two Steps Back and Begin Again?', *China Quarterly*, No. 81, 1980, p. 10.
3. Ibid.
4. At the Fifth TAR Conference on Education, Chairman Gyaltsen Norbu was still discussing the need 'gradually to turn teachers of *minban* schools into teachers of *gongban* schools'. See Gyaltsen Norbu, 'Education in Tibet', Speech to Fifth Regional Meeting on Education in the TAR on 26 October 1994, *Xizang Ribao* (Tibet Daily), 30 October 1994, pp. 1–4.
5. Keith M. Lewin and Wang Ying Jie, *Implementing Basic Education in China* (UNESCO, 1994), p. 153; see also Internal Party discussion paper, 1995.
6. Jin Lin, *Education in Post-Mao China* (Praeger, London, 1993), p. 40.
7. Announcement by the TAR People's Government, 20 June 1980, cited in *Modern China's Tibet*, part 2, p. 679.
8. Paper on Education Development among Tibetans, by Tibetan scholar in China, 1995.
9. State Education Commission Circular, 25 January 1996.
10. 1995 TAR Statistical Yearbook.
11. See Hu Yaobang, 'Report to TAR Regional Party Committee Cadres', Lhasa Radio, 1430 gmt, 30 May 1980 [SWB 4/6/80].
12. In 1981 the rural population was 90.16 per cent of the total population;

in 1994 it was 83.41 per cent of the total. See 1995 TAR Statistical Yearbook, p. 38.

13. Pepper, 'Chinese Education After Mao'.

14. For an analysis of the problems of data collection and statistical analysis in China see Tsui Kai-yuen, 'Economic Reform and Attainment in Basic Education in China', *China Quarterly*, No. 149, March 1997, pp. 104–27.

15. Interview with educationalist, 2 February 1997.

16. The explanatory notes on the calculation of enrolment rate in the 1995 China Statistical Yearbook state the following: 'the enrolment rate of primary school-age children refers to the proportion of school-age children enrolled at schools in the total number of school-age children both in and outside schools (including retarded children, but excluding blind, deaf and mute children)' p. 654.

17. Lewin and Wang Ying Jie, *Implementing Basic Education in China*, p. 35.

18. See among others: Lewin and Wang Ying Jie, op. cit., p. 5; and Yat Ming Leung, 'The People's Republic of China', in *Education and Development in East Asia* (Garland Press, London, 1995), p. 220; Pepper, 'Chinese Education After Mao', p. 7.

19. Melvyn Goldstein and Cynthia Beall, 'China's Birth Control Policy in the Tibet Autonomous Region: Myths and Realities', *Asian Survey*, Fall 1990.

20. Pressure usually took the form of reduced bonuses and benefits, see Catriona Bass, *Inside the Treasure House: A Time in Tibet* (Gollancz, London, 1990), p. 133.

21. Gyaltsen Norbu, 'Education in Tibet', Speech to Fifth Regional Meeting on Education in the TAR on 26 October 1994, *Xizang Ribao* (Tibet Daily), 30 October 1994.

22. Yang Wanli does not give population figures for the different prefectures. According to the 1990 Census, the population of Ngari was 61,639 and the population of Lhasa Municipality was 375,968.

23. Yang Wanli, '*Xizang Kecheng Jiaocai Yanjiu De Teshuxing Jiqi Duice*' (The Countermeasure and Particularity of Research on Teaching Materials), *Xizang Yanjiu* (Tibet Studies), Vol. 58, No. 1, 1996.

24. Although the most recent statistical data provide a rural/urban breakdown for certain educational criteria in the TAR, the statistics are incomplete and do not give information on enrolment rates, therefore we have to look back to statistical data from the 1980s to find enrolment rates in each prefecture. (See 1995 China Statistical Yearbook; and 1995 TAR Statistical Yearbook.)

25. Note: there appears to be an error in the statistics for Chamdo (*Changdu*): identical figures are given for both years. Reports in the Tibetan press in 1993 suggest that the enrolment rate in Chamdo was around 34 per cent; see Xiang Xiaoli and Zhang Qing, 'Courage of Conviction Consists of Tackling the Reality of the Situation Today with a Clear Vision for the Future', *Chamdo Daily*, 15 July 1993.

26. See Yang Wanli, 'The Countermeasure and Particularity of Research on Teaching Materials'.

27. Chen Kuiyuan, 'Speech on Education in Tibet', Fifth Regional Meeting

on Education in the TAR, 26 October 1994, *Xizang Ribao* (Tibet Daily), 28 October 1994.

28. Xiang Xiaoli and Zhang Qing, 'Courage of Conviction'.

29. *Xinhua*, 5 June 1994 [SWB 8/6/94].

30. *Xinhua* (in English), 12 January 1994 [SWB 17/1/94].

31. Internal Party discussion paper, 1995; the scholar Jiang Weizhu shares this view. See Jiang Weizhu, *'Shi Lun "San Bao" Jiaoyu Zhengce De Li Yu Bi Ji Qi Zhengce Duice'* (Advantages and Disadvantages and Reform Measures of the 'Three Guarantees' Education Policy), *Xizang Yanjiu* (Tibetan Studies), Vol. 58, No. 1, 1996.

32. Illiteracy and semi-illiteracy, for Chinese, is defined as 'those who cannot read, or can read only very little – normally less than 1500 characters – those who cannot read popular books or newspapers, or write short notes'. For Tibetans, the definition of illiteracy is the inability to read popular books or newspapers, or write short notes. See *Population Atlas of China* (Oxford University Press, Oxford, 1987).

33. Speech by Xu Zhijian, Deputy Secretary General of the State Council and Vice-President of the National Working Committee for Women and Children (NWCWC) at press conference on child development in China; *Beijing Review*, 16–22 December 1996.

34. *Xinhua* (in English), 17 June 1996 [SWB 19/6/96].

35. Paper on Education Development among Tibetans, by Tibetan scholar in China, 1995.

36. Report by the Literacy Section, TAR Education Commission, *Xizang Ribao* (Tibet Daily), 23 October 1990.

37. Save the Children Fund (UK), Education Project Information Sheet, November 1996.

38. 'Outline of the TAR's Five-Year Plan for Economic and Social Development and Its Long-term Target for 2010, Approved by the Fourth Session of the Sixth Regional People's Congress on 24th May 1996', *Xizang Ribao* (Tibet Daily), 7 June 1996, pp. 1–4 (TAR Ninth Five-Year Plan 1996).

39. Paper on Education Development among Tibetans, by Tibetan scholar in China, 1995. County populations vary between 12,000 and 60,000 but most are around 25,000–35,000. See *Encyclopaedia of Chinese Counties*, Vol.: South-West China (China Social Publishing House, 1993).

40. Save the Children Fund (UK), Education Project Information Sheet, November 1996.

41. Report by the Literacy Section, 1990.

42. *Xizang Ribao* (Tibet Daily) (Chinese), 16 April 1990.

43. Pama Namgyal, *'Xianjieduan Xizang Zongjiao de Diwei He Zuoyong'* (Lamaism in the Tibet Autonomous Region), *Xizang Yangjiu* (Tibet Studies), No. 1, 1989. Trans. in J. Seymour and Eugen Werli (eds), *Chinese Sociology and Anthropology, A Journal of Translations*, Spring 1994, p. 70.

44. Julia Kwong and Hong Xiao, 'Educational Equality Among China's Minorities', *Comparative Education*, Vol. 25, No. 2, 1989.

45. Edward Kormondy, 'Observations on Minority Education, Cultural Pres-

ervation and Economic Development in China', *Compare*, Vol. 25, 1995. See also: Gerard Postiglione, 'Implications of Modernization for the Education of China's Minorities', in R. Hayhoe (ed.), *Education and Modernization – The Chinese Experience* (Pergamon Press, London, 1992); and Bernhard Dilger, 'The Education of Minorities', *Comparative Education*, Vol. 20, No. 1, 1984.

46. See Xiang Xiaoli and Zhang Qing, 'Courage of Conviction'; see also Report by the TAR Education Commission Literacy Section, 1990; Jiang Weizhu, '... the "Three Guarantees" Education Policy'.

47. Dalu Yin, 'Reforming Chinese Education: Context, Structure and Attitudes in the 1980s', *Compare*, Vol. 23, No. 2, 1993, p. 117.

48. Xiang Xiaoli and Zhang Qing, 'Courage of Conviction'.

49. 'Looking Back at 1994 and Looking Forward to 1995: Raising High the Banner of Development', Lhasa Radio, 19 January 1995 [FBIS 27/1/95].

50. Gyaltsen Norbu, Work Report on the TAR Ninth Five-Year Plan, *Xizang Ribao* (Tibet Daily), 16 May 1996.

51. Dalu Yin, 'Reforming Chinese Education'.

52. Internal Party discussion paper, 1995.

53. In 1990, 40 per cent of children in TAR were said to be receiving grants; see *Xinhua*, 2 May 1990 [SWB 4/5/90].

54. See Jiang Weizhu, '... the "Three Guarantees" Education Policy'.

55. See, among others, Yang Wanli, 'The Countermeasure and Particularity of Research on Teaching Materials'; Paper on Education Development among Tibetans, by Tibetan scholar, 1995; see also Teng Xing, '*Wo Guo Shaoshu Minzu Diqu Jiaoyu Zhengti Gaige Guanjian*' (The Essence of Overall Educational Reform in China's Minority Regions), *Qiu Shi*, No. 7, April 1989, pp. 19–24; Interview with former Western educationalist in the TAR, January 1996.

56. Yang Wanli, 'The Countermeasure and Particularity of Research on Teaching Materials'.

57. Dalu Yin, 'Reforming Chinese Education'.

58. Lei Yongsheng, '*Xiandaihua Jiaoyu Fazhan Yu Xizang Jiaoyu Gaige*' (The Development of Modern Education and the Reform of Tibetan Education), *Xizang Yanjiu* (Tibet Studies), Vol. 58, No. 1, 1996.

59. See among others: Teng Xing, 'The Essence of Overall Educational Reform', pp. 19–24; Yang Wanli, 'The Countermeasure and Particularity of Research on Teaching Materials'; Yang Chunjing, '*Qiandan Zang Yuwen Jiaoxue Zai Fazhan Minzu Jiaoyu Zhong de Zhongyao Xing*' (A Tentative Study on the Importance of Teaching in the Tibetan Language for Developing National Education), *Xizang Yanjiu* (Tibet Studies), Vol. 59, No. 2, 1996; Dalu Yin, 'Reforming Chinese Education'.

60. Teng Xing, 'The Essence of Overall Educational Reform', pp. 19–24.

61. Yang Wanli, 'The Countermeasure and Particularity of Research on Teaching Materials'.

62. See accounts of inspection tours of education by Vice-Premier Li Langqing in Northern China, *Xinhua*, 5 July 1996 [SWB 9/7/96]; and Qinghai, *Xinhua* (in Chinese), 20 October 1996 [SWB 22/10/96].

63. *Xinhua* (in Chinese), 20 October 1996 [SWB 22/10/96].

64. Premier Li Peng, addressing participants of Third National Working Conference on Vocational Education, 17 June 1996 in *Xinhua*, 17 June 1996 [SWB 19/6/96].

65. Yang Chunjing, 'A Tentative Study'.

66. Interview with Tibetan educationalist, 7 August 1996.

67. Save the Children Fund (UK) Tibet, China Education Project Information Sheet, November 1996.

68. Interview with Tsering Shakya, Tibetan historian, 24 July 1997.

69. Paper on Education Development among Tibetans, by Tibetan scholar in China, 1995, p. 48.

70. Internal Party discussion paper, 1995.

71. Duojie Caidan (Dorje Tseten), *Xizang Jiaoyu* (Education in Tibet) (China Tibetology Publishers, Beijing, 1991).

72. See 'Raidi and Gyaltsen Norbu Summarize Tibet Work Forum Conclusions', *Xizang Ribao* (Tibet Daily) (in Chinese), 2 August 1994.

73. Yang Wanli, 'The Countermeasure and Particularity of Research on Teaching Materials'; see also Jiang Weizhu, '... the "Three Guarantees" Education Policy'.

74. Yang Wanli, op. cit.; see also Chen Kuiyuan, 'Speech on Education in Tibet'.

75. Interview with Tibetan educationalist, 7 August 1996; see also Lisa Keary, Interview for Doctoral Thesis, 1996.

76. Interview with Tibetan educationalist, 7 August 1996.

77. Yang Wanli, 'The Countermeasure and Particularity of Research on Teaching Materials'.

78. Duojie Caidan (Dorje Tseten), *Education in Tibet*.

79. See Yang Wanli, 'The Countermeasure and Particularity of Research on Teaching Materials'; interview with former Western educationalist in the TAR, January 1996.

80. Ibid.

81. Summary Print Quality Report (*Yinshua Zhiliang Jiance Jianbao*), 1 June 1995, cited in ibid.

82. Ibid.

83. Ibid.

84. Ibid.

85. Ibid.

86. Ibid.

87. Ibid.

88. This statement is part of the new directives for increasing 'unity' issued by the Central Committee; see ibid.

89. Yenming Zhang, *Effects of Policy Changes on College Enrolment of Minority Students in China, 1949–1989*, Doctoral Thesis (Harvard University, 1991).

90. 'Actively Guide Religion to Accommodate itself to Socialist Society', *Xizang Ribao* (Tibet Daily), 4 November 1996; see also Yang Wanli, 'The Countermeasure and Particularity of Research on Teaching Materials'; Jian Weizhu, '... the "Three Generation" Education Policy'.

91. See Yang Wanli, op. cit.; Teng Xing, 'The Essence of Overall Educational Reform', pp. 19–24.

92. Pama Namgyal, 'Lamaism in the TAR', p. 64.

93. Kham is the name of one of the three provinces that made up Tibet before 1950. Today its territory is divided between the TAR, Sichuan, Gansu and Yunnan.

94. Yang Wanli, 'The Countermeasure and Particularity of Research on Teaching Materials'.

95. Pama Namgyal, 'Lamaism in the TAR', p. 67.

96. Janet Upton, 'Home on the Grasslands? Tradition, Modernity, and the Negotiation of Identity by Tibetan Intellectuals in the PRC', in Melissa J. Brown (ed.), *Negotiating Ethnicities in China and Taiwan*, China Research Monograph 46 (Center for Chinese Studies, University of California, 1996), p. 118.

97. *Tibet Daily* [date unknown], cited in Teng Xing, 'The Essence of Overall Educational Reform'.

98. Ibid.

99. Upton, 'Home on the Grasslands?', p. 118.

100. Former TAR government cadre, interview, 28 July 1997.

101. Upton, 'Home on the Grasslands?', p. 118.

102. Pama Namgyal, 'Lamaism in the TAR', p. 70.

CHAPTER 6

Funding of Primary Education: Urban Versus Rural

Government funding

It is agreed by experts both inside and outside China that the lack of funding is the main cause of low enrolment in primary education, particularly in rural areas. In 1993 Zhu Kaixuan, Minister in charge of the State Education Commission, said in a report to the National People's Congress: 'Funding shortages have always been the prime factor impeding the development and reform of our country's educational services.'[1] In the same year, the 'Programme for China's Educational Reform and Development' stated that education funding was not sufficient either to provide for current basic educational needs or to provide the human resources for the further development of the economy.[2]

As mentioned in Chapter 4, the 1980s' educational finance reforms in China were planned on two levels. First, they were intended to shift funding from the central government to provincial-level governments and below and, second, they aimed to make the people play a role in the direct funding of education. Villages were to become responsible for the financing of primary schools, township governments for junior secondary schools and county governments for senior secondary schools.[3] However, the fiscal decentralization of education funding formed part of the wider economic decentralization which urged local governments to invest in projects that provided quick profits and generated tax revenues (such as town and village enterprises) and therefore, in reality, investment in education came into conflict with what is perceived as the greater priority of income generation.

The financial reforms included an educational surcharge to be added to local taxes. The educational surcharge was levied from production tax, business tax and VAT at a rate of 1 per cent in 1986, rising to 3 per cent in 1993.[4] According to the 1985 'CCP Decision on Education', the 'Programme for China's Educational Reform and Development', and later the 1995 Education Law, the educational surcharge has to be used primarily for funding compulsory education.[5] The 1995 Education Law allowed provincial and prefectural-level governments to set their own educational surcharge in accordance with central government guidelines. Township-level governments were to make arrangements for collecting educational surcharges for township-run schools under regulations set at the provincial level.[6] Initially, in the mid-1980s, there was a surcharge on agricultural taxes, although this proved extremely unpopular and was later abandoned.[7] Nevertheless, some local governments continued to impose a surcharge on agricultural taxes, leading the State Council to issue a circular in June 1996 prohibiting the imposition of tax surcharges on the agricultural population. According to the circular, 'some township and rural governments have solicited money from farmers in the name of building schools, which has affected farmers' living standards'.[8] In May of the same year, Zhu Kaixuan, Minister of the State Education Commission, reiterated: 'no governments are allowed to impose levies on local farmers to raise education funds.'[9]

Since the reforms, the state at county level has paid the salaries of state primary teachers and a subsidy for community primary teachers. Other expenditures are taken from donations, fees and school-generated incomes. Capital investment, mainly the construction of school buildings and the purchase of furniture, is funded by local donations under an incentive system known as the 'fishing policy' whereby the local government provides a small sum to encourage donations from villagers, or promises to furnish buildings if villagers undertake the construction. Expenditures such as the improvement of school facilities and repairing buildings are funded by schools through farms, orchards, school-operated factories, shops, or the rental of part of the school premises.[10]

The effect of these reforms has been to make education funding dependent not only on the prosperity of the region, as was shown in Chapter 4, but also on the prosperity of the individual prefecture, county and even village in the case of primary schools. What this means in the TAR, where there has been virtually no rural industrialization, is that county governments have very little revenue and thus little to invest in education in terms of teachers' salaries or incentives for local donations.[11] Furthermore, given the essentially agricultural economy, there is little to be levied as an educational surcharge, particularly since in many rural areas a partial barter economy still operates. As shown in the previous chapter, parents are often too poor to pay miscellaneous fees, for example to pay for exercise books, and they are too poor to provide free labour for construction.[12]

The reforms of the 1980s and early 1990s not only resulted in a disparity in the funding of education at the regional or provincial level

Table 6.1 Student–teacher ratio in primary schools, 1994

	Urban	County level	Rural
China average	20:1	22:1	24:1
TAR average	12:1	14:1	23:1

Source: Figures based on 1995 China Statistical Yearbook.

but also increased the discrepancy between the provision of education in urban and rural areas. Most of the state primary schools, which receive more government funding, are to be found in urban areas. This means that the state effectively subsidizes education to a greater extent in urban areas than in rural areas. At a meeting of the TAR branch of the CPPCC in May 1994, one delegate raised the issue of the inadequate funding of rural education. He noted that in some cases the funding required to make improvements was not substantial and implied that underfunding may be due to a lack of will among urban decision-makers.[13] A similar point is made by Yang Chunjing:

> It is necessary to give consideration both to stressing city and town educa-tion, and remote mountainous, pastoral areas and forest area education. The tendency in existing work of giving priority to cities and towns and devaluing farming and pastoral areas, in valuing secondary schools and giving low priority to primary schools, must be resolutely overcome in order to avoid the appearance of backward regions which become forgotten corners. We must work hard to lessen the gap between small cities and the countryside, progressively to realise the Tibetan people's ascendancy to the ranks of the advanced nationalities, and to realise a flourishing prosperity.[14]

The problem of rural underfunding is exacerbated by the fact that unit costs are higher in rural areas; schools tend to be small and the remoteness of many of them makes transportation costs high – this is particularly true in mountainous regions where the population is scattered.[15] For example, the population density of the TAR as a whole is 1.8 people per square kilometre, but in Nagchu and Ngari prefectures it drops to 0.8 and 0.2 people per square km, respectively. Furthermore, the TAR has only 17.6 km of road per 1,000 square km, which is 17 per cent of the average for the whole of China. To reduce costs in counties where there is a low population density, schools recruit only every two or three years. Many rural primary schools consequently practise multi-grade teaching.[16] Table 6.1 gives teacher–pupil ratios for urban and rural areas in the TAR in comparison with China as a whole. It shows how class sizes in the TAR are much lower than the national average, apart from in rural areas where multi-grade teaching is practised.

Grants Tuition for compulsory education is free in China and the TAR. In 1984, following the Second Forum, the Central Committee introduced a policy for the TAR whereby children from certain poor areas in the region would be eligible for free board, lodging and clothing from the fourth grade of primary school onwards.[17] This is known in Chinese as *san bao* (the three guarantees). In 1990, according to government sources, 40 per cent of students in the TAR were receiving free board and lodging in schools, as well as a monthly grant. The grant amounted to 29 yuan per month for primary school pupils, and 39 yuan per month for secondary school pupils;[18] in 1994 grants were raised to between 57 and 95 yuan per month.[19] However, the Chinese educationalist Jiang Weizhu suggested that the benefits of the increase were cancelled out by the increase in the cost of living.[20] Furthermore, most rural schools, where 75 per cent of primary pupils study, provide education to grade 3 at most and therefore these students are not eligible for the grant. An additional subsidy known as the *renmin zhuxuejin* (people's study grant) was introduced in the TAR in 1994 to provide funding for students in state (and a few community) primary schools below grade 4. The grant was issued by county governments directly to schools and amounted to 15–22 yuan per student per month. Although schools could only receive the *renmin zhuxuejin* for 60 per cent of their pupils, they sometimes managed to assist the other 40 per cent of pupils by providing clothing or food.[21]

Jiang Weizhu identifies several general problems in the grant scheme in the TAR. He suggests that the grants cannot keep pace with inflation and, given the limited funds available for education, there is no possibility of increasing them. Furthermore, Jiang Weizhu believes that the *san bao* system is using up funds on individuals which would be better spent on the improvement of the overall provision of education. Jiang Weizhu calls for a re-examination of eligibility for the *san bao*. He recommends that cadres' children and children from urban areas should not be entitled to the food grant, that the clothing grant should be abolished entirely, and that children who live within a five-mile radius of their school should not be eligible for free accommodation. In Jiang's view, one of the major failures of the scheme is that many parents simply send their children to school in order to obtain the grant and therefore the children are believed to lack motivation.[22]

It appears that in some areas of the TAR, the population is so poor that the children's bursary becomes the family's means of survival. In

1993, an article in the *Chamdo Daily* criticized parents for using their children's bursary to buy staple foods, instead of using it for educational purposes:

> In the pastoral and farming areas, families send their children to schools in order to get the *san bao*, 'the three guarantees' [board, lodging and clothing], and the pupil bursary. The over 30 yuan per month given as the fulfilment of the nation's 'three guarantees' has become the families' monthly salary. The families euphemistically call this the child's monthly income, and use the amount to buy their rations, such as tea and salt. As regards the child's education, they do not even bother to make enquiries. Had there been no 'three guarantees' or bursary, the children would surely have been withdrawn from school. How can there be improvement of knowledge in such a state of affairs? In sadness, we continue to worry and mourn over the sad state of education in Chamdo.[23]

In general, it appears that the state of the economy in the TAR at present has led to a situation where there are serious shortfalls in the government funding of education. As a result, the state is unable to provide adequate assistance to the poorest students, and turns increasingly to society, including its poorest members, to make up the shortfall in the education budget.

Non-government funding

Despite the poverty of rural China, and rural areas in the TAR in particular, the 1985 reforms emphasized the public's responsibility for funding education. In 1991, almost 40 per cent of education expenditure in China came from non-government sources.[24]

Although tuition is free for compulsory education, parents are faced with a number of costs. Children have to pay a registration fee and for textbooks each year as well as other items. Families in rural areas are often obliged to make payments in kind to supplement rural teachers' salaries, and to supply construction materials and voluntary labour. The cost of educating a child varies considerably depending on several factors:

- whether the family lives in an urban or rural area
- whether the family belongs to a state work-unit or not
- whether the child's school is a state or community school
- whether the child goes to a school within the region designated by the family's residence permit

Voluntary labour and payment in kind The statistical yearbooks do not calculate the cost of education for rural families since tuition is technically free, and poor children receive grants. Labour and payment in kind are not registered as payment but as voluntary contributions, despite the fact that they represent considerable cost to rural families in terms of loss of production and saleable assets. Indeed, the burden on the rural population of voluntary labour was recognized by the First Forum in 1980. In his speech to TAR government officials, Hu Yaobang said that peasants and nomads should no longer have to provide voluntary labour.[25] It is not clear the extent to which this policy was implemented in the 1980s, but by 1994 it appears to have been reversed. The Fifth TAR Conference on Education outlined a system by which the funding of schools in rural areas would depend directly on voluntary labour and the donation of materials by local people: 'Whenever possible, local governments should mobilize and organize peasants and herdsmen to reconstruct unsafe village schools, build new schools, and improve teaching conditions by contributing their labour service or construction materials on a voluntary basis.'[26]

Urban families rarely have to provide voluntary labour. When they do, only families who do not work for a state work-unit are affected in terms of loss of earnings or production. Families who work for the state are guaranteed a monthly salary and therefore a day of voluntary labour has no financial implications for them.

'Miscellaneous' fees Chinese law does not allow tuition fees to be charged for compulsory education, but it does allow what are termed 'miscellaneous' fees. These fees include book charges, food, electricity and extra tuition. Since 1993, schools have been required to seek the approval of the financial department of the local government before charging their students a particular type of fee.[27] Box 6.1 gives an example of costs for compulsory education (primary and junior secondary) in Lhasa in 1993, as well as costs for children who do not have a Lhasa residence permit; it also provides a comparison with senior secondary costs which include tuition fees.

After the 1985 'CCP Decision on Education', the government began promoting the positive value of community-funded education. In the TAR, the increasing cost of education was presented as a sign of progress. The cost to rural communities of building schools was positively compared with donations to monasteries, which were termed a sign of backwardness.[28] 'The general public showed unprecedentedly great enthusiasm in raising and donating money to build schools', was how a Lhasa Radio broadcast described public funding of education in 1994.[29] In the same year *Xinhua* published a survey on expenditure

---

Box 6.1 Educational expenses for students in compulsory
education in Lhasa, 1993

1. *Beginning in 1993, primary school students have to pay 15 yuan
and 10 yuan for exercise books, totalling 25 yuan per student per year.
Those from outside Lhasa will have to pay 100 yuan at the time of
admission to this school. Between the school sessions, more money is
collected, on a number of occasions.*

   2. *At junior secondary school students pay 25 yuan each, then they
have to pay 20 yuan for textbooks and exercise books, totalling 45 yuan
per student. Students from outside Lhasa have to pay 100 to 500 yuan
at the time of admission.*

   *Senior secondary school students have to pay 30 yuan tuition fee
and 30 yuan for text and exercise books, totalling 60 yuan per student.
Fees for the new recruits from outside Lhasa are similar to the above
fees (100–500 yuan per student).*

Source: Interview with Lhasa primary school teacher, April 1993.

---

among families in the Lugu district of Lhasa. The report stated that
altogether Lugu families spent more than 11,000 yuan on education,
which was 4.5 times the amount spent the previous year. According to
the report, the growth rate in education expenditure was much greater
than other daily expenditures.[30] In 1996, an article on education in the
TAR reported that funding 'donations from the people amounted to
105.23 million yuan ($12.36m) over the past six years'.[31]

However, the cost of education to families in the TAR is not equal,
even among urban families. The 1995 TAR Statistical Yearbook details
education expenditure for urban households in 1994. Figures 6.1 and
6.2 show the annual expenditure on education by families of different
income brackets in urban areas in the TAR in 1994, as well as education
expenditure as a percentage of total expenditure. As the graphs show,
households with the highest income pay less for education those with
average incomes or below. The reason for this is that state workers,
who are in the wealthiest sectors of society, have their children's educational costs paid for by their work-unit. Non-state workers have to pay
their own educational costs. In 1994, the highest-income households
paid 51.43 yuan per capita in educational costs, which represented
0.6 per cent of their annual per capita income and 0.8 per cent of their
annual per capita expenditure, while 'below middle income' households

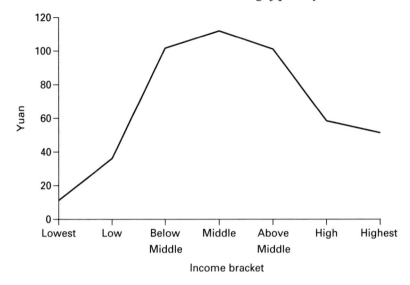

Figure 6.1 Annual per capita expenditure on education in urban households in the TAR, 1994 (*Source*: 1995 TAR Statistical Yearbook)

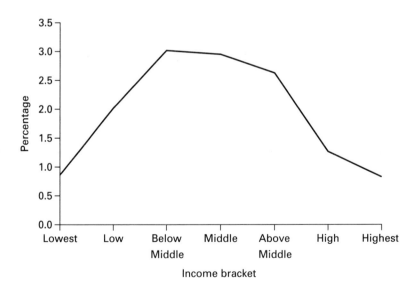

Figure 6.2 Annual per capita expenditure on education in urban households in the TAR as a percentage of total expenditure, 1994 (*Source*: 1995 TAR Statistical Yearbook)

paid almost twice the amount per capita: 101.75 yuan. This represented 3.3 per cent of their per capita income and 3 per cent of their annual per capita expenditure. The poorest households paid 11.25 yuan, or 1.2 per cent of income and 0.9 per cent of expenditure – a higher percentage than the highest-income households.

'Excessive' fees By the late 1980s the acute lack of state funding in education, together with the official encouragement of public funding of education, led to schools charging pupils increasing amounts in miscellaneous fees. A child interviewed from a rural primary school in Kongpo Prefecture in 1994 described collecting fungi and medicinal herbs to sell, in order to pay for educational costs.[32] Box 6.2 gives an illustration of the situation in one state primary school in Lhasa in 1996.

By the end of the 1980s, voices began to be raised about excessive fees and corruption in education throughout China. Similar complaints were being made in the TAR.[33] In May 1989, an article appeared in the Beijing newspaper, the *Economics Weekly*, which outlined the poor state of education funding as well as the misuse of funds: 'The authorities in charge of education have not realised how important it is to develop education. While much has been spent on luxury commodities such as refrigerators, colour TV sets, imported cars and new buildings, education has been neglected.'[34]

Box 6.2 Miscellaneous charges made by a Lhasa state primary school, 1996

Recently children have been told that they have to stay after class to do their homework in the classroom. Then parents are told they have to pay 15 yuan per month for the use of the classroom. Sometimes children are made to stay at school until 9 o'clock in the evening. I often see parents waiting for their children outside the school when it is already dark. The problem is that teachers have very low salaries and so they need to find ways of supplementing it, and this is one of the ways in which they do that. Another way is in the distribution of vaccinations and medicine to children. Last year, my son was told he had to have a certain number of vaccinations. We told the school that we had already had him vaccinated, but the school told us that we had to pay for the vaccinations anyway.

Source: Interview with Tibetan parent, 7 August 1996.

Box 6.3 Extract from TAR government investigation report into the charging of exorbitant fees, 8–17 June 1993

Fees of schools … Following complaints from the masses, our committee carried out an investigation and found that there are some exorbitant fees charged by schools and hospitals. In this school term, schools in Lhasa City have charged for 13 items and among them there are six items with exorbitant fees.

1. *Borrowing money from students' parents to build a store house for the school.*
2. *Charging peasants' and nomads' children fees for their textbooks and other items at the same rate as city children.*
3. *Collecting money from children's parents.*
4. *Charging pupils fees for joining a class in the middle of the term.*
5. *Charging fees for re-taking exams, and for failing to go up to the next grade.*
6. *Charging fees for making up lessons.*

The total sum of these 6 unreasonable fees is 175,000 yuan.

Source: Report to the TAR Party Committee and Government of 'Investigation into Unhealthy Tendencies in Pricing, Industries and Exorbitant Fees', 4 July 1993.

In the early 1990s, schoolchildren in the TAR responded to the increasing costs of education by staging protests, particularly at secondary level. In 1993, a number of reports referred to a demonstration in a secondary school in Lhasa which was fuelled by the imposition of school fees of 20 yuan per month for each student – one of the banners carried by marchers called for a decrease in school fees. A similar incident is reported to have taken place in the secondary school in Nyemo county on 1 January 1993.[35] On 4 May 1993 there were reports of a demonstration in the town of Tsethang, south of Lhasa, by 100 pupils at Lhokha Secondary School No. 1. They were reportedly protesting about poor conditions and the lack of jobs for school-leavers.[36]

In response to public protest in 1993, the TAR Party Committee set up an inquiry into the charging of exorbitant fees by government departments and other public organizations. The investigation committee, drawn from various departments of the TAR and Lhasa city governments, found schools to be particularly prone to exacting excessive fees. Box 6.3 is an extract of the investigation committee's report with regard to schools.

As a result of this investigation, the TAR Education Commission cancelled six kinds of educational fees, and published a report which was to be distributed to all county-level governments. The report included the stipulation that textbooks and other charges should be reduced or free for people on low incomes, and that fees should be both standardized and checked by the TAR regional-level finance department.[37] However, the charging of unlawful fees continued to be a cause of concern at the highest levels of government. Between 1993 and 1997 the State Council issued at least four circulars about curbing the random collection of fees.[38] The circulars drew attention to increasing corruption in some cities where the school authorities demanded 'expensive gifts' from their students, forced them to pay for insurance, set quotas of fees to be collected 'under the pretext of building schools', indiscriminately demanded contributions in cash or in kind by 'compulsory or covert means'.[39]

Reassessment of funding reforms in the 1990s: recentralization and renewed emphasis on government funding

By the late 1980s it was becoming clear that the rapid market reforms were having serious repercussions on the funding of education, particularly basic education. Recession gripped China and inflation was running at 20 per cent; the entrepreneurial spirit that had been so encouraged at the start of the reform period was now threatening to wreak havoc on the education system as administrators and teachers tried to bring market forces into schools.

Dalu Yin quotes Deng Xiaoping as saying in 1989: 'The greatest mistake we made in the last ten years was that in education.' Although he goes on to write that the implications of this statement need to be examined, his own conclusion is that the outcome of the reforms far from matched expectations, that the system had proven 'ruinous to the quality of primary education on the one hand and, on the other, had failed to produce the qualified personnel needed for China's socialist Four Modernisations'.[40]

By the early 1990s, the problems that the market economy had brought to the education system were being recognized at the highest levels of government. In 1993, Zhu Kaixuan told the National People's Congress:

The current accelerated shift from a planned economy to a socialist market economy has posed many new problems regarding educational reform and development, and brought to light some glaring difficulties ... The main problems and difficulties we currently encounter in primary education, especially primary education in the countryside, include funding shortages, arrears in payment of teachers' salaries, the collection of unwarranted fees and the rising drop-out rate among primary and secondary school students.[41]

The previous year, the 'Programme for China's Educational Reform and Development' had stated that educational funding was not only insufficient to meet the demands of the development of China's economic reform programme, it was also insufficient 'to meet the basic needs for developing the present educational work'.[42] In the TAR, like other remote rural regions, the situation was particularly acute. In June 1994, Gyaltsen Norbu, chairman of the TAR government, announced: 'about one third of school-age children could not afford to go to school in the TAR by the end of 1993.'[43]

In its 1993 report on the investigation into extortion, the TAR government investigation committee also explained the particular problems that the transition to a market economy had created in the TAR. These problems were said to be largely connected with the fact that the market economy had brought the freeing of prices in the TAR, and yet the Tibetan economy was not strong enough to increase government expenditure in areas such as health and education in order to offset rising costs. Schools and universities therefore found themselves in the position of either having to cut courses or find other ways of making up significant budget shortfalls. In its report to the TAR Party Committee, the TAR government investigation committee made the following analysis of the situation:

> During the transition from a planned economy to a market economy, it is inevitable that prices will rise. The finance department cannot keep prices artificially low as they did in the past. At the same time, as our region's economy is not strong enough to appropriate funds for departments and enterprises, they have to charge fees to make up the difference.
>
> At present, the economic system has been reformed in our region, but the regulatory system is incomplete so that there is no standardisation for the charging of fees. Some organisations have had great difficulty in meeting the funding levels set by higher levels of government, and have consequently turned to the community to make money by charging all sorts of fees...
>
> Due to the development of the commodity economy, some units have become enthusiastic entrepreneurs. But these units do not have a wide range of opportunities for making money, so they depend on charging different sorts of fees to one community. In this way they give their whole attention to economic results without considering moral issues.[44]

Indeed, the ruinous effect of economic reforms on education, particularly in 'minority' nationalities regions, had been highlighted by educationalists such as Teng Xing as early as 1989. In his paper for *Qiu Shi*, he argues like Dalu Yin that the underfunding of education (particularly in these areas) is not only short-sighted but results in a wastage of resources, since the education system is unable to produce either the quality or quantity of personnel needed to be effective. In the TAR, similar criticisms of what is perceived as the short-sightedness of the current policies are made by several Tibetan intellectuals and officials.[45] The only solution, as Teng Xing sees it, is a recentralization of control and a return to greater state funding:

> The State should designate a definite amount of funds to develop the educational enterprises in the minority nationality areas to train a large number of talented people of different types, standards and grades for use by the state in developing the great south-west and the great north-west by the end of this century and the beginning of the next century. This is a long-term policy with a strategic goal, because from now until the end of this century there are eleven years. Children of school-age now will be the main production force at that time. If by this time we still do not understand the important nature of this problem and adopt the necessary effective measures, then we will have been guilty of having committed an irremediable error in history, in the development of the macro-economic strategy.
>
> At present, the main source of funding in minority nationality regions is the revenues of the autonomous regions, provinces, cities and counties. The pattern of investment is that the local communities provide the big share and the state provides the small share. Despite the fact that each year, the state has accorded special treatment to education in the nationality regions, in the majority of these regions total educational expenditure has been unable to meet the cost of teachers' salaries. Furthermore, yearly gross expenditure has been insufficient for the rebuilding of schools in a critical and dangerous condition, or to provide school equipment.
>
> Hence, in order to realise the state's goal of socio-economic development in minority nationality regions by the end of the century, the state should make an effective input into education in these regions, on the precondition that local governments do not cut their educational budgets. The so-called effective input refers to the minimum level of investment in order to achieve certain fixed educational targets of training qualified personnel of sufficient quality and quantity. If investment is lower than this, the quality achieved will be low and therefore there will be a large amount of 'educational wastage'.[46]

With the change in the political climate in the 1990s, and the ascendancy of hardline conservatives in the Chinese government, the path of education development moved towards recentralization. At the same time, the government began to give greater publicity to the importance of state funding, particularly in compulsory education in state primary schools. The 1995 Education Law stipulated that 'the state should establish a system of appropriating budgetary funds as the main part of outlays for education, and gathering supplementary funds from various channels'. The Ninth Five-Year plan describes 'a new framework with respect to education finance in which fiscal allocations by the government constitute the main source to be supplemented by funds raised through multiple channels ... It is envisaged that by the year 2010 a framework for educational provision will basically take shape in which most schools are run by the state, supplemented by NGO-sponsored/ private schools, facilitating the pooling of resources from various quarters of society.'[47] However, there is no mention in either of these documents that education expenditure should represent 4 per cent of GDP, as the 1993 'Programme for China's Educational Reform and Development' had recommended.

In the TAR, at the Fifth TAR Conference on Education in 1994, new guidelines were set out which incorporated the Chinese government's directives on increased state funding and recentralization of control. From 1995, operating expenses for education were to amount to 17 per cent of the annual TAR government expenditure, and capital construction for education was to take a further 17 per cent of the TAR government expenditure. By the year 2000, expenditure would be increased to 20 per cent. Prefectural governments were directed to increase education expenditure 'to the extent that their financial resources allow',[48] although other sources state that local government expenditure should be 15 per cent of their annual revenue.[49] In 1994, Chamdo and Ngari prefectures did indeed spend 15 per cent of their annual revenue on education and these prefectures were held up as an example for others to follow.[50]

At the same conference, the chairman of the TAR government, Gyaltsen Norbu, announced a new recentralized structure of education administration. Henceforth, the TAR government would be responsible for organizing the assessment, planning, monitoring and implementation of primary education in the TAR, including curriculum development, selection of text materials and 'revision of textbooks compiled by Tibetan scholars'. Prefectural governments would provide an outline for the implementation of compulsory education and vocational education in their respective areas. County governments would be responsible for organizing the implementation of compulsory education and the development of vocational education. This would include regulating the use of funds, being responsible for school heads and teachers, including their transfer. Responsibilities of *xiang* (township) governments would include ensuring school attendance and enrolment at the required age.[51]

These new policies were aimed at tightening control of education fund-raising and of the expenditure of funds. It appears that the fund-raising powers of the township-level governments have been curtailed and thus, in this respect also, the policies mark a retreat from the funding reforms of the 1980s. The number of regulations with regard to collection of fees from students and raising funds from local people also increased. In 1994, the state set categories under which schools could collect fees; schools were forbidden to set their own categories, to charge for unnecessary commodities or books, or to fine students.[52]

In 1994, Gyaltsen Norbu told delegates at the Fifth TAR Conference on Education: 'the goal of reforming the system of running schools is to establish a system under which governments play a dominant role in running schools with active participation by various circles in society.'[53]

Educational trusts As part of the new direction of education reform, the central government and the TAR government turned to encouraging the development of 'educational trusts and investment companies' to supplement state funding of education.[54]

In the TAR, ordinary people and enterprises were encouraged to organize fund-raising events in order to collect money for educational purposes. In June 1994, in a report for *Xinhua*, Gyaltsen Norbu, chairman of the TAR government, wrote that since 'governments at different levels have only small budgets', people should be encouraged to contribute to educational trusts. In the article, he gave suggestions for fund-raising which included 'auctions, benefit performances and charity bazaars'. These, he said, had been effective in other parts of China.[55]

In 1992 the 'Hope Project' was established in the TAR to help return drop-outs to school, as described above. By 1994, 300,000 people (almost 15 per cent of the population of the TAR) were said to have contributed to the Tibetan branch of the 'Hope Project'.

In October 1994 the Tibet Education Foundation was established. It is affiliated to the China Youth League and is intended to fund Tibetan students in secondary and higher education in other parts of China. Organizations, institutions and individuals are encouraged to contribute to the fund. In 1994 it had 5.3 million yuan, part of which had been donated by the Bank of China and the Lhasa Customs.[56]

Namling County Primary Schools Project was established in 1991 by Tashi Tsering, a former English lecturer from Tibet University. By 1996 it had built thirty primary schools in Namling county, Shigatse Prefecture, at a total cost of 770,000 yuan ($96,000). Two thousand two hundred children had enrolled in the schools with on average ninety students in each, resulting in a rise in the area's enrolment rate from 37 per cent in 1990 to 68 per cent in 1996.[57] In 1993, the Namling County Schools Project received funding from the USA-based Boulder–Lhasa Sister City Project. However, most of the funding has come from Tashi Tsering himself. The rest of the funding has come from three sources: donors, Namling county government, which also provided materials and transport, and villagers who provided voluntary labour.[58] The schools are maintained and operated by the Namling County Education Department which also pays the salaries of the teachers. In 1994, students in the Namling County Project schools achieved the best results in the whole county.[59]

The Tibet Development Fund (TDF) is the most important, and indeed the first, so-called NGO that was established in the TAR. It was set up in 1987 at the initiative of the late Panchen Lama and Ngapo Ngawang Jigme, vice-chairman of the national CPPCC. TDF has an office in Beijing and an office in Lhasa. It has become the main liaison organization with foreign NGOs. According to its own literature, it was set up 'in order to support projects for the social, cultural and economic development of the TAR and the Tibetan areas in the surrounding provinces of Sichuan, Qinghai, Gansu and Yunnan, and to ensure that they are effectively carried out with a minimum of bureaucratic red tape and a maximum of financial reliability'. In 1993 its education projects included two Tibetan medicine schools, one in Shigatse and one in Lhokha (*Shannan*). These are to be partly funded until 1999 by the Swiss Red Cross. TDF also undertakes the building and funding of community schools. Future plans include setting up a Tibetan medicine school in every prefecture, and further development of primary schools.

New procedures promulgated in 1997 set out the regulations for education trusts and the pooling of voluntary donations. According to the regulations, the collection of donations in rural areas should be carried out only on a voluntary basis and should be dependent on the financial means of the local people. Under the terms of the new regulations, towns and townships in poor 'minority' nationality areas are not allowed to raise funds from the public if the local government financial appropriation, together with the additional funds for the compulsory education programme, are sufficient for rural education development. Pooled funds should be used only to build or repair schools for compulsory education, they must not be used for non-compulsory education purposes, nor for teachers' wages, or other benefits for teachers or administrative staff. Pooled funds must be kept in a special account in the township-level government, which must seek the approval of county governments before collecting such funds. Accounts of pooled funds must be made public.

Foreign aid Plans to alleviate the education funding crisis in the 1990s in China and the TAR included encouraging agreements with foreign funders.[60] Foreign aid organizations providing educational funding in the TAR include Swiss Red Cross; Misereor, Germany; Save the Children Fund, UK; World Concern, USA; Médicins Sans Frontières, France; Caritas, Hong Kong; Unicef. Among the foreign funders of education in the TAR are several foundations established by Tibetans now living in the West, who have set up trusts to build schools in their home regions in the TAR and other provinces with Tibetan populations. These include: Rokpa, UK; Provinz Drayab, Germany; Tsewang Tsultrim, Switzerland; Namkhai, Italy.

UNICEF Since 1998, Unicef has supported twelve educational programmes in the TAR at a cost of $4.39 million. These include in-service community teacher training courses, literacy programmes and programmes to increase primary enrolment.[61] One such programme involved the establishment of fifteen tent schools in Namtso township (*Namco xiang*), Damshung (*Damxung*) county, Lhasa Municipality. Each school is provided with teaching equipment, a tent (10,000 yuan; $1,176) a horse (5,000 yuan; $588) a lamp, a stove, a blackboard and some cushions. Unicef provided a grant of $250,000 for the project which included videos and televisions. According to government statistics, enrolment in the *xiang* rose from 19 per cent before the programme to 79 per cent.[62]

SAVE THE CHILDREN FUND Save the Children Fund's education programme was established in the TAR in 1992. It focuses on community schools in the Lhasa Municipality. It works with the Lhasa Education Bureau in running teacher training courses in the counties in Lhasa, as well as, on a smaller scale, in Shigatse and Nagchu prefectures. It has funded the translating of teaching materials into Tibetan, and is currently involved in several pilot projects including adult literacy classes, primary school libraries, pre-school teacher training and income-generation projects.[63]

ROKPA Ropka was established in 1980 by Akong Rinpoche, Buddhist teacher and the head of Samyeling Tibetan Centre in Scotland. In 1996, Rokpa was funding education projects in the TAR as well as in Tibetan areas of Qinghai, Sichuan and Yunnan; these projects included eight medical colleges and ten primary and secondary schools. In 1996, Rokpa invested $72,852 on primary education projects and $159,061 on secondary education and other education projects. A further $68,191 was committed to several new education projects for 1997.

'PROVINZ DAGYAB' 'Provinz Dagyab' (Dragyab) was founded in 1993 by Dragyab Kyabgon Rinpoche, the former spiritual leader of Dragyab county, who now lives in Germany and works at Bonn University. In 1994 the organization made plans to fund the construction and operation of four schools in Dragyab in Chamdo Prefecture, in association with the TDF. The organization planned to invest 31,890 DM in 1995, and gradually increase investment to 61,050 DM by the year 2001.[64]

EUROPEAN UNION PANAM PROJECT In 1994, China made a proposal to the European Commission (EC) for funding for a rural development project in Panam county, 200 km south-west of Lhasa. The project did not include an education component. This was later added by the EC and accounted for 11.33 per cent of the 7.6 million ECUs ($9.2 million). Agreement on the project was held up in 1995 when the European Parliament passed a motion urging the EC to divert the funds to small local projects run by non-government organizations (NGOs). In the revised implementation proposal, the Chinese government objected to the involvement of any foreign NGOs. At the time of writing the project is suspended until the issue of NGO involvement is resolved.

Summary

The economic policies instituted after 1985 made village communities largely responsible for the funding of primary education, with some assistance from county-level governments for capital construction and teachers' salaries. Local communities were expected to raise funds through school-run enterprises, voluntary contributions and labour. This resulted in a sharp rural–urban disparity in educational provision with education funding increasingly dependent not simply on the wealth of the region but on the prosperity of the individual county and village. This disparity was further increased by the fact that most of the state-run schools, which receive substantially more government funding, are to be found in urban areas. Rural education in the TAR is severely underfunded, particularly in remote areas where unit costs are higher. Such underfunding is perceived to lead to wastage, since investment in education is not sufficient to produce either the quality or quantity of trained personnel needed for economic development.

Tuition is free for compulsory education but schools are allowed to charge what are termed 'miscellaneous' fees; these include fees for textbooks, electricity and extra tuition. As the market economy took hold, and schools in the TAR were unable to meet the rising costs of educational provision, many resorted to increasing the number and amount of fees charged to parents. Although a system of grants was introduced in 1985 and extended in 1994, the grants were unable to keep pace with the rising costs.

In 1991, almost 40 per cent of education expenditure in China came from non-government sources.[65] In the TAR, costs in terms of fees, voluntary labour and payment in kind were greater for rural families, and for families outside the state work-units (who are usually poorer), than for urban state workers. In 1980, the First Forum directed that peasants and nomads should not have to provide voluntary labour. However, this policy appears to have been reversed in the 1990s. The Fifth TAR Conference on Education in 1994 directed that schools in rural areas should be supported by voluntary labour and by the donation of materials by local people, including peasants and nomads.[66]

By the early 1990s, an element of corruption had emerged in schools' finances, which mirrored trends in China as a whole, and provoked demonstrations by school pupils in the TAR in 1993. They eventually led to an official investigation into the charging of 'exorbitant fees' by the TAR Party Committee. By the mid-1990s there were new efforts on the part of the central government and the TAR government to regulate education funding. This brought a recentralization of control and led to plans to increase state funding. Pronouncements made at the Fifth TAR Conference on Education in 1994 included the following targets: 17 per cent of TAR government expenditure to be invested in educational operating costs, and 17 per cent for educational construction costs. The public funding of education was still encouraged but was henceforth to be more effectively regulated by the establishment of educational trusts.

In the 1990s a number of foreign aid projects were established in the TAR. Of the $43.697 million given to the TAR in foreign aid since 1980, around 12 per cent has been given to educational projects, including $4.39 million from Unicef.[67] However, the foreign funding of education has not developed as fast as might have been expected. This is partly due to the fact that education has become a sensitive political issue in the TAR in recent years. The Chinese government is reluctant to allow foreigners to get too closely involved, while international organizations often require foreign educational advisers to administer funding and monitor projects.

Notes

1. Zhu Kaixuan, 'Report to the Fourth Session of the Eighth National People's Congress Standing Committee on Educational Work', *Xinhua*, 28 October 1993 [SWB 10/11/93].

2. See 'Programme for China's Educational Reform and Development', issued by the CCP Central Committee and the State Council, *Xinhua*, 25 February 1993 [SWB 5/3/93].

3. Cheng Kai-Ming, 'The Changing Legitimacy in a Decentralizing System: The State and Education Development in China', *International Journal of Educational Development*, Vol. 14, 1994, p. 266.

4. See 'Programme for China's Educational Reform and Development', 1993.

5. Education Law of the People's Republic of China, article 57, *Xinhua*, 21 March 1995 [SWB 29/3/95].

6. Education Law, 1995.

7. See Tsui Kai-yuen, 'Economic Reform and Attainment in Basic Education in China', *China Quarterly*, No. 149, March 1997, p. 105; and Cheng Kai-Ming, 'Changing Legitimacy in a Decentralizing System', p. 266.

8. *Xinhua*, 7 June 1996 [SWB 10/6/96].

9. Zhu Kaixuan, announcing the introduction of a 10 billion yuan programme to introduce compulsory education in poor regions. Reported in *China Daily*, 8 May 1996.

10. Cheng Kai-Ming, 'Changing Legitimacy in a Decentralizing System', p. 266.

11. In 1996 industrial production accounted for 18.1 per cent of total output of the TAR, the remainder being agricultural production; see Jiang Weizhu, '*Shi Lun "San Bao" Jiaoyu Zhengce De Li Yu Bi Ji Qi Zhengce Duice*' (Advantages and Disadvantages and Reform Measures of the 'Three Guarantees' Education Policy), *Xizang Yanjiu* (Tibet Studies), Vol. 58, No. 1, 1996.

12. Several county education bureaux in the TAR have reported recently that villagers refuse to provide labour unless they are paid. (Interview with educationalist, 2 February 1997.)

13. TAR CPPCC, 'Thirteenth Bulletin of the Second Plenary Session of the Sixth TAR CPPCC', Secretariat of the Conference, 17 May 1994.

14. Yang Chunjing, '*Qiandan Zang Yuwen Jiaoxue Zai Fazhan Minzu Jiaoyu Zhong de Zhongyao Xing*' (A Tentative Study on the Importance of Teaching in the Tibetan Language for Developing National Education), *Xizang Yanjiu* (Tibet Studies), Vol. 59, No. 2, 1996.

15. See Jiang Weizhu, '… the "Three Guarantees" Education Policy'.

16. Internal TAR government planning document, October 1996. This document outlines plans to expand multi-grade teaching by the end of the century, in order to deal with current education shortages. Part of the plan involves giving training in multi-grade teaching for primary school teachers.

17. Report by Sonam Dorje, Deputy Party Secretary of the TAR govern-

ment, *Xinhua*, 2 March 1994 [SWB 4/3/94]; see also Jiang Weizhu, '... the "Three Guarantees" Education Policy'.

18. *Xinhua*, 2 May 1990 [SWB 4/5/90].

19. Sonam Dorje, Deputy Party Secretary of the TAR Government, March 1994.

20. Jiang Weizhu, '... the "Three Guarantees" Education Policy'.

21. According to one prefectural education official interviewed in December 1997, the *renmin zhuxuejin* was abolished in March 1997 following a meeting of the TAR Education Commission and the TAR People's Congress. It is not yet clear whether funding will be made available to primary schools in a different form as discussed by Jiang Weizhu above. The official believed that, if it was not, up to 30 per cent of children in the TAR would drop out of primary school because of this change.

22. Jiang Weizhu, '... the "Three Guarantees" Education Policy'.

23. Xiang Xiaoli and Zhang Qing, 'Courage of Conviction Consists in Tackling the Reality of the Situation Today with a Clear Vision for the Future', *Chamdo Daily*, 15 July 1993.

24. State Education Commission and Shanghai Institute of Human Resources Development, 'Annual Development Report of China's Educational Finance, 1992', cited in Cheng Kai-Ming, 'Changing Legitimacy in a Decentralizing System', pp. 265–9.

25. Hu Yaobang, 'Report to TAR Regional Party Committee Cadres', Lhasa Radio, 1430 gmt, 30 May 1980 [SWB 4/6/80].

26. Gyaltsen Norbu, 'Education in Tibet', Speech to Fifth Regional Meeting on Education in the TAR on 26 October 1994, *Xizang Ribao* (Tibet Daily), 30 October 1994, pp. 1–4.

27. State Education Commission of the PRC, Report on the 'Circular on Firmly Correcting the Practice of Random Collection of Fees at Secondary and Primary Schools', *Xinhua*, 27 August 1993 [SWB 20/9/93].

28. See Chen Kuiyuan, 'Actively Guide Religion to Accommodate Itself to Socialist Society', *Xizang Ribao* (Tibet Daily) (in Chinese), 4 November 1996 [SWB 16/11/96].

29. Lhasa Radio, 'Looking Back at 1994 and Looking Forward to 1995: Raising High the Banner of Development', 1100 gmt, 19 January 1995 [FBIS 27/1/95].

30. *Xinhua*, 10 June 1996 [SWB 13/6/96].

31. *Xinhua*, 9 December 1996 [SWB 10/12/96].

32. Lisa Keary, Interview with Tibetan child, 29 December 1994, undertaken during research for a doctoral thesis.

33. Internal Party discussion paper, 1995.

34. *Xinhua* (in English), 1 May 1989 [SWB 5/5/89].

35. Interview, 17 January 1993; Interview, 5 March 1993.

36. Interview, 18 August 1993.

37. 'Report to the TAR Party Committee and Government of "Investigation into Unhealthy Tendencies in Pricing, Industries and Exorbitant Fees"', 4 July 1993.

38. 'Circular on Firmly Correcting the Practice of Random Collection of Fees at Secondary and Primary School', *Xinhua*, 27 August 1993 [SWB 20/9/93]; 'Circular on Managing Funds Raised for Building New Schools, and Regulating Fees Collected in Primary and Secondary Schools', *Xinhua*, 20 December 1994 [SWB 5/1/95]; Opinions on Carrying out Work Across the Nation in 1996 to Remedy the Practice of Collecting Unwarranted Fees in Primary and Middle Schools', *Xinhua*, 7 June 1996 [SWB 10/6/96]; 1997: 'Procedures for the Management of Educational Fund Pooling in Rural Areas', *Xinhua*, 11 March 1994.

39. See 'Circular on Managing Funds'; 'Opinions on Carrying out Work Across the Nation'.

40. Dalu Yin, 'Reforming Chinese Education: Context, Structure and Attitudes in the 1980s', *Compare*, Vol. 23, No. 2, 1993, p. 124.

41. Zhu Kaixuan, 'Report to Fourth Session of Eighth National People's Congress Standing Committee on Educational Work'.

42. 'Programme for China's Educational Reform and Development', 1993.

43. Gyaltsen Norbu, *Xinhua*, 5 June 1994 [SWB 8/6/96].

44. 'Report to the TAR Party Committee and Government of "Investigation into Unhealthy Tendencies in Pricing, Industries and Exorbitant Fees"', 4 July 1993.

45. Yang Chunjing, 'A Tentative Study'; Internal Party discussion paper, 1995.

46. Teng Xing, '*Wo Guo Shaoshu Minzu Diqu Jiaoyu Zhengti Gaige Guanjian*' (The Essence of Overall Educational Reform in China's Minority Regions), *Qiu Shi*, No. 7, April 1989, pp. 19–24.

47. State Education Commission of the PRC, 'Ninth Five-Year Plan for Educational Development toward the Year 2010' [sic], Beijing, 1996 (China Ninth Five-Year Plan for Education 1996).

48. Gyaltsen Norbu, 'Education in Tibet'.

49. He Guanghua, 'Briefing from the TAR Education Commission', *Renmin Ribao* (People's Daily), 1 November 1994 [SWB 21/11/94].

50. Gyaltsen Norbu, 'Education in Tibet'.

51. Ibid.

52. State Education Commission, 'Circular on Managing Funds'.

53. Gyaltsen Norbu, 'Education in Tibet'.

54. Zhu Kaixuan, 'Television Debate to Discuss Educational Projects in 1994', *Xinhua*, 11 January 1994 [SWB 14/1/94].

55. *Xinhua*, 5 June 1994 [SWB 8/6/96].

56. *Xinhua*, 28 October 1994 [FBIS 31/10.94].

57. 'Man Devoted to Improving Education', *Xinhua*, 8 January 1997.

58. Namling County Schools Project Prospectus, 1993.

59. Melvyn Goldstein, William Siebenschuh and Tashi Tsering, *The Struggle for Modern Tibet, The Autobiography of Tashi Tsering* (M. E. Sharpe, New York, 1997), p. 192.

60. See 'Programme for China's Educational Reform and Development', *Xinhua*, 25 February 1993 [SWB 5/3/93]; and China Ninth Five-Year Plan for Education, 1996.

61. *Xinhua*, 10 October 1996 [SWB 12/10/96].

62. Internal government education planning document, November 1995.

63. Save the Children Fund: China Programme Prospectus, 1996.

64. 'Provinz Dagyab', Annual Report for 1994.

65. State Education Commission and Shanghai Institute of Human Resources Development, Annual Development Report of China's Educational Finance, 1992; cited in Cheng Kai-Ming, 'Changing Legitimacy in a Decentralizing System', pp. 265–9.

66. Gyaltsen Norbu, 'Education in Tibet'.

67. *Xinhua*, 10 October 1996 [SWB 12/10/96].

CHAPTER 7

General Secondary Education

Elite versus mass education

This chapter deals with secondary education in the TAR since 1978, focusing on the impact on development of the prevailing 'quality'-oriented strategies. In 1978, key schools and the practice of streaming within schools were formally reinstated by the State Council with the aim of bringing education in China up to 'advanced world standards'.[1] Consideration is given to the effect of the return to these strategies on secondary education in China as a whole, and at the form their implementation has taken in the TAR, with particular reference to the extension and adaptation of the key schools policy into the programme of sending selected Tibetan secondary students to schools in Central China. This chapter also examines the way streaming in schools in the TAR operates, and assesses the extent to which the system is weighted against Tibetan students, given the fact that secondary education is in Chinese medium.

Enrolment in secondary education

The process of the 'consolidation' of schools throughout China was aimed at increasing efficiency, as was noted in relation to primary education in Chapter 5. Although 'consolidation' affected secondary schools in the TAR it appears not to have had such a dramatic effect on enrolment as in primary education (see Figures 7.1 and 7.2). The number of secondary schools increased in the TAR between 1978 and 1980, with fourteen new general secondary schools being opened. However, between 1981 and 1983, when the communes were being disbanded, twenty-four general secondary schools closed. Between 1979 and 1982, enrolment in general secondary education fell from 19,788 students to 16,767 students. After 1982, however, secondary enrolment rose steadily with a minor dip around the recession of 1989–90. Over the sixteen-year period between 1978 and 1994, secondary enrolment

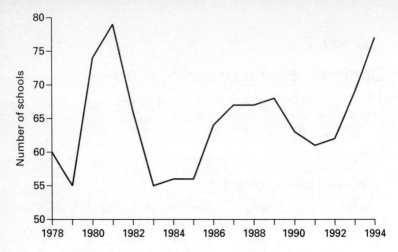

Figure 7.1 General secondary schools in the TAR, 1978–94 (*Source*: 1995 TAR Statistical Yearbook)

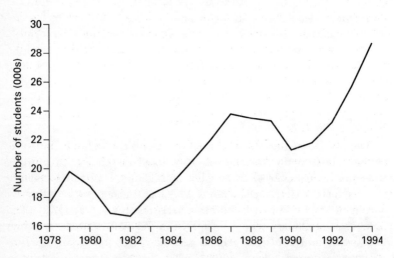

Figure 7.2 Enrolment in general secondary education in the TAR, 1978–94 (*Sources*: 1995 TAR Statistical Yearbook; 1989 TAR Statistical Yearbook)

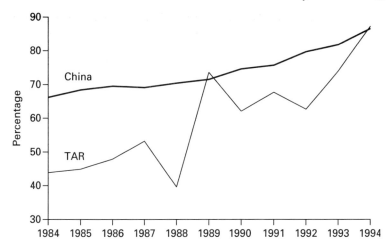

Figure 7.3 Promotion rate from primary school to junior secondary
in China and the TAR, 1984–94 (*Sources*: Figures calculated from 1995
China Statistical Yearbook and 1995 TAR Statistical Yearbook)

has increased significantly, according to the official statistics. In 1994,
the TAR had in total seventy-seven secondary schools with 28,725
students. This represents an increase of 62 per cent in sixteen years. In
addition, by 1994, a further 5,190 were enrolled in vocational secondary
education, and 13,000 students from the TAR were enrolled in secondary education in Central China.[2] Targets for the year 2000 include
providing each of the TAR's seventy-six counties with one secondary
school,[3] although some of these secondary schools will be primary
schools which have been extended to include one year of junior
secondary education.[4]

The TAR Statistical Yearbooks do not provide enrolment rates at
secondary level. What they provide instead are promotion rates from
primary to junior secondary school and from junior secondary to senior
secondary school. Figure 7.3 gives a comparison of promotion rates in
China and the TAR between 1984 and 1994. Promotion rates have
improved considerably in the TAR over this ten-year period. In 1994,
the promotion rate in the TAR was 87.3 per cent compared with 86.6
per cent for China as a whole. However, promotion rates are misleading
as an indicator of the enrolment rate of children in secondary
education. They simply indicate the percentage of students in the final
year (grade 6) of primary school who graduate and go on to junior
secondary school. Since most students in the TAR receive only three
years of education, the total number of students in grade 6 is extremely

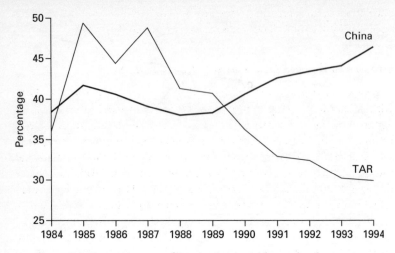

Figure 7.4 Promotion rate from junior secondary school to senior secondary in China and the TAR, 1984–94 (*Sources*: Figures calculated from 1995 China Statistical Yearbook; 1995 TAR Statistical Yearbook)

small. This was shown by the statistics in Chapter 5 (Table 5.2) above.

Despite the achievements in enrolment growth, the enrolment rate of secondary school-aged children in the TAR remains low. A government report published in *Xizang Ribao* (Tibet Daily) in 1995 put the enrolment rate of junior secondary school-aged children at 12.3 per cent. Targets to increase the enrolment rate by the end of the century are similarly modest. The same report indicates that by the year 2000 the enrolment rate of junior secondary school-aged children will be 14.1 per cent.[5]

Official statistical publications do not provide the enrolment rate of senior secondary school-aged students, nor drop-out rates from secondary school. Again, promotion rates from junior to senior secondary school are the only indicators of progress provided in the TAR statistical yearbooks (see Figure 7.4). It is therefore difficult to get a clear indication of the percentage of children of senior secondary school age in school. Figure 7.4 none the less provides some interesting insights. It indicates that while promotion rates in the TAR compared favourably with China as a whole during the 1980s, there has been a significant decline in the 1990s. In 1994, 29.9 per cent of students who graduated from the final year of junior secondary school enrolled in senior secondary education. The comparable figure in 1985 was just under 50 per cent. This may indicate an absolute decline in senior secondary enrolment or an increasing diversion of senior secondary students into vocational education. The statistics do not make this clear.

Urban–rural distribution of secondary schools

Secondary schools are unevenly distributed throughout the TAR, with urban areas being better provided for than rural areas. In 1995, eighteen of the TAR's seventy-seven general secondary schools were to be found in the Lhasa Municipality, as well as six of the region's eighteen senior secondary departments.[6] Enrolment figures show a similar bias towards urban areas, particularly at senior secondary level. Targets for the year 2000 in Lhasa Municipality include a 35 per cent enrolment rate for the secondary school-aged population, which would include 9,500 students in junior secondary school, and 2,550 in senior secondary school. This target enrolment rate is almost twice the 14.1 per cent target for the TAR as a whole.

The educational reforms of the 1980s have led to the increasingly uneven distribution of resources between schools and between different streams within schools. The student elite in key schools, and in the 'fast' stream of secondary schools throughout China, benefit from higher funding, better facilities and higher quality teaching than is provided for the majority of students in ordinary schools and in the 'slow' stream. The student elite may include the brightest students but, in a society that operates largely by a system of connections (*guanxi*), it increasingly includes students whose parents have contacts with those in authority.

Key schools

The key school policy was re-established in China after the Cultural Revolution in line with the economic strategy of capitalizing on existing assets. The rationale behind investing in key schools was that they would, among other things, improve the quality of secondary education and therefore provide the necessary qualified personnel for economic development; and set up examples for ordinary schools to follow.[7]

Typically, key schools receive up to twice the funding of non-key schools.[8] They are allocated the best available teachers and significantly better facilities. At the national level in China, there are twenty key schools under the direct supervision of the State Education Commission. At the provincial, prefectural and county levels, local governments are authorized to run key schools under their own jurisdictions. One to six key schools are recommended for each county or city district. On

Box 7.1 Palden Gyal: a secondary school career in Tongren 'Minority' Nationality Secondary School, Huangnan Tibetan Autonomous Prefecture, Qinghai

In July 1980 I sat the secondary school entrance exam with my primary school class mates at Tongren Minority Nationality Secondary School in Rongwo. This was a Tibetan medium secondary school. The exam was in Tibetan and we had to pass three subjects: maths, Tibetan and Chinese. Tongren Minority Nationality Secondary School was a key school so it was quite difficult to get into, but my primary school was the best in the county. Out of fifteen pupils who took the exam from my class twelve passed, including all six of the girls.

The school covered a large area. All the teachers and all the students lived in the school. We slept 25 to a dormitory in long rows of bunk beds. In 1983 a very good new three-storey building was constructed for the school. When I first went to the school it was only a junior secondary school; in 1983 it was extended to include a senior secondary school as well. There were about 40 students per class and 4 classes in each year. Every year a few students were expelled for poor study or for smoking or drinking; discipline was very strong in the school. There were about 100 teaching and non-teaching staff at the school. Almost all the teachers were Tibetan – there were only about 15 Chinese teachers but most of the non-teaching staff were Chinese.

We did not have to pay fees, but we had to buy our bedding, and textbooks, and we had to give the school 30 pounds of grain each month for our food. There was a small market garden in the school in which potatoes were grown. The older students had to look after the land, digging the soil in Spring and planting, often during lesson times.

In the first year we studied maths and Tibetan. Our maths textbooks were in Chinese until 1983 when they were translated into Tibetan. But I've always been no good at maths because I didn't understand anything in those first two years when we studied in Chinese and I was never able to catch up. We studied Chinese for the whole 3 years junior secondary school. We also studied Chinese history, geography, politics, physics, chemistry and sports.

By 1983, apart from classes on the Chinese language, we were taught everything in Tibetan. Even the Chinese teachers spoke Tibetan.

After three years at Tongren National Minorities Secondary school (it was still only a junior secondary school), we took the exam to Huangnan National Minorities Teacher Training School which was a senior secondary level teacher training school. Each county secondary

> *school in the prefecture could send the students to Tongren to take the exam for Huangnan National Minorities Teacher Training School. Those who didn't get in were sent back to their villages and that was the end of their education. Only 10 students in 150 passed. I didn't pass the exam. But the year that I took it, the education department decided to extend Tongren Minority Nationality Secondary School. And so the best 50 students of those who had failed to get into the teaching school were given two years of senior secondary education and then we took the university entrance exam. We still paid only for books and clothes. We had to work in the school garden in spring and autumn; once we had to dig a deep trench to lay a pipe-line from the school down to the river to improve the water supply.*
>
> Source: *Interview with Palden Gyal, 20 October 1996.*

average, each medium or large city has between one and six key schools. In 1981, 24.1 per cent of schools in the TAR were officially designated key secondary schools, which was far higher than the national average of 4 per cent, although in fact this reflects the scarcity of secondary schools in the TAR rather than a preponderance of key schools.[9] Boxes 7.1 and 7.2 give examples of the situation in two secondary schools. One is a key Tibetan medium secondary school in Qinghai province in the early 1980s; the other is an ordinary secondary school in a poor Tibetan area of Gansu province in the 1990s.

At the start of the Four Modernizations period, key schools could be designated at any level of education: primary, junior secondary, or senior secondary. However, it became clear that the drive to get pupils into key schools was having a negative effect on the education they were receiving. Teaching was becoming restricted to coaching for examinations, and students were being put under considerable pressure. During the 1980s, resistance to the designation of key schools increased, particularly at lower levels. In 1985, *Beijing Review* quoted a primary school headmaster who called for the abolition of all key schools, which the newspaper said had 'the academic advantages of the best teachers and facilities'. The headmaster also called for the abolition of the secondary school entrance exam. In the same article, the Minister for Education, He Dongchang, is quoted as saying: 'We should let our children be more playful, or we'll see no creative talent. Children are now too serious, rather than too frivolous as some people have complained. Most of our teachers are responsible people but some have

Box 7.2 A rural county secondary school, Gannan Tibetan
Prefecture, Gansu province, 1995

*X county secondary school was established in 1982. The school serves 8
counties some of which are 150 kms away. Transport in the area is poor.
The nearest tarmac road is 55 kms away. In 1995 there were 150
students in the school. 95 per cent of the students come from nomad
families with an average annual income in 1995 of 3,000 yuan. Most of
the students board at the school during the term. There is accommodation for up to 150 students in the school. Students sleep 8 to a dormitory
which is 12 sq. m; other students stay with relatives in the town.*

*The school receives money from the local county education bureau
for teachers' salaries, but is largely dependent on donations for other
expenses. In 1983 it received 10,000 yuan from a high Tibetan lama;
and in 1990 the headmaster donated 10,000 yuan. It largely runs on
donations from the local community.*

*The school has four classrooms, all of which are in a bad state of
repair. Several have broken windows. They have desks and chairs, some
of which are broken. Students sit four to a desk. In 1995 a new building
which would house 6 classrooms and teachers' rooms was under construction. It was being funded by donations collected over the years
from the local community. However, the money had run out before the
inside of the building was complete.*

*There are six grades in the school with about 30 students per class.
However, due to the lack of classroom space, multigrade teaching takes
places with students taught together in groups of 60. According to the
teachers, this affects the students' progress. 20 students failed the end-
of-year exams in 1995.*

*The school has 35 teachers, most of whom teach part-time. Because
the town is so remote, the school has difficulty finding full-time teachers.
Many of them are simply taken from the local community and devote
two to three hours a week to teaching at the school. 15 of the teachers
have received higher education.*

*The monthly salary is on average 300 yuan for full-time teachers.
The highest salary is 600 yuan and the lowest is 200 yuan.*

*The school spends 100 yuan per student per year on textbooks. The
students have to buy other materials such as pens and notebooks themselves.*

*The academic year is divided into two semesters, with 2 holidays
per year, one in the summer and one in February at Tibetan New Year.
Each lasts for 40 days. Eleven subjects are taught in the school, in-*

cluding Tibetan, mathematics, geography, history, astrology, Chinese, science, music and sport. But the school has no facilities for science, music or sport, and it also has no library.

The headmaster is now seeking outside funding from non-government and foreign education funds to repair the classrooms and complete the new classrooms, as well as to build facilities for science, music and sport.

Source: *Interview, 1995.*

restrained the children too much. As a result, the pupils lack creativity, and the teachers are worn out.'[10]

At that time, the Beijing Education Bureau announced that key schools would gradually be phased out.[11] However, although by the 1990s key schools were no longer officially designated at primary level, in many places, including the TAR, the best primary schools – all former key schools – continued to get the best teachers and facilities and were, consequently, still very competitive. Key schools remained at secondary level. In 1996, the problems of divisiveness and of encouraging an exam-oriented education system, caused by their existence, were recognized in the State Education Commission's Ninth Five-Year Plan and Long-Range Development Programme to the Year 2010 (China Ninth Five-Year Plan for Education). Nevertheless, according to the plan, the key school system is set to continue into the next century, although provincial governments are now being urged to bring non-key schools up to the standard of key schools: 'Effective measures should be taken to rectify such long-standing problems as lopsided pursuit after high transition rates and the excessive workload of pupils and students. Steps should be taken to strengthen the weak secondary schools so as to gradually narrow the gaps between key schools and non-key schools.'[12]

Given the financial restrictions which still exist in education, this continuing endorsement of key-school education will make it extremely difficult to redistribute resources in order to upgrade non-key schools.

The streaming system in secondary schools

An examination-oriented education system, including the channelling of students into a fast stream or slow stream, is traditional in China, and can be traced back to 400CE. In the post-1949 period, streaming was deemed necessary in the 1950s and in the early 1960s, but it was abolished when the egalitarian policies of the Cultural Revolution took hold.

Streaming in schools is an important part of the 'quality' strategy, designed to invest most resources in those students who are likely to produce the best results. It reappeared as a result of the reintroduction of the university entrance examination in 1977. Although urban children have greater access to education than rural children, considerable inequality exists as a result of the streaming system. Compared with rural schools, urban schools have a more systematic streaming system. Students are divided into two groups that are treated differently in terms of educational opportunities, teachers and resources.[13] According to the Chinese educationalist Dalu Yin, 'the programmes of the 1980s are more elitist and more "talent" oriented than any that existed before'.[14] In an attempt to redress the balance of the Cultural Revolution, the pendulum swung far out in the other direction. Given the limited budget, not only rural schools but most urban schools have had to make sacrifices for the training of China's intellectual elite in the key schools and the fast stream.[15]

The two-tier system, with its emphasis on teaching for examinations, has created problems for the education system as a whole. Although there have been repeated calls in government documents and from Chinese leaders for a more rounded education with less emphasis on examinations, educational administrators at lower levels have not changed their priorities.[16] The 1993 'Programme for China's Educational Reform and Development' directed primary and secondary schools to move away from a system that taught solely for examinations.[17] In 1996, during an inspection tour of education in Qinghai, Li Lanqing (Vice Premier of the State Council) reiterated that 'primary education should be reformed to put less emphasis on passing examinations and more on the quality of education'.[18]

It is now believed that the two-tier system and what is known as the 'diploma disease' have reinforced traditional modes of rote learning rather than encouraging creative independent thinking. Furthermore, the ranking of schools by examination pass rates has encouraged teachers to make students who are unlikely to perform well repeat grades, or even drop out of school altogether. It is also believed to have restricted curriculum development.[19] The educationalist J. Unger writes:

> The results of such a misorientation of education can be crippling. The great majority of pupils can never 'make the grade' and find themselves deemed 'failures' of a system skewed toward the narrow upper reaches of

the educational ladder. They are the products of schools ... that had in-fluenced students to regard the most common occupations of their society with disdain and then consigned most of them to those very occupations.[20]

In the next section, we look at how the streaming system operates in the TAR. Here, because Tibetan students in secondary school have six hours of Tibetan tuition per week while Chinese students have six hours of English tuition, streaming operates along racial lines. Furthermore, because secondary education is in the Chinese medium, Tibetans tend to perform less well. The Chinese classes are thus treated as the fast stream, the Tibetan classes as the slow stream, and they are resourced accordingly, irrespective of the ability of the individual students.

The streaming system in Tibetan secondary schools After the Second Forum in 1984, the TAR government began reforming the education structure with the stated aim of eventually implementing a system of Tibetan medium education for Tibetans in the TAR. The summary report of the Forum stipulated that 'teaching and learning should give priority to the Tibetan language, that primary schools should be wholly in Tibetan language; secondary schools can include the Chinese language'.[21] The 'Provisions on the Study, Use and Development of Spoken and Written Tibetan (for trial implementation)', which were promulgated in 1987, included the gradual introduction of Tibetan medium education in secondary schools.[22] From 1984 onwards, primary schools were divided according to nationality. In principle, Tibetans were to study in Tibetan medium primary schools and Chinese children were to study in Chinese medium primary schools, although as the reform process slowed up and it became clear that a Tibetan medium primary education created obstacles for further educational advance-ment, Tibetans with sufficient contacts to by-pass the system enrolled their children in Chinese medium schools. The introduction of Tibetan medium primary schools was to be the first stage of the reforms: Tibetans were to be taught entirely in Tibetan at primary school and were to be given Chinese classes from the third or fourth grade. How-ever, the plans to extend Tibetan medium education into secondary schooling have never been implemented, and secondary education in the TAR continues to be taught in Chinese. Since 1984, therefore, Tibetan children, having received no Chinese teaching until the age of nine or ten, have had to compete for entrance to secondary school in a second language, against children using their mother-tongue.[23] The result of the piecemeal implementation of these Tibetan language reforms has been to give Han Chinese children in the TAR a considerable advantage over Tibetans in educational advancement. Although a concession is given to Tibetan children in the secondary school entrance examination because of the language difficulties, and those who pass the secondary school entrance examination have an additional preparatory year before the first grade to improve their Chinese, the percentage of Tibetan children entering secondary school is extremely low. This is largely as a result of poor mastery of Chinese.[24] According to directives on compulsory education laid out by the State Education Commission, primary school pupils must master 2,500 Chinese characters by the time they graduate from primary school. However, according to a survey carried out in the TAR in 1989, Tibetans in primary schools in Lhasa (which have the highest standards of Chinese teaching in the TAR) had mastered on average around 800 characters. Furthermore, this was only in a test of character recognition – in listening, reading and writing, comprehension was found to be lower still.[25]

As a result of the language difficulties for Tibetans learning in Chinese, Tibetans tend to perform less well than Chinese students in secondary school, as mentioned above. The Tibetan classes are therefore considered to be the lower stream classes.[26] A study published in the journal *Xizang Yanjiu* (Tibet Studies) in 1996 reports:

National minority students when they enter secondary school do not have anywhere near the required levels of Chinese to cope with classes in other subjects. In addition, after students have entered junior secondary school and are being taught various subjects in Chinese, because the spoken and written language is an obstacle, the students either do not understand, or do not completely understand the lesson content. Therefore, study becomes excessively difficult, the burden of studying increases and the students' interest and confidence in studying decreases, even to the extent that their desire to study is crushed. Students suffer real hardship while studying and teachers teach until they are exhausted. This results not only in reduced marks in school work and a reduction in teaching quality but it also affects students' physical and mental health and all round development.[27]

Thus the Tibetan classes, like lower-stream classes throughout China, become part of a system which, justified by the strategy of gaining maximum returns, assigns them poorer facilities and less qualified teachers. This means that Tibetan students who embark on a secondary school career have not only to contend with learning in a second language, but also with inferior teaching. In the graduation examinations and the university entrance examinations, Tibetan students (those who do not drop-out before then) are given a concession to make up for the disadvantages they face. Although this helps to some extent, the way the allowance is given reinforces prejudice and resentment. It is presented, even in official documents, as being designed to help Tibetan children because they are less intelligent.[28] Although Tibetan scholars continue to point out that Tibetan children are not backward but face problems with the language barrier, the perception that they are persists. Lei Yongsheng writes:

> We must work hard to eradicate students' mental and emotional negative self-image and their fears ... Teachers must deal fairly and correctly with each student, preventing and avoiding all kinds of prejudices towards students. They must oppose racial prejudice and particularly take the correct view on the differences between Chinese students and Tibetan students. While admitting objectively that these differences exist, on no account must these differences be artificially exaggerated. What must be understood is that Tibetan and Chinese students are all normal people who possess great and limitless potential.[29]

In short, the streaming system, which is already inequitable in the rest of China, becomes racially inequitable in the TAR, due to the piecemeal implementation of policies on 'minority' nationality education. The lower stream in Tibetan secondary schools is made up almost entirely of Tibetans who are there not necessarily because they are less intelligent but because they are less fluent in Chinese. Furthermore, it appears that the structural problem in the school system is feeding into Tibetan society and leading to growing prejudice and resentment. One parent interviewed in Lhasa in 1990 described the situation thus:

> In the end, in a natural way there is a comparison between the Tibetans and the Chinese pupils; a Chinese pupil will wonder why a Tibetan in the same year has less knowledge than he has, so he will easily conclude that the Tibetans are backward and stupid. The seed is also planted for the Tibetan children to consider themselves as stupid.[30]

The education of children from the TAR in Central China

One obvious example of the prioritizing of elite education over mass education is the programme of sending selected secondary students to be educated in central China. The designation of key schools is relative, and all schools in the TAR are considered to be of an inferior quality compared with the rest of China.[31] To address this problem, using the argument of the need for cost effectiveness and the need to produce skilled manpower quickly, the Education of Tibetan Children in China Programme was set up following the National Planning Conference in

November 1984. The programme was part of the broader policy, set out at the First Forum in 1980, of repatriating Han Chinese cadres in the TAR and training Tibetans to take their place. Among other things, it was said to be designed to increase the enrolment of Tibetans in higher education, since children studying in China would be better prepared than if they attended secondary schools in Tibet, and they would be more likely to succeed at university if they had had several years to adjust to life in Central China. In 1989, the State Education Commission (SEC) expanded the programme by opening classes for technical/vocational education. The first batch of graduates returned to the TAR in 1992.[32] By 1994, there were 13,000 Tibetan students in 104 schools in twenty-six provinces throughout China, and 75 per cent of Tibetans students graduating from these junior secondary schools in China went on to technical secondary schools.[33]

The majority of Tibetan students in Central China are in special Tibetan classes attached to local secondary schools. However, eighteen schools have been constructed known as 'Tibet Secondary Schools'.[34] Three of the schools have junior and senior secondary programmes – these are located in Beijing, Chengdu and Tianjin – the rest are junior secondary schools only. The Beijing Tibet Secondary School is described as a model school; it was built in 1989 to resemble the Potala Palace in Lhasa and by 1994 it had 700 students (100 in each year). Students are selected for this school by a special board set up by the TAR Education Commission. The selection procedure for other Tibet secondary schools appears to be less formal – in the Chengdu school, for example, it is undertaken solely by the headmistress.[35]

Tibetan students who go to senior secondary school remain in Central China for seven years and during that time they return home only once. The first year provides a foundation course with emphasis on Chinese language and mathematics. From the second year the students follow the standard national curriculum, with classes in Chinese, English, mathematics, physics, chemistry, history, geography, politics, music, art and sport. All these subjects are taught in Chinese. Tibetan is, in principle, taught to the students, although according to Tibetan students and educationalists these classes are not considered a priority and are often abandoned.[36] One Tibetan scholar writing in 1995 urged the Chinese government to give priority to the Tibetan language, saying that the failure to do so would lead to accusations of cultural assimilation: 'The twenty secondary schools in Beijing and other places must take the Tibetan language as the main course. The State Ministry of Education should pay attention to this work, so that we can crush the fabrication of [people] saying that "to set up Tibetan secondary schools in central China is to assimilate the next Tibetan generation".'[37]

In 1994, in line with the new political climate which no longer made positive discrimination in favour of Tibetans a priority, TAR Executive Deputy Secretary Ragdi announced to the Third Forum that the children of Han Chinese officials in the TAR would henceforth be able to enrol on the programme.[38] This is likely to result in a significant reduction in the number of Tibetans on the programme since, as mentioned above, students in the Han Chinese classes tend to perform better in examinations. Furthermore, with Chinese students on the programme, Tibetan language classes are likely to become even less of a priority.

Funding and enrolment Operating costs for the Tibetan schooling in Central China programme are paid by the central government, which spent 53 million yuan on the programme between 1984 and 1991.[39] Tuition funding comes from the twenty-six provincial governments that run the Tibetan classes; student stipends are provided by the TAR government, and the students receive free board and lodging. In 1991, operating costs, excluding student living costs, amounted to 2 million yuan; and tuition costs amounted to 300–500 yuan per student[40] and student stipends amounted to 706 yuan ($81.2) per student per year. In 1994, the TAR government allocated 17.35 million yuan to increase student grants to 1,050 yuan ($120.7) per year.[41]

By 1994, there were 13,000 Tibetans on the programme, which means that over 28 per cent of Tibetan students participating in secondary education were being educated outside the TAR (see Table 7.1). The proportion of students studying in technical secondary schools was even higher: 3,600 students were studying in Central China in 1991, which equalled the number of students in technical secondary schools in the TAR.[42]

The education of Tibetans in Central China is justified by the same cost effectiveness argument and the need to produced skilled manpower quickly that have been seen elsewhere in the education system. In 1996, the rationale for the programme was outlined once again in the TAR Ninth Five-Year Plan:

> Since China initiated reforms and opening up to the outside world, the State has made a series of plans for speeding up economic development, traffic, telecommunications, energy construction and major construction and other fields [in the TAR]. A great number of specialised personnel are needed to achieve the goal. As the TAR could not afford to train so many specialised personnel, the Central Government decided to call on more developed provinces and cities.[43]

Table 7.1 Enrolment of TAR secondary students in Central China compared with secondary enrolment in the TAR, and as a percentage of total enrolment

	1986	1990	1991	1993	1994
Secondary students in the TAR	25,011	22,478	26,187	30,641	33,915
TAR secondary students enrolled outside TAR	4,000	5,000	7,000	10,000	13,000
Percentage of TAR students enrolled outside TAR	14	18	21	25	28

Sources: 1986: *100 Questions about Tibet*, Jing Wei (ed.) (Beijing Review Press, 1989), pp. 42–3; 1990: *The Change in Education in Tibet*, pamphlet distributed at UN by PRC (New Star Publishers, Beijing, 1992); 1991: *Tibet from 1950–1991*, compiled by China's *Tibet and Beijing Review* (New Star Publishers, Beijing 1992); 1993: China's Report to UN Committee on the Rights of the Child; 1994: 'Tibet Special', *Beijing Review*, 7–13 August 1995.

At the same time the programme is described as a continuing priority for the future: there are plans to expand and develop it.[44]

Tibetan views of the programme It is clear from the Tibetan media that the programme was unpopular among Tibetans when it began in 1984. According to Liu Boqing, an official with TAR Education Commission who organized the classes: 'when the classes were first offered, Tibetans were not as enthusiastic about enrolling their children ... Parents worried that their children would be unaccustomed to living with strangers, such as the Han people, or that they would find themselves helpless in strange circumstances.'[45]

This view is confirmed by interviews with Tibetans; they go further in pointing out the negative effects on children brought up away from their families and outside their own culture. These include:

- loss of family environment at a sensitive age
- loss of mother-language and culture
- problems of cultural reintegration on return
- lack of relevant job opportunities on return
- high costs for parents despite student grants
- reduced funding for the development of education in the TAR[46]

Liu Boqing went on to say that the programme had in recent years become more popular. The reason he gave was that the attitude of parents towards education had changed: 'The change in Tibetans' attitude toward their children's education, from the preference for mon-asteries to inland classes, has been remarkable and positive.' The article cited others as saying that the change was the result of 'increasingly frequent exchanges between Tibetan people and the rest of the coun-try'.[47] Nevertheless, on 24 September 1992, Tibet TV broadcast an interview with Tibetan children studying in Central China that caused an uproar in Lhasa after the children complained about their living and studying conditions in Chinese schools.[48]

Data collected through interviews also suggest that the programme is now more popular among Tibetans. However, the change in attitude includes reasons other than those presented above. They include the perception that schools in urban areas in the TAR have deteriorated to such an extent, and that in rural areas educational provision remains so poor, that sending children to China is the only way of providing them with a reasonable education. Tibetans' concern about the drawbacks of the programme appear not to have decreased. However, the alternative – children receiving a substandard education, or no education, in the TAR – is of even greater concern. Other parents have taken the risk of serious sanctions by the authorities and clandestinely sent their children to India to be educated in schools in the Tibetan exile community.[49]

Since 1990, almost half the new intake of Tibetan secondary students each year has been sent to be educated in China. Given the higher costs in the TAR, there may be financial benefits in the programme in terms of the provision of secondary education for the students who get selected. However, in terms of the general provision of secondary education, the costs are none the less significant, particularly if we consider that the average county government in the TAR has 2 million yuan per year to spend on the education of its whole population (1995 figures).[50] Furthermore, the programme appears to have changed from being an interim measure to being a long-term strategy.

Summary

Enrolment in secondary education is low in the TAR. In 1995, 12.5 per cent of secondary school-aged children were in school; by the end of the century the enrolment rate is scheduled to rise by less than 2 per cent to 14.1 per cent.[51] The distribution of schools shows a marked urban/rural disparity, as in primary education, with almost 25 per cent of secondary schools and 30 per cent of senior secondary departments in the Lhasa Municipality. The education reforms of the 1980s included the reintroduction of key schools and streaming within schools through-out China, with the aim of improving the quality of education. Key schools receive twice the funding of ordinary schools and are able to recruit the best teachers as well as to provide better resources. Key schools at primary level were gradually phased out after 1985, although at secondary level they continued through the 1990s and were further endorsed in the State Education Commission's plans for education up to the year 2010. Towards the end of the 1980s, there was growing concern among educators that the key school policy, and the policy of channelling students into a fast or slow stream depending on their ability, were having a detrimental effect on the development of the education system as a whole. These particular policies were also held responsible for encouraging what became known as 'the diploma disease'. In the TAR, the streaming system operates along racial lines because Tibetans and Chinese students study different subjects in secondary school and, because Chinese is the medium of secondary education, Tibetan students tend to perform less well. The dislocation between the medium of instruction in secondary schools (Chinese) and the medium of the instruction for Tibetans in primary schools (Tibetan) has created considerable obstacles to the educational advancement of Tibetan children. Tibetan children, who receive no Chinese teaching until the fourth grade of primary school, not only have suddenly to study in a foreign language, they also have to compete for places in secondary school against Han Chinese children using their mother-tongue. In 1997, Chinese language was introduced from grade 1 for Tibetans in urban primary schools but not in rural schools.

In the TAR, the key school system has been extended into the programme of sending selected secondary students to schools in Central China. In 1994, 28 per cent of Tibetan secondary students were enrolled in schools outside the TAR. Educational standards are significantly higher in Central China and the selected students have a much greater chance of being able to enrol in higher education than those who remain in the TAR. The shortcomings of the programme include considerable investment in a relatively small percentage of the secondary school population, and loss of facility in their mother-tongue for the selected students. The programme was initiated in 1984 as part of a policy designed to repatriate Han Chinese personnel in the TAR and to train Tibetans to take their place. However, at the Third Forum in 1994, TAR Executive Deputy Party Secretary Ragdi announced a change in policy, which would allow Han Chinese students on the programme.[52]

Official statistics and basic facts 1994

Table 7.2 Secondary school terminology in Tibetan, Chinese and English

English	Tibetan	Chinese
General secondary	Dring-rim lobdra	Putong zhongxue
Junior secondary	Ma-dring lobdra	Chuji zhongxue
Senior secondary	Tho-rim lobdra	Gaoji zhongxue

Table 7.3 Number of secondary schools, students, teachers and students per teacher in the TAR, 1994

	Total	Urban	County town	Rural	Tibetans etc.
Secondary schools	77	14	61	2	
Senior secondary	18	7	11	0	
Secondary students	28,725	9,944	18,426	355	28,239
Senior secondary	4,521	2,504	2,017	0	
Teachers	2,691	857	1,813	21	
Students:teacher	10.7	11.6	10.2	16.9	

Sources: 1995 China Statistical Yearbook; see also China's Ethnic Statistical Yearbook, 1995.

Table 7.4 Enrolment rate of secondary school-age children in the TAR

Year	Enrolment rate (%)
1995	12.5
2000	14.1 (projected)

Source: TAR Child Development Programme, 1996.

Table 7.5 Length of secondary education

	Junior secondary		Senior secondary	
Stream	Tibetan	Chinese	Tibetan	Chinese
Length of education (years)	4	3	3	3

Table 7.6 General secondary curriculum

Tibetan stream	Chinese stream
Ideology/politics	Ideology/politics
Chinese	Chinese
Tibetan	English
Sport	Sport
Mathematics	Mathematics
History	History
Politics	Politics
Music	Music
Science	Science
Art	Art

Notes

1. *Xinhua*, Beijing, 1 March 1978.
2. 'Tibet Special', *Beijing Review*, 7–13 August 1995.
3. Gyaltsen Norbu, Work Report on the TAR Ninth Five-Year Plan, *Xizang Ribao* (Tibet Daily), 16 May 1996.
4. 'Outline of the TAR Child Development Programme for the 1990s', *Xizang Ribao* (Tibet Daily), 11 July 1996, p. 2.
5. Ibid.
6. Internal government planning document, October 1996.
7. Jin Lin, *Education in Post-Mao China* (Praeger, London, 1993).
8. Keith Lewin and Xu Hui, 'Rethinking Revolution: Reflections on China's 1985 Educational Reforms', *Comparative Education*, Vol. 25, No. 1, 1989.
9. Keith M. Lewin, Xu Hui, Angela Little and Zheng Jiwei, *Educational Innovation in China* (Longman, Harlow, 1994), p. 87.
10. *Beijing Review*, 6 May 1985.
11. Ibid.
12. State Education Committee of the PRC, 'Ninth Five-Year Plan for Educational Development Toward the Year 2010' [sic], Beijing, 1996, p. 44 (China Ninth Five-Year Plan for Education, 1996).
13. Jin Lin, *Education in Post-Mao China*, p. 49.
14. Dalu Yin, 'Reforming Chinese Education: Context, Structure and Attitudes in the 1980s', *Compare*, Vol. 23, No. 2, 1993, p. 126.
15. Ibid.
16. Ibid.
17. 'Programme for China's Educational Reform and Development', issued by the CCP Central Committee and the State Council, *Xinhua*, 25 February 1993 [SWB 5/3/93].
18. *Xinhua*, 20 October 1996 [SWB 22/10/96].

19. See among others: Lei Yongsheng, *'Xiandaihua Jiaoyu Fazhan Yu Xizang Jiaoyu Gaige'* (The Development of Modern Education and the Reform of Tibetan Education), *Xizang Yanjin* (Tibet Studies), Vol. 58, No. 1, 1996; Dalu Yin, 'Reforming Chinese Education'.

20. J. Unger, *Education Under Mao* (Columbia University Press, 1982).

21. 'Summary Report of Second Reform', cited in Duojie Caidan (Dorje Tseten), *Xizang Jiaoyu* (Education in Tibet) (China Tibetology Publishers, Beijing, 1991).

22. 'Provisions on the Study, Use and Development of Tibetan Language', 1987, cited in Luo Qun, *The Tibetan People's Right of Autonomy*, New Star Publishers, Beijing, 1991, p. 6.

23. In 1997, when plans to introduce Tibetan medium secondary education were abandoned, new plans were promulgated to start teaching Chinese to Tibetan children in urban primary schools from the first grade instead of the third grade; see Chen Kuiyuan, 'Speech on Literature and Art', *Xizang Ribao* (Tibet Daily), 11 July 1997; see also Han Zihong, Director of Primary Education at TAR Education Commission, quoted in *Agence France Presse*, 7 May 1997.

24. Gendian Ciren (Gendun Tsering) (ed.), *'Xizang Shuang Yu Jiaoyu de Shijian yu Tansuo'* (Exploration and Practice of Double Language Education in Tibet), *Xizang Yanjiu* (Tibet Studies), Vol. 58, No. 1, 1996.

25. Ibid.

26. Jane Peek (VSO Teacher at Tibet University 1987–89), 'Discrimination in Education in Lhasa', unpublished paper, June 1989. Catriona Bass, *China's Education Policy in Tibet*, Submission to the 'Hearing on the Respect for Human Rights in Tibet', before Human Rights Sub-Committee of the Political Affairs Committee, European Parliament, Brussels, 25 April 1990.

27. Gendian Ciren, '… Double Language Education in Tibet'.

28. Internal Party discussion paper, 1995; see also Lei Yongsheng, 1996.

29. Lei Yongsheng, 'The Development of Modern Education'.

30. Interview with Tibetan parent, 1990.

31. Interview with Tibetan educationalist, 7 August 1996; TAR CPPCC bulletin, 15 July 1993.

32. *China Daily*, 4 July 1992.

33. *Beijing Review*, 7–13 August 1995; *Xinhua* in SWB, 2 August 1994.

34. Edward Kormondy, 'Observations on Minority Education, Cultural Preservation and Economic Development in China', *Compare*, Vol. 25, 1995.

35. Ibid.

36. Interview with Tibetan educationalist, 7 August 1996.

37. Internal Party discussion paper, 1995.

38. 'Raidi and Gyaltsen Norbu Summarize Third Tibet Work Forum Conclusions', *Xizang Ribao* (Tibet Daily; in Chinese), 2 August 1994.

39. *Xizang Ribao* (Tibet Daily), 28 February 1991.

40. *Xinhua*, 27 October 1991.

41. *Xinhua*, 2 March 1994 [SWB 4/3/94].

42. *Xinhua*, 27 October 1991.

43. Ibid.

44. 'Outline of the TAR's Five-Year Plan for Economic and Social Development and Its Long-term Target for 2010, Approved by the Fourth Session of the Sixth Regional People's Congress on 24th May 1996', *Xizang Ribao* (Tibet Daily), 7 June 1996, pp. 1–4 (TAR Ninth Five-Year Plan, 1996).

45. *Xinhua*, 18 July 1996 [SWB 19/7/96].

46. Interview with Tibetan student, 23 October 1994; Interview with Tibetan educationalist, 7 August 1996; Internal Party discussion paper, 1995.

47. *Xinhua*, 18 July 1996 [SWB 19/7/96].

48. Interview, 1993.

49. According to officials of the Tibetan government-in-exile, during the ten years after 1984, between 6,000 and 9,000 Tibetans (including young adults) left Tibet, many clandestinely, to seek educational opportunities in India and Nepal. About 5,000 were said to have joined monasteries and nunneries, while some 4,000 had joined exile lay schools. See Tibetan Centre for Human Rights and Democracy, *The Next Generation: The State of Education in Tibet Today* (Dharamsala, 1997), p. 7.

50. Paper on Education Development among Tibetans, by Tibetan scholar in China, 1995.

51. 'Outline of the TAR Child Development Programme for the 1990s', *Xizang Ribao* (Tibet Daily), 11 July 1996, p. 2.

52. See: 'Raidi and Gyaltsen Norbu Summarize Third Tibet Work Forum Conclusions', *Xizang Ribao* (Tibet Daily; in Chinese), 2 August 1994.

CHAPTER 8

Vocational Secondary Education

The development of vocational secondary education in the TAR since 1978

The economic reforms of the 1980s brought the full-scale revival throughout China of the dual-track senior secondary education system (i.e. the channelling of students at senior secondary level into either general education and vocational education). The system had been abandoned during the Cultural Revolution for its discrimination against the children of workers and peasants. At the National Conference on Education in April 1978, Deng Xiaoping defined the main goal of education as being 'to meet the requirements of our country's economic development'.[1] This necessitated the rapid development of vocational secondary education for the training of skilled technicians and scientists.

Since then, the laws and policy documents on education drafted by the Chinese government have all underlined the vital importance of vocational training. The 1985 'CCP Decision on Education' stated: 'Our socialist modernization not only requires senior scientific and technical experts but also urgently requires millions of intermediate and junior engineers, managerial personnel and technicians who have received adequate vocational and technical education as well as urban and rural workers who are well-trained vocationally.'[2]

The 'CCP Decision on Education' set a target of equal numbers of students going into general and vocational senior secondary education by 1990. In June 1996, Premier Li Peng announced plans to the effect that vocational students would make up 70 per cent of all senior secondary students by the end of the century.[3] In September 1996, the Law on Vocational Education was promulgated, which set out the general principles for the development of vocational education as well as the administrative structure and sources of funding.[4]

By 1996, specialized secondary schools providing vocational education constituted 58 per cent of all senior secondary schools in China.[5] In the TAR, 60 per cent of senior secondary students were said to be in specialized or technical education, which was higher than the national average.[6] Nevertheless, China as a whole still had an acute shortage of senior skilled workers; in 1996, only 2 per cent of skilled workers were senior skilled workers.[7] The situation in minority nationality areas such as the TAR was worse: in 1981, 'minority' nationalities in the whole of China had over four times fewer skilled personnel than Han Chinese. Among the Han Chinese population there was one senior engineer for every 100,000 people, while in 'minority' nationality regions there was only one senior engineer for every 480,000 people.[8]

Although the diversification of secondary education was vigorously promoted in government documents and in the media throughout the 1980s and 1990s, it became evident that the policies on vocational education were not being implemented. There were several reasons for this. First, vocational and technical education are more expensive to provide than general secondary education. In the TAR, even now, there are few teaching materials or resources available for vocational secondary education.[9] Second, teachers trained before the 1980s are not trained to teach vocational skills. In the TAR, for example, with the acute shortage of ordinary teachers, there is little funding available for training vocational teachers; in 1994, 26 per cent of teachers in specialized secondary schools had received only secondary education, and some had not even graduated.[10] In 1996, Li Peng described the lack of appropriately qualified teachers as being the main hindrance to the development of vocational secondary education, and directed education departments to 'redouble their efforts to cultivate a great number of teachers committed to vocational secondary education'.[11]

Furthermore, despite the promotion of vocational secondary education in the media and in government circulars, it continues to be considered a second-class education. The persistence of the so-called 'diploma disease' has meant that people and, more importantly, education administrators continue to give priority to academic education. In the 1985 'CCP Decision on Education', the Central Committee described the situation thus:

> We have failed to make a genuine breakthrough in the development of vocational and technical education, although we have stressed its need for many years. An important reason for this failure lies in the fact that for a long time we have not set political, cultural and technical standards for those to be employed and that the out-worn concept of belittling vocational and technical education is deeply rooted.[12]

The education funding reforms had a further negative effect on the implementation of the vocational education policy. The diversification of education funding in the 1980s resulted in the industrial and commercial organs being made largely responsible for vocational secondary education. The 1993 'Programme for China's Educational Reform and Development' stated that, by the end of the century, every trade in every major city and county should establish a vocational training school or centre, and that 'trades, enterprises and institutions will chiefly be relied upon to run schools for vocational-technical education'.[13] However, in reality, the industrial bureaux concentrated on production and showed little concern for the revived vocational education scheme.[14] Enterprises were supposed to provide vocational training for their workers and for people they were intending to employ, but few took up these responsibilities, leading Vice Premier Li Lanqing to tell a meeting of senior government leaders in 1996: 'In the past few years, only a small number of enterprises have taken part in running schools, and a large number of medium and small enterprises, rural enterprises and foreign-funded enterprises have still not undertaken their obligations in vocational education.'[15]

China's Ninth Five-Year Plan for Educational Development reiterated the need to reverse this trend, stipulating that specialized secondary education should be developed 'energetically', in contrast to general secondary education and higher education which were to be developed 'moderately'.[16] Furthermore, in 1996, Li Peng announced plans to expand vocational education into primary and junior secondary education.[17]

In the TAR, government chairman Gyaltsen Norbu, in a speech to the Fifth Regional Meeting on Education in the TAR in 1994, told delegates that the only way to promote the development of vocational education was to introduce a system that 'attaches equal importance to a diploma showing one's record of formal schooling and a certificate of vocational qualifications'.[18]

However, it seems unlikely that vocational education will easily shake off its reputation as an education for those who have failed in the academic system, since that is how it continues to be presented. The Ninth Five-Year Plan for the TAR, for example, states:

> In the cities, all primary and secondary school graduates who fail to enter a higher school are to receive vocational and technical training; in the rural areas, more than 50 per cent of the primary and secondary school graduates who fail to enter a higher school are to receive vocational and technical training; and in the pastoral areas, vigorous efforts are to be made to conduct vocational and technical training for primary and secondary school graduates according to local conditions.

Funding of vocational secondary education

Vocational secondary education is the area where the industrial and business sector is supposed to play the greatest role in funding. The 1985 'CCP Decision on Education' stipulated:

> we should bring into full play the initiative of enterprises and establishments as well as the departments concerned with developing vocational and technical education. We should encourage individuals, collectives and other sectors to run schools and urge all units and departments to set up vocation and technical schools on their own in co-operation with each other or with educational departments.[19]

The 1996 Vocational Education Law stated that funds for vocational education should be gradually increased at all levels of government. Nevertheless, the law also stipulated that enterprises were to provide specialized technical and vocational education for their employees. They could independently, or jointly, run schools and training courses; alternatively, they could commission schools to provide vocational education for their workers and employees. Whatever strategy they used, enterprises were required by the 1996 law to fund this type of education for their workers. Fees could also be collected from students for secondary and tertiary vocational education, although those with economic difficulties were to be exempt, or allowed to pay less.[20]

In the TAR, plans drawn up at the the Fifth TAR Conference on Education in 1994 included the designation of a separate fund for vocational education within the regional government's education budget. This was to provide funds for the construction of a TAR Vocational Secondary Education Centre, and for vocational schools in all prefectures 'in the next few years'.[21]

Enrolment in vocational secondary education in the TAR

In the TAR, specialized technical and vocational schools are largely state-run. Nine of the TAR's specialized secondary schools, including the agricultural school, finance school and the art school, are run directly by educational institutions in the ministries and commissions under the State Council.[22] Other vocational schools are run by the TAR government and several are run by prefectural governments. The TAR has seventeen specialized secondary schools, including five teacher training schools. It also has two specialized secondary classes attached to higher education institutions: the TAR Institute of Agriculture and Animal

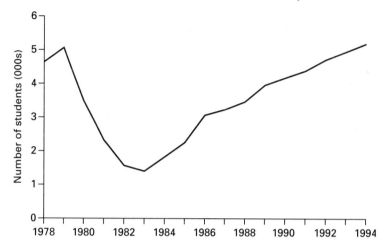

Figure 8.1 Enrolment in senior secondary specialized education in the TAR, 1978–94 (*Source*: 1995 TAR Statistical Yearbook)

Husbandry has one secondary-level class, and the Tibet Nationalities Institute has a secondary-level teacher training class; there are also seven specialized technical classes attached to general secondary schools.

Like enrolment in all senior secondary education in the TAR, enrolment in specialized education is low. However, it has been increasing since 1985 at an average annual growth rate of 14.4 per cent, as is shown in Figure 8.1. This compares well with the national annual average growth rate of 6.9 per cent.[23]

Junior secondary vocational schools have not been developed at all in the TAR. In 1994, there was one vocational secondary school in the whole region with 103 students, compared with an average of 340 vocational secondary schools per province for the whole of China.[24] We can only speculate as to the reasons for this, but they may be connected with the fact that the TAR, like other poor regions, is still struggling to provide basic three-year primary education. There are not the funds available to train specialist teachers, or to develop the relevant teaching materials.

Senior secondary specialized schools in the TAR

Teacher training dominates specialized senior secondary education in the TAR. The acute shortage of primary teachers, which continues to be cited as one of the major causes of low enrolment in primary education in the TAR, has resulted in considerable pressure being put

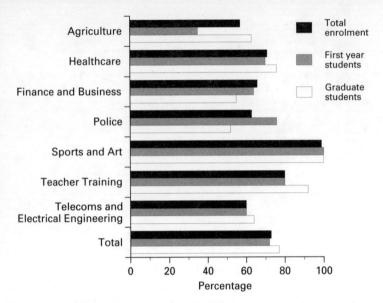

Figure 8.2 Enrolment of Tibetans and other non-Han Chinese students in senior secondary specialized education in the TAR as a percentage of total enrolment, 1994 (*Source*: 1995 TAR Statistical Yearbook)

on junior secondary school graduates to go on to teacher training. Students enrolled in the TAR's five teacher training schools and one teacher training class make up 46.97 per cent of the total enrolment in specialized senior secondary education. The remaining 53 per cent of the enrolment in specialized secondary education is made up as follows: finance/business – 15.66 per cent; agriculture – 11.77 per cent; healthcare – 8.47 per cent; police training – 6.06 per cent; telecommunications/ electrical engineering – 5.85 per cent; art and sport – 5.18 per cent.

Table 8.2 (see p. 174) gives official enrolment figures for different types of specialized secondary education in 1994; it also shows the number of Tibetans and other non-Han Chinese students in the total enrolment for each type.[25] Figure 8.2 presents the proportion of Tibetans and others in the total enrolment. In 1994, non-Han Chinese students made up 73 per cent of the total enrolment in specialized education. A comparison of the first-year enrolment with the number of graduates indicates an overall lower percentage of non-Han Chinese nationalities in the first-year enrolment, although in some subjects the percentage is higher. In 1994, 76.9 per cent of the total number of students who graduated were Tibetan or from another non-Han

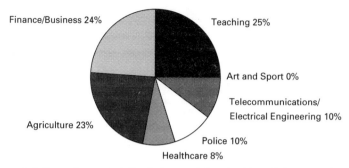

Figure 8.3 Secondary specialized courses taken by Han Chinese students in the TAR, 1994 (*Source*: 1995 TAR Statistical Yearbook)

Chinese nationality, while in the new enrolment for that year 71.4 per cent were non-Han Chinese.

During the early 1980s, the government elaborated plans to train large numbers of skilled personnel among 'minority' nationalities, and particularly in the TAR. Much publicity was given to the importance of the training of Tibetans in vocational and technical skills in order to enhance economic development of the TAR. However, Table 8.2 suggests that reality lagged behind policy statements in secondary-level specialized education. Given that official statistics put the Han Chinese population of the TAR at just over 2 per cent,[26] the fact that 28 per cent of the enrolment in specialized secondary education are Han Chinese suggests that a disproportionate number of Han Chinese students are being trained on programmes supposedly designed to raise the level of skilled personnel among Tibetans in specialities vital to the development of the Tibetan economy.

In teacher training, Tibetans and other non-Han Chinese nationalities do, in fact, predominate. In most of the teacher training schools, non-Han Chinese nationalities make up over 90 per cent of the students, apart from in the Lhasa teaching school where, in 1994, 76 per cent were Tibetan or other non-Han Chinese. However, in technical, financial and business education, all areas vital to the Tibetan economy, up to 50 per cent of the places in some classes were taken by Han Chinese students in 1994. More significantly, given the TAR's dependence on agriculture and the considerable government publicity about the particular importance of agricultural education, there is a low proportion of non-Han Chinese nationalities in agricultural classes.[27] In 1994, only 45 per cent of the students in the first year enrolment at the TAR School of Agricultural and Animal Hubandry were Tibetan or other non-Han Chinese nationalities.

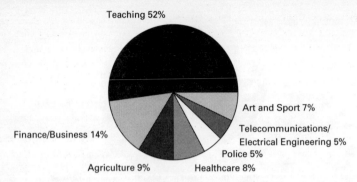

Figure 8.4 Secondary specialized courses taken by Tibetans and other non-Han Chinese students in the TAR, 1994 (*Source*: 1995 TAR Statistical Yearbook)

Figures 8.3 and 8.4 give an indication of enrolment patterns of Han Chinese students in specialized secondary education in the TAR compared with enrolment of non-Han Chinese students. In the 1990s, there were no Han Chinese students studying in the Art School or the School of Tibetan Medicine, and only one was enrolled in the Sports School. Chinese students are channelled equally into teaching, finance/business and agriculture, with lower numbers going into healthcare, police training and telecommunications and engineering. By contrast, over 52 per cent of 'minority' nationality students are channelled into teaching, with significantly lower enrolment figures for all other training courses. For example, 13 per cent of 'minority' nationality students enrol in finance and business schools, just over 8 per cent in healthcare and agriculture, and only 4.75 per cent into telecommunications and electrical engineering.

In recent years, some Tibetan officials have called for greater controls on the number of Han Chinese students from outside the TAR enrolling in Tibetan secondary schools. Figure 8.2 indicates that in some of these key areas – finance, banking and telecommunications, for example – the percentage of non-Han Chinese nationalities is indeed higher in the new enrolment. These Tibetan officials make two points about the training of relatively high numbers of Chinese students in Tibetan schools. The first is that the practice results in a 'brain drain', since Chinese students are unlikely to remain in the TAR after they have finished their training. The second is that the training of Chinese students at the expense of Tibetan students means that the TAR will continue to be dependent on Central China for the development of its economy.[28] In an interview with the journal *Qiushi* in 1994, TAR government chairman Gyaltsen Norbu acknowledged that the TAR 'had suffered a serious brain drain over the past few years'.[29] One Tibetan intellectual makes the same point, but ends his consideration of vocational education with the observation that if Tibetans are trained in specialized technical skills, there is no guarantee that they will remain in their local area either, particularly those who have been trained in Central China:

> Among vocational workers and technicians, our own nationality people are few in number and poor in quality. There is the worrying trend of secondary and senior level vocational workers and technicians, who have been trained at great expense or have been sent to work in Tibetan areas after having graduated from college or university, and who have now left Tibetan areas for various reasons. Some might have worked for about seven or eight years and have become quite professional, but then left. Some have been funded out of the education budget for Tibetan areas and have been to the interior parts of China for higher education as part of the enrolment quota for Tibetan areas. But after they got their qualifications or academic degrees they then wanted to leave the area. Ironically, in this way the Tibetan areas became a basic place for training vocational workers who then leave the region for the advanced and developed provinces of our country. Many people say that in future we should only educate and train local people and not those who want to leave the area after their education. This is easy to say, but hard to practise.
>
> Furthermore, among Tibetans with scientific and technological training, there have been many people who have gone to interior parts of the country to work, which has led to a shortage of talented people in their own local area. This has caused Tibetan areas to become more backward.[30]

Summary

Vocational education was intended to play a vital role in the Chinese government's drive to improve the economy after the Cultural Revolution. In the 1980s and 1990s the Chinese government has made considerable efforts to re-establish vocational training in China and the TAR to make up for the acute shortage of skilled personnel. In 1996, the Vocational Education Law was promulgated, and a target was set to channel 70 per cent of senior secondary students into vocational education by the end of the century. Nevertheless, during the past eighteen years, a number of obstacles to the successful implementation of vocational education have arisen. These include the fact that the education finance reforms made commercial enterprises responsible for financing vocational education, and most of them are still failing to take up this responsibility.[31] This has led to a lack of funding being available for the purchase of equipment and, most seriously, for the training of teachers. In 1994, 26 per cent of teachers in specialized secondary schools in the TAR had received only secondary education, and some had not even graduated from secondary school.[32] Furthermore, there continues to be a reluctance on the part of schools, teachers and students to engage in vocational training since it is still considered to be a second-class education; even in official documents it is described as being intended for those who fail in the academic system.[33]

In the TAR, enrolment in vocational education is low, as it is in all secondary education, although the proportion of senior secondary pupils in vocational education is 60 per cent, which is higher than the national average. Teacher training dominates vocational education in the TAR, with 47 per cent of the total number of students being channelled into this field. In the early 1980s, considerable publicity was given to the importance of training Tibetans in vocational and technical skills. However, by 1994, Han Chinese (according to official statistics, comprising just over 2 per cent of the population of the TAR) occupied 28 per cent of the places on senior secondary specialized courses. Furthermore, the enrolment patterns of Han Chinese and non-Han Chinese students differ quite considerably. In 1994, 52 per cent of Tibetans and other non-Han Chinese students were taking courses in teacher training; only 9 per cent were taking courses in agriculture and 5 per cent in telecommunications and engineering, whereas 23 per cent of Han Chinese students were in agricultural schools and 10 per cent were in telecommunications and engineering schools. Several Tibetan educationalists and officials have called for greater controls on the number of Han Chinese being trained in the TAR, arguing that the practice will result in a 'brain drain' as the Han Chinese students are unlikely to remain in the TAR after training; it will also mean that the TAR will continue to be reliant on Central China for the development of its economy.

Official statistics and basic facts

Table 8.1 Number of senior secondary specialized and technical schools, students and teachers in the TAR, 1994

Schools		Students			Teachers		
Schools	Classes	Total	Women	Tibetans etc.	Total	Women	Tibetans etc.
17	9	5190	2302	3829	744	307	427

Source: 1995 TAR Statistical Yearbook.

Box 8.1 Types of vocational secondary education

1. *Specialized Education includes technical education and teacher train- ing; it exists at senior secondary and higher education levels.*

    i. *Specialized Senior Secondary Schools* (Zhongdeng Zhuanye Xue- xiao). *These schools are sponsored and run by ministries and commissions under the State Council, or professional departments at provincial level.*

    ii. *Secondary Technical Schools* (Zhongdeng Jishu Xuexiao). *Tech- nical schools are run by large or medium-sized enterprises or by provincial government departments to train technical workers. After graduation, students are usually recruited by the enterprises that run the schools. Technical schools used to be junior secondary level, but today they are almost all senior secondary. Courses offered in- clude engineering, agriculture, forestry, medicine, economics, finance and economics, law, sports and art.*

    iii. *Senior Secondary Teacher Training Schools* (Zhongdeng Shifan Xuexiao). *These schools provide teacher training for pre-school and primary-level teachers.*

2. *Vocational Secondary Education may be at junior or senior secondary levels, and provides a lower level of training than specialized education.*

    i. *Vocational Schools* (Zhiye Zhongxue). *Vocational schools were an innovation of the 1980s reforms. Courses are directly based on the needs of local economic development. Vocational schools include agricultural schools* (Nongye Zhongxue) *which are mainly at junior secondary level. Courses offered include agriculture, forestry, farm machinery and public health.*

Table 8.2 Senior secondary specialized and technical schools in the TAR, and number of Han Chinese, Tibetans and other non-Han students, 1994

Schools	Total students	Tibetans etc.
Lhasa Teacher Training School	833	633
Chamdo Teacher Training School	261	235
Lhoka Teacher Training School	303	268
Nagchu Teacher Training School	132	132
TAR Agriculture & Animal Husbandry School	332	201
TAR Healthcare School	329	207
TAR School of Tibetan Medicine	52	52
Shigatse Healthcare School	59	53
TAR Finance School	313	192
TAR Banking School	319	210
TAR Telecommunications School	240	147
TAR Business School	181	131
TAR School of Economics	64	35
TAR Police School	315	199
TAR Sports School	137	136
TAR Art School	132	132

Source: 1995 TAR Statistical Yearbook

Notes

1. Deng Xiaoping, Speech to National Conference on Education, 22 April 1978, in Deng Xiaoping, *Speeches and Writings* (Pergamon Press, London, 1984).

2. CCP Central Committee, 'Decision of the CCP Central Committee on the Reform of China's Education Structure' (Foreign Languages Press, 1985).

3. Vice-Premier Li Lanqing, *Xinhua*, 19 June 1996 [SWB 21/6/96].

4. 'The Law of the People's Republic of China on Vocational Education', *Xinhua*, 16 May 1996 [SWB 8/6/96].

5. Li Peng, addressing participants of the Third National Working Conference on Vocational Education, 17 June 1996, *Xinhua*, 17 June 1996 [SWB 19/6/96].

6. *Xinhua*, 20 March 1996 [FBIS 28/3/96]. Note: Statistical tables for the TAR present aggregate figures for junior and senior secondary enrolment, so the graphs presented in this document cannot reflect this percentage.

7. Vice-Premier Li Lanqing, *Xinhua*, 19 June 1996 [SWB 21/6/96].

8. Kuang Kuolin, '*Minzu jinyi yao fazhan, minzu jiaoyu yao xianxing*' (1989), cited in Gerard Postiglione, 'Implications of Modernization for the Education of China's Minorities', in R. Hayhoe (ed.), *Education and Modernization – The Chinese Experience* (Pergamon Press, London, 1992), p. 332.

9. Research document on education in Tibet by Tibetan scholar, 1996.

10. 1995 TAR Statistical Yearbook, p. 289.

11. Premier Li Peng, addressing participants of Third National Working

Conference on Vocational Education, 17 June 1996, *Xinhua*, 17 June 1996 [SWB 19/6/96].

12. 'CCP Decision on Education', 1985.

13. CCP Central Committee and the State Council, 'Programme for China's Educational Reform and Development', 25 February 1993, *Xinhua*, 25 February 1993 [SWB 5/3/93].

14. Dalu Yin, 'Reforming Chinese Education: Context, Structure and Attitudes in the 1980s', *Compare*, Vol. 23, No. 2, 1993, p. 121.

15. Li Lanqing, Vice-Premier of State Council and Member of Political Bureau of CCP, Report of speech to meeting of senior government leaders, *Xinhua* (in Chinese), 22 May 1996 [SWB 7/6/96].

16. State Education Commission of the PRC, 'Ninth Five-Year Plan for Educational Development Toward the year 2010' [sic], Beijing, 1996 (China Ninth Five-Year Plan for Education, 1996).

17. Li Peng, 17 June 1996.

18. Gyaltsen Norbu, 'Education in Tibet', Speech to Fifth Regional Meeting on Education in the TAR on 26 October 1994, *Xizang Ribao* (Tibet Daily), 30 October 1994, pp. 1–4.

19. 'CCP Decision on Education', 1985.

20. Vocational Educational Law, 1996.

21. Gyaltsen Norbu, 'Education in Tibet'.

22. Dai Yannian, 'Helping Tibet Train Its People', *Beijing Review*, Vol. 30, No. 42, 19 October 1987, p. 4.

23. Figures calculated from 1995 China Statistical Yearbook and 1995 TAR Statistical Yearbook.

24. 1995 China Statistical Yearbook.

25. Tibetans account for 99.2 per cent of the non-Han Chinese population of the TAR. See 1995 TAR Statistical Yearbook, p. 39.

26. In 1994, the official figure for the number of Han Chinese in the TAR was 65,749, which represents 2.84 per cent of the total population. See 1995 TAR Statistical Yearbook, p. 39.

27. See, for example, Li Peng, 'Speech on 20th Anniversary of the Founding of the TAR', *Xinhua*, 31 August 1985 [SWB 4/9/85]; see also Yang Wanli, '*Xizang Kecheng Jiaocai Yanjiu De Teshuxing Jiqi Duice*' (The Countermeasure and Particularity of Research on Teaching Materials), *Xizang Yanjiu*, Vol. 58, No. 1, 1996.

28. See TAR CPPCC, 'Thirteenth Bulletin of the Second Plenary Session of the Sixth TAR CPPCC', Secretariat of the Conference, 17 May 1994.

29. Gyaltsen Norbu, 'Tibet: Development Plans to Overcome Natural Enclosed Economy', interview in *Qiushi*, Beijing, 11 August 1994 [SWB 15/8/94].

30. Internal Party discussion paper, 1995.

31. Li Lanqing, 22 May 1996.

32. 1995 TAR Statistical Yearbook, p. 289.

33. 'Outline of the TAR's Five-Year Plan for Economic and Social Development and Its Long-term Target for 2010, Approved by the Fourth Session of the Sixth Regional People's Congress on 24th May 1996', *Xizang Ribao* (Tibet Daily), 7 June 1996 (TAR Ninth Five-Year Plan, 1996).

CHAPTER 9

Higher Education

With the end of the Cultural Revolution in China, higher education became one of the priorities in education for the new leadership. After ten years in which universities either had been closed down or had been enrolling students according to non-academic criteria, tertiary education was said to be in a worse state than either primary or secondary schooling. In order to rebuild the system and to compensate for the acute shortage of urgently needed high-level manpower, the Chinese government made two fundamental changes to the existing policy: (1) higher education would become a priority in education funding, and (2) enrolment to university would be made competitive according to academic criteria.

In 1978, the university entrance examination was reintroduced. In the same year, the number of higher education institutions throughout China increased from 404 to 598 (including those that reopened), and by 1990, 477 new universities had been built, bringing the total to 1,075. Indeed, the Chinese leadership boosted tertiary education at such a speed that full-time university enrolment in China jumped from 1.1 million to 2 million between 1980 and 1990, an increase of 80 per cent, while enrolment at secondary level declined by 10 per cent and primary enrolment declined by 16 per cent.[1] In the TAR, patterns of enrolment growth in higher education during the 1980s follow trends similar to those in China as a whole: between 1979 and 1990 tertiary enrolment increased by 37 per cent, secondary enrolment by 2 per cent while primary enrolment declined by 37 per cent.[2] Of course, it should be remembered that we are dealing with very low numbers of students in higher education in the TAR (see Figure 9.1). During the 1990s, enrolment in higher education in the TAR increased more rapidly than in China as a whole. Between 1990 and 1994 enrolment at tertiary level in the TAR increased by 61 per cent at an average annual growth rate of 15 per cent, compared with the national annual average of 8 per cent.[3] Over the same period, enrolment in secondary and primary education in the TAR grew by 33 per cent and 48 per cent respectively.[4]

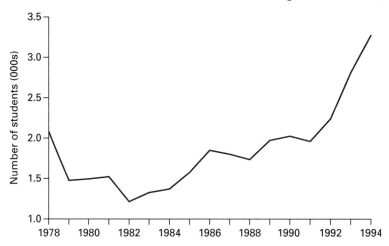

Figure 9.1 Enrolment in higher education in the TAR, 1978–94
(*Source*: 1995 TAR Statistical Yearbook)

These statistics, however, tell us nothing about the percentage of Tibetans and other non-Han Chinese students in tertiary enrolment in the TAR. This chapter traces the pattern of enrolment in higher education since 1978, and provides an examination of the factors that have affected the enrolment of non-Han Chinese nationalities. After the end of the Cultural Revolution, the rejection of 'leftist' policies did not initially include a rejection of those policies that had undermined the education of non-Han Chinese nationalities, i.e. the disregard for cultural differences and the imposition of the so-called 'Han model' on 'minority' education. Immediately after the end of the Cultural Revolution, the Chinese government tried to synchronize the educational development of border areas with that of Central China, most dramatically, as far as tertiary education is concerned, in the introduction of the standardized university entrance examination; this led to a sudden decline in 'minority' nationality enrolment. By the early 1980s, a number of policies had been drawn up in an attempt to reverse the decline: they gave preferential treatment to 'minority' nationalities in higher education, and granted the autonomous regions the right to establish a separate education system with their own examinations. However, the emergence of 'leftist' policies in 1990s has resulted in renewed rejection of cultural distinctiveness, further emphasis on the importance of ideological education over professional education, and an apparent rejection of the policy of training Tibetans to take over from Chinese professionals in the TAR.[5]

Before addressing the issue of enrolment, this chapter provides a description of investment in higher education in China and the TAR, with particular reference to the arguments about funding higher education at the expense of basic education, especially in areas where educational levels are generally low. The rapid increase in the number of universities and in enrolment in the 1980s led to what was officially termed an over-expansion and a decline in quality; this, combined with the new conservatism of the 1990s, led to a reassertion of central government control in enrolment planning and the administration of higher education.

Funding of higher education in the 1980s: higher education versus basic education

Throughout China, the 1980s saw an over-investment in higher education at the expense of basic education. In 1991, university students, who comprised 8.3 per cent of the total student population, consumed 21.5 per cent of the total education expenditure (see Table 9.1). Even in underdeveloped areas like the TAR, where educational levels are generally low, higher education was made a priority in education funding.[6] It is not clear why this should be the case, since there is much discussion in China about the importance of funding basic education for the long-term development of the system, and particularly in the TAR.[7] Indeed, on a visit to the TAR in 1985, Li Peng told regional leaders that 'emphasis should be placed on primary and secondary education and particularly the former'.[8] One author suggests that the prioritizing of tertiary education in 'minority' regions might, in part, be politically inspired: 'minority' students studying in colleges and universities in 'minority' areas are a very visible sign of achievement, since there was none fifty years ago.[9] However, such a policy runs counter to research on education in other developing countries, which shows that the most efficient use of education funding in a poor economic environment lies in raising the general educational level and in training large numbers of low-grade technical personnel.[10] Making higher education a priority in under-developed regions not only means that there is less funding available for lower levels of education, it also results in a 'brain drain', since there is no established infrastructure in which highly trained personnel can use their skills.[11] Teng Xing writes:

> Due to wrong priorities in Minority Education over the last ten years a large number of senior technical personnel have been trained. They are unable to put their skills to use in the low economic environment of

Table 9.1 Education expenditure in China by level of education

Level	% of student population	% of total expenditure
Higher education	8.3	21.54
Secondary education	20.1	35.78
Primary education	44.6	35.02
Pre-school education	8.9	1.34
Other	18.1	6.32

Source: Yat Ming Leung in 'Education and Development in East Asia,' Garland Press, London 1995; 1992 Chinese Statistical Yearbook.

minority nationality regions. The result is an outflow of trained personnel, and educational wastage. Moreover, spending the limited funds in minority nationality regions on higher education means that there is no money for training the low-level technical personnel that minority nationality regions urgently need. This kind of 'educational wastage' is alarming. Research has shown that in a low economic environment, the lower the education level receiving funding priority, the greater the economic and social benefits.[12]

In the TAR, a breakdown of educational expenditure by level is not available. However, as early as 1981 there was concern among some educators and officials in the TAR that resources for higher education were being over-extended in relation to secondary schooling, and that secondary schools were not able to provide enough qualified college entrants.[13] Israel Epstein writes of that period:

Too many teachers, in the opinion of some local educators, were concentrated in the higher schools and not enough lower down, so their downward redistribution was necessary to provide a reliable foundation for future advance. (In fact senior secondary schools themselves were not getting enough entrants, since some junior secondary school leavers went straight to work and others into secondary-level technical schools).[14]

By the end of the 1980s, concern was growing in the TAR about the funding of higher education at the expense of basic education,[15] although by then the universities were being pressed to produce more graduates than their budgets would allow and were also facing financial difficulties.[16] In a television debate about education, broadcast on Lhasa TV during the Fifth Session of the Fourth TAR People's Congress in 1988, one of the participants pointed out the long-term damage caused to the education system in the TAR by not making primary education a priority: 'Primary education is so inadequate and since this is the basis of all education we cannot make any improvement in secondary schools and in higher education until we improve the quality of lower schools.'[17]

By the 1990s, the effect of underfunding primary education was beginning to show in the poor quality of students enrolling in higher education institutions in the TAR. The issue was raised in May 1996 at a meeting of the TAR CPPCC, where one member complained:

> due to the low level of marks required in the entrance exam to the TAR University, the real academic standard of the students is low; and some students lack even the standard comparable to that of a junior secondary pupil in Central China. Consequently, they cannot follow the lectures, and thus adversely affect the academic standard of universities in the Tibet Autonomous Region.[18]

Perhaps the most serious consequence of these funding priorities in the TAR is that the poor quality of primary and secondary education has led to a situation in the 1990s where Tibetan students cannot compete with Han Chinese students, many of whom come to the TAR having studied in secondary schools in Central China. Therefore, despite the preferential policies promulgated in the 1980s there is a danger that, in the future, higher education in the TAR will provide training for growing numbers of Han Chinese students in place of Tibetans.

Funding crisis in higher education in the 1990s: recentralization of control

By the 1990s, the strains of fast growth in higher education in China were beginning to show. The rapid expansion of enrolment led to serious financial problems in institutes and universities all over the country. Education officials began to argue for a readjustment and a slowdown.[19] In 1993, Zhu Kaixuan, Minister in Charge of the State Education Commission, reported to the National People's Congress:

> In the past two years, higher education has developed swiftly. While the general development is favourable, we cannot afford to overlook some problems. Some localities and departments have failed to assess, in a clear-headed manner, potential trouble caused by the exceedingly fast pace at which higher education is being developed, a pace that outstrips local economic development and is too fast for schools to cope with. Considering our country's national conditions, the development of higher education must keep pace with economic development and be based upon internal factors.[20]

The financial problems were partly due to the high unit costs of university education in general, and partly to an increase in the number of small-scale higher education institutions. In 1994, Vice Premier Li Lanqing told a Hong Kong newspaper that China had too many universities and that most of them were small and comprehensive rather than vocational. He went on to say that many of them were 'redundant and of poor quality'.[21]

Furthermore, the 1985 'CCP Decision on Education' had made higher education adapt to market forces, to a greater extent than lower levels of education. From 1985 onwards, state-enrolled students accounted for only part of the enrolment; universities were responsible for recruiting 'self-supported students', and 'commissioned students' who were sponsored by businesses and industries with a need for graduates.[22] In addition, since 1985, universities have had to supplement their state budget by other means, including selling their services outside the state plan and developing technology for industry.

The introduction of market forces into the higher education system has meant that universities with good reputations and well-developed research departments in areas with obvious industrial applications have been most successful at income generation both in terms of commissioned students and contracts from industry. Universities in Shanghai, for example, developed over 1,000 items of technology for industry between 1985 and 1987: Tongji University made 13.5 million yuan in one year from such contracts, which accounted for 40 per cent of its expenditure.[23]

In the TAR, by contrast, institutions of higher education have experienced financial shortages in the 1990s. With little research, and few industries to pay either for technological developments or to commission students, the TAR's universities been forced to expand enrolment with diminishing funds.[24]

In 1994, Tibet University received a budget of 7 million yuan ($823,530) which was 2 million yuan less than the previous year, although enrolment had increased. This was a budget cut of 28.5 per cent, not taking inflation into account. The TAR Institute of Agriculture & Animal Husbandry School also faced financial difficulties in that year; its budget had been reduced by 1 million yuan ($117,650), and this had led to cuts in the teaching programme.[25] In 1996, the TAR's higher education institutions continued to face financial constraints, leading members of the TAR CPPCC to urge the government, in May, to make savings in other parts of the economy in order to fund education:

> The main reason why it is difficult to cultivate highly trained people in our region is that our educational budget is too low. This year, although Tibet

University needed a budget of 12.71 million yuan they only got 12.30 million yuan. They still need a further 410,000 yuan. The situation of the TAR Institute of Tibetan Medicine was even worse. Their annual budget was only 2.4 million yuan. This only covered the teachers' wages and a fraction of the running costs. The budget shortage has badly affected educational work and the fostering of high level personnel. We hope that the government will cut down on unnecessary expenses and spend the limited budget on education as much as possible.[26]

China's Ninth Five-Year Plan for education addresses the issue of financial shortages in higher education. Indeed, plans for the next fourteen years indicate a slowing-up of higher education enrolment. Predicted annual average growth to the year 2010 is 3.8 per cent, which is considerably less than the 8 per cent growth for the period 1990–95. Strategies to increase cost effectiveness include the merging of institutes of higher education, increasing student–teacher ratios, and expanding links with industry.[27] At the same time, in January 1996, the State Education Commission announced that 10 billion yuan would be spent on the improvement of 100 key universities by the year 2000.[28]

In 1994, the State Education Commission introduced a system whereby students paid part of their fees for higher education. The system was extended in April 1996 to a full fee-paying system for all universities, to take effect from 1997. Grants for poor students are to be instituted at the same time. The system is intended to raise further revenues for higher education, and also to eliminate the inequalities of the present system where fee-paying students require lower scores to enter university than state-funded students.[29] Certain categories of university, however, are instructed to continue to charge low tuition fees or to remain free. Among the universities that are to remain free are teacher training universities, agricultural universities, naval colleges, 'minority' nationality universities and physical education colleges. Low fee universities include colleges of hydraulic engineering, geological mining, police, meteorology and topography.[30]

China's Ninth Five-Year Plan also outlines the need to rationalize university courses further. According to the plan, emphasis should henceforth be placed on undergraduate courses, and on those which cater to the manpower needs of rural regions, rural enterprises, small enterprises and the service sector. Courses with an industrial application are also to be made a priority, as are courses which provide manpower for 'key industrial enterprises, educational and research institutions and the defence sector'.[31]

In the TAR, in line with Chinese government policy, the Fifth TAR Conference on Education in 1994 cited as a priority the readjustment of university courses in order to bring them in line with economic development: 'It is necessary for institutions of higher learning to go further towards meeting the needs of the TAR's economic and social development by rationally readjusting their departments, special fields of study, and curriculum, widening the base of special fields of study, broaden students' knowledge, and accelerate the training of qualified, suitable personnel.'[32]

Enrolment in higher education

After the end of the Cultural Revolution, the new leadership was concerned not simply to expand tertiary education, but, in particular, to restore its function of providing high-level academic and technical training rather than ideological education for workers, peasants and soldiers. The first step in restoring universities' academic status was to reinstate the entrance examination. The National Unified Higher Education Enrolment System was introduced in 1978; it stipulated that there should be one standard university entrance examination drawn up by the Ministry of Education, with one set of answers and common methods of grading. Throughout the country, in early July each year, millions of candidates would enter examination halls to sit identical papers in every subject.

Each subject had a 100-point test; the total score for Humanities subjects was 500 points and the total for the Sciences was 600 points. The foreign language paper was not counted in the compiled scores, although it was used as a reference in selection. In the Chinese paper, the Ministry of Education stipulated a 60 per cent pass mark; candidates gaining a lower score than this would not be eligible for enrolment in higher education.[33]

The reintroduction of the university entrance examination marked a return to the policies of the 1960s, although now, unlike in the earlier period, there were far more applicants than there were university places available, and therefore competition was much greater. The new system was a dramatic revalidation of the quality-oriented strategies which favoured urban areas, eastern provinces and Han Chinese children over other nationalities. By 1980, the bias could be seen in enrolment patterns in different regions and among different nationalities: in China as a whole, tertiary enrolment rose from 856,000 to 1.14 million between 1978 and 1980, yet in the TAR enrolment fell from 2,081 to 1,494.[34] The proportion of non-Han Chinese nationalities among students in higher education also declined: at the national level it fell from 6.5 per cent in 1976 to 3.7 per cent in 1979. In the TAR, in that year, only 10 per cent

Table 9.2 Subjects of the standardized university entrance examination

Humanities	All courses	Sciences
History	Politics	Physics
Geography	Chinese	Chemistry
	Mathematics	Biology (added in 1981)
	Foreign language	

of the quota of students sent from the region to universities in China were Tibetan although Tibetans comprised over 97 per cent of the total population.[35] At the Tibet Nationalities Institute, the percentage of Tibetans and other non-Han Chinese students fell from 90.7 per cent in 1976 to 32.6 per cent in 1979.[36] Box 9.1 is an account, by a Tibetan class teacher, of life in the TAR Healthcare School at the time of the introduction of the unified university entrance examination in 1978. It provides an example of what was taking place in higher education institutions all over China, when the students who had joined the universities during the Cultural Revolution had their studies abruptly curtailed and were sent back to their villages to make way for young secondary school graduates. At the TAR Healthcare School, the process resulted in an immediate sense of racial discrimination, since the students who were sent back to their villages were all Tibetan and, of the 120 new students, all but two were Chinese.

The introduction of a unified university entrance examination put non-Han Chinese nationalities, including Tibetans, at an immediate disadvantage in enrolment in higher education. It was not just that the quality of secondary education was inferior in 'minority' regions; the examination itself set other obstacles. First, foreign languages were not taught to non-Han nationalities, and so they were unable to take the foreign language test; even though the grade was not counted in the compiled scores, it was used as a reference in the selection prodecure. Second, an age restriction was put on tertiary enrolment, which meant that most students would be selected from the twenty-year-old cohort, and no one could be selected over the age of twenty-five. This again put students from 'minority' regions at a disadvantage since they are likely to start school later than in Central China (primary enrolment is delayed to the age of nine in some parts of the TAR); furthermore, 'minority' nationalities have an additional preparatory year at the beginning of secondary school to improve their command of Chinese. Thus, 'minority' students tended to be older than their Han Chinese

---

Box 9.1 Life in the TAR Healthcare School

In 1977, after I left university, I was sent to teach in the TAR Healthcare School in Kongpo Prefecture. At that time it was still a secondary level medical school teaching western-style basic medical care, but in 1977 it was accorded tertiary status.

There were six classes in the school with around 150 students. I was in charge of one class, and I also taught Chinese and Mathematics. The students were almost all adults, some over the age of thirty; most of them had a very low level of education and many of them were illiterate. Teaching was quite difficult, because we had to teach the secondary school curriculum although many of the students had not even received primary school education.

In 1978 when the university entrance examination was reintroduced, most of these students were sent back to their villages. It was terrible, they were all very upset and came to see me to ask me if I could persuade the leaders not to make them leave as they were only half way through their studies, but it was not possible.

New teachers had been sent from Shanghai to run the university courses, and I was kept on to run one preparatory class. Of the 120 students in the first year in 1978, only two were Tibetans; they were two girls from aristocratic Tibetan families in Lhasa. One was called Yangzom, the other was from the Shatra family and now lives in Canada.

Source: *Interview with Dakar, teacher at TAR Healthcare School, 1977–79, 13 August 1997.*

---

counterparts, and so were less likely to be selected. However, the most important reason why 'minorities' were less successful in the unified entrance examination was that all the papers were in Chinese, and however well they studied Chinese at secondary school, they could not hope to compete with native speakers. Furthermore, if they failed to score the 60 per cent required in the Chinese paper they would not be eligible for enrolment, even if they passed the other papers.[37]

By 1979, voices began to be raised about the unequal treatment of 'minority' nationalities, and about the continuing decline in tertiary enrolment among them, at a time of record enrolment for Han Chinese students. There was concern that the 'leftist' influence on 'minority education' still existed.[38] 'Leftism' in the context of 'minority education' meant several things: (1) little attention was paid to the education of 'minority' nationalities; (2) the distinctive culture of the different nationalities, and the disparity in educational development was not recognized (i.e. a unified education system was imposed on them); (3) 'minority' nationalities did not have the autonomy to establish their own educational systems.[39] Some of these opinions were expressed in two authoritative magazines, *Unity of Nationalities* and *Nationality Studies*, which resumed publication in 1979. It was also argued that the unified university entrance examination was having an adverse impact on education in 'minority' nationality regions, because it disproportionately excluded 'minority' applicants for university. The fact that these views were also expressed in *Red Flag* suggests that the issue was, by this time, being taken seriously by the Chinese government.

In May 1979, the State Nationalities Affairs Commission convened its first conference in Tianjin. The conference announced the shift in the Chinese government's 'nationality work' from emphasis on politics to concentration on economic and educational development in minority regions.[40] For the first time since 1949, nationality institutions were allowed to give equal weight to the training of professionals and the training of political cadres.[41] In the previous thirty years, higher education for 'minority' nationalities had consisted of teacher training and in-service or pre-service training of political cadres. Although the Minister of Nationalities Affairs, Yang Jingren, still emphasized the importance of education in ensuring national security in 'minority' regions, training for socialist modernization became part of the role of education of 'minority' nationalities in the early 1980s.[42] In other words, the training of scientific and technical professionals and management personnel became more important than before.

In 1980, in an attempt to reverse the decline in the enrolment of 'minority' students, which had been precipitated by the entrance examination, the Ministry of Education revised the enrolment regulations of the previous three years and put forward five new measures:

1. National key institutions, including Beijing University, would set up 'minority' nationality classes, and would take a quota of students who were outstanding in their own region but who might have failed the unified entrance examination.
2. Departments of education in the autonomous regions could set their own entrance examinations for enrolment in colleges in their own regions.
3. Non-Han Chinese students could take the university examination in their native language for subjects such as geography, mathematics, physics and chemistry.

4. The pass mark could be lowered slightly for 'minority' students.
5. Students from 'minority' nationalities in Han areas would take priority in admission if they had the same scores as their Han counterparts.[43]

The 1984 Law on Regional Autonomy gave further pledges to increase enrolment of non-Han Chinese nationalities in higher education. New enrolment regulations in 1984 stipulated not the 'slight' lowering of the pass mark for minority students recommended by the previous regulations, but an evaluation of minority students according to local teaching conditions and a policy of taking those who were 'outstanding' in their own regions, regardless of their performance relative to Han Chinese students.[44]

By the early 1980s, the predominant cadre training programmes in each of the eleven nationality institutes in China were giving way to undergraduate and graduate courses in humanities and natural sciences that were on higher academic levels and were enrolling and training more professionals. Also, research institutes or research offices were established in nearly all the nationality institutes to carry out research on 'minority' history, language, culture and so on.[45] With more institutions open to 'minority' students, there were, in principle, more opportunities for higher education; indeed, the ratio of 'minority' students in higher education grew to 5 per cent by 1985. However, there were indications that the implementation of the policy favouring minorities soon faltered and the increase in the proportion of non-Han Chinese students slowed.[46] Tertiary enrolment patterns in the TAR and the ratio of Tibetans and others to Han Chinese are examined below, and a few suggestions are made as to why, despite the preferential policies drawn up in the early 1980s, the proportion of Tibetans in higher education has never come close to their proportion in the population, which is the stated aim of the Chinese government.[47] In 1984, Tibetans and other non-Han Chinese nationalities were said to make up 48.6 per cent of tertiary enrolment in the TAR. In 1993, the ratio had increased to 57.8 per cent, but by 1994 it had fallen to 49.6 per cent; yet Tibetans and non-Han Chinese nationalities constituted 97.16 per cent of the population.[48] As the statistics are incomplete, it is not possible to present an overall picture of trends in the enrolment of Tibetans in higher education. However, a few observations are presented below, as well as a summary of the options available for higher education in the TAR, the process by which students enrol, and the distribution of enrolment among fields of study.

Enrolment in higher education in the TAR

Since the introduction of the preferential policies for 'minority' nationalities, discussed above, Tibetan secondary school graduates have had, in principle, a variety of options available for higher education. They may apply for enrolment to (1) 'minority' nationality classes attached to key national universities in Central China; (2) 'minority' nationality classes attached to regular universities in Central China; (3) one of the eleven nationalities institutes which include the Central Nationalities Institute in Beijing, the Northwest Nationalities Institute in Lanzhou, the Qinghai Nationalities Institute in Xining, the Southwest Nationalities Institute in Chengdu or the Tibet Nationalities Institute in Xianyang; (4) higher education institutes in the TAR.

Statistics for higher education in the TAR do not indicate the proportion of Tibetan university applicants who apply to comprehensive or technical universities outside the region, nor to the size of the quota of successful candidates. The best students from the TAR are said to apply to such universities rather than to nationalities institutes or to universities in the TAR. Gongkar Gyatso, formerly a teacher at Tibet University, describes the university preferences of secondary school graduates in the TAR:

> Students with the highest marks will always apply to major universities in big cities in China, such as Beijing or Shanghai. If Tibetans have good marks they will get in to those universities quite easily, because there is a special quota for students from 'minority' nationalities. The second choice for Tibetans would be universities or the nationalities institutes in Sichuan, Gansu and Qinghai provinces. Students who don't get in to those universities would apply to Tibet University. TAR Agriculture & Animal Husbandry School would be the last choice: no one wants to study agriculture, and the TAR Agriculture & Animal Husbandry School is far from the city. Only students who couldn't get in anywhere else would apply to go there.[49]

Table 9.3 gives details of the students who, in 1994, enrolled in the four institutions of higher education that come under the jurisdiction of the TAR. According to official statistics, there were 3,280 students in higher education in the TAR; 1,226 students were enrolled in Tibet University (representing 37 per cent of the total enrolment in 1994), 35.5 per cent were enrolled in the Tibet Nationalities Institute, 7.8 per cent in the TAR School of Tibetan Medicine and 19.2 per cent in the TAR Agriculture & Animal Husbandry School.

Given the considerable government publicity about the importance of agriculture to the Tibetan economy and the urgent need to modern-

Box 9.2 A Visit to the TAR School of Tibetan
Medicine, 1993

Until 1989, the TAR School of Tibetan Medicine was a part of Tibet University. However, in 1989 it was given its own site on the road running north out of Lhasa towards Sera Monastery. At that time it had the status of a specialized senior secondary-level school; in 1993, the school was accorded university status.

When the school moved to its present site it received a one-off payment of 7 million yuan ($823,539) from the government, which was used for the construction and establishment of the new school. The TAR Education Commission now provides funding for running costs, which in 1993 amounted to one million yuan ($117,647) per year. Most of this sum is spent on salaries, food for the students and electrical costs.

The new buildings are extensive with well-furnished classrooms, still in good condition, and spacious student accommodation. It is set in large grounds which include a sports field. There is the formal library, as well as the one regularly used by the students. The library is very peaceful and beautifully decorated, with medical texts, as well as other religious texts, stored in the cupboards lining the walls. However, the collection of written materials is incomplete. In total there are around 500 writers on Tibetan medicine – mostly from east Tibet, but the library does not have a full collection of their works because the institute cannot afford them. Furthermore, the institute only possesses forty of the ninety-five medical thankas (paintings) used in the teaching of Tibetan medicine. The institute also has a museum which was built in 1992 to house the eight collections of flora, fauna and mineral specimens used in teaching medicine. In 1993, the school needed to buy a camera since some of the specimens were poorly preserved and it was thought to be easier for the students to identify plants and other specimens from photographs. However, funding was said not to be available for this type of expenditure. The school also lacked the equipment and a workshop to allow the students to practise making medicines.

In 1993, the institute had three hundred students and thirty-two teachers; fifteen teachers taught on the secondary-level course and seventeen taught on the university-level course. Each year one prefecture was given a chance to put forward more students – in 1992, it was the turn of Chamdo Prefecture. The ages of students on admission range from 20 to 22 years. For the university-level course the students must have passed the senior secondary school exam, and for the senior secondary-

level course they must have passed the junior secondary school exam. In 1993, the enrolment included five students from Gannan Tibetan prefecture in Gansu province and five students from Inner Mongolia.

The secondary-level course is a four-year course, including three years' theoretical training and one year practical training. Since the institute acquired university status, the secondary-level course has been scaled down, although there are no plans to close it completely. The university-level course is a five-year course, including four years' theoretical training and one year practical. There are twenty subjects taught in total. In addition to the standard Tibetan medical subjects, students are taught astrology, Chinese, politics, Tibetan language, English language, and Western medicine. A set of three Tibetan medical books are distributed to each student; however for some practical lessons like making moxibustions or classes in Western medicine, students lack sufficient equipment. For their practical training, half the students are sent to the Shigatse Tibetan Medical Hospital and the other half go to the Lhasa Tibetan Medical Hospital.

The graduation examinations at the School of Tibetan Medicine have a sliding pass rate, according to the general level of the students. On graduation, students will be allocated to county hospitals or town hospitals; today, increasing numbers of students are being sent to the county hospitals since the need is greater in the rural areas.

Source: *Visit to the school in 1993.*

---

ize farming methods and provide agricultural education, the percentage of enrolment in the Agriculture & Animal Husbandry School would seem to be rather low. Furthermore, only 3.7 per cent of TAR graduates in 1994 were from the Agriculture and Animal Husbandry School; none of them was from a 'minority' nationality. Reasons why this is the case are speculative but likely to be connected with the fact that (1) educational advancement is still seen as a means of getting out of the rural economy, and therefore university-level agricultural courses are unpopular; (2) the TAR Agriculture & Animal Husbandry School is situated in Kongpo, 300 miles from Lhasa; (3) science subjects are taught in Chinese at secondary school and are therefore more difficult for Tibetans and other non-native Chinese speakers to follow.[50]

Table 9.3 also gives an indication of the number of Tibetans and other nationalities in higher education in the TAR in 1994: 49.6 per

Table 9.3 Distribution of enrolment in the TAR's higher education institutions, 1994

	1st year enrolment			Graduates			Total enrolment		
	Total	H	T	Total	H	T	Total	H	T
Tibet University	396	69	327	409	15	394	1,226	208	1,018
TAR School of Tibetan Medicine	85	30	55	28	0	28	259	60	199
TAR Agriculture School	236	180	56	23	23	0	630	446	184
Tibet Nationalities Institute	378	311	67	161	138	23	1,165	938	227

Key: H = Han Chinese; T = Tibetans and other Non-Han Chinese Nationalities.
Source: 1995 TAR Statistical Yearbook.

cent of the total enrolment consisted of students from a 'minority' nationality; in the first year enrolment, 46.1 per cent were of non-Han Chinese origin, while 71.1 per cent of the graduates were Tibetan or from another non-Han Chinese nationality. These figures seem to indicate that, unless 'minority' students performed better in the graduation exam than Chinese students, which general evidence from the entrance examination as well as interviews with educators suggest is not the case, there was a greater percentage of 'minority' students in the final year than in the first year. It would appear therefore that there has been a decline in the proportion of students from 'minority' nationalities enrolled in higher education; indeed, in 1993, 58 per cent of students enrolled in higher education were from 'minority' nationalities, compared with 49.6 per cent in 1994.[51]

Non-Han Chinese nationalities are particularly poorly represented in the Agriculture & Animal Husbandry School and in the Tibet Nationalities Institute, accounting for 29.2 per cent and 19.5 per cent of the total enrolment respectively. In the TAR School of Tibetan Medicine, 76.8 per cent of the total students were from 'minority' nationalities: yet while 100 per cent of the graduates were of non-Han Chinese origin only 65 per of the first-year enrolment were from 'minorities'. This suggests that even in Tibetan subjects like Tibetan medicine, an increasing number of university places in the TAR are being taken by Han Chinese students.

Tables 9.4, 9.5 and 9.6 provide more detail about enrolment patterns of Tibetans and other non-Han Chinese nationalities in higher educa-

Table 9.4 Ratio of Tibetans and other Non-Han Chinese in Tibet Nationalities Institute for selected years between 1976 and 1994

	1976	1979	1980	1981	1982	1983	1988	1989	1994
Total	486	175	338	374	239	426	702	490	1,165
Han Chinese	45	118	22	113	45	81	301	367	938
Tibetans etc.	441	57	316	261	194	345	401	123	227
Tibetans etc. (%)	90.7	32.6	93.5	69.8	81.2	81.0	57.1	74.9	19.5

Sources: Introduction to Tibet Institute of Nationalities, 1989, cited in Yenming Zhang, *Effects of Policy Changes on College Enrolment of Minority Students in China, 1949–1989*, Doctoral Thesis (Harvard University, 1991), p. 138; 1995 TAR Statistical Yearbook.

tion. Table 9.5 is taken from a report by Tibet University's examination office, giving information about the selection procedure to the university in 1992. In accordance with national policy, the pass mark was set at different levels for Han Chinese students and 'minority' students. The pass mark for Han Chinese was set at 350; for 'minority' students it was set at 240 for humanities subjects and 230 for science subjects.[52] It appears that places were given to Tibetans in proportion to the number of applicants, rather than in proportion to their numbers in the population: 46 per cent of the applicants were Tibetan and 54 per cent were Han Chinese; of those candidates who were selected, 45 per cent were Tibetan and 55 per cent were Chinese. Furthermore, the data presented in this table indicate that Tibetan students enter humanities departments rather than science departments: 26 per cent of the successful science candidates were Tibetan compared with 70 per cent of humanities candidates; other reports of previous years at Tibet University point to the same phenomenon.[53] At the same time, 56 per cent of the places were given to science candidates although they constituted 44 per cent of the total candidates. The table indicates that Tibetans achieved considerably lower scores than Han Chinese students: only three Tibetans got more than 350 marks which was the pass mark for Chinese students.

Table 9.6 gives an indication of the number of Tibetans who enrolled on the English course at Tibet University in the first four years after the university was made a tertiary institution. The sudden rise in the number of Tibetans enrolling in 1986 is likely to be connected with the establishment of a six-month British Council project which provided course books, audio-visual materials and two teachers/teacher trainers to develop the teaching of English to Tibetans at the university. The

Table 9.5 Selection procedure in Tibet University, 1992

	Total			Sciences			Humanities		
	Total	Tibetans	Tibetans (%)	Total	Tibetans	Tibetans (%)	Total	Tibetans	Tibetans (%)
Candidates	1,699	781	46	749	–	–	950	–	–
Candidates successful	312	139	45	180	46	26	132	93	70
Distribution of marks in entrance examination:									
540	1	0	0	1	0	0			
450–539	10	0	0	10	0	0			
400–450	50	1	2	37	0	0	13	1	7.7
350–399	115	2	1.7	87	1	1.1	28	1	3.6
250–350	136	136	100	45	45	100	91	91	100

Source: Taken from a report by the Tibet University Students Examination Office, 5 October 1992.

Table 9.6 Ethnic background of students in the English section of Tibet University

Year of enrolment	Han Chinese	Tibetan	Tibetan/Chinese
1985	12	2	2
1986	0	20	4
1987	11	8	2
1988	33	7	0

Source: Jane Peek (VSO teacher at Tibet University 1987–89), 'Discrimination in Education in Lhasa', unpublished paper, June 1989.

number of Tibetans enrolled in the English section declined considerably in the two subsequent years. The main reason for the low number of Tibetans on the English course is that only those Tibetan students who get into the Chinese stream in secondary school are able to study English, and therefore the number of Tibetans able to pass the English paper in the university entrance examination is extremely low, although the all-Tibetan class of 1986 included a quota of ten Tibetan villagers who had learned no English at all (see Box 9.4).[54]

Table 9.4 presents the proportion of non-Han Chinese nationalities in the enrolment at the Tibet Nationalities Institute between 1976 and 1994, which provides a slightly fuller picture of enrolment in the post-Cultural Revolution period. It shows, for example, the effect on enrolment of the unified entrance examination when the proportion of 'minority' nationalities declined from 90.7 per cent in 1976 to 32.6 per cent in 1979. Similarly, in 1980, the sudden rise in 'minority' enrolment to 93.5 per cent can be explained by the implementation of the preferential policies drawn up by the Nationalities Affairs Commission in 1979. Through the 1980s, when government documents emphasized the training of 'minority' nationality professionals to take over from Han Chinese in the TAR, the ratio was relatively high, reaching 74.9 per cent by 1989. However, in the 1990s, it appears to have declined significantly, falling to an all-time low of 19.5 per cent in 1994. This coincides with the new political climate where Han Chinese are no longer repatriated to make way for Tibetans but are encouraged to go to the TAR and engage in the process of economic development;[55] and where the educational goal for Tibetans has once more been made to emphasize ideological allegiance to China over professional qualifications in order to ensure stability in the region.[56]

Low enrolment of Tibetans in higher education: factors involved

In practice, since the Cultural Revolution, the proportion of Tibetans in higher education in the TAR has never come near their percentage in the population. At the 1984 TAR Regional Conference on Student Enrolment, a target was set to increase enrolment of 'minority' nationality students in the TAR to 60 per cent of the total enrolment. Three reform measures were introduced in an attempt to achieve this: (1) Tibetans resident anywhere in China would be able to enrol for higher education in the TAR; (2) the age limit for enrolment would be increased to twenty-eight; and (3) particular attention would be paid to the enrolment of 'minority' nationalities in higher education.[57] Despite these reforms, however, the enrolment of Tibetans has remained relatively low. There appear to be several reasons for this, which are connected both with the poor implementation of 'minority' tertiary education policy, and with shifting political priorities. However, the main reason, as we have seen, is that the majority of Tibetans drop out of the education system before the start of secondary school; by secondary graduation, the ratio of Tibetans to Han Chinese is already far lower than their proportion in the population. The low enrolment of Tibetans on science courses can be attributed, at least in part, to the particular difficulty of learning science subjects through a second language in secondary school. Indeed, throughout China, non-Han Chinese nationalities are enrolled predominantly in humanities rather than sciences.

Implementation of Chinese government policy

QUOTA SYSTEM In setting out the criteria by which the quota of students from 'minority' regions should be selected for Central Chinese universities, the 'Rules on the Enrolment of Students in Ordinary Schools of Higher Learning', promulgated in 1984, state: 'The grade requirement for minority candidates coming from the frontiers, mountainous and pastoral regions where "minority" nationalities live in compact communities can be lowered in accordance with local conditions and those who are outstanding will be selected.'[58]

In the TAR, there are several problems in the way the quota system operates. First, despite the wording of the regulation, the quota is not restricted to students of 'minority' nationality; it is in fact open to Han Chinese residents of the TAR. Indeed, in publishing the number of successful students each year, TAR newspapers give a breakdown of the number of Tibetans, Han Chinese and other nationalities.[59] If the system is open to Han Chinese students, the criterion of selecting 'those

---

Box 9.3 An urban secondary school in the TAR: students from Central China enrol unofficially in the final year

There are two streams at my school. One stream is for ordinary Tibetans, the other stream is called the 'Chinese section', but actually many of the students are Tibetan. They are the sons and daughters of officials, both Chinese and Tibetan, and there are also some children of mixed marriages.

In the 6th grade, when the students in the Chinese section have to take their final examination, a lot of Chinese students from mainland China join the class and take part in the same exam. This is because the level of education at Chinese schools in Central China is much higher than at the Chinese schools in the TAR. These students from outside pretend that they live in the TAR, that their parents work there and in this way they can occupy the places which are meant for 'minority' nationalities or for Chinese living in the TAR. Since their educational background is much stronger because they have been to better schools, they can really come up among the other students and pass the final examinations very well. With good exam results they get much better opportunities in China than if they had had mediocre results at their own school. With good exam results they might get a job in a city or big town, with poor results they might get a job in the countryside. That's why they try to get a high percentage by taking their exam in the TAR.

But they take the places of the Tibetan students who cannot compete with them when they apply for places at universities. Some of these Chinese have relatives in Tibet and organize it through them. In some ways the school wants these students because they give the school a good name because they get very high marks.

We all talk about this, but there's nothing we can do. Teachers, parents and students have complained about it and sent letters to the Chinese People's Political Consultative Conference. We also wrote to the Regional People's Congress. But it has had no effect.

Source: *Interview with secondary school teacher, 1995.*

---

who are outstanding' in the local region will inevitably favour Han Chinese students, due to the obstacles faced by Tibetans in secondary schools as described above. Furthermore, it appears that the system has been increasingly open to corruption; there have been complaints in recent years that Han Chinese students from Central China who do not

Table 9.7 Pass Mark Set by Tibet University in university entrance examination

| | Han Chinese | | 'Minority' nationalities | |
	Humanities	Sciences	Humanities	Sciences
1985	–	–	210	170
1992	350	350	240	230
1997	330	310	300	280

Sources: 1985: Zhou Runnian,'My Humble Opinions on Developing Minority Education in Tibet', *Nationality Studies*, No. 5, 1988, cited in Yenming Zhang, *Effects of Policy Changes*, p. 239; 1992: Report by the Tibet University Students Examination Office, 5 October 1992; 1997: Tibet TV, 25 July 1997. The figures presented in this report are projected figures, which might fluctuate according to the general quality of the applicants. The report also announced the pass mark for the one-year foundation course which is open only to 'minority' nationalities (humanities: 280; science: 230).

achieve high enough marks from their secondary schools to enrol in universities have their resident permits transferred to the TAR through 'back-door' connections, and then apply to those same universities, taking advantage of the quota system and of the lower standards required of applicants from the TAR. In July 1993, according to a report by the Lhasa City CPPCC, '2000 Chinese students came to Lhasa, and by dubious means took the university entrance exams'.[60]

Furthermore, Han Chinese students resident in the TAR who, even with the advantage of the quota system, do not have the ability to enrol in Central Chinese universities can apply to higher education institutions in the TAR where the pass mark is significantly lower. In 1992, the pass mark for Chinese students applying to Tibet University was 350;[61] in Central China, by 1985, admissions scores were already around 400.[62] Table 9.7 presents the pass mark set by Tibet University over several years between 1985 and 1997. The table demonstrates that while the pass mark for 'minority' nationalities has risen since 1985, the pass mark for Han Chinese students has dropped. This suggests perhaps that Tibetans' fears about increasing numbers of Han Chinese students taking the place of Tibetans in higher education are not unfounded.

The quota system, with the lowering of the pass mark for certain categories of student, has become somewhat controversial for other reasons as well. For example, the enrolment of significant numbers of students on higher education courses with lower marks than the stand-

---

Box 9.4 Practical problems with the quota system at Tibet
University: the experience of an English teacher, 1988

*In the second year class there were 15 students who were all Tibetan.
They fell into two categories. (1) About ten seem to come from small
villages and have received a poor quality basic education – even in
Tibetan their skills are basic (and Chinese). They are not, to be blunt,
at an educational standard required by a university – through no fault
of their own, for them Lhasa is the big city and they are easily
distracted from work, and lured into tea-houses! This was the group
known as the 'slow class' – they were my responsibility and had six
hours' alternate tuition at a lower level. They were a delight to teach
but forever hopeless, I'd say, at least in English. Many wanted to change
their subject but were not allowed to. Other English teachers said they
were stupid because they were Tibetan. One referred to the Tibetan
practice of inter-marriage within families which then produced 'stupid
children' … We asked ourselves why the students were humiliated in
this way and they were not allowed to change their subject. The answer
seemed to be 'quota', according to a Chinese teacher … These boys are
expected to graduate next year and teach English themselves in a middle
school – the idea terrifies them so much that one or two I got to know
a little indicated that the future they see before them makes their life
now unendurable. (2) The rest of the second year were somewhat
better suited to their pre-determined fates. Many enjoyed English and
made excellent progress.*

Source: *Julie Brittain, 'Experience of an English Teacher at Lhasa
University', Tibetan Review, April 1988.*

---

ard is seen by some to be a sacrifice of quality to quantity. Even in the
TAR, there are those who are against the system, suggesting that it
lowers the standard of Tibet's universities.[63] Administered properly,
there is no doubt that it could increase the number of professionals
among 'minority' nationalities in the short term, although it does have
a number of drawbacks. It certainly causes practical problems for
teachers attempting to teach classes of mixed ability; at the same time
it perpetuates a situation where those who have enrolled through the
quota system are considered less intelligent, as the example provided in
Box 9.4 demonstrates.

LANGUAGE AND CONTENT OF UNIVERSITY ENTRANCE EXAMINA-
TION Although the 1984 regulations allowed autonomous regions to
set their own university entrance examination in the local language, in
the TAR all papers apart from the Tibetan-language paper are in fact
set in Chinese.[64] It appears, furthermore, that the TAR government
does not set its own examination but uses the unified entrance examination and simply sets a lower pass mark.[65]

*The changing political climate and its effects on 'minority' nationality
enrolment* When Hu Yaobang came to the TAR in 1980, he promised
the repatriation of Han Chinese and the training of Tibetans to take
over from them the economic development of the region.[66] However,
by the Second Forum in 1984, it became clear that the economy was
not developing as rapidly as planned; a lack of adequately qualified
personnel was partly blamed for this. From that time, the policy of
repatriating Han Chinese was replaced by the active encouragement of
Han Chinese to go to the TAR to take part in economic development.
According to official sources, 60,000 official Han Chinese workers
entered the TAR in the first three months of 1985, many of whom
stayed on in the region after the completion of their projects.[67] In
addition, according to incomplete statistics, from the summer of 1984
to the beginning of 1985, at least 10,000 entrepreneurs entered the
TAR.[68] Many of the Han Chinese from both groups came with their
children who had to be accommodated in schools and universities in
the TAR. In his 1985 Work Report, Wu Jinghua announced an ambitious
plan to boost Tibet's economy, aiming to raise per capita income to
1,200 yuan by the year 2000 and to create a skilled labour force in the
region. Wu Jinghua still made a commitment to the specific training of
Tibetans, announcing that the TAR would train 15,000 professional and
technical personnel to enable the region to dispense with the need to
import large numbers of skilled personnel from China.[69] This priority
given to the training of Tibetans in the TAR in the early to mid-1980s
is now associated with the liberal leadership both in the TAR, under
Wu Jinghua, and in the Chinese government with leaders such as Hu
Yaobang, and in the policies which gave more autonomy in education
planning to autonomous regions.

In the 1990s, statements about the importance of training Tibetans
to take over from Han Chinese skilled personnel are no longer evident
in government documents and broadcasts. Emphasis is given to the
need for higher education institutions in the TAR to make greater efforts
to adjust to the needs of the economy and 'to accelerate the training
of qualified, suitable personnel'.[70] It appears that, in practice, the rapid

development of the economy has taken precedence over policies of positive discrimination in favour of higher education for Tibetans. Indeed, in the political climate of the 1990s, there appears to have been renewed emphasis on the pre-reform goals of primarily providing ideological education for non-Han Chinese nationalities. In this context Chen Kuiyuan's speech of October 1994, which was quoted above, is particularly relevant:

> The success of our education does not lie in the number of diplomas issued to graduates from universities, colleges, polytechnic schools, and secondary schools. It lies, in the final analysis, in whether our graduating students are opposed to or turn their hearts to the Dalai clique and in whether they are loyal to or do not care about our great motherland and the great socialist cause.[71]

Plans for education in the TAR to the end of the century outline continued growth for tertiary education; indeed, they indicate a higher growth in enrolment than the national average. The TAR Ninth Five-Year Plan indicates a 70 per cent increase in tertiary enrolment by the year 2000 (compared with 74 per cent growth in primary and secondary).[72] This represents an average annual growth of 11.7 per cent, compared with the national annual average of 3.8 per cent.[73] However, despite the fact that the media still describe the high-level training of Tibetans (although no longer in the context of replacing Han Chinese personnel),[74] there is nothing in government planning documents or in the media to indicate that the problem of declining enrolment of Tibetans and other non-Han Chinese nationalities in the TAR is being addressed either currently or in future enrolment strategy.

Summary

After the end of the Cultural Revolution, higher education became one of the main priorities in education, even in non-Han Chinese nationality areas where education levels are generally low. In the TAR, between 1979 and 1990, tertiary enrolment increased by 37 per cent (although the number of students is still small), secondary enrolment by 2 per cent while primary enrolment declined by 37 per cent.[75] By the beginning of the 1990s, voices began to be raised about the funding of tertiary education at the expense of primary and secondary education, the consequence of which was said to be a decline in the quality of students and also a decline in the proportion of Tibetans and other non-Han Chinese students in enrolment.

By the 1990s, it was declared that higher education had been over-expanded throughout China. New directives issued by the Chinese government were aimed at rationalizing courses, closing small comprehensive universities in favour of technical universities, and making universities themselves play a greater role in raising revenue. In 1997, a full fee-paying system was introduced (although certain categories of university were exempt from having to charge fees). The system allowed for poor students to receive grants; some other students were to be funded by industries. Universities were expected to raise further funds by making contracts with relevant industries to undertake research. In the TAR, the introduction of market forces into higher education led to a situation where institutions (which had few research departments and were therefore poorly equipped to make contracts with industries or to encourage them to sponsor students) were forced to expand enrolment with diminishing funds.

The reintroduction of the standardized national university entrance examination in China in 1978 led to a sudden decline in the enrolment of non-Han Chinese nationalities. By the early 1980s, a number of policies had been drawn up in an attempt to reverse the decline. For the first time since the communist government came to power, nationality institutions were allowed to give equal weight to political and professional training. The new policies gave preferential treatment to non-Han Chinese nationalities in higher education, and granted the autonomous regions the right to establish a separate education system with their own examinations. The aim of these policies was to increase the enrolment of non-Han Chinese students in proportion to their percentage in the population. In the TAR, the new commitment to the enrolment of Tibetan and other non-Han Chinese nationalities (a target of 60 per cent was set initially) included raising the enrolment age to twenty-eight, and allowing Tibetans living outside the TAR to enrol in universities in the region.

The percentage of Tibetan students and other non-Han Chinese nationalities in the total tertiary enrolment rose by 9 per cent between 1983 and 1993. However, by 1994, it had declined by 8 per cent to around 50 per cent, while the proportion of Tibetans and other non-Han Chinese nationalities in the population of the TAR remained at 97 per cent. Several reasons can be suggested for the failure to implement these preferential policies successfully: (1) the quota, set for the enrolment of students from the TAR to universities in Central China, was open to residents of the TAR, not only to non-Han nationalities. As a result, Han Chinese students began to predominate, their numbers increasing as students from other parts of China found a way of enrolling in the final year of secondary school in the TAR; (2) Tibetan students in the TAR have to sit the unified national university entrance examination in Chinese (despite central government recommendations for autonomous regions) even to enter universities in the TAR; (3) most Tibetan students drop out of school before secondary level.

Since the beginning of the 1990s, the implementation of preferential policies for non-Han nationalities in the TAR has further been affected by the re-emergence of 'leftism' in politics. Increasingly, this has involved a rejection of cultural distinctiveness in the education system, renewed emphasis on the importance of ideological education over professional education for Tibetans, and an apparent rejection of the policy of training Tibetans to take over from Chinese professionals in the TAR.[76]

Official statistics and basic facts

Table 9.8 Types of higher education institution: terminology in Tibetan, Chinese and English

English	Tibetan	Chinese
Higher education institute	*Tho-rim lob-ling*	*Gaodeng xuexiao*
Specialized higher education institute	*Che-nyer tho-rim lobdra*	*Gaodeng zhuanke xuexiao*

Table 9.9 Proportion of Tibetans and other non-Han Chinese nationalities in higher education in the TAR

Year	1984	1993	1994
Percentage	48.6	57.8	49.6

Sources: 1984: Yenming Zhang, *Effects of Policy Changes*, p. 217; 1993: *China's Ethnic Statistical Yearbook*, 1995; 1994: 1995 TAR Statistical Yearbook.

Table 9.10 Number of institutes of higher education, students and teachers in the TAR

Institutes	Students				Teachers			
	Total		Tibetans etc.		Total		Tibetans etc.	
		Women		Women		Women		Women
4	3,280	1,215	1,628	699	777	246	373	102

Source: 1995 TAR Statistical Yearbook.

Box 9.5 Institutes of higher education in the TAR

Tibet University *acquired university status in 1985. It had been founded a decade earlier at the instigation of the late Panchen Lama as the TAR Teachers College.* Tibet University is now a comprehensive higher education institution offering seventeen specialities in seven academic departments covering the humanities and sciences. The departments are: Chinese & English Department, Tibetan Department, Politics & History Department, Art & Music Department, Mathematics Department, Chemistry, Biology & Geography Department, and the Economic Management Department.*

The TAR School of Tibetan Medicine *began as part of Tibet University. In 1989 it acquired its own site in Lhasa as a senior secondary-level institution, providing training in Tibetan medicine. In 1993 it was upgraded to university level. Prior to this the* TAR Healthcare School *had provided tertiary-level Western medical training between 1976 and 1982. The* TAR Healthcare School *was established in Kongpo (Linzhi) Prefecture, 300 miles south-east of Lhasa. It was upgraded from a secondary-level school in 1976. In 1982 it moved to Lhasa and returned to providing secondary-level education. However, in 1995 it re-established two university-level classes and was planning further expansion of its tertiary programme.*

The TAR Agriculture & Animal Husbandry School *is also situated in Kongpo Prefecture. It was originally founded as a branch campus of* Tibet Nationalities Institute, *and became an independent higher education institution in 1978. It offers five specialities in four departments. These are: Animal Husbandry & Veterinary Science Department, Hydroelectricity Department, Agronomy Department, Forestry Department.*

The Tibet Nationalities Institute *is in Xianyang, Shaanxi province, although it is under the jurisdiction of the TAR Education Commission. It is a comprehensive university and was founded in 1965, having been established as a secondary-level institution in 1957. It has eight departments including Chinese, Economics, History, Medicine, Physical Education, Politics. It also has one research institute.*

Yang Xin and Duo Fen, 'Random Notes from Tibet University', Beijing Review, Vol. 31, No. 47, 21–27 November 1988.

Table 9.11 Number of students and teachers in institutes of higher education in the TAR

Institutes	Students		Teachers	
	Total	Tibetans etc.	Total	Tibetans etc.
Tibet University	1,226	1,018	322	241
TAR Institute of Tibetan Medicine	259	199	54	54
Tar Institute of Agriculture and Animal Husbandry	630	184	169	60
TAR Nationalities Institute	1,165	227	232	18

Source: 1995 TAR Statistical Yearbook.

Notes

1. Figures calculated from 1995 China Statistical Yearbook.

2. 1995 TAR Statistical Yearbook and 1989 TAR Statistical Yearbook. Note: the figures for secondary and tertiary enrolment do not include Tibetan students educated in China.

3. State Education Commission of the PRC, 'Ninth Five-Year Plan for Educational Development Toward the Year 2010' [sic], Beijing (China Ninth Five-Year Plan for Education, 1996).

4. Percentages calculated from 1995 TAR Statistical Yearbook.

5. See Chen Kuiyan, 'Speech on Education in Tibet', Fifth Regional Meeting on Education in the TAR, 26 October 1994, *Xizang Ribao* (Tibet Daily), 28 October 1994; 'Chen Kuiyan in Chamdo Says Prosperity Will Drive Out Religion', Tibet People's Broadcasting Station, Lhasa, 28 November 1994 [SWB 5/12/94]; Chen Kuiyan, 'Speech on Literature and Art', *Xizang Ribao* (Tibet Daily), 11 July 1997; see also Yang Wanli, '*Xizang Kecheng Jiaocai Yanjiu De Teshuxing Jiqi Duice*' (The Countermeasure and Particularity of Research on Teaching Materials), *Yizang Yanjiu* (Tibet Studies), Vol. 58, No. 1, 1996.

6. Teng Xing, '*Wo Guo Shaoshu Minzu Diqu Jiaoyu Zhengti Gaige Guanjian*' (The Essence of Overall Educational Reform in China's Minority Regions), *Qiu Shi*, No. 7, April 1989, pp. 19–24.

7. See Israel Epstein, *Tibet Transformed* (New World Press, Beijing, 1983), p. 359; also 'Fully Affirm Xinjiang's Great Achievements', 17 October 1990 [FBIS-CHI-90-201]; Teng Xing, op. cit., pp. 19–24.

8. Li Peng, 'Speech on 20th Anniversary of the Founding of the TAR', *Xinhua*, 31 August 1985 [SWB 4/9/85].

9. Yenming Zhang, *Effects of Policy Changes on College Enrolment of Minority Students in China, 1949–1989*, Doctoral Thesis (Harvard University, 1991), p. 249.

10. For a survey, see e.g. T. Paul Schultz, 'Education Investments and Returns', in H. Chenery and T. N. Srinivasan (eds), *Handbook of Development Economics* (Elsevier Science Publishers, Amsterdam, 1988), pp. 543–630.

11. See internal Party discussion paper, 1995; see also Lei Yongsheng on the importance of primary education: Lei Yongsheng, '*Xiandaihua Jiaoyu Fazhan Yu Xizang Jiaoyu Gaige*' (The Development of Modern Education and the Reform of Tibetan Education), *Xizang Yanjui* (Tibet Studies), Vol. 58, No. 1, 1996; see Gyaltsen Norbu on the seriousness of the 'brain drain' in the TAR: Gyaltsen Norbu, 'Tibet: Development Plans to Overcome Natural Enclosed Economy', interview in *Qiu Shi*, Beijing, 11 August 1994 [SWB 15/8/94].

12. Teng Xing, 'The Essence of Overal Educational Reform', pp. 19–24.

13. Epstein, *Tibet Transformed*, p. 359; Yang Jingren, '*Jianjue Guanche Zhongyang Zhishi Zuo Hao Xizang Gongzuo*' (On the Correct Implementation of the Central Committee's Directive and Carrying Out Work for Tibet Well), *Honqui* (Red Flag), No. 15, 1980.

14. Epstein, op. cit., p. 359. See also Jiang Weizhu, '*Shi Lun "San Bao" Jiaoyu Zhengce De Li Yu Bi Ji Qi Zhengce Duice*' (Advantages and Disadvantages and Reform Measures of the 'Three Guarantees' Education Policy), *Xizang Yanjiu* (Tibet Studies), Vol. 58, No. 1, 1996; and Duojie Caidan (Dorje Tseten), *Xizang Jiaoyu* (Education in Tibet) (China Tibetology Publishers, Beijing, 1991); Yang Jingren, op. cit.

15. Yang Chunjing, '*Qiandan Zang Yuwen Jiaoxue Zai Fazhan Minzu Jiaoyu Zhong de Zhongyao Xing*' (A Tentative Study on the Importance of Teaching in the Tibetan Language for Developing National Education), *Xizang Yanjiu* (Tibet Studies), Vol. 59, No. 2, 1996.

16. Yenming Zhang, *Effects of Policy Changes on College Enrolment of Minority Students in China, 1949–1989*, Doctoral Thesis (Harvard University, 1991), p. 251.

17. Television debate on education, Lhasa TV, 30 July 1988.

18. Wang Bing, Report of Fourth Meeting of the Sixth Executive Committee of TAR, CPPCC, 11 May 1996, Issue 9, edited by the Assembly Secretariat Office.

19. Jean Robinson, 'Stumbling on Two Legs: Education and Reform in China', *Comparative Education Review*, Vol. 35, No. 1, February 1991, p. 183.

20. Zhu Kaixuan, Education Minister, 'Report to Fourth Session of Eighth National People's Congress Standing Committee on Educational Work', *Xinhua*, 28 October 1993 [SWB 10/11/93].

21. Xu Hong, 'An Interview with Vice-Premier Li Lanqing: Vocational Education Can Invigorate the Country', *Tzu Ching* (Hong Kong), No. 10, 5 October 1994 [SWB 14/11/94].

22. Dalu Yin, 'Reforming Chinese Education: Context, Structure and Attitudes in the 1980s', *Compare*, Vol. 23, No. 2, 1993, p. 121.

23. D. G. Yang, *Higher Education Development Strategy* (Shanghai, Fudan University Press, 1987), cited in Dalu Yin, op. cit.

24. According to a report by Lhasa Radio, in the TAR, in 1994, 113 research projects were undertaken in the fields of agriculture, biology and mineral resources; 64 of them received awards from the TAR government. However, it is not clear whether they had direct industrial application or funding. See 'Looking Back at 1994 and Looking Forward to 1995: Raising High the Banner of Development', Lhasa Radio, 19 January 1995 [FBIS 27/1/95].

25. TAR CPPCC, 'Report of Second Committee Meeting of the Sixth Session of TAR CPPCC', CPPCC News Bulletin, 18 May 1994.

26. TAR CPPCC, 'Summary Report of the Fourth Plenary Session of the Sixth TAR CPPCC', compiled by the Secretariat of the Conference, 15 May 1996.

27. China Ninth Five-Year Plan for Education, 1996.

28. *Xinhua*, 23 January 1996 [SWB 24/1/96].

29. State Education Commission, 'Report on Decision on Higher Education Fees', March 1996, *Xinhua*, 31 March 1996 [SWB 1/4/96].

30. Ibid.

31. China Ninth Five-Year Plan for Education, 1996.

32. Gyaltsen Norbu, 'Education in Tibet', Speech to the Fifth Regional Meeting on Education in the TAR on 26 October 1994, *Xizang Ribao* (Tibet Daily), 30 October 1994, pp. 1–4.

33. Yenming Zhang, *Effects of Policy Changes*, p. 162.

34. 1995 China Statistical Yearbook, Table 18-5; 1995 TAR Statistical Yearbook.

35. Melvyn Goldstein, William Siebenschuh and Tashi Tsering, *The Struggle for Modern Tibet, The Autobiography of Tashi Tsering* (M. E. Sharpe, New York, 1997), p. 188.

36. *Introduction to Tibet Institute of Nationalities*, 1989, cited in Yenming Zhang, *Effects of Policy Changes*, p. 138.

37. Robert Barendsen, 'The 1978 College Entrance Examination in the PCR' (US Dept of Health, Education and Welfare, 1979), cited in Yenming Zhang, *Effects of Policy Changes*, p. 162.

38. Zhang Boping, 'Steadily Develop Minority Education in the Period of Readjustment', *Red Flag*, 16 June 1981.

39. Ibid.; Wei Shiyuan and Zhou Guanda, 'The Development of Educational Progress in Mountainous Regions to Enhance the Culture and Knowledge of "Minority" Nationalities', *Bulletin of Studies in Minority Nationality Theory*, No. 3, 25 August 1984; and 'Opinions on Minority Education, Ministry of Education and the State Nationality Affairs Commission, October 9th 1980', *Almanac of Chinese Education, 1949–1981*, cited in Yenming Zhang, *Effects of Policy Changes*, p. 201.

40. Zhang Ru, 'The Starting Point of Nationality Work', *Unity of Nationalities*, No. 1, 1979, cited in Yenming Zhang, op. cit., p. 173.

41. Ibid., p. 168.

42. See Yang Jingren, 'Tasks of Nationality Work in the New Socialist Period', 1979, cited in Yenming Zhang, op. cit., p. 173.

43. Zhao Sheng, 'Regulations of College Enrolment in 1980 Concerning Minority Candidates', *Unity of Nationalities*, No. 6, 1980, cited in Yenming Zhang, op. cit., p. 178.

44. 'Rules on the Enrolments of Students in Ordinary Schools of Higher Learning', *State Council Bulletin*, No. 7, 30 April 1984, cited in Yenming Zhang, op. cit., p. 211.

45. Ibid.

46. Ibid., p. 198.

47. Ibid., p. 233.

48. Ibid., p. 217; 1995 TAR Statistical Yearbook; Economic Department of State Ethnic Affairs Commission and Department of Integrated Statistics of State Statistical Bureau of PRC (eds), *China's Ethnic Statistical Yearbook* (1995).

49. Interview with Gonkar Gyatso, teacher at Tibet University 1985–92, 2 February 1997.

50. Ibid.

51. *Chinas's Ethnic Statistical Yearbook* (1995). (Figures for the TAR presented in this publication are said to be for 1994; however, comparing them with more comprehensive statistics provided in the 1995 TAR Statistical Yearbook suggests that they are actually for 1993.)

52. The total possible score in humanities was 500 and in sciences 600.

53. See Jill and Charles Hadfield (British Council teachers at Tibet University 1986–87), 'Talk on Tibet for Great Britain–China Association', January 1988; see also Jane Peek (VSO teacher, Tibet University 1987–88), 'Discrimination in Education in Lhasa', unpublished paper, June 1989; Catriona Bass, *Inside the Treasure House*, p. 79.

54. Julie Brittain, 'Experience of an English Teacher at Lhasa University', *Tibetan Review*, April 1988.

55. See 'Chen Kuiyuan in Chamdo'.

56. See Chen Kuiyuan, 'Speech on Education in Tibet'.

57. Report of 'TAR Regional Conference on Student Enrolment', Lhasa Radio, 28 May 1984 [SWB 4/6/84].

58. 'Rules on the Enrolment of Students in Ordinary Schools of Higher Learning', *State Council Bulletin*, No. 7, 30 April 1984.

59. Interview with Gongkar Gyatso, teacher at Tibet University, 1985–92, 2 February 1997.

60. See Lhasa City CPPCC, Bulletin No. 2, 'Problems About Which People Have Serious Complaints', July 1993; see also Peek, 'Discrimination'.

61. Report by the Tibet University Students Examination Office, 5 October 1992.

62. Zhou Runnian, 'My Humble Opinions on Developing Minority Education in Tibet', *Nationality Studies*, No. 5, 1988, cited in Yenming Zhang, *Effects of Policy Changes*, p. 239.

63. Wang Bing, 'Report of Fourth Meeting of the Sixth Executive Committee of TAR, CCCP'; see also Ye Zhaoyang, 'Colleges Enrolling Students Throughout the Country Should Set a Unified Test Score Requirement and Practise Unified Admissions', *Higher Education Front*, No. 10, 1984, pp. 13–14.

64. Interview with Gongkar Gyatso, teacher at Tibet University, 1985–92, 2 February 1997; see also Goldstein et al., *The Struggle for Modern Tibet*, p. 188.

65. See Zhou Runnian, 'My Humble Opinions'; see also Goldstein et al., op. cit. p. 188.

66. Hu Yaobang, 'Report to TAR Regional Party Committee Cadres', Lhasa

Radio, 1430 gmt, 30 May 1980 [SWB 4/6/80]; see also Wang Yao, 'Hu Yaobang's Visit to Tibet, May 22–23 1980', in R. Barnett and S. Akner (eds), *Resistance and Reform in Tibet* (Hurst & Co., London, 1994).

67. 'Zhongguo Renkou, Xizang Fince' (p. 153), cited in Tseten Wangchuk Sharlho, 'China's Reforms in Tibet: Issues and Dilemmas', *Journal of Contemporary China*, Vol. 1, No. 1, 1992, p. 50.

68. Ibid.

69. Party Secretary Wu Jinghua, TAR Regional Government Work Report, 1985.

70. Gyaltsen Norbu, 'Education in Tibet'.

71. See Chen Kuiyuan, 'Speech on Education in Tibet'.

72. Figures calculated from 1995 TAR Statistical Yearbook; 'Outline of the TAR's Five-Year Plan for Economic and Social Development and Its Long-term Target for 2010, Approved by the Fourth Session of the Sixth Regional People's congress on 24th May 1996', *Xizang Ribao* (Tibet Daily), 7 June 1996 (Tar Ninth Five-Year Plan).

73. TAR Ninth Five-Year Plan, 1996, pp. 1–4.

74. See *Beijing Review*, 28 July–3 August 1997, p. 20.

75. 1995 TAR Statistical Yearbook and 1989 TAR Statistical Yearbook. Note: the figures for secondary and tertiary enrolment do not include Tibetan students educated in China.

76. See Chen Kuiyuan, 'Speech on Education in Tibet'; 'Chen Kuiyuan in Chamdo'; Chen Kuiyuan, 'Speech on Literature and Art'; see also Yang Wanli, 'The Countermeasure and Particularity of Research on Teaching Materials'.

CHAPTER 10

Pre-school Education, Education for Girls, and Special Needs Education

Pre-school education

Pre-school education is only just beginning in the TAR. At present it is confined to urban areas, and caters mainly to the children of Han Chinese residents. In 1993, according to official statistics, there were 2,365 children in pre-school education in the TAR, 1,420 (60 per cent) of whom were Han Chinese children.[1]

Kindergartens exist only in the cities of Lhasa and Shigatse. The pre-school curriculum in these kindergartens focuses on play, art and singing. Children may also begin reading, writing and counting. Most schools outside Lhasa have no provision for pre-school education, although a few run a pre-school class where the children begin the grade 1 primary school curriculum.[2]

In 1995, the TAR Regional Kindergarten in Lhasa charged pupils 600 yuan for five months, including milk and lunch each day. The Lhasa City Kindergarten charged similar fees. Kindergartens run by state work-units for their staff charged considerably less: 200 yuan and below for the same period.[3]

Lhasa Teacher Training School runs a four-year pre-school teacher training course. The course includes teaching reading, writing, handicraft, general knowledge and outdoor activities. In 1996, the TAR Regional Kindergarten ran a twenty-day pre-school teacher training course which was attended by teachers from the Lhasa Municipality, including ten teachers from Medrogongkar and Daktse counties. The course focused on teaching games, songs, art and handicraft, using locally available materials such as stones, leaves and earth. A longer course was planned for 1997.[4]

Targets set in 1996 for pre-school education for the end of the year included a 35 per cent enrolment rate in urban areas and a 10 per cent enrolment rate in rural areas. The 'TAR Child Development Programme for the 1990s' states that the enrolment rate is to increase to

50 per cent in urban areas and 20 per cent in rural areas by the end of the century. Work-units, businesses and collectives are to be encouraged to set up kindergartens.[5] The TAR's Ninth Five-Year Plan and long-term target to the year 2010 include plans for universal pre-school education in cities, and for the provision of 'one or two kindergartens in each county', and also plans to increase the number of children attending kindergartens to over 25,000 by the year 2010.[6]

Education for girls

There is little information available on the extent of access to education for girls in the TAR. Table 10.1 gives an indication of the percentage of girls in enrolment in 1990. At university and in general secondary education the percentage of girls in the total enrolment in the TAR is in fact higher than the national average. Nevertheless, there are reports that girls are more likely to drop-out from primary schools than boys, as girls are seen as more useful in carrying out domestic work.[7] Furthermore, illiteracy among women is significantly higher than among men. In 1990, 84.2 per cent of Tibet women in the TAR were illiterate or semi-illiterate compared with 73.3 per cent of Tibetans in general.

In 1996, according to a government report, the TAR Women's Federation set up a 30 million yuan literacy campaign, involving 86,000 women in 876 literacy courses and vocational training courses. The funding was also reportedly being used to help female drop-outs get back into schools.[8]

Special needs education

The TAR is the only province or region in China which, as yet, does not provide a special school for handicapped children although, according to official statistics, the TAR has the highest proportion of handicapped people in China: 7.24 per cent of the population which amounts to 146,000 people.[9] There were plans to build a special school in Lhasa in the early 1990s but the assigned money ran out; similar plans were reiterated in the Ninth Five-Year Plan; the planned completion date is now said to be 1999.[10] According to official reports in 1997, 16.1 per cent of handicapped primary school children attend school (2,400 children) and forty-five handicapped secondary students were in school.[11] By September 1995 there were three workshops which provided training for handicapped people in Lhasa. They had a total of 55 participants who were selected from senior secondary school graduates

Table 10.1 Percentage of girls in educational enrolment, 1990

Enrolment	China	TAR
Total	45.1	41.4
University	32.6	37.2
Vocational university	39.9	34.0
Specialized senior secondary	47.9	41.7
General senior secondary	39.8	47.1
Junior secondary	42.9	44.2
Primary	46.2	40.8

Source: Tabulation on China's National Minorities (Data of 1990 Population Census), May 1994.

in Lhasa. The Lhasa City government runs a handicapped people's workshop employing about fifty people. In 1997, the Lhasa Cuiquan Welfare School was established; it combines some general education with training in making handicrafts and tourist souvenirs.[12]

Government documents highlight the importance of providing special education for disabled children. The 'Outline of the TAR Child Development Programme for the 1990s' stipulated: 'During the Eighth Five-Year Plan the relevant departments should be assisted in building a school for special needs. All prefectures, cities and counties with the appropriate conditions should provide ordinary classes or special needs classes for disabled children.'[13]

Notes

1. *China's Ethnic Statistical Yearbook*, 1995 (figures for the TAR presented in this publication are said to be for 1994; however, comparing them with more comprehensive statistics provided in the 1995 TAR Statistical Yearbook suggests that they are actually for 1993).

2. Paper on Education Development among Tibetans, by Tibetan scholar in China, 1995.

3. Ibid.

4. Save the Children Fund (UK), Education Project Information Sheet, November 1996.

5. 'Outline of the TAR Child Development Programme for the 1990s', *Xizang Ribao* (Tibet Daily), 11 July 1996, p. 2.

6. 'Outline of the TAR's Five-Year Plan for Economic Development and Its Long-term Target for 2010, Approved by the Fourth Session of the Sixth Regional People's Congress on 24 May 1996', *Xizang Ribao* (Tibet Daily), 7 June 1996.

7. Save the Children Fund (UK), Education Project Information Sheet, November 1996.

8. *Xinhua*, 28 February 1997 [SWB 10/3/97].

9. Wu Yi, 'Undertakings for the Disabled in Tibet', *China's Tibet*, No. 5, 1997, p. 12; 1995 China Statistical Yearbook.

10. Interview with educationalist, 2 February 1997.

11. Wu Yi, 'Undertakings for the Disabled in Tibet', p. 12.

12. Ibid.

13. 'Outline of the TAR Child Development Programme for the 1990s', *Xizang Ribao* (Tibet Daily), 11 July 1996, p. 2.

CHAPTER II

Teachers and Teaching

'Both Tibetans and Chinese say that they would rather take a letter to the ends of the earth than become a teacher.' (Television debate on education, Lhasa TV, 30 July 1988)

The teaching profession, traditionally esteemed since Confucian times, has lost popularity and people's respect in the last few decades. The result of this is that, today, just when the Chinese leadership is urging the development of education for socialist modernization, people are flooding out of the teaching profession, and those who are joining, for the most part, join reluctantly. The low status that teachers have today is due to a combination of financial and political factors. This chapter begins with an exploration of those factors and continues with an assessment of the extent to which they are responsible for a decline in teaching quality in recent years. The chapter ends with a description of the process of teacher training and the measures taken by the TAR government to improve it.

Teachers and the Communist Party

The anti-intellectual movements of the late 1950s and the Cultural Revolution hit teachers particularly badly. Unlike technical and scientific professionals, who were vital for economic production and thus were protected from the worst excesses of the Cultural Revolution, teachers were considered irrelevant to the economy and therefore they could be attacked with impunity. During the Cultural Revolution, they were said to form the 'stinking ninth category'. The post-Cultural Revolution leadership has given considerable publicity to rehabilitating teachers. In 1978, Deng Xiaoping told the National Conference on Education that 'we must raise the political and social status of teachers. They should command the respect not only of their students but also of the whole community.'[1] Since then, the Communist Party has tried to re-establish the value and importance of teachers in society, but it has not been entirely successful.

In the TAR, the Party's relationship with the teaching profession is particularly ambivalent, especially since the resurgence of nationalist resistance in 1987. On the one hand, teachers are vitally important for the training of personnel for socialist modernization; they are also the means whereby the 'correct' ideology is transmitted to the younger generation. On the other hand, as intellectuals who have a chequered relationship with the Party, they are not entirely trusted. Furthermore, their position of influence over young people makes them especially vulnerable.

In the current political climate in the TAR, teachers come under particular scrutiny. They have been accused of allowing 'splittism' (the official term used to describe the pro-independence movement) to enter the classrooms. Since, in recent years, even the issue of Tibetan medium education and the cultural relevance of the curriculum have been linked to Tibetan nationalism by the Communist Party, teachers find themselves in a particularly difficult position.[2] In the televised education debate on Lhasa TV in 1988, mentioned above, one of the participants complained that 'when we speak about Tibetan education, about using the Tibetan language, we are accused of wanting to separate the motherland'.[3] In November 1994, at the Fifth TAR Conference on Education in Tibet, Chen Kuiyuan, the General Secretary of the TAR Communist Party, told delegates:

> The Dalai clique is desperately competing with us to win over the youths – the people of the next generation. Splittist elements try to infiltrate the educational circle by using narrow nationalism and religion … In a few units, some teaching staff have not changed their attitude but publicly impart splittist ideology among students … As a place for cultivating people, schools are not a forum on 'freedom'. Schools should be captured by socialism. We should not allow splittist elements and religious idealism to use the classrooms to poison people's sons and daughters.[4]

Between 1983 and 1995, there have been twenty-one known arrests of teachers. Most of these appear not to be connected with their work as teachers, although one teacher, a twenty-six-year-old woman from the Lhasa Cement Factory Primary School named Dawa Dolma, was given a three-year prison sentence for 'writing reactionary songs on the blackboard and teaching them to her students'.[5]

The economic status of teachers

Teachers' salaries are both relatively and absolutely low. In 1994, the average teacher's salary in China was comparable with the GNP per capita. In low-income countries as a whole, primary teachers' salaries have a median value 6.1 times GNP per capita and the mean is 4.9 times.[6]

Until the economic reforms of the 1980s, teachers' economic position, although low, was relatively secure. This was particularly true of rural community school teachers whose salaries were paid by the local production brigade. But the market economy has brought a growing divide in people's income and, in urban areas, teachers have found themselves earning less than the average worker.[7] In rural areas, as has already been mentioned, the break-up of the communes meant that in some places salaries for teachers disappeared altogether.

In the new Chinese culture where income determines status in society, teachers have found themselves slipping further down the social ladder. The effect on schools has been dramatic. By the late 1980s, Party officials and educators began issuing warnings to government administrators at every level instructing them to improve conditions for teachers:

> When we look at the field of education it is true that there have been many improvements. However, if we look at it in terms of the attitudes of high and low government officials, there is a lack of serious commitment in education. If you look at lower schools there is a shortage of qualified teachers, for example in one class there are sixty or seventy students. In such a situation how can we improve the quality of the students? Likewise the status of the teachers is very low. If you think about it, the role of a teacher is very important. A teacher has to work for many years. The work of a teacher is unending. If you look at schools in towns teachers are badly off: there is no canteen and their reward is small. These points were also raised at the Fifth Congress of the TAR. Economic improvement and everything else is dependent on education. In every direction we must pay special attention to educational needs …
>
> Even though we cannot improve everything in education, it is urgent that we should raise the status of teachers.[8]

Furthermore, not only are teachers' salaries low in general, but community school teachers' salaries are low in comparison with state school teachers' salaries. In some cases a community school teacher may get less than a third of the basic salary of a state school teacher, who will receive, in addition, free housing, bonuses and other incentives. Table 11.1 below illustrates the difference between the annual income of community and state primary school teachers in the Lhasa Municipality in 1994; it also shows how teachers' salaries compare with the average income in the TAR as a whole. For community teachers, their salary is their only income, although they may in some cases be given

Table 11.1 Average annual salary of primary school teachers in Lhasa Municipality compared with average annual income in urban and rural areas in the TAR, 1994

Educational qualifications	Community teachers' salary (yuan)	State teachers' salary (yuan)	Av. rural income (yuan)	Av. urban income (yuan)
Completed:			1,183	4,163
Primary school	960			
Junior secondary	1,080			
Senior secondary	1,320	3,600		
Passed LMEB exam	+10 per month			

Sources: Interview with education official, October 1994; 1994 TAR Statistical Yearbook.

a plot of land or grain in addition to, or in lieu of, part of their salaries. Since the reforms, state teachers' income has consisted of two parts: a basic salary (shown below), and a number of bonuses, which include a seniority subsidy, free housing and other emoluments.

Since 1987, bonuses and the quality of the housing that teachers receive depend primarily on their workload, the success of their pupils, and their rank.[9]

In his report to the National People's Congress in October 1993, the Education Minister announced a reform plan for teachers' pay to be implemented in November 1993, which stated that the average teacher's pay should not be less than that of a government worker and that it should 'rise gradually to keep pace with national income'.[10] In the 1993 'Programme for China's Educational Reform and Development' it was stipulated that the average teacher's salary should be higher than the average salary of employees in state-owned enterprises.[11]

Low salaries are a concern not only for primary and secondary school teachers; university teachers' salaries are also low in comparison with those of other professions. The new ranking system, while designed to provide an incentive to improve teaching quality, is constrained by the fact that the number of teachers of a particular rank is limited in each school or college. Box 11.1 gives an illustration of some of the problems for teachers at tertiary level in the TAR in 1996.

The 1993 'Programme for China's Educational Reform and Development' stipulated that a preferential policy for teachers in housing and welfare should be implemented. Teachers were to be given priority in the distribution of housing and were to be entitled to a house 'the

---

Box 11.1 A meeting on how to stabilize the teaching force,
14 May 1996

We should stabilize the contingent of teachers by good means. If we want our regional educational work to take a new step forward, we must have a contingent of teachers who are qualified and who have a sense of responsibility. Unfortunately, at present there is a serious trend of key teachers being transferred to other jobs. The cause of this trend is that teachers' incomes are too low, while cadres of other departments can enjoy extra benefits with their wages. Due to this unequal income that teachers have, they look for jobs with a higher salary.

Teachers don't have enough opportunities to improve their rank. The number of people in a certain rank is [artificially] limited. In Tibet University there were 68 people qualified for a lecturer's rank, but the number of people to receive this rank was limited to five people. This means that the assessment and distribution of ranks is unfair. Having a particular rank for a teacher is a way of improving his income. Therefore we request the distribution of ranks to be done according to each school's reality, and if possible to show some special consideration for the teachers to bring the initiative of the teachers into full play.

Source: *TAR CPPCC, 'Report of the Fourth Plenary Session of the Sixth CPPCC of the TAR', 15 May 1996.*

---

average size of urban residents' homes'. Local governments were to be responsible for the construction of teachers' housing and for setting up a security system for teachers, including medical care and retirement insurance; funds were to be collected 'through various channels'. At the same time the programme directed that state subsidies for community school teachers should be increased, to 'gradually enable them to receive the same wages as teachers of state schools'.[12]

In September 1994, the TAR regional government launched a public campaign to raise money to improve teachers' living conditions. According to official sources, 2 million yuan was raised in five months. Other benefits said to have been offered to teachers included preferential medical treatment, commodities at reduced prices and other material rewards.[13] However, teachers' salaries continue to be an issue, as is indicated by Gyaltsen Norbu in his 1996 work report: 'The people's teachers are hardworking engineers of the human soul. We should respect them, gradually raise the wages for them, and give priority to improving working and housing conditions for them.'[14]

Teacher shortages

By the late 1980s, so many teachers all over China were leaving the profession to find more rewarding work that schools were having to close.[15] The 1985 'CCP Decision on Education' stipulated that 'no government departments or any other units shall be allowed to transfer qualified teachers from secondary or primary schools to other jobs'.[16] The regulation was reiterated at the Fifth TAR Conference on Education in 1994.[17] But this regulation appears to have done little to stem the flow, either in the TAR or in the rest of China.

In May 1994, a meeting of the TAR Chinese People's Political Consultative Conference (CPPCC) raised the problem of trained teachers leaving the profession. Members at the meeting gave the following examples of the transfer of teachers to jobs outside the teaching profession in the previous three years:

- Kongpo (*Linzhi*) Prefecture: 170 teachers
- Lhasa No. 1 Secondary School: 18 teachers
- Tibet University: 98 teachers[18]

In the TAR, the 'intellectual aid' scheme instituted in 1984, part of which included sending teachers to the TAR from other parts of China, is an additional cause of instability in the teaching force. According to a *Xinhua* report in 1996, 6,640 teachers have been sent to the TAR from Central China since 1957 on contracts of varying length.[19] Despite the obvious benefit of increased numbers of trained teachers, one of the problems with the system is that it produces a high turnover of staff in schools, as teachers come to the end of their contracts and return to Central China and new teachers arrive to take their place. Furthermore, the teachers are given six months' home leave after every year and a half, and are known to make every attempt to postpone their return to work in the TAR. The result of this is that large numbers of unqualified temporary teachers are employed in schools in the TAR. According to a report by an English teacher at Tibet University, there were four different heads of the English section between 1987 and 1989: 'two left on account of "a weak heart" and one left because of an opportunity to study in the USA. Two female teachers left because they were pregnant and one was given six months' marriage leave. Another teacher left because of personal problems with the head of department and a further three went back to China on home leave.'[20] In 1986, in an attempt to prevent cadres and teachers leaving their posts in the TAR or delaying their return from home leave in Central China, TAR government chairman, Dorje Tsering, announced that personnel returning late from vacation in Central China would have their salaries reduced or stopped. Those wishing to seek medical treatment in Central China would require 'a hospital certificate and approval by higher levels'; furthermore, those who did not have serious medical conditions would not be allowed 'to have long rests and to stay in the interior for long periods of time'.[21] By 1994, the problem of high teacher turnover was raised again at a meeting of the TAR CPPCC. Members of the committee suggested that the only way to avoid the teacher shortages caused by the system was to train more Tibetan teachers.[22]

The problem of teacher shortage is compounded by the reluctance of young people to go into the profession. Teaching is unpopular as a profession not only because of its low economic and social status, and its political vulnerability; its most serious drawback, particularly for better qualified urban young people, is the likelihood of being sent to live and work in rural areas. In the 1988 Lhasa television debate on education, an education official claimed that not one of the 1988 graduates from Tibet University was going into teaching. Although he proved not to be accurate, his comments are an indication of the seriousness of the problem; he blamed the government for not giving them better living conditions.[23]

In the late 1980s, the TAR government began to take steps to attract teachers into the profession and to prevent those in it from leaving. In 1988, all state teachers in the TAR were given an extra 23 yuan per month, which was described as an incentive to encourage people to join, and to remain in the teaching profession.[24] Other measures included, for example, the stipulation that all graduates of Tibet University in 1988 and 1989 should become teachers; in 1990, half the graduates were to become teachers. By 1996, however, only one of the 1988 graduates of the English department of Tibet University was still in teaching.[25]

In Tibetan areas of Qinghai province, local governments have also been urged to work out preferential policies for teachers. They have been directed to raise teachers' salaries and improve their living conditions in order to encourage people to teach in less desirable rural areas. In 1994, new incentives in Qinghai for teachers working in remote areas for over fifteen years included 'more favourable treatment in work and the possibility for their children to take part in university enrolment examinations'.[26] It appears, however, that such efforts have not been enough to provide teachers with a genuine sense of material and social improvement. In 1996, concerns of low salary, low status and poor living conditions were still being raised in the TAR.[27]

Teaching quality

The low economic and social status of teachers since the start of economic reform have had a deleterious effect on the teaching quality in schools all over China, particularly at primary and secondary levels. To a large extent, those who have the ability (or the connections) to avoid the teaching profession do so. According to a report by the State Statistical Bureau, during the 1980s there was a 'a continuing drop in the quality of students entering the teaching profession'.[28]

The situation has been particularly disastrous for primary schools in rural areas where the existing teaching force consisted of unqualified teachers recruited during the period of community school expansion in the 1970s. Efforts to retire older unqualified teachers have been hampered by the fact that there are not enough well qualified new teachers to replace them. Box 11.2 contains an anecdote about a primary school teacher in Chamdo who is caught out by the arrival of a team of school inspectors.

At the Fifth Regional Meeting on Education in the TAR in November 1994, Chen Kuiyuan, the general secretary of the TAR Communist Party, told delegates: 'Following educational development, the lack of qualified personnel on the education front is a prominent contradiction. Tibet's universities, secondary and elementary schools and various types of special schools generally lack qualified backbone leaders as well as key teaching and scientific research personnel.'[29]

The concept of a 'qualified' teacher was introduced as part of the education reforms designed to raise teaching standards after the Cultural Revolution. Table 11.2 shows the length of education necessary for a teacher to be considered qualified for each particular level of teaching.

In China as a whole, 80 per cent of teachers are qualified; the TAR has a significantly lower percentage of qualified teachers. In Lhasa Municipality, in 1995, 60 per cent of senior secondary teachers were qualified; 72 per cent of junior secondary teachers were qualified; and 57 per cent of primary teachers were qualified. Forty-three per cent of primary teachers in Lhasa Municipality are unqualified community school teachers. Again, this figure disguises discrepancies between counties in the prefecture. In Lhundrup county, for example, 29 per cent of community school teachers were qualified, while 70 per cent of state primary school teachers were qualified. In Toelung (*Duilong*) county, 65 per cent of community school teachers were qualified, while in

Box 11.2 'Teachers Steeped in Old Thought'

'When the bell struck to begin school, it was already very late in the day and sun rays beamed into the class-rooms from all directions. As the teacher sat, leaning on his chair, an unimaginable thing happened: a school inspection team came! When members of the team looked at the teacher's lesson plan, they saw the words "Go through the textbook" scribbled on it. It is indisputable that the teacher is the basic textbook for the students. Although there is nothing wrong in the mere reading of textbooks by the students, the question still remains as to what things the teachers could teach apart from merely telling the students what pages of the textbooks they are required to read.' The above is an eye-witness observation made by an Inspection Team of the Chamdo (Changdu) Prefectural Sports and Education Department in a County Secondary School in the Autumn of 1991.

Speaking about the state of the teaching profession, there are those whose knowledge of Tibetan is no higher than that of third year primary school level; those who know over one hundred Chinese characters are eligible to become teachers. According to what we have learnt, the knowledge of a substantial proportion of the 1,134 community school teachers is woefully poor, and the literacy of many of them is extremely low. The educational level of many of them is below that of a fifth grade primary school student. Such being the situation, it is not surprising to find people heave a sigh of disappointment, saying, 'These teachers don't resemble teachers; isn't it a great offence to harm the children of others?'

Out of the total of 1,441 teaching and other staff in schools, over 70 per cent are people with specialized higher and secondary-level qualifications; most of them are teachers in secondary schools. Why then is the capacity of the teaching community so woefully poor? Regarding this, many young teachers said that when sitting for their examination, university students do not opt for Teacher Training Course. Therefore, students who fail in their studies in other schools are made to teach even though they do not want to. Likewise, can we fault some people who say, 'Could someone who is himself not qualified as a teacher teach others?'

To seek other jobs or transfer of posting or to want to run fish shops are practices which today enjoy much enthusiasm; these have led to a continuous decline in dedication to the teaching profession. While teaching is a profession of unrivalled nobility, business people are characterized by utter mercilessness. When these two things come

> *together in the same arena, would not there be a danger of assimilation of the pre-eminent by the mundane? … This is the teaching environment that we have found.*
>
> Source: Xiang Xiaoli and Zhang Qing, 'Courage of Conviction Consists in Tackling the Reality of the Situation Today with a Clear Vision for the Future', Chamdo Daily, July 15, 1993.

Medrogongkar only 8 per cent were qualified. In Taktse (*Dadze*) county, only 39 per cent of primary school teachers had more than primary education.[30]

Furthermore, what is not publicly acknowledged is that a significant proportion of the teaching force consists of unqualified Han Chinese teachers from Central China. Some of these teachers are temporary teachers, replacing Chinese teachers who fail to return from home leave in Central China, others are women who come unofficially to the TAR to join their husbands and, despite their lack of qualifications, get teaching jobs to legitimize their position. Indeed, in 1986, one of Lhasa's key schools, the No. 1 Secondary School, was nicknamed by students *'Jiashu Xuexiao'* ('Housewives' School').[31] According to Jane Peek, an English teacher trainer who observed English classes in Lhasa secondary schools in 1988, out of five Han Chinese English-language teachers at No. 3 Secondary School in Lhasa, only one had received higher education; at No. 5 Secondary School, none of the Chinese English-language teachers had received higher education.[32] Box 11.3 contains Jane Peek's views on the issue of teacher training in Lhasa.

Table 11.2 Level of education required for qualified teaching status

Teacher of:	Graduate of:
Primary	Senior secondary, or normal school
Junior secondary	Junior college of teacher training
Senior secondary	Normal college or normal university

Source: Keith M. Lewin, Xu Hui, Angela Little and Zheng Jiwei, *Educational Innovation in China* (Longman, Harlow, 1994).

Box 11.3 The experience of an English teacher trainer at
Tibet University, 1987–89

*It is clear that while there is no large pool of well-trained Tibetans to
teach in both secondary and tertiary institutions, nevertheless it is
equally true than many of the Chinese imported to staff the schools
are neither 'expert' nor 'qualified'.*

*Even if one assumes for a moment that there is a present need for
teachers to be brought from China, only lip-service is paid to training
Tibetans so that this dependency can be reduced. My job description
included teacher training. Despite my repeated offers, no training
scheme materialized. Furthermore, in contrast to the usual four-year
degree course in China, students at Tibet University are only provided
with a three-year course. They therefore graduate, not with a BA but
with a Certificate of Graduation. Many Tibetans arriving at the university with little or no prior English background, studying for only
three years and being given no teacher training (except for their one
month practical experience), are therefore cast into the role of secondary
school teachers with totally inadequate training.*

Source*: Jane Peek, 'Discrimination in Education in Lhasa', unpublished paper, June 1989.*

Teacher training

China operates two systems of teacher training: pre-service training
and in-service training.

Pre-service training   Pre-service training takes place in senior secondary-
level teacher training schools, higher education colleges and universities.
Training for primary and pre-school teachers takes place in senior
secondary-level specialist schools. The curriculum is set nationally and
is similar to general senior secondary education with an added pedagogy
and methodology component as well as a period of teaching practice
which consists of eight weeks for three-year programmes and ten weeks
for four-year programmes. The courses include Chinese, mathematics,
politics, physics, chemistry, history, geography, psychology, pedagogy,
biology, physical education, art, music, television education and basic
agriculture (not all these subjects are compulsory). Additional subjects
for the pre-school training course include language, handwriting, handi-

crafts and general knowledge.[33] Training courses for junior and senior secondary teachers (since the student-teachers have already completed secondary education) focus on psychology, methodology and theory of education.

In 'minority' nationality areas, teacher training courses include train-ing in the nationality's language; in the TAR, all other courses are taught in Chinese. This presents particular problems for teachers in primary schools where the teaching medium is Tibetan and few children in rural areas speak Chinese. Most student-teachers who graduate from the secondary-level teacher training schools will be sent to township (*xiang*) level state primary schools in counties throughout the TAR. Since these teachers have been taught in Chinese not only at junior secondary school but also on their teaching course, their standard of written Tibetan and their ability to read in Tibetan is generally poor. Tibetans who have been sent to schools in China for training are often unable even to speak correct Tibetan. They are given some language training by local county education bureaux before they take up their post;[34] however, according to one educationalist, the level of Tibetan among primary school teachers in general is so low that '95 per cent of rural in-service training courses focus on teaching primary school teachers Tibetan. Most of them know too little Tibetan to be effective as teachers.'[35]

In 1989, in recognition of this problem, Tibet University recalled all the previous year's English graduates to give them a year of Tibetan-language coaching before sending them back to teach in schools;[36] and from 1990 all new graduates were to be given a one-year course in Tibetan language.[37] According to a report by the TAR Education Commission, since 1993, the TAR government has trained 500 teachers to teach in Tibetan, ninety-nine of whom are qualified to teach both in Tibetan and Chinese.[38] By 1998, there were said to be 360 bilingual teachers[39] (out of a total of approximately 15,000). Since 1989, regulations have stipulated that young teachers who qualify for Tibetan medium teacher training at secondary level must attend Tibet Univer-sity's teacher training section, or that of other institutions, to be trained to teach in Tibetan.[40] From 1989, all graduates of Tibet University were to have one year's Tibetan-language training.[41] However, in 1997, the plans to extend Tibetan-medium education in schools were replaced with new plans to introduce Chinese classes into Tibetan schools from the first grade of primary school. Given the controversy that currently surrounds the use of the Tibetan language, it is possible that, at least in the present political climate, Tibetan language training will not be a priority.

Box 11.4 Lhasa Teacher Training School: profile of four-year primary school teacher training course, 1996

<u>Timetable</u>
Term: 20 weeks
Lesson: 45 minutes
Day: 6 lessons   *Morning Session: 4 lessons*
                         Afternoon Session: 2 lessons
                         Evening Session: 1½ hours' private study

<u>Curriculum</u>

<u>Core curriculum</u> – 4 years	<u>No. of lessons per week</u>
Tibetan language	6
Chinese language	6
Mathematics	5
Politics	2
Sports	2
Drawing	
Singing	

<u>Additional Courses</u>

Year 1	Biology	
	Geography (2 terms)	
	History (3 terms)	
Year 2	Physics	
	Chemistry	
Year 3	Psychology for primary school level	
	Teaching skills/methodology	
Year 4	Electrical equipment operation	2
	Drawing	4
	Teaching skills	2
	Sports	2
	Biology/natural science	2

<u>Textbooks</u>

Year 2 to 4: national primary school teacher training handbook
Year 4 (one term): primary school textbooks are studied

<u>Teaching Practice</u>
One month (reduced from three months in 1996)

<u>Student Costs</u>
Accommodation: 80 yuan per month
Food: 3 yuan per meal

Source: *Interview with educationalist, April 1997.*

In-service training In 1996, the TAR Education Commission, in line with the 'Programme for China's Educational Reform and Development', set a target of ensuring that all teachers will be qualified by the year 2000. Given that in 1995, in the Lhasa Municipality alone, 43 per cent of primary school teachers were unqualified, and 28 per cent of junior secondary teachers were unqualified, in-service training has become the main form of teacher training in the TAR.[42]

The TAR Education Commission has recently introduced a qualifying exam for community school teachers which gives those who pass the status of state primary school teachers. County education bureaux run courses to help prepare teachers for this exam. The exam consists of the three main subjects taught in primary school: Tibetan, mathematics and Chinese. In 1995, the pass mark was 97 out of a total of 300 marks, which means that the teachers who only just pass are not highly qualified. In March 1996, a new ruling was introduced that gave teachers three chances to pass the TAR Education Commission exam. If they fail the third time they are not allowed to continue as teachers.[43] On the basis of these exams, some teachers are being promoted and others retired.

There is little information available on in-service teacher training programmes in areas outside the Lhasa Municipality. In the Lhasa Municipality, with continued emphasis on improving quality in the 1990s, teaching training has become a priority, at least in policy documents.

Although general statements were made through the 1980s about upgrading community school teachers, it is only with the 1990s that more publicity has been given to the need to implement these policies. In the 1980s, county education bureaux sent selected teachers to Lhasa Teacher Training School, but little training was done at county level and below. In the 1970s, in-service teacher training was carried out in county headquarters, but some areas abandoned county-level teacher training altogether after 1979.[44] Since 1990, however, emphasis has been placed on training primary school teachers at the county and township levels. Counties have been urged to run their own courses. In the Lhasa Municipality each county has run one or two five-month courses training about thirty teachers on each, since 1991. The courses focus essentially on the subjects taught at primary school: Tibetan, mathematics and sometimes Chinese. They also provide coaching for the TAR Education Commission exams, as well as basic methodology and school management, and basic training in multi-grade teaching.[45]

Again, like the literacy programmes, these programmes have run into funding problems. County education bureaux are expected to save money from their existing budget, or seek funding from other depart-

---

Box 11.5 A county's success in primary school
teacher training, 1996

*The result of having a definite purpose, of setting the appropriate
curriculum, and of taking strict exams was that we achieved the goal
of training. Lots of local primary school teachers only knew a little
written Tibetan language and no mathematics or written Chinese
language when entering the training class. Through training their
Tibetan improved, they gained some knowledge of mathematics and
understood a bit of the written Chinese language, so that they actually
strengthened their relevant knowledge by widening their general knowledge. For instance, teacher Y from X village primary school said with
deep feeling when the training course was completed: 'The achievement
was great. I am a teacher who had just graduated from a primary
school and I don't even know Tibetan grammar. In the training class
I learned Tibetan and mathematics, which I didn't know before. Now,
going back to my own work post, I have the basis on which to carry on
the studies by myself.' Teacher Y returned to his school, worked hard
and due to the improvement of his professional standard he soon
became a key teacher in his school.*

Source: *Unpublished report on teacher training by a county education
bureau, December 1995*

---

ments, to run training programmes. There is no money to pay for the
travel and accommodation of teachers on training programmes, or to
pay substitute teachers in their absence.[46] Nevertheless, teacher training
continues to be a priority in government education documents. In 1995,
the Lhasa municipal government announced that every county in the
Lhasa Municipality should submit detailed plans for teacher training for
1996 to the Lhasa City Education and Sports Commission before the
end of March 1996. The plans were to include an ideology guide for
training, as well as training objectives, the number of trainees, enrolment criteria, the timetable, courses offered, teaching materials, the
date and duration of each course, the status of the teachers, teaching
methods, methods of assessment, the setting and correcting of students'
exams, the students' accommodation and a plan of funding allocation
including teachers' allowances. The Lhasa City Education and Sports
Commission was to act in a supervisory role in the planning and
executing of teacher training programmes.[47]

Future plans set out by the Lhasa municipal government for the Lhasa Municipality include: (1) increasing the use of multi-grade classes to keep down unit costs; (2) translating material into Tibetan, and publishing material that would be useful for teacher training from the Tibetan edition of the journal *Lhasa Education*, including material produced by UNICEF; (3) creating a system of course assessment and teacher assessment for rural areas; and (4) increasing funds for teacher training centres at county and municipal levels. Plans up to the end of the century include expanding Lhasa Teacher Training School, and building teacher training centres in each county.[48]

It is generally agreed that teacher training is the key to improving education in the TAR. It is also agreed that the TAR has a long way to go to upgrade its teaching force. In Lhasa Municipality alone, 43 per cent of teachers are unqualified community school teachers.[49] The Ninth Five-Year Plan sets targets for the year 2000 of 80 per cent of teachers having achieved the educational qualifications required for the level at which they teach, and 70 per cent having obtained the relevant teaching credentials. New teachers are to have a qualified educational background. Plans are said to include the training of more than 6,000 new teachers, bringing the teaching force to 21,000.[50] Whether these targets can be reached remains to be seen. Box 11.5 gives an example of small successes in one county in the TAR.

Summary

Since the end of the Cultural Revolution, the teaching profession in the TAR has been dogged by difficulties in recruiting teachers, by a high turnover of teaching staff and by an increasing outflow of teachers into other professions. Reasons for these problems include: (1) the low status of teachers in society; (2) poor remuneration compared with other professions; (3) the likelihood of being sent to work in rural areas; (4) the precarious position of teachers *vis-à-vis* the Communist Party, particularly since the resurgence of nationalist unrest when they have been accused of allowing 'splittism' to enter the classrooms. The consequence of the increasing unpopularity of the profession is a deterioration in the quality of teaching. In the Lhasa Municipality in 1995, 43 per cent of primary school teachers, 28 per cent of junior secondary teachers, and 40 per cent of senior secondary teachers were unqualified. This compares with 20 per cent of teachers at all levels in China as a whole.[51]

In 1984, in an effort to improve teaching quality in the TAR, the Chinese government introduced the 'intellectual aid scheme' through which teachers were sent from Central China to teach in the region. In terms of increasing the number of qualified teachers, the programme has been beneficial. Nevertheless, factors such as the high turnover of teachers and frequent absenteeism, which leads to the use of temporary unqualified teachers, as well as the fact these teachers do not speak Tibetan, are the negative side effects of the programme.

During the 1990s, further measures were taken by the TAR government to improve teaching quality. These included the introduction of an examination for community school teachers to enable them to qualify as state teachers and the exclusion from further teaching of those who failed the exam after three attempts. Efforts were also made to enhance the system of pre-service and in-service teacher training. One of the particular problems of the teaching system in the TAR is that teachers are taught in Chinese in secondary school and for their teacher training. Although they are given Tibetan-language classes at teacher training school, most teachers have difficulty teaching in Tibetan. The in-service teacher training programmes focus on Tibetan-language training; by 1998, official sources indicated that 360 teachers in the TAR were qualified to teach in Tibetan and Chinese.[52] However, since the total of number of teachers is around 15,000, the figure is still extremely low. As in other areas of the education system, these teacher training programmes are hampered by a lack of adequate funding.

Official statistics and basic facts

Box 11.6 Secondary-level teacher training schools

Teacher training schools in the TAR

Lhasa (Lasa) Teacher Training School
Chamdo (Changdu) Teacher Training School
Lhokha (Shannan) Teacher Training School
Shigatse (Xigaze) Teacher Training School
Nagchu (Naqu) Specialist Secondary School

Teacher training schools outside the TAR which train TAR students

Tibet Nationalities Institute Teacher Training Class, Shaanxi province
Jiang Xiang Teacher Training School, Shanxi province
Hefei Teacher Training School, Anhui province
Shijiazhuang Teacher Training School, Hebei province

Table 11.3 Teacher training: educational requirements, institutions and qualifications

Educational level	Institution	Qualification	Teaching level
Graduates from universities and colleges (22–23)	Teacher training universities (postgraduate)	Master's degree and doctorate (3 years each)	University and college
Graduates from senior secondary school (18–19)	Teacher training universities and colleges; other universities and colleges	Bachelor's degree (4 years)	Senior secondary and specialized secondary
Graduates from senior secondary school (18–19)	Junior colleges for teacher training	Diploma (2–3 years)	Junior secondary
Graduates from junior secondary school (15–16)	Senior secondary level teacher training schools; pre-school training schools	Certificate (3 years)	Primary and kindergarten

Source: Lewin et al., *Educational Innovation in China.*

Table 11. 4 'Minority' nationality teachers in the teaching force in the TAR

	Total	Tibetans etc.	Tibetans etc. (%)
University	761	371	48.7
Specialized secondary	685	313	45.4
General secondary	2,342	1,924	82.2
Primary	11,500	11,027	95.9

Source: *China's Ethnic Statistical Yearbook*, 1995.

Notes

1. Deng Xiaoping, Speech to National Conference on Education, 22 April 1978, in Deng Xiaoping, *Speeches and Writings* (Pergamon Press, London, 1984), p. 59.

2. See Chen Kuiyuan, 'Speech on Literature and Art', *Xizang Ribao* (Tibet Daily), 11 July 1997.

3. Television debate on education, Lhasa TV, 30 July 1988.

4. Chen Kuiyuan, 'Speech on Education in Tibet', Fifth Regional Meeting on Education in the TAR, 26 October 1994, *Xizang Ribao* (Tibet Daily), 28 October 1994.

5. Lhasa Radio, 8 December 1989.

6. Keith M. Lewin and Wang Ying Jie, *Implementing Basic Education in China* (UNESCO, 1994), p. 160.

7. *Economics Weekly, Xinhua*, 1 May 1989.

8. Television debate on education, Lhasa TV, 30 July 1988.

9. A new four-point ranking system was introduced in 1987 whereby teachers are graded according to their teaching qualifications, and receive extra income accordingly. This was a shift from the 'iron rice bowl' system where teachers' salaries increased automatically with seniority, to a system where salary is directly related to work and talent. See also CCP Central Committee and the State Council, 'Programme for China's Educational Reform and Development', 25 February 1993, *Xinhua* [SWB 5/5/93].

10. Zhu Kaixuan, Education Minister, 'Report to Fourth Session of Eighth National People's Congress Standing Committee on Educational Work', *Xinhua*, 28 October 1993 [SWB 10/11/93].

11. 'Programme for China's Educational Reform and Development', 1993.

12. Ibid.

13. *Xinhua*, Lhasa, 11 February 1995 [FBIS 13/2/95].

14. Gyaltsen Norbu, 'Work Report on the Outline', 5 June 1996.

15. *Economics Weekly, Xinhua*, 1 May 1989.

16. CCP Central Committee, 'Decision of the CCP Central Committee on the Reform of China's Educational Structure' (Foreign Languages Press, Beijing, 1985).

17. Gyaltsen Norbu, 'Education in Tibet', Speech to Fifth Regional Meeting on Education in the TAR on 26 October 1994, *Xizang Ribao* (Tibet Daily), 30 October 1994, pp. 1–4.

18. TAR CPPCC 'Report of the Second Committee Meeting of the Sixth Session of the TAR CPPCC', *CPPCC News Bulletin*, 18 May 1994.

19. *Xinhua* (in English), 20 March 1996 [FBIS 28/3/96].

20. Jane Peek, 'Discrimination in Education in Lhasa', unpublished paper, June 1989; see also Catriona Bass, *Inside the Treasure House: A Time in Tibet* (Gollancz, London, 1990), p. 169.

21. Dorje Tsering, 'Report on Economic Problems and Policies in Tibet', Lhasa Radio, 31 March 1986 [SWB 7/4/86].

22. TAR CPPCC, 'Thirteenth Bulletin of 2nd Plenary Session of the Sixth TAR CPPCC', Secretariat of the Conference, 17 May 1994.

23. Television debate on education, Lhasa TV, 30 July 1988.

24. Interview with Tibetan teacher, 10 October 1996.

25. Interview with a graduate of Tibet University, 2 February 1997.

26. *Xinhua*, 25 February 1994 [SWB 1/3/94].

27. TAR CPPCC, 'Summary Report on the Fourth Plenary Session of the Sixth TAR CPPCC', Secretariat of the Conference, 15 May 1996.

28. State Statistical Bureau, 'Education in Present Day China', *Beijing Review*, 17 July 1989.

29. Chen Kuiyuan, 'Speech on Education in Tibet'.

30. Internal government education planning document, November 1995.

31. Bass, *Inside the Treasure House*, p. 169.

32. Peek, 'Discrimination'.

33. Internal government education planning document, November 1995.

34. Ibid.

35. Interview with former educationalist in the TAR, 30 January 1996.

36. Interview with Tibetan teacher, 10 October 1996.

37. Dayang, 'To Further the Study, Use and Development of the Tibetan Language: The Lhasa Education and Sports Committee Makes Additional Provisions on Relevant Concerns', *Lhasa Wanbao* (Lhasa Evening News), 25 August 1990.

38. Education Committee of TAR, 'Report on the Work of Experimental Teaching in Tibetan Language at Middle Schools', *Tibet Education*, Vol. 4, 1995.

39. *Xinhua* (Beijing, in English), 18 January 1998.

40. Education Committee of TAR, 'Report on the Work of Experimental Teaching'.

41. Dayang, 'To Further the Study, Use and Development of the Tibetan Language: The Lhasa Education and Sports Committee Makes Additional Provisions on Relevant Concerns', *Lhasa Wanbao* (Lhasa Evening News), 25 August 1990.

42. Internal TAR government document on teacher training in agricultural and pastoral areas, December 1995.

43. Paper on education development among Tibetans, by Tibetan scholar in China, 1995.

44. Internal government education planning document, November 1995.

45. Ibid.

46. Ibid.

47. Internal TAR government document on teacher training in agricultural and pastoral areas, December 1995.

48. Internal government education planning document, November 1995.

49. Ibid.

50. 'Outline of the TAR's Five-Year Plan for Economic and Social Development and Its Long-term Target for 2010, Approved by the Fourth Session of the Sixth Regional People's Congress on 24th May 1996', *Xizang Ribao* (Tibet Daily), 7 June 1996.

51. Internal government education planning document, November 1995.

52. *Xinhua*, 18 January 1998.

CHAPTER 12

Tibetan Language Policy in Education

An overview

The Tibetan language policy has been one of the most important issues in education in the TAR since 1950, and particularly since 1980. In 1991, the Deputy Party Secretary of the TAR, Dorje Tseten, described Tibetan-language education as a 'critical issue' over which there are 'strong differences of opinion'.[1] Debate has centred on the interpretation and implementation of Chinese government policy more than on changes in the policy itself since, from the first constitution of the PRC, the 1949 'Common Programme', China's nationalities have had, in principle, the right to use their own languages in administration and education. The 'Common Programme' stated: 'all minority nationalities have the freedom to develop their languages and writing scripts, and to maintain or modify their customs and religious beliefs.'[2] Article 121 of the 1982 Constitution allows 'minority' nationalities to employ the written and spoken language in common use.[3] The Law of the PRC on Regional Autonomy (1984) includes the right of 'minority' nationalities to conduct their affairs in their own languages, and to 'independently develop education for nationalities'.[4] In education, the option for 'minority' nationalities to provide teaching in their own languages became part of the 1995 Education Law. Article 12 of the law states that 'schools and other educational institutions primarily for "minority" nationalities may use the spoken or written language in common use among the ethnic group or in the locality as the language of instruction'.[5]

However, despite the fact that language rights are enshrined in Chinese law, because language is so closely connected with national identity it has borne the brunt of attacks against non-Han Chinese culture during 'leftist' periods in China's history over the last five decades. This is particularly true of the Tibetan language. In 1987 the Panchen Lama described the development of the Tibetan language thus: 'in the thirty or more years since the peaceful liberation of Tibet, the study, use and development of the Tibetan language has followed a tortuous course.'[6]

The Tibetan language first came under attack in the crushing of the Lhasa Uprising in 1959, which coincided with the ascendency of Mao's Anti-Rightist Campaign and the Great Leap Forward in Central China.[7] The Tibetan language became associated with the former Tibetan government and denounced, along with all manifestations of the old society; it was described as a relic of feudalism and of no use in the modern world. In the early 1960s, when Mao's authority temporarily waned and education policy swung back to allowing for the distinctive nature of 'minority' education, attempts were made to extend Tibetan-medium education in Tibet. In 1960, the Tibet Educational Materials Translation and Editing Committee was set up under PCART to compile and translate textbooks for community schools in the region. The committee was directed to use the Han Chinese textbooks as models, but to include stories and characters from Tibetan literature as well as real Tibetan figures; the committee was also told it had to avoid 'all religious superstition'. By 1963, complete sets of primary school textbooks for community schools had been compiled and translated into Tibetan as well as textbooks for adult literacy and a textbook on agricultural accounting.[8]

However, in 1966 when Mao launched the Cultural Revolution, Tibetan language once more came under attack, as did non-Han Chinese languages all over China. The dominant ideology of waging 'class struggle' made Tibetan particularly vulnerable since it is a highly stratified language with two complete sets of terms: one set constitutes the honorific language that is used when speaking to a person of higher social standing. Honorific terminology was specifically banned both in spoken and written Tibetan during the 1960s and 1970s. From the early 1960s, various propaganda campaigns, such as 'Tibetan Written Language is Useless, Only the Han Language is an Advanced Language', sought to denigrate Tibetan in the eyes of Tibetans.[9] Schools taught in Chinese and Chinese became the language of administration;[10] Dorje Tseten blames the lack of Tibetan-language education during this period on 'the rapid expansion of education, the shortage of teachers and textbooks and the interference of leftist ideology'.[11] The Tenth Panchen Lama and Ngapo Ngawang Jigme go further in saying that during this time 'the nationality policies of the Party and State were wrecked'.[12]

By the beginning of the 1980s, the Chinese government once more began taking steps to enshrine in law the rights of non-Han Chinese nationalities to use their own languages. In the TAR, several committees and administrative bodies were established to realize the 'minority education' policies promulgated by the central government. As mentioned in Chapter 5, the 'Five Provinces and Region Jointly Published Teaching Materials' Committee (*Wu Sheng Qu Tongbian Jiaocai*) was established in 1982 to co-ordinate the compilation of textbooks in Tibetan and the development of Tibetan-language education in the TAR and the four provinces with significant Tibetan populations.[13] At the Second Forum in 1984, plans were drawn up teach Tibetans at primary level in the Tibetan medium.[14] In 1987, at the instigation of the Tenth Panchen Lama and Ngapo Ngawang Jigme, the TAR People's Congress issued the 'Provisions on the Study, Use and Development of Spoken and Written Tibetan (for trial implementation)' (Provisions on the Use of Tibetan).[15] This was a detailed document which set out procedures for implementing Tibetan language policy in education and public life. The regulations allowed the use of both Tibetan and Chinese, but Tibetan was to be the first language. All official meetings were henceforth to be held in Tibetan and Chinese; official documents were to be written both in Tibetan and Chinese, including court documents, public notices and signs; the media were also to use both Tibetan and Chinese; the procuracy and the courts were to guarantee the right of Tibetans to use spoken and written Tibetan.[16] The examination for government service could henceforth also be taken in Tibetan. The 1987 'Provisions on the Use of Tibetan' also included the gradual introduction of Tibetan medium education in secondary schools.[17] In July 1991, the first 'Regional Conference on Tibetan Language Teaching' took place in Lhasa during which officials were urged to make greater efforts in implementing central and regional government policies regarding Tibetan language education.[18]

Following the promulgation of the 1987 'Provisions on the Use of Tibetan', the Guiding Committee on Work in Spoken and Written Tibetan was set up under the TAR government to oversee the implementation of the Tibetan language policy. At the prefectural, municipal and county government level, parallel structures were established for the development of the Tibetan language and the translation of Chinese government documents and other texts into Tibetan.[19] By 1988, the TAR was said to have 500 translators divided between the departments of the regional government, the prefectural, city and county governments.[20] In the same year, the TAR Regional People's Congress announced that Tibetan would be the official language of the TAR from July.[21] In 1991, the State Council issued a directive, known as Document 32, which again stressed the importance of using 'minority' nationality languages in order to enhance the 'second stage' of economic development in China.[22]

In theory, the restoration of the Tibetan language in government policy and law was deemed important not only in terms of the preservation of Tibetan culture, but also in terms of economic development and for the dissemination of government policy and information. Given that the majority of Tibetans do not speak Chinese (in 1998, 90 per cent of Tibetans were said to use Tibetan),[23] neither socialist modernization nor the economic development of the TAR could take place without the use of Tibetan.[24] In 1993, in a speech to the Guiding Committee on Work in Spoken and Written Tibetan, TAR Deputy Party Secretary Tenzin gave his view on the economic importance of developing the use of Tibetan language in the TAR:

> Our region is not only an autonomous region where the Tibetan nationality constitutes 95 per cent of the population, it is also where spoken and written Tibetan is used by the majority of people. Therefore, according to our region's circumstances, to develop science and technology, to raise up the nationality's educational level, we have to depend on spoken and written Tibetan. In other words, we have no alternative but to aim at translating scientific technological knowledge and the advanced experiences of fraternal nationalities into the Tibetan language, and then to spread this amongst the people, especially amongst the broad masses of peasants and herders to improve the whole of the Tibetan nationality's educational level. If this issue isn't properly sorted out, then the construction of the TAR's four modernisations will meet an obstacle. From this point of view, the work relating to the Tibetan language is not only an issue of implementing policy, but is an important condition in leading the people on the road to prosperity through constructing Tibet's four modernisations, and it has great present and future significance.[25]

However, despite the law and government policy on the use of 'minority' languages, reality has lagged far behind the state goals of Tibetan language development in the TAR. Furthermore, despite the fact that successive leaders, including Hu Yaobang, Yin Fatang, Li Peng, Ngapo Ngawang Jigme, the Panchen Lama, Wu Jinghua, Dorje Tsering, Dorje Tseten and Tenzin, have emphasized the importance of Tibetan language in the development of education and the economy, it appears that, even at the height of the reforms in the 1980s, directives to implement the Tibetan language policy met with apathy or resistance from many officials and leaders. Through the 1980s, speeches by the leaders mentioned above and meetings of the Lhasa CPPCC raised the issue of the failure by officials to implement government policy.[26] Talking at the TAR People's Congress in 1985, Ngapo Ngawang Jigme said: 'The use of the nationality language has not yet attracted sufficient importance ... The key to attaching importance to the use of the nationality language lies in the leadership.' Again in 1987, he repeated that 'there has been no fundamental change in the use of the Tibetan language'.[27] In 1991, at the Conference on Tibetan Language Teaching, TAR Deputy Party Secretary Tenzin described the implementation of the Tibetan language policy as 'not working and at a stalemate'. He blamed the Cultural Revolution for the interruption to the development of Tibetan language, but in the same speech he described strengthening the leadership over the Tibetan language issue as the 'key task'.[28]

By the mid-1990s, the problem of implementing the Tibetan language policy appeared to be not so much a question of the resistance of individual officials, but rather that the political climate had changed. The notion of cultural distinctiveness, which had allowed the Tibetan language policy to be formulated in the 1980s, was replaced in the TAR by a Central Committee directive to use 'the guiding spirit of close connection with the Interior'.[29]

The next section describes the implementation of the Tibetan language policy in education, assessing the achievements and the more salient problems that it currently creates for the education of Tibetan children.

Provision of Tibetan medium education

The issue of the provision of Tibetan medium education cannot be divorced from the Tibetan language policy in the TAR in general. Not only is the development of Tibetan education dependent on the wider implementation of the policy, but a failure to implement the Tibetan language policy in society – i.e. to give Tibetan the same status and usage as Chinese in government, commerce and society – has serious consequences for those whose only education is in Tibetan.

Statistically, the provision of Tibetan medium primary education in the TAR has been very successful; however, as discussed in Chapter 5, there is likely to be a gap between the apparent statistical success of the policy and the ability of schools to implement it, due to a lack of textbooks and teachers qualified to teach in Tibetan.[30] By 1996, 98 per cent of primary schools were said to be Tibetan medium.[31] Although the available statistics do not allow one to make conclusive comparisons with all Tibetan areas, this percentage compares favourably with Qinghai where, according to official statistics in 1992, only 40 per cent of primary schools for 'minority' nationalities provided education in their mother-tongue. In Gannan Tibetan autonomous prefecture in Gansu province, 34 per cent of schools for Tibetans provided education in Tibetan in 1996.[32]

However, Qinghai province (in contrast to the TAR) provides secondary education in the Tibetan medium. Tibetan medium education has been available both at primary and secondary level since the 1970s. In 1992, there were eighty-one secondary schools for 'minority' nationalities in Qinghai, who make up 42 per cent of the population in that province.[33] Forty of these secondary schools provided education in 'minority' languages.[34] In 1994, in Huangnan Tibetan autonomous prefecture in Qinghai, 61 per cent of secondary students were taught in Tibetan; in addition there was a senior secondary-level teacher training school with 557 students studying in Tibetan.[35] In the same year, the Qinghai government announced plans for a special fund to boost education for 'minority' nationalities in Qinghai, and to 'provide free textbooks in minority languages'. The Qinghai government announced an annual expenditure of 6 million yuan for this fund, which was also intended to attract donations from foreign funding agencies. The programme gave priority to building six key senior secondary schools, thirty key junior secondary schools and 191 key primary schools in the province's six national 'minority' autonomous prefectures. Preferential treatment in funds, facilities and training teachers was to be granted to these six prefectures.[36] Again, it is not possible to determine the extent to which the preferential policies are actually implemented, since it is widely agreed even by officials at the highest levels, that implementation of policy is the greatest problem.[37]

In the TAR itself, the process of implementing the Tibetan language policy in education began in 1984 after the Second Forum with the introduction of Tibetan medium primary schools for Tibetan children. The TAR Conference on Student Enrolment in the same year issued a statement to the effect that 'Primary schools whose pupils are mainly of Tibetan nationality must all use the Tibetan language as the medium of instruction. The secondary schools can additionally run courses in Han language.'[38] The introduction of Tibetan medium education included twelve hours of Tibetan language tuition each week at primary school, five hours per week at junior secondary school and three to four hours per week at senior secondary school. Chinese children in the TAR were also to learn Tibetan at primary and secondary school; by the time they graduated from senior secondary school, Chinese students were supposed to have mastered Tibetan to the standard of junior secondary school.[39] In 1990, the Lhasa Municipal Education and Sports Committee issued a directive to the effect that students who did not pass the Tibetan examination would not be able to graduate from secondary school.[40] However, all secondary education for Tibetans in the TAR continued to be taught in Chinese.

At tertiary level, at the instigation of the Panchen Lama, the TAR Teachers' College was turned into a comprehensive university in 1985, and renamed Tibet University. The original plan behind this development was to orient higher education in the TAR towards 'maintaining and developing Tibetan culture'. Three of the university's departments were to include Tibetan subjects: the Tibetan Language Department, the Tibetan Art Department and the Tibetan History Department. That teaching should be conducted in Tibetan was a particular aim.[41] In practice, however, as at primary level, the teaching of university classes in Tibetan was hampered by the delays in translation and an inadequate supply of textbooks, but more significantly by the fact that Han Chinese students were enrolled on most courses and therefore it was impractical to teach in Tibetan since these students did not speak Tibetan while most Tibetan students could understand Chinese.[42] At the beginning of December 1996, thirty students formally complained about the fact that the Tibetan history course, which is part of the Tibetan language department, was being taught in Chinese. In 1997, the specifically Tibetan nature of the university's inception was further jeopardized by the China-wide government directives to rationalize the courses of comprehensive universities and relate them more closely to the needs of China's economic development. In a speech to a TAR Conference on Education, in 1997, Deputy Party Secretary Tenzin told the meeting that 'older specialities in higher education are not suited to modern social needs'.[43]

Experimental Tibetan medium secondary schools

In 1982, with new policies allowing the development of an education system for Tibetans in Tibetan medium, a pilot project was set up in three secondary schools in Lhasa, Gyantse and Lhokha (*Shannan*) to test the relative merits of teaching Tibetan students in Tibetan and Chinese. According to the educationalist Dorje Tseten, students studying in the Tibetan class in the Gyantse school achieved, on average, twice as many marks in examinations as Tibetan students studying in the Chinese class. However, according to another report, the experiment was subsequently closed down due to 'a lack of teaching materials, qualified teachers and poor management'.[44]

In 1989, another attempt to establish a pilot project to test the benefits of Tibetan medium secondary schooling was established under the Guiding Committee on Work in Spoken and Written Tibetan. Four schools took part in the project: two in Lhasa, one in Shigatse and one in Lhokha. One hundred and sixty-one students were enrolled on the project, sixty-three were from rural peasant or nomad families, fifty-three were from the families of rural officials and forty-five were urban children. All subjects were taught in Tibetan including physics, chemistry, mathematics and Chinese. The classes used textbooks compiled by the Five Provinces and One Region Jointly Published Teaching Materials Committee, although subsequently these books had to be abandoned at the senior secondary level due to changes in the graduation examination.

After the first year, the Tibetan medium secondary school project was generally recognized as being extremely successful, and thereafter continued to receive glowing reports.[45] As TAR Deputy Party Secretary Tenzin told a meeting of the Guiding Committee on Work in Spoken and Written Tibetan on 16 March 1993:

> Some of our regional junior secondary schools carried out an experiment of teaching in the Tibetan language, and found that results and grades were increasingly and distinctively higher than those of students taught in the Chinese language. There was conclusive evidence that nothing could substitute the effect of using Tibetan language to raise the educational quality and improve the nationality's cultural level through popularising science and technology in our region. Therefore it is apparent that we should use the Tibetan language for communication more than ever.[46]

A similar trial project was carried out in one primary school in Gannan Tibetan prefecture of Gansu province. Two classes of Tibetan students from the same grade took part in the trial. One class was taught in Chinese and the other in Tibetan. The students who had been taught in the Tibetan class all finished the syllabus on time and passed the exams. However, by the end of the project, the students in the Chinese class had not completed the syllabus, and a third of them were still unable to count from one to one hundred in Chinese.[47]

However, at the same time, there were other educationalists and officials who believed that the only successful means of developing education for Tibetans was for them to learn Tibetan and Chinese simultaneously from the first grade of primary school. In the early 1990s, a parallel project was set up in a primary school in Lhasa to test what was called 'bilingual' education from grade 1 of primary school.[48] The two experiments ran concurrently with their different supporters.

In 1995, the TAR Education Commission called for greater financial support for the Tibetan medium secondary education project. In a report for the journal *Podjong Lobsu* (Tibet Education), the TAR Education Commission announced plans for the gradual expansion of Tibetan medium secondary education into rural schools, 'when conditions are appropriate'. The decision on implementation was to be made at the local government level, not at the regional government level; however, the commission suggested that at least one class in each school should be taught in the Tibetan medium.[49]

In 1995, the Tibetan secondary school pilot project in the TAR ended with the students passing the senior school graduation exams with an average of 80 per cent, compared with an average of 39 per cent for Tibetan students in Chinese medium secondary schools. Even in the Chinese paper, the students in the Tibetan medium classes were more successful than Tibetan students in the Chinese medium classes: 66 per cent of Tibetan medium students passed the Chinese paper, compared with 61 per cent of Tibetan students in Chinese medium classes.[50]

The project was extended for a further year; however, in 1996, despite its success and despite earlier decisions to generalize Tibetan medium education for Tibetans at secondary level, plans for implementing Tibetan medium secondary education were abandoned.[51] The Lhasa Municipal Education Bureau cited financial reasons for the decision to abandon the project. It acknowledged that the pilot scheme had been very successful, but that there were no resources to broaden the scope of Tibetan medium secondary education, or even to continue the pilot project. Apart from an absence of financial resources, a general lack of teachers qualified to teach in Tibetan was cited as the main reason for the failure to develop the programme.[52] It has been suggested by other educationalists in the TAR that the abandonment of Tibetan medium secondary education, and the apparent lack of commitment to resolving the problems that partial implementation of Tibetan medium education engenders, are both signs of a shift in funding priorities due to a change in the political climate. By 1997, teaching Chinese to Tibetans from the first grade of primary school was deemed by the TAR government to be more appropriate than extending Tibetan medium teaching into secondary education.[53]

Problems of implementation

Despite the statistical success of the Tibetan medium education programme at primary level, research papers and reports of government meetings in the 1980s and 1990s suggest that the Tibetan language policy in the TAR was not being implemented successfully. In fact, there is a common saying in Tibet that 'Central Government policy is like *chang* [Tibetan barley beer]: the first brew is strong but the more water that is added the weaker it gets until it has no strength at all.' The meaning of this is that policy drafted by officials in Beijing has some strength but by the time it reaches the people who are to implement it, the momentum has been lost and the policy measures fail to materialize. It appears that there are several reasons for this, which are described in the next section below.

Lack of financial and human resources The cost of funding Tibetan-medium education is obviously greater than the standard Chinese education. It is not just a question of economies of scale, and the expense of translation; there is the additional cost of providing Tibetan-language training for teachers. Since junior secondary teachers have received all their education from junior secondary level, including teacher training, in Chinese, even Tibetan teachers in the TAR have to be provided with Tibetan-language courses before they begin teaching.[54]

Lack of will on the part of local government officials In the 1980s and 1990s it was widely suggested that the government authorities lacked the will to implement the Tibetan-language policy, partly because the officials concerned were unable to speak Tibetan themselves.[55] In the 1950s, Han Chinese officials were given Tibetan language training before arriving in the TAR. In fact, until the 1980s, Tibetan departments in Chinese universities existed solely to provide language training for Han Chinese officials who were to be sent to work in Tibetan areas.[56] By the 1980s, however, although Han Chinese officials were encouraged to learn Tibetan once they arrived in the TAR, it was no longer a prerequisite. Furthermore, with increasing numbers of Han Chinese entrepreneurs arriving in the TAR as the economy developed, the Chinese-speaking culture became stronger. At the same time, significant numbers of Tibetans in government office were also unable to speak Tibetan, particularly those who had been brought up in the 1960s and 1970s, or who had been educated in China. In 1987, the 'Provisions on the Use of Tibetan' stipulated that all Tibetan cadres under forty-five and Tibetan workers under forty who did not know Tibetan should 'take lessons in Tibetan and strive to be capable of using basic Tibetan language in three years' time'.[57] One survey carried out in 1987 gave the following results: out of 6,044 Tibetan government officials in one particular prefecture who were educated beyond primary level, 991 could speak Tibetan. This represented 16.5 per cent of the total number of Tibetan government officials.[58] A similar survey of a Tibetan school in Lhasa Municipality revealed that among twenty teachers, ten of whom were Tibetan, only three were qualified to teach in Tibetan, and two of these spoke such poor Tibetan that the students could not understand them.[59]

Disparity between the programme in schools and the requirements for advancement in society The failure to implement the Tibetan language policy successfully in society has a detrimental effect on the implementation of Tibetan education in schools. In a situation where Chinese continues to be the dominant language, knowledge acquisition in Tibetan and the devotion of a substantial proportion of a student's school career to the learning of the Tibetan language will not enable him or her to compete in society on an equal footing with his or her Han Chinese peers.

Since the 1985 reforms, parents have been faced with a situation where they have to send their children to a Tibetan medium primary school in which the education is culturally more relevant and the child is likely to perform better, on the one hand, but, on the other hand, he will be less well equipped to compete for secondary education, or to compete in the work market. Although since 1986 Tibetans have been able to take the examination for government service in Tibetan, Chinese is still the working language, and therefore fluency in Chinese is of vital importance. Employment in a state work-unit not only allows the opportunity for career advancement to jobs and salaries at the highest level; it also significantly reduces the cost of living: ordinary citizens receive lower rations of basic foods than state workers, and commodities such as bicycles and electric cooking facilities are much more difficult and costly to obtain.

Some parents in urban areas – if they have sufficient contacts to bypass the system – enrol their children in Chinese medium primary schools, where they study in Chinese from the first grade. This will give them greater access to secondary and tertiary education, as well as enable them to compete for jobs in the state sector, although they still have to master the language before they can learn other subjects. However, most Tibetans who have been through Chinese medium education lose the ability to read and write Tibetan. Some even lose facility in spoken Tibetan.

In recent years, therefore, Tibetan medium education has lost popularity, partly because it is considered inferior to Chinese medium education and partly because of the obstacles it creates to further academic and social advancement. The continuing failure to increase the use of Tibetan in Tibetan society has led to a situation where Tibetan medium education is seen as a hindrance to many students, as is shown in Box 12.1.

Obstacles created by the partial implementation of Tibetan medium education The 'Provisions on the Use of Tibetan', promulgated in 1987, included a clause providing for schools 'to systematically institute

---

Box 12.1 What is the point of learning Tibetan?

How do the students look at this? Students say what the teachers say is correct. What benefit is there in learning Tibetan? Tibetan is no use after we leave school. It is not used in offices, so what is the point of learning it? In the end we are faced with difficulties: when you have finished school where can you go? To the Tibetan Medical Institute. You can't go to the Academy of Social Sciences (only a few have). As a teacher I face this problem with my students all the time. Of course, the Party has good policies but a few leaders have not put this into practice.

But we should learn Tibetan. Of course, some teachers seem to think that we are saying that we shouldn't learn Chinese. We should learn Chinese. Of course Chinese is the dominant national language in our country. But the TAR is an autonomous region. I have not been to Xinjiang or other places. But I am told that when they have big meetings they talk in their own language. This is not the case in the TAR. In all the meetings here, whatever it is, we talk in Chinese. Take the example of the higher leaders. They need to practise what they preach. That would be beneficial. For example, because teachers have such low status, high officials take no notice of what they have to say.

Source: *Television debate on education, Lhasa TV, 30 July 1988.*

---

an educational system whereby teaching is done principally in the Tibetan language'.[60] However, the system has been only partially implemented, and there are currently no plans to develop it further. Therefore, it lacks the coherence needed for it to function properly. As all secondary and tertiary education is still taught in Chinese, mother-tongue education for Tibetans at primary level creates an obstacle to further educational advancement. In 1997, plans were drawn up to tackle this problem by teaching Chinese to Tibetans from the first grade of primary school instead of from grade 3; these plans, however, were said to apply only to urban schools.[61]

Most Tibetan children study entirely in Tibetan to the end of primary school. Many rural schools provide no Chinese tuition at all. Urban primary schools currently provide three hours of Chinese language tuition per week for Tibetan children from the age of nine (grade 3). However, even this is insufficient to allow Tibetan children to compete with Han Chinese children in exams. Although a concession is given to

Tibetan children in the secondary school entrance examination because they are competing against Chinese children using their mother-tongue, they still have to achieve a certain competence in the Chinese paper to enable them to progress to secondary school. Indeed, the 12.3 per cent enrolment of junior secondary school-aged children in 1995 suggests an extremely high failure rate, given that enrolment rate in primary school in that year was 63 per cent.[62]

Another disadvantage for Tibetans studying at secondary schools is that since they continue to have six hours per week of Tibetan tuition and six hours per week of Chinese tuition, they are unable to study a foreign language. Universities in China require students to take a foreign language paper in the entrance examination and, although the marks are not counted in the total, the paper has a bearing on the success of the candidate; this means, in practice, that Tibetan students are blocked from many higher education courses, and particularly science and foreign language courses.

This dislocation between primary and secondary education lies at the centre of the debate over Tibetan-medium education. It is this that has provoked the division between those who advocate extending Tibetan medium education up to tertiary level and those who argue for increasing Chinese at primary level.[63] Some educationalists and officials argue the benefit of starting the teaching of Chinese from the first grade of primary school.[64] At a meeting of the TAR CPPCC in 1994, one delegate expressed the following view:

> In some primary schools, students are taught in the Tibetan language during the first and second years, and they are taught Chinese only after reaching higher standards. Because of this, it is difficult to improve the class grades in these schools. We should learn from the Lhasa Experimental Primary School and start to teach the students both the Tibetan and Chinese language from the first year. It will then help the students receive an all-round education and help students improve their grades.[65]

The 1997 proposal to increase the teaching of Chinese in primary education rather than to extend Tibetan medium teaching into secondary education, in effect, signifies a reversal of the plans laid out in the 1987 'Provisions on the Use of Tibetan'. Funding considerations undoubtedly play an important role in the new plans, since increasing the teaching of Chinese at primary level would be considerably cheaper than extending the Tibetan medium education into secondary school. However, as mentioned earlier, these plans also accord with the political climate of the 1990s which has led to the gradual reduction of the concessions given to Tibetan cultural distinctiveness.

Changing political climate   The return to a policy of 'politics in control', which was seen throughout China after 1989, came earlier in the TAR. The policy is still prevalent today, to a greater extent than in the neighbouring provinces with smaller Tibetan populations.[66] The resumption of pro-independence demonstrations after 1987 linked Tibetan culture and Tibetan language with Tibetan separatism. Consequently, in the TAR, the economic logic of using Tibetan medium education to provide a skilled work-force has been overridden by political notions of security.

The primary political role of 'minority education' was reasserted, making the unity of the motherland the leading ideology in education; anything that was deemed to subvert that came under threat. Tibetan language was increasingly associated with Tibetan nationalism and 'splittism', with the result that efforts to develop its use in society and education were increasingly undermined. In 1997, in a speech on literature and art, TAR Party Secretary Chen Kuiyuan described Tibetan language in terms reminiscent of the Cultural Revolution when ethnic characteristics had been attacked for emphasizing nationality differences and creating nationality tensions which were contrary to the concept of Communism. In his speech, Chen said: 'separatists now go all out to put religion above the Tibetan culture and attempt to use the spoken language and culture to cause disputes and antagonism between nationalities, and this is the crux of the matter.'[67]

In education, some officials still called for the extension of Tibetan medium education to secondary and tertiary level into the mid-1990s. At the Fifth TAR Conference on Education in 1994, government chairman Gyaltsen Norbu talked of 'attaching importance to Tibetan language teaching and actively promoting bilingual teaching'. At the Third Forum in the same year, Executive Deputy Party Secretary Ragdi also stressed that the government should 'earnestly promote bilingual teaching so that students will have a good command of Tibetan and standard Chinese'. By 1996, it appeared that those who advocated increasing Chinese tuition were in the ascendancy. Unlike the policy documents of the 1980s, or indeed Deputy Party Secretary Dorje Tseten's book published in 1991, which suggested that Chinese need not be taught at all in rural primary schools and that Tibetan medium education should gradually be implemented up to tertiary level,[68] the Ninth Five-Year Plan for the TAR appears to put more emphasis on learning Chinese than on learning Tibetan: 'Attention is to be paid to the teaching and study of the Tibetan language, and vigorous effort is to be made to promote the teaching and study of the Han language.'[69]

In his speech on art and literature, Chen Kuiyuan said that the policies on Tibetan language drawn up in the 1980s will continue to be followed in the future. However, in 1996, the 'Guiding Committee on Work in Spoken and Written Tibetan' was downgraded from a prefectural-level organ to county level, and the number of its members was reduced.[70] There were subsequent indications that it was to be abolished altogether.[71] In 1996, the CPPCC continued to raise the issue of the failure to implement Tibetan language policy in Tibetan society, laying the blame on the government as a whole, rather than on the failure of individual officials as had been the case earlier:

> Tibet is an autonomous region where the Tibetan nationality live in compact communities and 95 per cent of its population live in farming and pastoral areas. The masses of peasants and herders use the Tibetan written language to study the Party's policies and to study the country's laws and regulations. The written Tibetan language itself has a glorious history of more than a thousand years. All the world accepts the Tibetan written language as an advanced written language, and in the history of the world's culture it has its own important position.
>
> In 1987, according to the proposals of the two vice chairmen of the People's National Congress, the regional People's Congress not only adopted laws and regulations to enhance work on written and spoken Tibetan, but also established translation teams in all departments of county level of the whole region. These departments quietly made a certain contribution to Tibet's stability and development. Even so, in recent years the government at all levels didn't attach much importance to using spoken and written Tibetan.
>
> Work on spoken and written Tibetan must be strengthened. The Law on Regional Autonomy and the Party's Nationality Policy must be seriously implemented. At present it is not clear whether the 'Guiding Committee on Work in Spoken and Written Tibetan' will continue, or whether it will be abolished. If it is to be abolished, then the reasons should be properly explained in order to convince the people.[72]

Several Tibetan intellectuals describe what appear to be irreconcilable arguments about cause and effect in relation to the Tibetan language issue. One Tibetan scholar believes the problem lies in the fact that the Tibetan language has always been seen politically as 'a tool of "separatists"', and thus at different periods use of the language has been more or less actively discouraged. So, while Chinese law and economic sense call for a more general use of Tibetan language in the TAR, the perception that it is politically threatening undermines its actual development:

> There are many complicated reasons why Tibetan was prohibited for a long time, but there are two main reasons: One reason is that the educational leaders and government officials didn't pay enough attention to Tibetan

language. The second is that in the old Tibetan society only a few people could read and write Tibetan, and these people were largely from the aristocracy or other high-class leaders and important people in monasteries. These people have mostly escaped to India and are involved in the movement to separate from the Motherland. Since people who knew the language were mostly likely to be involved in such activity, the Government thinks of the Tibetan language in a political sense. The Government thinks that Tibetan society was at the feudal-slave stage of economic development. And they think that within that there was a strong class struggle, and that Tibetan language was a tool to maintain the feudal-slave system. This is one reason the government doesn't want to improve the conditions for Tibetan language.[73]

In the 1988 Lhasa television debate, as mentioned earlier, one of the speakers suggested that even the discussion of Tibetan medium education can lead to accusations of separatism: 'When we speak about Tibetan education, about using the Tibetan language, we are accused of wanting to split the motherland.' There is another group of officials and scholars, including Deputy Party Secretary Tenzin, who reverse the argument by suggesting that undermining the Tibetan language in fact causes nationalist unrest.[74] One scholar writes that serious implementation of the Tibetan language policy, including Tibetan medium education up to university level, could go a long way towards resolving the nationalist issue in the TAR. This author concludes:

> An important cause of nationalist unrest is that the oral and written Tibetan language is not accorded due status; nor is it effectively implemented ... The Socialist period is a period of development and improvement of all nationalities together and it is not a period to wither away the nationalities. But when 'Left' thinking played the main role in our country, they pushed forward a policy to create a fusion of nationalities, by making the Han the key nationality. They didn't recognize the specific character of different nationalities' cultures, they prohibited 'minority' nationalities from using their written language, and severely damaged minority nationalities' self-respect and feelings. In this way they laid the foundation for potential calamities to stir up national conflicts.[75]

Summary

The language rights of all China's nationalities have been enshrined in Chinese law since China's first constitution. Nevertheless, the Tibetan language was denounced in education and society during the Great Leap Forward and again in the Cultural Revolution. In the early 1980s attempts were made to reinstate it as the official language of the TAR.

The 1984 Law on Regional Autonomy and the 1995 Education Law both guarantee the right of 'minority' nationalities to use their own language in education. In 1987, detailed procedures were drawn up for implementing Tibetan language policy in education and public life in the TAR.[76] Given that, in 1998, official statistics indicated that 90 per cent of the population in the TAR still communicated in Tibetan,[77] the use of the language was deemed to be important not just for the preservation of Tibetan culture but for economic development and for the dissemination of government policy and information.

However, despite the law and government directives on the use of 'minority' languages, the implementation of the Tibetan language policy has been relatively unsuccessful. The reasons behind the failure to implement the policy include: (1) reluctance on the part of officials to use Tibetan, many of whom (including Tibetan officials) are unable to speak it themselves; (2) financial considerations; and (3) a change in the political climate after the resumption of pro-independence demonstrations in 1987. Since that time, the Tibetan language has been increasingly associated with Tibetan nationalism and the economic logic of using Tibetan language to provide a skilled work-force has been undermined during the 1990s by political notions of security.

The process of implementing the Tibetan language policy in education began after the 1984 Second Forum with the introduction of Tibetan medium primary schools for Tibetan children. Statistically, implementation has been very successful, although there is a gap between the apparent statistical success of the policy and the ability of schools to implement it. This is due to a lack of textbooks and teachers qualified to teach in Tibetan.[78] By 1998, 99.42 per cent of primary schools in the TAR were said to be Tibetan medium.[79] However, all secondary education for Tibetans in the TAR has continued to be taught in Chinese. It is this dislocation between primary and secondary education that lies at the centre of the debate over Tibetan-language education. For the last twelve years, parents have been faced with a situation where they have had to send their children to a Tibetan medium primary school in which the education is culturally more relevant and the child is likely to perform better, but he is then less well equipped to compete for secondary education, or to compete in the work market. This situation has led to the declining popularity of Tibetan medium education among urban Tibetans, partly because it is said to be of inferior quality and partly because of the obstacles it creates to further academic and social advancement.

Two groups have emerged among officials and educationalists over the Tibetan-language issue. One group, which was dominant in the mid-1980s, advocates the importance of developing Tibetan as the language of education and commerce, including the extension of Tibetan medium education up to tertiary level. The other group argues for increasing the teaching of Chinese at primary level.[80] In the political climate of the 1990s, with the overriding importance given to economic development and the de-emphasis of Tibetan culture, the views of this second group now dominate government policy and implementation. In 1996, plans for generalizing Tibetan medium secondary education were abandoned.[81] In 1997, new plans were drawn up to introduce Chinese classes from grade 1 in urban primary schools.[82]

Notes

1. Duojie Caidan (Dorje Tseten), *Xizang Jiaoyu* (Education in Tibet) (China Tibetology Publishers, Beijing, 1991).

2. 'Common Programme of the Chinese People's Consultative Conference', Item 53, 1949.

3. Constitution of the People's Republic of China (Foreign Languages Press, Beijing, 1982), pp. 70–1.

4. 'Law on Regional Autonomy for "Minority" Nationalities of the People's Republic of China', 1984, Article 37.

5. 'Education Law', 18 March 1995, *Xinhua*, 20 March 1995 [SWB 19/3/95].

6. Ngapo Ngawang Jigme and Panchen Lama 'Proposal on the Study, Use and Development of the Tibetan Language', delivered at Fifth Session of Fourth TAR People's Congress, 9 July 1987, Lhasa Radio, 12 July 1987.

7. Duojie Caidan (Dorje Tseten), *Education in Tibet*; see also Ngapo Ngawang Jigme and Panchen Lama, op. cit.

8. Duojie Caidan (Dorje Tseten), op. cit.

9. Internal Party discussion paper, 1995.

10. Ngapo Ngawang Jigme and Panchen Lama, 'Proposal on the Study, Use and Development of the Tibetan Language'.

11. Duojie Caidan (Dorje Tseten), *Education in Tibet*.

12. Ngapo Ngawang Jigme and Panchen Lama, 'Proposal on the Study, Use and Development of the Tibetan Language'.

13. Ibid.

14. 'Summary Report of Second Work Forum', cited in ibid.

15. TAR People's Congress, 'Provisions on the Study, Use and Development of Spoken and Written Tibetan (for trial implementation)', 'Provisions on the Use of Tibetan', 1987.

16. Ibid.

17. Ibid.

18. 'Report on First Regional Conference on Tibetan Language Teaching', 16–21 July 1991, *Xizang Ribao* (Tibet Daily), 23 July 1991.

19. In Lhasa, the department that oversees the implementation of the

Tibetan language policy falls under the jurisdiction of the Prefectural Education and Sports Committee.

20. Tenzin (TAR Deputy Party Secretary), 'Speech to Meeting of TAR Guiding Committee on Spoken and Written Tibetan', 16 March 1993, *Dakpo* (The Owner), No. 2, 1993.

21. Television debate on education, Lhasa TV, 30 July 1988.

22. Tenzin, 'Speech to Meeting of TAR Guiding Committee'.

23. *Xinhua*, 18 January 1998.

24. Li Peng, 'Speech on 20th Anniversary of the Founding of the TAR', *Xinhua*, 31 August 1985 [SWB 4/9/85]; Ngapo Ngawang Jigme and Panchen Lama, 'Proposal on the Study, Use and Development of the Tibetan Language'; see also Phunstok Tsering, TAR CPPCC, Eleventh Bulletin of the Second Plenary Session, May 1994; see also Teng Xing, 1988 Internal Party discussion paper, 1995.

25. Tenzin, 'Speech to Meeting of TAR Guiding Committee'.

26. See Li Peng, 'Speech on 20th Anniversary of the Founding of the TAR'; Yin Fatang, Lhasa Radio, 4 June 1980; Hu Yaobang, May 1980; Ngapo Ngawang Jigme, 'Increasing Official Use of the Tibetan Language', Lhasa Radio, 21 July 1985; Tenth Panchen Lama, 'Tibetan Language and Religion', *Xinhua*, 31 August 1985; also Lhasa Radio, 16 August 1986; Ngapo Ngawang Jigme and Panchen Lama, 'Proposal on the Study, Use and Development of the Tibetan Language'; Dorje Tsering, Speech to Fifth Session of TAR Fourth Regional People's Congress, 4 July 1987, reported on Lhasa Radio, 4 July 1987 [SWB 8/7/87]; Wu Jinghua, Speech to Fifth Session of TAR Fourth Regional People's Congress, 4 July 1987, reported on Lhasa Radio, 4 July 1987 [SWB 8/7/87]; see also comments on him by Tseten Wangchuk Sharlho, 'China's Reforms in Tibet: Issues and Dilemmas', *Journal of Contemporary China*, Vol. 1, No. 1, 1992, p. 54.

27. Ngapo Ngawang Jigme, 'Increasing Official Use of the Tibetan Language', July 1987.

28. Tenzin (TAR Deputy Party Secretary), 'Report of Speech to First Regional Conference on Tibetan Language Teaching', *Xizang Ribao* (Tibet Daily), 23 July 1991.

29. See Yang Wanli, '*Xizang Kecheng Jiaocai Yanjiu De Teshuxing Jiqi Duice*' (The Countermeasure and Particularity of Research on Teaching Materials), *Xizang Yanjiu* (Tibet Studies), Vol. 58, No. 1, 1996.

30. See Duojie Caidan (Dorje Tseten), *Education in Tibet*; also Gendian Ciren (Gendung Tsering), '*Xizang Shuang Yu Jiaoyu de Shijian yu Tansuo*' (Exploration and Practice of Double Language Education in Tibet), *Xizang Yanjiu* (Tibet Studies), Vol. 58, No. 1, 1996.

31. Percentage calculated from *Xinhua* report which stated that 95 per cent of all schools in the TAR provided teaching in the Tibetan language. Since there is currently no Tibetan medium education above primary level, it would suggest that 98 per cent of primary schools are Tibetan medium. *Xinhua*, 20 March 1996 [FBIS 28/3/96].

32. Yang Chunjing, '*Qiandan Zang Yuwen Jiaoxue Zai Fazhan Minzu Jiaoyu*

Zhong de Zhongyao Xing' (A Tentative Study on the Importance of Teaching in the Tibetan Language for Developing National Education), *Xizang Yanjiu* (Tibet Studies), Vol. 59, No. 2, 1996.

33. 48 per cent of 'minority' nationalities in Qinghai are Tibetan. See *Tabulation on China's Nationalities* (China Statistical Publishing House, Beijing, 1994).

34. *Qinghai Statistical Yearbook 1993* (Qinghai Provincial Statistical Bureau, China Statistical Publishing House, Beijing, 1993).

35. Huangnan Prefecture Statistics, 1994–1995.

36. *Xinhua*, 25 February 1994 [SWB 1/3/94].

37. 'Conclusion of the First Regional Meeting on Tibetan Language Work, Basang and Others Attend, Speech Made by Tenzin', *Xizang Ribao* (Tibet Daily), 23 July 1991.

38. Lhasa Radio, 28 May 1984.

39. Dayang, 'To Further the Study, Use and Development of the Tibetan Language: The Lhasa Education and Sports Committee Makes Additional Provisions on Relevant Concerns', *Lhasa Wanbao* (Lhasa Evening News), 25 August 1990.

40. Ibid.

41. Yang Xin and Duo Fen, 'Random Notes from Tibet University', *Beijing Review*, Vol., 31, No. 47, 21–27 November 1988.

42. Interview with former teacher at Tibet University, 2 February 1997.

43. Tenzin, 'Speech to TAR Education Conference', *Tibet Education*, No. 2, 1997, pp. 2–7.

44. Duojie Caidan (Dorje Tseten), *Education in Tibet*.

45. *Xizang Ribao* (Tibet Daily), 11 August 1990; CPPCC News Bulletin, 18 May 1994.

46. Tenzin, 'Speech to Meeting of TAR Guiding Committee'.

47. Yang Chunjing, 'A Tentative Study'.

48. There is a certain confusion in the way the term 'bilingual' is used in the Tibetan context. The term is used somewhat indiscriminately to mean both the teaching of Tibetan and Chinese language and teaching in Tibetan and Chinese medium. See Gendian Ciren, '… Double Language Education in Tibet'.

49. TAR Education Commission and Guiding Committee on Spoken and Written Tibetan, 'Report on Tibet Medium Secondary Education', *Podjong Lobsu* (Tibet Education), No. 4, 1995.

50. Ibid.

51. Interview with education official, 10 November 1996.

52. Ibid.

53. See Chen Kuiyuan, 'Speech on Literature and Art', *Xizang Ribao* (Tibet Daily), 11 July 1997.

54. 'To Further the Study, Use and Development of the Tibetan Language – Supplementary Comments by the Lhasa Municipal Education and Sports Committee', *Lhasa Wanbao* (Lhasa Evening News), 25 August 1990.

55. See among others: Duojie Caidan (Dorje Tseten), *Education in Tibet*, 1991; Ngapo Ngawang Jigme and Panchen Lama, 'Proposal on the Study, Use and Development of the Tibetan Language'; Paper on Education Development in

Tibet, by Tibetan scholar, 1995; TAR CPPCC, 'Report of the Fourth Plenary Session of the Sixth CPPCC of the TAR', 5 May 1996; Television debate on education, Lhasa TV, 30 July 1988.

56. Interview with Palden Gyal, 20 October 1996.

57. 'Provisions on the Use of Tibetan', 1987.

58. Internal Party discussion paper, 1995.

59. Duojie Caidan (Dorje Tseten), *Education in Tibet*.

60. 'Provisions on the Use of Tibetan', 1987.

61. Han Zihong, Director of Primary Education at TAR Education Commission, quoted in *Agence France Presse*, 7 May 1997.

62. 'Outline of the TAR Child Development Programme for the 1990s', *Xizang Ribao* (Tibet Daily), 11 July 1996, p. 2.

63. See Tenzin, 'Speech to Meeting of TAR Guiding Committee'; Duojie Caidan (Dorje Tseten), *Education in Tibet*.

64. TAR CPPCC, Report of the Second Committee Meeting of the Sixth Session of the TAR CPPCC, *CPPCC News Bulletin*, 18 May 1994.

65. TAR CPPCC, Thirteenth Bulletin of Second Plenary Session of the Sixth TAR CPPCC, Secretariat of the Conference, 17 May 1994.

66. Interview with Tsering Shakya, Tibetan historian, 1 January 1997.

67. Chen Kuiyuan, 'Speech on Literature and Art'.

68. Duojie Caidan (Dorje Tseten), *Education in Tibet*.

69. 'Outline of the TAR's Five-Year Plan for Economic and Social Development and Its Long-term Target for 2010, Approved by the Fourth Session of the Sixth Regional People's Congress on 24th May 1996', *Xizang Ribao* (Tibet Daily), 7 June 1996 (TAR Ninth Five-Year Plan, 1996), pp. 1–4.

70. Interview with Lhasa government official, 1997.

71. TAR CPPCC, May 1996.

72. Ibid.

73. Paper on Education Development in Tibet, by Tibetan scholar, 1995, p. 85.

74. Tenzin, 'Report of Speech to First Regional Conference on Tibetan Language Teaching'.

75. Internal Party discussion paper, 1995.

76. 'Provisions on the Use of Tibetan', 1987.

77. *Xinhua*, 18 January 1998.

78. See: Duojie Caidan (Dorje Tseten), *Education in Tibet*.

79. *Xinhua*, 18 January 1998.

80. See: Tenzin, 'Speech to Meeting of TAR Guiding Committee'; Duojie Caidan (Dorje Tseten), *Education in Tibet*; Chen Kuiyuan, 'Speech on Literature and Art'; Ragdi, August 1994.

81. Interview with education official, 10 November 1996.

82. See Chen Kuiyuan, 'Speech on Literature and Art'.

CHAPTER 13

Concluding Comments

This book has considered the developments in each sector of education in the TAR since the start of China's economic reforms, set against the background of education history in the TAR and the wider background of education in China since 1950. This final chapter gives an overview of developments since 1980, looking at the goals that were set at the beginning of the period, at what has been achieved and at the extent to which the goals have been changed by the economic and political developments of the last two decades. It would be interesting, here, to compare conditions for Tibetans in the TAR with educational conditions in similar communities in other parts of the world, but that is beyond the scope of this study. Nevertheless, an attempt is made to draw some conclusions about where conditions in the TAR mirror conditions in poorer areas of China and where circumstances in the region are unique. A few comparisons are also made with efforts to develop a Tibetan education system across the border in the Tibetan refugee community in India.

After the end of the Cultural Revolution, the tenor of Chinese policy in the TAR changed, as did policies in China as a whole. The First Forum on Work in the TAR convened in Beijing in April 1980 set the new tone. Following the First Forum, China's top leaders came to the TAR to apologize personally for the 'mistakes of the past'. In May of that year, Hu Yaobang himself, the General Secretary of the CCP Central Committee, told a gathering of 5,000 cadres in Lhasa: 'We feel that our Party has let the Tibetan people down. We feel very bad! ... We have worked for nearly thirty years, but the life of the Tibetan people has not been notably improved. Are we not to blame?'[1]

The main thrust of the First Tibet Forum was to set Tibetans in the TAR on the path to increased prosperity, and to re-establish what was known as the 'national regional autonomy' of the TAR within China.[2] The TAR was said to be 'an even more special autonomous region than the others and thus even more entitled to autonomy rights'.[3] Regional autonomy included the right to develop Tibet's traditional culture and language, and to reject any central government policy that did not accord with the TAR's 'special conditions'.[4] The report by Yang Jingren, head of the State Commission for Nationalities Affairs, stated: 'Everything must be done in line with ethnic and regional conditions rather than vague generalizations or arbitrary uniformity.' Hu Yaobang set target dates by which improvements in living standards were to be achieved: (1) Two to three years to 'make the first steps in improving its poor and backward situation'; (2) Five to six years to exceed 'the best level attained in the last 30 years'; (3) Ten years to achieve 'greater affluence'.[5]

The pledges and policies that emerged from the First Forum included a tax exemption for peasants and nomads and an exemption from meeting state quotas. They also included an increase in state funds from the Central government to the TAR for what was termed the 'one development and two improvements', that is the development of the economy and the improvement of living standards and education. As far as education was concerned, new policies included the use of Tibetan as the first language in schools and society, an emphasis on primary and secondary education and on the state funding of education, and an emphasis on education for Tibetans. One of the main pledges of the First Forum was the transfer of Han Chinese personnel out of the TAR, and the training of Tibetans to take their place. 'Putting more Tibetans in the Saddle' was the slogan of the period.

The economic and cultural concessions made at the First Forum created a mood of cautious optimism among Tibetan officials and educationalists in Lhasa in the early 1980s. However, with hindsight, it appears that although there may have been the desire to grant the TAR a measure of autonomy at the First Forum, it proved impossible (as it had in the past) for the TAR to be divorced from the economic and political developments of central China. From the start, the First Forum set up a conflict between policies made for the benefits of Tibetans in the TAR and policies which furthered China's broader economic and strategic interests. In education, the see-saw effect which was noted in earlier periods continued through the 1980s and 1990s. During the 1980s, significant advances were made in the development of a distinctive Tibetan education system, and yet the lack of funding – principally brought about by China's economic reforms – led to a serious decline in enrolment. On the other hand, during the 1990s, as the economy in the TAR took off, educational funding increased and there were new achievements in school construction, teacher training and enrolment. But the growing economy brought into the region increasing numbers of Han Chinese whose children had to be accommodated into the education system; at the same time, new conservative influences entered the political arena. The result of these factors was that overall enrolment in the TAR increased in the 1990s, but the commitment to providing an education system specifically for Tibetans was eroded.

Education in the TAR and China's broader economic concerns

At the end of the Cultural Revolution, China's economy was in such a parlous state that finding an efficient way to modernize and develop it became an overriding priority. As one of the poorest regions of China, the TAR was set to suffer, along with the other less developed regions, from the choices made by the Chinese government in the interests of the country as a whole. The experience of the TAR and other poor regions in China was similar to that of the poor in many countries around the world in the 1980s as governments turned from socialism and central planning to embrace a free market economy. In China, the economic reforms hit the underdeveloped regions doubly: not only did they entail a overall reduction in central government funding, but the funds that were available were primarily invested in the more developed eastern provinces. This resulted in a growing divide between the economies of the rich and poor regions of China, and an increasing discrepancy between the funds available for education. The wider economic decentralization which took place at this time coincided with the fiscal decentralization of education funding, and this resulted in several major contradictions. While the financial reform of education achieved considerable success in the wealthier eastern regions of China, in poor regions like the TAR it led to a serious decline in investment in education, which had a negative impact on both the quality and the extent of the education provided. This, in turn, affected enrolment. Thus, in the TAR, the economic reforms, instead of improving quality and efficiency, increased what became known as 'educational wastage'.

As discussed in Chapter 4, the TAR was only scheduled to join China's economic development plan during the 1990s and yet from the start of the reforms, the TAR (as every province and region in China) had to take financial responsibility for its own educational development. The pledge of increased central government funding made at the First Forum proved to be insufficient to meet the commitment to state-sponsored education, also made at the First Forum. This appears to have been the case in other poor regions of China, and particularly in 'minority' nationality areas.[6] Furthermore, the economic reforms set up a conflict of interests at local government level between investment in education and income generation. One of Deng Xiaoping's key slogans in the 1980s was *'Zhi Fu Guangrong'* (To Get Rich is Glorious). On the one hand, full responsibility for education funding devolved from the central government to provincial, prefectural and county governments. On the other hand, local governments were being encouraged to invest in projects that provided quick profits and generated tax revenues (such as town and village enterprises). As a result, investment in education was, to a certain extent, sacrificed to what was perceived as the greater priority of income generation.

The situation was made worse in the TAR by the fact that although the government lacked the funding to extend state education, and although the First Forum had stipulated that the TAR should develop education in accordance with the particular conditions in the region, the TAR followed the China-wide policy of closing and merging community-funded primary schools. With few state schools to replace the community schools, there was a 70 per cent reduction in the number of primary schools between 1978 and 1985 and a 55 per cent decline in enrolment. Indeed, by 1994, the enrolment rate was 67 per cent, still 9 per cent lower than it had been in 1982.

As economic recession hit China at the end of the 1980s, regional, prefectural and county governments throughout the country had fewer resources available for education: an increased burden of responsibility for funding education therefore fell on ordinary people. In the TAR, the First Forum had stipulated that nomads and peasants should no longer be obliged to provide labour and materials without recompense.[7] However, this directive was often overlooked; indeed, as was seen in Chapter 5, the cost of education was often greater for the poorer sections of society than for the wealthier sections. This appears to have had a significant affect on enrolment, leading the TAR Government Chairman to announce, at the end of 1993, that one-third of children in the TAR were unable to afford to go to school.[8]

However, in the early 1990s the TAR was brought into the second stage of China's economic development plan, as had been determined at the beginning of the reform period. In 1992, the TAR was made a 'special economic zone'; tax concessions and low land-use fees were given to encourage investment. Nineteen ninety-three was designated the Year of Education in the TAR during which financial resources increased at every level. In 1994, government expenditure on education in the TAR amounted to 282.72 million yuan, almost double the expenditure for 1990.[9] Furthermore, funding priorities were reassessed in the light of the failure of the reforms to deliver improvements during the 1980s. Indeed, perhaps for the first time, the TAR did not follow national strategies but put more funding into increasing the number of schools in the region rather than improving efficiency in existing schools. The 1990s saw achievements in programmes to reduce illiteracy and drop-out, and in training courses to improve the quality of teaching in primary schools as well as new plans to provide training for multi-grade teaching, which is still a feature of education in sparsely populated rural areas.

There is no doubt that significant improvements were made in the general provision of education in the 1990s, although the education system continues to be under serious financial strain. With current levels of investment, the financial problems in the education system seem set to continue for, unlike Central China, where the one-child family planning policy has led to a decline in the school-age population, the school age population of the TAR is still expanding and is being swelled by the children of Han Chinese settlers arriving in the region. One of the major challenges for the future in the TAR is to achieve and maintain *effective* levels of funding, most crucially in those sectors where there is currently under-performance (i.e. in rural primary schools and in Tibetan classes in secondary schools), for the repucussions of not providing sufficient funding are likely be significant.

Probably the most significant instance of the policies made at the beginning of the 1980s for the benefit of Tibetans in the TAR conflicting with China's broader economic concerns lies in the issue of providing personnel for economic development. One of the major commitments made after the First Forum was that Han Chinese would be transferred out of the region. As the Minister for Nationalities Affairs, Yang Jingren, wrote in his 1980 report: 'In the next few years, the Han nationality will be transferred out of Tibet in large numbers.'[10] At the same time, a commitment was made to the high-level training of Tibetans and other non-Han nationalities in the TAR so that they could play a role in the development of their own region. Yang Jingren's report directed that 'an autonomous region must develop the scientific, cultural and educational undertakings of its own nationality'.[11]

The extent to which the transfer of Chinese personnel out of the TAR took place in the 1980s is unclear. As noted in Chapter 9, large contingents of Han Chinese government workers were being sent into the TAR by 1985. By the end of the decade, all mention of Han Chinese personnel being transferred out of the TAR had disappeared from public announcements. Instead, statements encouraging Han Chinese from other parts to China to take part in the economic development of the TAR dominated the media; in the new market economy, large numbers of individual entrepreneurs found the TAR a particularly profitable place in which to engage in business.[12]

By the 1990s, it appears that the development of the TAR economy had begun to taken precedence over the longer-term goal of training Tibetans to enable to them to play a role in economic development. Moreover, the increasing Han Chinese population (brought in by economic growth, particularly in the cities) has had to be accommodated within the education system. As their numbers have grown, their educational needs and priorities have carried ever more weight. As a result, additional pressure has been placed on an educational system that is already under considerable strain. This has had particular ramifications for the education of Tibetans in secondary schools, where Chinese is the medium of instruction. As was seen in Chapter 7, the linguistic obstacle faced by Tibetans not only gives Han Chinese children an advantage in enrolment, but also enables them to enter the fast stream, which is provided with better resources and better teachers.

As regards Tibetan and other non-Han nationalities in senior secondary and higher education, progress was made during the 1980s in increasing their proportion in enrolment. However, in the mid-1990s, their proportion of the total enrolment appeared to decline, and was low relative to their percentage of the population. The fact that their enrolment was especially low in areas of study that are vital to the Tibetan economy, such as agriculture, is a particular cause for concern. The mid-1990s also saw a dilution of the concessions drawn up after the First Forum that were intended specifically to promote the education of Tibetans. From 1994 onwards, the programme of sending Tibetan children to school in Central China was extended to include the children of Han Chinese residents in the TAR.[13] In 1996, efforts to develop Tibetan-medium education at secondary level were abandoned. While financial considerations, as well as political factors, are likely to have been relevant to the latter decision, the increasing number of Han Chinese children in the TAR undoubtedly played a role in these recent policy changes.

There is always a conflict between equity and efficiency in the funding of education systems. As has been shown, the education system in China has swung from one extreme to the other over the past five decades. In the current period, the quest for efficiency has driven education planning both in China and in the TAR. But while the strategy may result in maximum efficiency for China as a whole, it is not necessarily efficient for the TAR. A lack of adequate funding for rural primary schools and for Tibetan classes in secondary schools is likely to perpetuate the vicious circle where funding them is perceived to be a waste of money and they thus fail to receive sufficient funding to enable them to improve. The dilemma is faced China-wide in terms of the disparity between urban and rural investment. However, in the TAR, insufficient funding has, perhaps, more serious social and political ramifications. Already, a lack of investment in the TAR education system as a whole has led to the perception that the TAR is unable to provide sufficient numbers of well-trained personnel for the economic development of the region and this, in turn, has led to the transfer of large numbers of Han Chinese from Central China. The TAR's adoption of the national 'quality'-oriented education policies (which give preferential funding to urban schools, key schools and the fast stream in secondary schools) has more serious implications. Because of the structure of the system in the TAR and because a good knowledge of the Chinese language is essential for educational advancement, in the current situation Han Chinese children are effectively given greater educational opportunities than Tibetan children. The extremely low enrolment of secondary school-aged children and the declining proportion of Tibetans in higher education is, in the long term, likely to hinder the participation of the Tibetan community in the economic development of the region. There is, thus, a danger that this could lead to a situation in which Tibetans are a poorly educated underclass and the administrative and skilled technical jobs are taken by resident Han Chinese. This would inevitably have political consequences and could lead to instability. Already there is a growing sense of social injustice in the Tibetan community and a sense of alienation among Tibetan youth. In 1993 riots broke out in Lhasa in which, for the first time, attacks were made on business premises of resident Han Chinese.

Education in the TAR and China's strategic concerns

The First Tibet Forum set the agenda for developing a distinctive, rounded Tibetan education system in the TAR. By the mid-1980s certain positive steps had been taken towards achieving this. Primary schools for Tibetans were made Tibetan-medium in 1984, and there were plans to extend Tibetan-medium education into secondary schools. In 1985, the TAR Teachers' College had become Tibet University – a comprehensive university that aimed to provide Tibetans with a scientific education but was also to focus on preserving and developing Tibetan culture. Plans were being drawn up for Tibetan to become the official language of the TAR, and the *Wu Sheng Qu* textbook committee was producing textbooks in Tibetan that were increasingly sympathetic to Tibet's history and cultural traditions. Moreover, in 1986, the Chinese government allowed the *Monlam Chenmo* (Great Prayer Festival), the most important festival in the Tibetan religious calendar, to be celebrated for the first time since the early 1960s. This was intended to be the ultimate indication of the Chinese government's tolerance of the TAR's distinctive religious, cultural and historical traditions.

However, the policies proposed in the early 1980s for the TAR eventually came into conflict with China's perceived strategic needs. If in terms of the conflict of economic interests, the position of the TAR has been similar in many ways to that of other less developed regions of China, in the conflict between China's perceived security concerns and the development of an appropriate education system, the problems of the TAR are more specific.

In 1987, a new series of pro-independence demonstrations began, which continued into the 1990s. A large proportion of the demonstrators were young people – in fact, many of them were of school age – and central to the demonstrations was the survival of a Tibetan cultural identity. There are several factors which may have contributed to the re-emergence of Tibetan nationalism into public life, after more than a decade during which it had disappeared underground. The rapid pace of change during the late 1980s and 1990s had a number of repercussions: the traditional face of the TAR was being transformed; increasing numbers of Han Chinese were moving into the region; perhaps most significantly, there was a perceived unfairness in the distribution of the economic benefits of change between the Han Chinese and the Tibetan communities. At the same time, the more liberal policies of the 1980s, which had allowed the rebuilding of monasteries and the rewriting of Tibetan textbooks, had given young Tibetans a new sense of cultural identity. For the first time, young people had been taught to appreciate the achievements of Tibetan history (albeit within the parameters of the Chinese motherland). They could talk to their parents openly about the past and learn about their religious and cultural heritage.

When the Chinese government made an attack on the Dalai Lama in September 1987, Tibetans mounted a public protest. This protest has been followed by over 150 demonstrations in the last ten years. The demonstrations have mostly been led by monks but have included large numbers of young people who, having been emboldened by the recognition their culture was at last receiving, were not prepared to see it criticized. (Western fascination with Tibet after the opening of the TAR to tourism in 1985 undoubtedly contributed to a new sense of self-worth.)

The repercussions of these demonstrations in education have been significant and serious. The renewed sensitivity of education, which the Chinese authorities are currently portraying as an arena in their battle with the Dalai Lama for Tibetan youth, has led to a dilution of the measures adopted after the First Forum for the development of a distinctive Tibetan education system. Furthermore, it has meant that attempts to make a balanced assessment of the advantages and disadvantages of Tibetan-medium education for Tibetans within the Chinese education system and society are distorted by political interference. It has also led to what could also be termed as 'educational wastage', on both the economic and educational levels. First, the perception that the monasteries pose a threat to China's security has meant that the role they had begun to forge for themselves in the development of basic education in rural areas has become impracticable in the TAR. In 1996, there were said to be 46,000 monks and nuns in monasteries throughout the TAR, which is over three times the number of teachers in the region.[14] Many of these monks and nuns live within reach of rural communities where there are no schools. They could, therefore, provide a vast free resource for the spread of basic literacy. Indeed, their contribution to the development of basic education was recognised as being significant in the 1980s, but although the clergy still continue to teach to some extent in Tibetan regions in other provinces, it is currently impossible for them to do so in the TAR.

Second, the perceived sensitivity of education in the current period has put in jeopardy the development of foreign funding in recent years. A number of projects have been delayed or suspended due to the reluctance of the Chinese authorities to allow foreign nationals to work as resident advisers on the projects.

Finally, the reassertion of the primary political role of 'minority education' is at present significantly narrowing the curriculum for Tibetan children, and has resulted in an erosion of time for academic study. In the current situation in the TAR, Chinese culture and language, and the Chinese state as the bearer of social and economic progress, are again being promoted at the expense of Tibetan culture and language in education.

In terms of political pressure on the education system, it appears that the situation is worse in the TAR than in Tibetan communities in other provinces. This is likely to be due to the fact that the proportion of Tibetans is smaller in other provinces and therefore that there is believed to be less danger of political instability. Furthermore, the TAR lies in a more sensitive position strategically, stretching as it does along the border with India.

Tibetan language policy: economic and strategic implications

The use of the Tibetan language was one of the key issues discussed at the First Forum. In his report, Minister Yang Jingren wrote:

> In autonomous regions the spoken and written language of the nationality exercising autonomy must be used as the first language, and it is through this medium that the local authorities are to exercise their functions and powers. The national language must be used as the principal language in conducting official business, issuing documents, making announcements, teaching ... etc. Reports and talks given in Han language must be translated into the national language. In Xizang [TAR] the first language is Tibetan; however, the Han language must also be used.[15]

Certain measures were taken by the TAR government to meet the Tibetan-language requirements of the First Forum. In 1985, Tibet University was established, and the policy of providing Tibetan-medium primary education for Tibetans was implemented. Two years later, the 'Provisions on the Use Of Tibetan' outlined the strategy for the introduction of Tibetan-medium education into secondary schools. However, as discussed in Chapter 12, this policy was never implemented; furthermore, the provision of Tibetan-medium tuition at Tibet University was largely abandoned.

There were both economic and political factors behind the failure to extend Tibetan-medium education into secondary schooling and to supply Tibetan-medium education at Tibet University. In the TAR, where the government has yet to provide any education for two-fifths of its children, the costs of bilingual education are particularly significant. Given the economies of scale in terms of textbook provision alone, Chinese-language education is considerably cheaper. Furthermore, the general failure to implement the First Forum policies regarding the Tibetan language in society has meant that it is increasingly impractical for Tibetan children to receive all their education in Tibetan. As for university-level teaching, increasing numbers of Han Chinese students who, despite TAR policy requirements, do not speak Tibetan have begun to enrol on courses at Tibet University. Since most Tibetans who reach university level can speak Chinese, only the most committed teachers persisted in teaching their courses in Tibetan. Moreover, as the political climate changed, these teachers became afraid that such a commitment to the original aspirations of the university would be reinterpreted as being unpatriotic.[16]

The issue of mother-tongue education in a society where a second language is dominant is a problem with which many governments have wrestled. Indeed, a brief look at a number of papers on education in the Tibetan refugee journal *Tibetan Review* suggests that the Tibetan government-in-exile may have been no more successful than the Chinese government in providing Tibetan-medium education for the children in the refugee community in India, even though the preservation of Tibetan culture is one of its primary goals. Although education in the Tibetan refugee community is not the subject of this book, the *Tibetan Review* articles reveal some interesting parallels with the situation in the TAR, which seem worth considering briefly here.

The Tibetan refugee community has its own system of Tibetan schools; nevertheless, they follow the standard Indian curriculum with teaching in the English medium. It was not until 1994 that the Tibetan government-in-exile endorsed the use of Tibetan as the language of instruction in primary schools.[17] Several reports suggest that many Tibetans have a poor command of written Tibetan when they graduate from school.[18] Indeed, one report predicted, on the basis of research carried out in the community, that the Tibetan language would not be spoken by the Tibetan refugee community at all by the middle of the twenty-first century.[19]

It is interesting to note that the problems facing educators in the Tibetan exile community in India are similar to those faced by educators in the TAR. Efforts to improve the system of Tibetan-medium education are said to be hampered by a lack of qualified teachers and a lack of textbooks. The existing textbooks are said to be dull and complicated, and their design is less appealing to students than the English-medium textbooks.[20] Most significantly, Tibetan students fear that a Tibetan medium primary education will reduce their chance of success in secondary schools as well as their career prospects.[21] Tenzin Sangpo writes: 'For Tibetan children to leave Tibetan education and find that Tibetan language has no market value will only, in time, create language disaffection and decay. There is the current danger of Tibetan becoming the language of the school and English or Hindi, language of the street and shop.'[22]

There does, however, appear to be one important difference between the Tibetan language debates in the TAR and in the Tibetan refugee community in India. According to the articles in the *Tibetan Review*, one of the major dangers to the survival of the Tibetan language in the exile community is that many young people consider Tibetan to be an old-fashioned and complicated language that is ill-suited to the needs of the modern world.[23] By contrast, in the TAR, where Tibetans have a sense that their culture is under threat from a Chinese-style modernization process, the language has become part of a powerful nationalist resistance movement. On the one hand, this is likely to be the surest way to keep the language alive. On the other hand, in the current political climate, it has meant that hardline officials in the TAR government have portrayed Tibetan-language education, and aspects of Tibetan culture in the curriculum, as potentially subversive.

The analysis presented in this book has identified the multiple factors and their complex interactions that have shaped the TAR education system. Over the fifty-year period reviewed here, the cycle of changes brought about by these interactions has led at some times to improvements in the education of Tibetan children and at other times it has greatly disadvantaged them. Today, the education system in the TAR is once again on a cusp. On one hand the Chinese economic boom has produced a great demand for the TAR's raw materials (indeed, *Xizang* – the Chinese name for the TAR – means 'the Western Treasure House'). With it have come renewed possibilities for improving the education system in the region. On the other hand, China's perceived strategic concerns and the disproportionate growth of the Han Chinese population in the TAR mean that the education system is weighted against Tibetans both in terms of their linguistic and cultural needs and in allowing them to compete on equal terms for educational advancement. The challenge for the future will therefore be to find a new synthesis that exploits the economic improvements in the TAR and China to realize the educational aspirations of both Han and Tibetan children in the TAR.

Notes

1. Wang Yao, 'Hu Yaobang's Visit to Tibet, May 22–23 1980', in R. Barnett and S. Akiner (eds), *Resistance and Reform in Tibet* (Hurst & Co., London, 1994).

2. The inspection tour was timed to coincide with the thirty-ninth anniversary of the signing of the Seventeen-Point Agreement. The notion of regional autonomy was defined in the context of that agreement.

3. Yang Jingren, *'Jianjue Guanche Zhongyang Zhishi Zuo Hao Xizang Gongzuo'* (On the Correct Implementation of the Central Committee's Directive and Carrying Out Work for Tibet Well), *Hongqi* (Red Flag), No. 15, 1980.

4. There was the following proviso: 'However, in doing this it must seek approval beforehand or report to the higher levels afterward.' See ibid.

5. Hu Yaobang, 'Report to TAR Regional Party Committee Cadres', Lhasa Radio, 1430 gmt, 30 May 1980 [SWB 4/6/80]; 'Raidi and Gyaltsen Norbu summarize Tibet Forum Conclusions,' *Xizang Ribao* (Tibet Daily; in Chinese), 2 August 1994 [SWB 21/8/94].

6. Keith M. Lewin, Xu Hui, Angela Little and Zheng Jiwei, *Educational Innovation in China*, p. 217.

7. Hu Yaobang, 'Report to TAR Regional Party Committee Cadres', Lhasa Radio, 1430 gmt, 30 May 1980 [SWB 4/6/80].

8. Gyaltsen Norbu (Chairman of the TAR government), in 'Tibet Government to Put Education at Top of Agenda', *Xinhua*, 5 June 1994 [SWB 8/6/94].

9. 1995 TAR Statistical Yearbook.

10. Yang Jingren, 'On the Correct Implementation of the Central Committee's Directive', p. 94.

11. Ibid., p. 99.

12. Wang Xiaoqiang, 'The Dispute Between the Tibetans and the Han', in Barnett and Akiner (eds), *Resistance and Reform in Tibet*.

13. 'Raidi and Gyaltsen Norbu Summarize Third Tibet Work Forum', *Xizang Ribao* (Tibet Daily; in Chinese), 2 August 1994 [SWB 21/8/94].

14. See 'Actively Guide Religion to Accommodate Itself to Socialist Society', *Xizang Ribao* (Tibet Daily), 4 November 1996. In 1995, there were around 15,000 teachers in the TAR.

15. Yang Jingren, 'On the Correct Implementation of the Central Committee's Directive'.

16. Interview with Gongkar Gyatso, teacher at Tibet University 1985–92, 2 February 1997.

17. Report by the Tibetan government-in-exile's Department of Education, cited in Tenzin Sangpo, 'The Case for Teaching Tibetan Children in Tibetan', *Tibetan Review*, March 1977, p. 17.

18. See Sherab Gyatso, 'The Crisis of Tibetan Language in Exile', *Tibetan Review*, September 1993, p. 16; Ngawang Phuntsog Sipur, 'Tibetan Secular Education: A Rude Awakening', *Tibetan Review*, June 1992.

19. Report by Centre for Applied Linguistics, Washington, cited in Sherab Gyatso, op. cit., p. 16.

20. Ibid.

21. Report by the Tibetan Exile Government's Department of Education, cited in Tenzin Sangpo, 'The Case for Teaching Tibetan Children in Tibetan', p. 17.

22. Ibid., p. 19.

23. Sherab Gyatso, 'The Crisis of Tibetan Language in Exile'.

Appendix 1

Administrative structure in China

	Administrative levels	Chinese	Tibetan
National level	The centre	*zhong yang*	
Province level	Provinces	*sheng*	
	Municipalities under the central government	*zhi xia shi*	
	Autonomous regions	*zi zhi qu*	
Prefecture level	Prefectures	*di qu*	*sa khul*
	Autonomous prefectures	*zi zhi zhou*	*khru'u*
	Municipalities or cities	*shi*	*grong khyer*
County level	Counties (in rural areas)	*xian*	*rdzong*
	Inner city (in urban areas)	*chengguanqu*	
Xiang level	Townships or village cluster	*xiang*	*grong*
	Village	*cun*	*seb/tsun*

Appendix 2

Population of the TAR and Tibetan Autonomous Prefectures and Counties in Qinghai, Sichuan, Gansu and Yunnan, 1990

Administrative area	Tibetan	Chinese	Other ethnic groups	Total
TAR	2,096,718	80,837	18,474	2,196,029
Lhasa Municipality (Lasa shi)	327,882	44,945	3,141	375,968
Lhasa inner city (Lasa chengguanqu)	96,431	40,387	2,9981	39,816
Chushul (Quxu) county	27,104	231	11	27,346
Damshung (Damxung) county	33,372	632	213	4,025
Lhundrub (Linzhou/Lunzhub) county	46,827	29	504	7,122
Medrogungkar (Maizhokungar) county	36,516	147	213	6,684
Nyemo (Nimu) county	26,170	7	26	26,248
Taktse (Daxi, Dagze) county	23,125	387	52	3,517
Toelung Dechen (Doilungdeqen)	38,337	2,794	79	41,210
Lhokha (Shannan) Prefecture	274,235	5,715	857	280,807
Kongpo (Linzhi) Prefecture	109,828	13,865	10,731	134,424
Shigatse (Xigaze, Rigaze) Prefecture	542,207	4,918	2,0435	49,168
Ngari (Ali) Prefecture	60,181	1,432	26	61,639
Nagchu (Naqu) Prefecture	290,771	2,954	117	293,842
Chamdo (Qamdo) Prefecture	491,614	7,008	1,540	500,162

Qinghai Province	912,160	2,578,912	965,874	4,456,946
Tsochang (Haibei) TAP	52,336	118,900	87,226	258,462
Malho (Huangnan) TAP	115,813	20,039	46,143	181,995
Tsolho (Hainan) TAP	194,399	136,255	30,701	361,355
Golog (Guoluo) TAP	105,645	12,127	2,201	119,973
Jyekundo (Yushu) TAP	219,336	7,186	776	227,298
Tsonub (Haixi) Mongol-Tibetan Autonomous Prefecture	30,899	236,970	44,458	312,327
Gansu Province	367,006	20,513,607	1,490,528	22,371,141
Pari (Tianzhu) Tibetan Autonomous County (in Wuwei Prefecture)	55,617	140,465	14,763	210,845
Gannan TAP	276,844	261,938	41,879	580,661
Sichuan Province	1,087,758	102,328,069	3,802,346	107,218,73
Ngaba (Aba) Tibetan-Qiang Autonomous Prefecture	375,551	244,205	156,024	775,780
Kandze (Ganzi) TAP	627,034	177,778	23,719	828,531
Muli (Mili) Tibetan Autonomous County (in Liangshan Yi Autonomous Prefecture)	34,616	32,405	48,237	115,258
Yunnan Province	111,335	24,614,533	12,246,742	36,972,610
Dechen (Diqing) TAP	104,366	50,880	160,070	315,316

Sources: Zhongguo minzu renkou ziliao (1990 nian renkou pucha shuju) [Tabulation on China's Nationalities (Data of 1990 Population Census)]. Beijing 1994. Zhongguo renkou tongji nianjian 1992 [China Population Statistical Yearbook, 1992]. Beijing 1993.

Appendix 3

Trends in society and education in China and the TAR, 1949–97

Society in China	Society in the TAR	Period	Education in China	Education in the TAR
Common Programme (1949) Economic rehabilitation Nationalization Land reform	17-Point Agreement signed between Tibetan and Chinese governments (1951)	1949–52	Adoption of Soviet model Expansion of higher education Development of community schools	First Conference on Minority Nationality Education, Beijing (1951) Lhasa Primary School opened (1952)
First Constitution (1954) Soviet industrialization Collectivization Professional/political struggle for control	Revolt in Eastern Tibet (1956) Preparatory Committee for the Autonomous Region of Tibet (PCART) (1956)	1953–57	Rapid enrolment expansion Introduction of degrees Urban bias in education Literacy campaigns	Second Conference on Minority Nationality Education, Beijing (1956) Lhasa Secondary School opened (1956)
Anti-Rightist campaign 'Walking on Two Legs' Rural industrialization People's communes	Lhasa Uprising (1959) 'Anti-Rebellion' campaign: suppression of Tibetan revolt (1959–60)	1958–59	Proletarian education Education with production Anti-intellectualism Community school expansion	'Walking on Two Legs' Programme (1959) Community school expansion
Break with USSR Economic liberalization Rehabilitation of 'rightists' Material incentives	First land reforms – disbanding of monastic and aristocratic estates (1960–61)	1960–62	Stress on academic quality Promotion of 'key schools' Less labour and politics Agricultural schools	Promotion of vocational education (1961) Closure of Community Schools

	Establishment of Mutual Aid collectives Famine (1961–62) Sino-Indian war (1962)			
Bureaucratic control Intellectuals valued	2nd phase of the Land Reform – redistribution of land/collectivization Inauguration of TAR (1965)	1963–65	Vocational schools Promotion of key schools	Tibet Nationalities Institute established (1965)
Cultural Revolution Mass confrontation Red Guard dominance Ultra-leftism	Cultural Revolution 'Elimination of 'Four Olds': thoughts, customs, habits, culture Total communization (1969)	1966–76	Teachers form the 'Stinking Ninth Category' Class origin over academic work Abolition of examinations Integration of vocational and general education	Special minority nationality education abolished Rapid expansion of community schools Expansion of primary and secondary education University entrance dependent on class origin
Deng Xiaoping in power De-collectivization Rural responsibility system Pragmatism Four Modernizations Fifth Constitution (1982) Law on regional autonomy (1984)	First Tibet Work Forum (1980) De-communization (1980) Wu Jinghua: TAR Party Secretary (1985) Greater religious freedom Opening of Tibet to foreign tourists Second Tibet Work Forum (1984)	1977–85	Redevelopment of higher education University examination reintroduced (1978) Departments of Minority Nationality Education set up in central and regional governments Reintroduction of 'key schools'	New minority nationality policies (1979) Five Provinces and Region Teaching Materials Committee (Wu Sheng Qu ...) established (1982) Tibetan medium primary schools (1985) Programme of sending Tibetans to secondary school in China (1984)

Trends in society and education in China and the TAR, 1949–97, continued

Society in China	Society in the TAR	Period	Education in China	Education in the TAR
	Law on regional autonomy (1984)		Provisional regulations on requirements for universalizing primary education (1983) CCP Decision on Education (1985)	Streaming in primary and secondary schools Decline in enrolment at all levels
'Open Door' policy Industrial responsibility system Special economic zones High economic growth Inflation	Economic liberalization Economic migrants from Central China Major nationalist demonstrations (1987) Hu Jintao: TAR Party Secretary (1988)	1986–88	Law on compulsory education (1986) Diversification of education funding Reduction of % of government funding Over-expansion of higher education Student loans Commissioned students More autonomy to school principals	Development of private tuition (1985) 'Provisions on the Study, Use and Development of Spoken and Written Tibetan' (1987) Third TAR Conference on Education (1987)
Recession Ideological conflict Leftist conservatives gain power	'Anti-Splittist' campaign (1989–90) Martial Law (1989–90) Death of the Tenth	1989–91	Patriotic Education campaigns Politics classes reintroduced Party dominant over professionals	Experimental Tibetan medium secondary schools (1989–96) Opening of Tibetan secondary school in Beijing (1989)

Politics in control	Panchen Lama (1989)		Recentralization	Conference on Tibetan Language Teaching (1991)
Return to high growth' Freeing of labour market 'Socialist Market Economy'	Chen Kuiyuan: TAR Party Secretary (1992) TAR made 'Special Economic Zone' (1992)	*1992–93*	'Programme for China's Educational Reform and Development' (1993) Law on Teachers (1993)	TAR Year of Education (1993) TAR Bill to introduce compulsory education on an experimental basis in 1994 (1993)
'Strike Hard' Anti-Crime Campaign (1996–97) Death of Deng Xiaoping (1997)	Third Tibet Work Forum (1994) 'Anti-Dalai Lama' campaign (1994–97) 'Propagation of Atheism' campaign (1996) Dispute over selection of Eleventh Panchen Lama (1995–96)	*1994–97*	'Guidelines for Patriotic Education' (1994) Development of private tuition Education Law (1995) Vocational Education Law (1996)	Fifth TAR Conference on Education (1994) Establishment of educational charities Upgrading community schools Target for compulsory education for nomadic areas reduced from 4 to 3 years (1996) De-emphasizing Tibetan cultural distinctiveness Decision to abandon experiment of Tibetan medium secondary education (1996) Introduction of Chinese language from first grade primary in urban schools (1997)

Source: China sections adapted and expanded from Keith M. Lewin et al., *Educational Innovation in China* (Longman, 1994).

Appendix 4

Extract from Report on Tibet following First Forum and Inspection Tour by Yang Jingren, member of Central Committee and head of State Commission for Nationalities Affairs

'Jianjue Guanche Zhongyang Zhishi Zuo Hao Xizang Gongzuo' (On the Correct Implementation of the Central Committee's Directive and Carrying Out Work for Tibet Well)[1]

What does national regional autonomy comprise and what rights of self-government are involved? They are mainly as follows:

1. The self-government organ must comprise mainly cadres of the nationality excercising regional autonomy. In Xizang (TAR), the self-government organ must be made up mainly of Tibetan cadres.

2. In autonomous regions the spoken and written language of the nationality exercising autonomy must be used as the first language, and it is through this medium that the local authorities are to exercise their functions and powers. The national language must be used as the principal language in conducting official business, issuing documents, making announcements, teaching … etc. Reports and talks given in the Han language must be translated into the national language. In Xizang the first language is Tibetan; however, the Han language must also be used.

3. In autonomous regions we must act according to the national character and the regional special requirements. Everything must be done in line with the ethnic and regional conditions rather than vague generalizations or arbitrary uniformity.

4. An autonomous region, in the light of its special conditions and needs, is allowed to formulate its special regulations and specific autonomy ordinances as well as mandatory decrees and stipulations under the general principle of the state constitution and laws.

5. An autonomous region has broader financial powers than other areas at the same level.

6. An autonomous region, as regards the administration and distribution of earnings from the forests, grasslands, and mineral deposits

within its jurisdiction, enjoys larger rights and interests than other areas at the same level.

7. Under normal conditions, an autonomous region bordering on foreign countries should have the right to conduct frontier trade.

8. An autonomous region must develop scientific, cultural, and educational undertakings of its own nationality.

9. An autonomous region has the right to refuse implementation of or to implement with appropriate adaptation instructions or regulations issued by the Centre or higher authorities that are out of keeping with local conditions. However, in doing this it must seek approval beforehand or report to the higher levels afterward.

The above nine points are roughly the basic contents of the rights of a nationality to autonomy and action on its own.

Only by fully exercising such rights, especially in the case of Xizang, which is an even more special national autonomous region than others and thus even more entitled to autonomy rights, can we effectively strengthen national solidarity, consolidate the motherland's unity and develop the political economic and cultural undertakings of various minority nationalities. In this way, the actual inequality among the nationalities can be gradually eliminated, and the minority nationalities can quickly become affluent and prosperous and able to rank among the advanced nationalities.

To make self-government a reality and do the work in autonomous regions well, we must also ethnicize the Party organs. Han nationality cadres working in the Party organs or other government units must respect the wishes of the minority people and act according to the special conditions of local minority nationalities and the autonomous region. Cadres of minority background and of the Han nationality must be closely united in a joint effort to successfully carry on revolution and construction in the autonomous region. This is very important.

Note

1. *Hongqi* (Red Flag), No. 15, 1980 (Nationalities Publishing House, Beijing).

Appendix 5

Text of speech by Chen Kuiyuan, secretary of the Tibet Autonomous Regional CCP Committee, at the Fifth Regional Meeting on Education in the TAR, 26 October 1994[1]

The Fifth Regional Meeting on Education held by the Tibet Autonomous Regional People's Government is an extremely important one. The major task of this meeting lies in conscientiously studying and carrying out the guiding spirit of the Third Forum on Work in Tibet held by the State Council, in the National Work Meeting on Education, and in striving to create a new situation for educational work in our region. On behalf of the Autonomous Regional CCP Committee and government, Comrade Gyaincain Norbu will make a keynote speech later. I would like to express some opinions about the current situation and tasks on the educational front in our region as well as some problems worthy of our attention.

Correctly analyse the situation of educational work in our region

1. *Tremendous achievements* which are recorded in history. Over the past forty and more years since the first primary school was set up in Qamdo in 1951, under the leadership of the Party, the educational front of our region has witnessed tremendous changes. Thanks to our efforts of past decades, schools of all levels and various kinds – ranging from primary schools to universities, from schools of fundamental education to those of higher education, professional education and adult education – were established, thus cultivating a large group of leading cadres for the party and the government as well as personnel of various professional fields. It is because our educational front has achieved major results that the illiteracy rate among Tibetan people decreased from more than 90 per cent during the early period of liberation to around 4 per cent now. The results helped free the people from ignorant and backward conditions created by serfdom, and enabled them to walk along the glorious path of modern civilization. The results have laid a

fairly good foundation for people in Tibet to realize socialist modernization along with people in other parts of the country. These results,
which are hard to come by, should be attributed to the Party and the
government for their concern and support of educational causes in
Tibet, to older-generation pioneers of Chinese, Tibetan and other
nationalities who blazed the trail of evolutionary and constructional
causes, and to educational workers who have worked diligently and
silently on the educational front over the past decades.

2. *The gap remains great.* Despite the tremendous results, our region
still lags far behind other provinces and municipalities with regard to
educational development, not being able to meet the need of economic
and social development. Comrade Deng Xiaoping once said: 'Only after
recognizing the backwardness are we able to change the situation. Only
by learning from the advanced people can we catch up with and surpass
them.' Our region is far behind other provinces and municipalities in
education. The gap in this respect remains great. Fundamental education
is not popular, and is not able to achieve, along with other provinces and
municipalities, the goal stipulated in the state's educational programme.
School-age children's attendance at primary schools is low and their
drop-out rate is high. As a result, the number of illiterate people remains
large. We only have a limited number of middle schools, high schools
and professional schools. Offering little professional training, they are
not able to meet the needs of social development. Many things are
waiting to be done in Tibet. But many undertakings cannot operate
properly because of a lack of managing and professional personnel.
Although we have set up many schools, the teaching level of various
schools at all levels is poor, as is the quality of their graduates.

If the situation continues, we will not be able to solve the basic
problems of having leading cadres and professional personnel at all
levels. Backward education will directly restrict Tibet's progress towards
economic and social modernization.

3. *Our performance in political and ideological work is poor and our moral
education is a weak link.* As pointed out by leading comrades of the
central authorities at the Third Forum on Work in Tibet, the Dalai
clique is desperately competing with us to win over the youths – the
people of the next generation. Splittist elements try to infiltrate the
educational circle by using narrow nationalism and religion. Scriptures
have entered some schools and become textbooks in the classrooms.
Some students have joined the ranks of monks. Some people purposely
interpret this phenomenon as a national feature in an attempt to legalize
religious interference in educational affairs. Considerably strong
nationalist sentiment exists among some college and middle school

students and teachers, and the political inclination of national splittism exists and develops among a handful of people. Therefore, we have arduous tasks in political and ideological work as well as heavy responsibilities in training constructors and successors who possess deep love for the motherland and socialist undertakings.

4. *We must urgently strengthen the building of leading bodies and the teaching force of education departments.* Tibet's vast number of cadres, teachers and educational staff have carried forward the old Tibetan spirit, and overcome difficulties to make great contributions to education for the people and country. Tibet's development and progress is a monument to their contributions. Following educational development, the lack of qualified personnel on the education front is a prominent contradiction. Tibet's universities, middle and elementary schools, and various types of special schools generally lack qualified backbone leaders as well as key teaching and scientific research personnel. A serious problem is that some leading cadres are not concerned about work for schools, resulting in the loss of qualified personnel in schools. Jealousy and pressure on qualified personnel is a phenomenon still existing in some departments and units. In a few units, some teaching staff have not changed their stand but publicly impart splittist ideology among students. Some teachers do not know the differences between socialist education and outmoded education. The teaching syllabi and formats they adopt are far from the requirements of modern education. All these indicate that it is urgent to strengthen the building of leadership and the teaching force on the education front.

5. *Many practical problems concerning poor school operating conditions and teachers' work and living must be solved.* I understand that the regional government and Chairman Gyaincain Norbu attach great importance to this issue. In a recent discussion of plans for 1995, we have placed education as one of the important daily work agenda items. The central government has greatly helped Tibet's educational undertakings. The autonomous regional party committee and government will also strive to solve problems. Comrade Gyaincain Norbu will talk about these issues in his report. The Third Forum on Work in Tibet has shown the correct direction and goal for our region's education as well as given us a series of practical support. Under the guidance of the Third Forum on Work in Tibet, our region's education will have a brighter future. We must redouble our efforts, address existing problems, rectify our thinking, and overcome difficulties and problems. We must work with all our might to promote positive and down-to-earth development for Tibet's education.

Resolutely implement the strategy of giving preference to educational development. Work relentlessly for training a large group of constructors and successors who possess deep love for the motherland and who are suited to the need of modernization

1. *Raise awareness and strive to realize the strategy of giving preference to educational development.* The task in educational development is not a special job of education departments, but the entire Party's job. There will be no healthy development in education if Party committees and governments at all levels do not attach importance to and support the task. When studying the issue of education reform in 1992, I stressed that the autonomous region's education department must jointly manage educational affairs with prefectural and county Party committees and governments. The education department alone cannot shoulder the heavy responsibilities in educational undertakings, and it will be difficult to ensure rapid development for education with only one department doing the job. Once we unify our thinking and depend on the entire society, it is possible to achieve an early goal of establishing middle schools in every county and elementary schools in every village as well as enrolling 80 per cent of school-age children. This proposal was forwarded during the Fourth Regional Meeting on Education and confirmed by the central government. I think the crux of our task lies in Party and government leaders at all levels, who must possess an awareness of a sense of urgency. First, we must address the issue of understanding. Developing education in accordance with the principle directed by Comrade Deng Xiaoping is in unanimity with the CCP's historical mission as well as an internal demand and final guarantee for realizing the basic line. Only when leading bodies and leaders have a correct understanding can educational undertakings be placed on a preferential position in practice. Party committees and governments at all levels must resolve to strengthen leading bodies on the education front. They must select outstanding personnel, improve school operating conditions, be concerned about teachers' hardships and implement relevant policies. In short, we must comprehensively implement the Party's and state's strategic principle for Tibet's education, and ensure that educational development must not only suit the needs of modernization but must also surpass previous achievements.

2. *We must comprehensively implement the Party's policy on education and train successors who have deep love for the motherland and will dedicate themselves to socialist modernization in Tibet.* The state and its people conduct education for the purpose of bringing up qualified personnel who will strive for their country's regeneration and for the benefit of

the people, and for the purpose of training them to become builders and successors conscious of socialism and having an educational background. The outcome of the struggle between us and the Dalai clique to win over successors will have a bearing on the future of Tibet. The success of our education does not lie in the number of diplomas issued to graduates from universities, colleges, polytechnic schools and middle schools. It lies, in the final analysis, in whether our graduating students are opposed to or turn their hearts to the Dalai clique and in whether they are loyal to or do not care about our great motherland and the great socialist cause. This is the most salient and the most important criterion for assessing right and wrong, and the contributions and mistakes of our educational work in Tibet. To successfully solve the problem, we must improve political and ideological work at schools and have political and ideological work run through all the teaching, study and work at schools. Moral education contains many things. It seems to me that, in the light of Tibet's actual conditions, the primary task of our moral education is to successfully solve this fundamental problem.

3. *We must further optimize the educational structure, improve the quality of education and bring up various qualified personnel who meet the needs of modernization.* We must integrate the bringing up of a new generation of people who have good moral ethics as well as the necessary knowledge of education and science with the improvement of the quality of education of the whole nationality. The connotation of education is very profound. It is not confined to bringing up a new generation of people. In addition, it must improve the quality of the whole nationality. To develop education in Tibet, we must adhere to the policy of walking on two legs. In respect of regular education, we must 'focus attention on improving elementary education, give priority to developing normal school education, continuously optimize higher education, and vigorously develop vocational, technical and adult education'. We must speed up the training of professional technicians at the primary and intermediate levels who are badly needed by Tibet for the development of its construction. Meanwhile, we must make efforts to obliterate illiteracy among young and middle-aged people, improve the quality of general education among labourers, and change the face of society in Tibet. Tibet has the highest illiteracy rate of all the thirty provinces, municipalities and autonomous regions in China, and the Zang [Tibet] nationality's illiteracy rate is the highest of China's fifty-six nationalities. Such an illiteracy rate makes the ancient Zang nationality, which boasts cultural traditions dating back several thousand years, lag behind modern social development. As a consequence, there are many outmoded

conventions and bad customs in our society. Instead of being done away with, they are still poisoning our nationality and posterity. It is related to the fact that the quality of general education of the whole nationality is still not high enough. Only by speeding up the process of educational development can we improve the quality of our nationality, promote development of various undertakings in Tibet as well as the Zang nationality in a better way, and bring about changes to the face of Tibet with each passing day. Addressing the Third Forum on Work in Tibet, General Secretary Jiang Zemin said: 'The Tibet Autonomous Region is a focal point of the work on minority nationalities in China and is, of course, a focal area for minority nationalities' education.' To develop education for minority nationalities, we must broaden our horizon and have a correct orientation. The policy on education for minority nationalities constitutes an integral part of, and is subordinated to, the Party's policy on minority nationalities. We must gain an understanding of and correctly promote development of education for minority nationalities in accordance with Comrade Deng Xiaoping's guiding ideology – 'uphold equality among nationalities and accelerate Tibet's development' – and the Party's policy on minority nationalities in the new period and, in accordance with the above-mentioned guiding ideology and policy, we must define or stipulate the tasks for minority nationalities' education and study new problems. The 'Opinions of the CCP Central Committee and the State Council on Accelerating Tibet's Development and Maintaining Its Social Stability' pointed out that 'in judging China's policy on minority nationalities and the Tibet issue, what counts is how to benefit the Tibetan people and enable Tibet to enjoy very rapid development. This is in the fundamental interests of the Tibetan people and constitutes the fundamental criterion for assessing the work in Tibet.' Likewise, in promoting the development of education for minority nationalities, what counts is how to benefit the Tibetan people and enable Tibet to enjoy very rapid development as it is in the fundamental interests of the Tibetan people. On the basis of this fundamental criterion, the purpose, orientation and principles of education for minority nationalities are quite clear at a glance. Our education for minority nationalities does not stick to the ways of the old society or return to the state of our ancestors. Instead, in conducting education for minority nationalities, we must keep abreast of the footsteps of history and make the promotion of our nationality's prosperity and progress our purpose. In this connection, we must also adhere to the principle of gearing our education to the needs of the world, the future and modernization.

4. *We should strengthen the construction of the contingents of leading*

bodies and teachers. The leading bodies of education departments and particularly those of schools – ranging from kindergarten and primary schools to university – should be firm in their political orientation. They should also promote their managerial standard and be versed in educational work. The leading bodies should be good at applying the Party's educational principle to imparting knowledge and educating people. To judge whether the Party secretary or principal of a school is qualified politically, we should observe their attitude towards major political issues. More importantly and practically, we should see whether or not the political climate in their school is healthy, what kind of ideology they use in nurturing and guiding the broad masses of teachers and students, whether its graduates are qualified builders of the country, and whose successors they become. As a place for cultivating people, schools are not a forum on 'freedom'. Schools should be captured by socialism. We should not allow splittist elements and religious idealism to use the classrooms to poison people's sons and daughters. Some prefectures, counties and townships in our region are hesitant to accept the graduates of some colleges and universities in our region. Although they are in urgent need of teachers, they do not want these graduates to teach in their schools. This is an issue which deserves our utmost concern. This is a test. If such a situation cannot be changed in the long run, we might as well not run these schools at all. Of course, we cannot say that most of these graduates are not welcome. Besides, in the final analysis, they are not the ones to be blamed. The crux of the matter is that we failed to carry out the Party's educational principles. If our sons and daughters are not up to par, it is us, instead of them, to be blamed. Schools' classrooms should be not turned over to, nor should they be shared by, others. They should be captured firmly only by socialism. Because of historical reasons, an extremely small number of teachers are influenced by the Dalai clique and religion. The behaviour of these people should be restricted because the law of the state does not allow them to wilfully disseminate harmful things in the classrooms so as to exert their influence on the students. It is necessary to strengthen ideological and political work among the contingents of teachers. We should encourage them to acquire progressive thinking, remould themselves, and foster a correct world outlook, outlook on life and national viewpoint. This does not mean that 'left' things can come back again. As you well know, former Premier Zou Enlai once said: 'It's never too late to learn and remould oneself.' Comrade Deng Xiaoping said: 'In our socialist society, all people have to go through the process of remoulding themselves. Moreover, all people should continue to remould themselves, study new issues, accept new things and conscientiously resist intrusion of the capitalist class so as to better shoulder the glorious and tremendous task of turning China into a socialist country that is strong and modern.' Remoulding means progress. Chairman Mao Zedong said that it is necessary to regularly clean up ideological dust. We do not mean that only comrades on the educational front should remould themselves. Comrades on other fronts should also remould themselves. Those comrades in grass-roots units are not the only people who should remould themselves. The higher a person's position is, the more frequently and conscientiously they should remould themselves. If a person loses contact with reality and is backward ideologically for failing to remould himself, how can they become a leader? Being unable to have a clear understanding of the situation, where will they lead the people? One should remould oneself with a clear objective in mind when meeting a problem. Ideological remoulding is an inevitable way for us to persist in the proletarian world outlook and in the materialist world outlook. Party committees and governments at all levels, educational organizations at all levels, Party leaders and administrators of schools, as well as all teachers, staff members and workers should have a profound understanding of the Third Forum on Work in Tibet, seize the opportunity, foster ambition, and accelerate educational undertakings in our region so as to make more contributions in promoting long-term peace, stability and prosperity in Tibet; in bringing about a fundamental change in Tibetan society; and in helping the Tibetan nationality walk even faster into the world of advanced nationalities.

(© BBC Monitoring Summary of World Broadcasts)

Note

1. *Xizang Ribao* (Tibet Daily) (in Chinese), 28 October 1994

Appendix 6

Transcript of Television Debate on Education, Lhasa TV, 30 July 1988

SPEAKER: Dorje Tsering talked about the Five-Year Plan originating from the Eleventh Party Congress in 1983. During these five years there have been improvements in living standards and production has greatly increased and during this five-year plan there have been improvements in the field of education. We must strive to continue to improve the quality of students' work, and improve the education of the masses.

When we look at the field of education it is true that there have been many improvements. However, if we look at it in terms of the attitudes of high and low government officials, there is a lack of serious commitment in education. If you look at lower schools there is a shortage of qualified teachers, for example in one class there are sixty or seventy students. In such a situation how can we improve the quality of the students? Likewise the status of the teachers is very low. If you think about it, the role of a teacher is very important. A teacher has to work for many years. The work of a teacher is unending. If you look at schools in towns, teachers are badly off: there is no canteen and their reward is small. These points were also raised at the Fifth Congress of the TAR. Economic improvement and everything else is dependent on education. In every direction we must pay special attention to educational needs ...

Even though we cannot improve everything in education, it is urgent that we should raise the status of teachers ...

NEW SPEAKER: I have come to attend the Fifth Congress of the TAR. By attending this congress I have learned that the main issue is increasing productivity in the TAR. There has been much discussion about generating economic productivity. As a person speaking about education, let us think what is the face of the TAR. The TAR has the appearance of an autonomous region, but what is an autonomous region? What is the basis of the autonomous region? The national language of the people is its identity. We will recognize it as genuinely autonomous when the language of the people is allowed to be practised. We need school education in the Tibetan language. Tibetan culture is old and different, and we need to teach younger generations to preserve this culture. But if we look at the constitution, it has beautifully guaranteed these rights. We need to put these into practice. But how do the students look at this? Students say what the teachers say is correct. What benefit is there in learning Tibetan? Tibetan is no use after we leave school. It is not used in offices, so what is the point of learning it? So in the end we are faced with difficulties. When you have finished school where can you go? Menzhikhang. You can't go into the Academy of Social Sciences (only a few have). As a teacher, I face this problem with my students all the time. Of course, the Party has good policies but a few leaders have not put this into practice.

But we should learn Tibetan. Of course, some teachers seem to think that we are saying that we shouldn't learn Chinese. We should learn Chinese. Of course Chinese is the dominant national language in our country. But the TAR is an autonomous region. I have not been to Xinjiang or other places. But I am told that when they have big meetings they talk in their own language. This is not the case in the TAR. In all the meetings here, whatever it is, we talk in Chinese. Take the example of the higher leaders. They need to practise what they preach. That would be beneficial. For example, because teachers have such low status, high officials take no notice of what they have to say.

Two members of the TAR government have stated that Tibetan will be the official language in the TAR from the first of July 1988. This was announced at the Congress of TAR. Now it is July already, and I want to know how it has been put into practice. Some people say that this is only rhetoric. People are sceptical because this has happened in the past. Everyone blames each other. Tibetan culture is a major culture of the motherland. If you preserve this culture it will benefit the motherland.

This is the first thing I want to say. Secondly I want to talk about the rights of the teachers. Primary education is so inadequate, and since this is the basis of all education, we cannot make any improvement in secondary schools and higher education until we improve the quality of teachers at lower schools.

NEW SPEAKER: All the teachers have made marvellous contributions and I have nothing else to say. I recognize that improvements have been made in education. Our primary aim is to improve the economy in the TAR. If we look at economic improvement and educational improvement there are big gaps. There can be no agricultural and economic development without making fundamental improvements in education. Without educational improvements, economic improvement and agricultural productivity is empty talk. It is impossible to have economic development without education. Therefore improving the educational quality of Tibetans is urgent and important. What is the present condition of education in the TAR? We are lagging behind, unable to graduate from school. If you look at the number of students leaving school it isn't low. But the standard of students leaving school is low. Everyone knows that in the old times education in the TAR was poor. We also have to recognize that even still today we are lagging behind. This is a very important issue. Of course we recognize that there are problems of having to learn science through another language. Tibet is dependent on aid from other provinces. It is good that they have to provide us with aid. But we must preserve this right to autonomy. This can be done by Tibetans administering this region. This year the first batch of students graduated from Tibet University. None of them was going on to a teacher training course. Both Tibetans and Chinese say that 'they'd rather take a letter to the ends of the earth than teach'. Where does this view originate? You have a lower salary and lots of work. Look at students stepping out of Lhasa University. Do we look at their living conditions? This is a question that cadres should be addressing ...

Others have stated other things that I wanted to say. But there is something that I wanted to say. The government of the TAR has adopted a resolution to use the Tibetan language. But the Chinese have great ideas which are never carried out. It is like an overture without the opera. People are now saying that there is thunder that never brings rain. What you preach must be practised. There are those who talk about lack of resources and many difficulties in implementing government policy. They put obstacles by saying that there is a lack of resources and that they are in difficulties. There are Tibetan cadres who don't know the Tibetan language. Maybe there are personal reasons for not seeing the Tibetan language used. Such thoughts are wrong, the use of Tibetan is for the benefit of all the people. There are difficulties in using Tibetan language in schools, e.g. in sciences, but they can be overcome, but I cannot see any reason why we can't use Tibetan language in administration.

Bibliography

Books

Barnett, Robert and Shirin Akiner (eds), *Resistance and Reform in Tibet* (Hurst and Co., London, 1994).

Bass, Catriona, *Inside the Treasure House: A Time In Tibet* (Gollancz, London, 1990).

Bell, Charles, *The People of Tibet* (Oxford University Press, 1968).

Brown, Melissa J. (ed.), *Negotiating Ethnicities in China and Taiwan*, China Research Monograph 46 (Center for Chinese Studies, University of California, 1996).

Chae Jin Lee, *China's Korean Minority*, (Westview Press, Boulder, CO, 1986).

Chenery, H. and T. N. Srinivasan, *Handbook of Development Economics* (Elsevier Science Publishers, Amsterdam, 1988).

China Statistical Yearbooks (China Statistical Publishing House, Beijing).

Conner, Victoria and Robert Barnett, *Leaders in Tibet: A Directory* (Tibet Information Network, London, 1997).

Deng Xiaoping, *Speeches and Writings* (Pergamon Press, London, 1984).

Dhondub Choedon, *Life in the Red Flag People's Commune* (Information Office of H.H. the Dalai Lama, 1978).

Duojie Caidan (Dorje Tseten), *Xizang Jiaoyu* (Education in Tibet) (China Tibetology Publishers, Beijing, 1991).

Economic Dept of State Ethnic Affairs Commission and Dept of Integrated Statistics of State Statistical Bureau of PRC (eds) *China's Ethnic Statistical Yearbook, 1995* (Ethnic Publishing House, Beijing).

Encyclopaedia of Chinese Counties, Vol.: South-West China (China Social Publishing House, 1993).

Epstein, Israel, *Tibet Transformed* (New World Press, Beijing, 1983).

Goldstein, Melvyn, William Siebenschuh and Tashi Tsering, *The Struggle for Modern Tibet, The Autobiography of Tashi Tsering* (M. E. Sharpe, New York, 1997).

Goldstein, Melvyn, *A History of Modern Tibet, 1913–1951, The Demise of the Lamaist State* (University of California Press, 1989).

Hayhoe, Ruth (ed.), *Education and Modernisation: The Chinese Experience* (Pergamon Press, Oxford, 1992).

Introduction of Institutions of Higher Education in China (Beijing Educational Science Press, 1982).

Jetsun Pema, 'Three Months in Tibet: A Personal View', *Methok* (Dharamsala, India).

Jiaoyu Nianjian 1985–86 (Education Yearbook of China).

Jin Lin, *Education in Post-Mao China* (Praeger, London, 1993).

Lamb, Alastair, *Tibet, China & India 1914–1950: A History of Imperial Diplomacy* (Roxford Books, 1989).

Lawasia and Tibet Information Network, *Defying the Dragon, China and Human Rights in Tibet* (March 1991).

Leung, Y. M., *China's Education System in Crisis: Can Structural Reform Help?* (University of Hong Kong, Department of Professional Studies in Education, mimeo, 1986).

Lewin, Keith M. and Wang Ying Jie, *Implementing Basic Education in China* (UNESCO, 1994).

Lewin, Keith M., Xu Hui, Angela Little and Zheng Jiwei, *Educational Innovation in China*, (Longman, Harlow, 1994).

Luo Qun, *The Tibetan People's Right of Autonomy* (New Star Publishers, Beijing, 1991).

McKay, Alex, *Tibet and the British Raj: The Frontier Cadre, 1904–1947* (Curzon Press, 1997).

Panchen Lama, '1962 Petition to Mao', in *A Poisoned Arrow, The Secret Report of the Tenth Panchen Lama* (Tibet Information Network, London, 1997).

Population Atlas of China (OUP, Oxford, 1987).

Qinghai Provincial Statistical Bureau, *Qinghai Statistical Yearbook 1993* (China Statistical Publishing Co., Beijing, 1993).

Shakya, Tsering Wangdu, *The Dragon in the Land of Snows, A History of Modern Tibet Since 1947* (Pimlico Press, London, forthcoming).

The Change in Education in Tibet (New Star Publishers, Beijing, 1992).

Tibet: From 1951 to 1991 (China's Tibet/Beijing Review, New Star Publishers, Beijing, 1991).

Tibet Autonomous Region Yearbooks, *Zhongguo Tongji Chubanshe* (China Statistical Publishing House, Beijing).

Tibet Information Network and Human Rights Watch/Asia, *Cutting off the Serpent's Head: Tightening Control in Tibet, 1994–1995* (Tibet Information Network, London, 1996).

Tibetan Centre for Human Rights and Democracy, *The Next Generation: The State of Education in Tibet Today* (Dharamsala, 1997).

UNESCO, *World Education Indicators* (World Education Report, Oxford, 1995).

Unger, J., *Education Under Mao* (Columbia University Press, 1982).

UNICEF, *Children and Women of China – A UNICEF Situation Analysis* (Beijing, 1989).

Wang Xiaoqiang and Bai Nanfeng, *The Poverty of Plenty*, trans. Angela Knox (Macmillan, London, 1991).

White, Gordon, *Party and Professional – The Political Role of Teachers in Contemporary China* (M. E. Sharpe, New York, 1981).

Zhang, Yenming, *Effects of Policy Changes on College Enrolment of Minority Students in China, 1949–1989*, Doctoral Thesis (Harvard University, 1991).

Articles

Bass, Catriona, *China's Education Policy in Tibet*, Submission to the Hearing on the Respect for Human Rights in Tibet, before Human Rights Sub-Committee of the Political Affairs Committee, European Parliament, Brussels, 25 April 1990.

Bastid, M., 'Chinese Educational Policies in the 1980s and Economic Development', *China Quarterly*, No. 6, 1984.

Brittain, Julie, 'Experience of an English Teacher at Lhasa University', *Tibetan Review*, April 1988.

Brittain, Julie, 'Britain Bows to Chinese in Tibet Teacher Project', *Hong Kong Standard*, 6 August 1988.

Cheng Kai-Ming, 'The Changing Legitimacy in a Decentralizing System: The State and Education Development in China', *International Journal of Educational Development*, Vol. 14, 1994.

Dai Yannian, 'Helping Tibet Train Its People', *Beijing Review*, Vol. 30, No. 42, 19 October 1987.

Dalu Yin, 'Reforming Chinese Education: Context, Structure and Attitudes in the 1980s', *Compare*, Vol. 28, No. 2, 1993.

Delany, Brian and Lynn Paine, 'Shifting Patterns of Authority in Chinese Schools', *Comparative Education Review*, Vol. 35, No. 1, 1991.

Dilger, Bernhard, 'The Education of Minorities', *Comparative Education*, Vol. 20, No. 1, 1984.

Epstein, Irving, 'Class and Inequality in Chinese Education', *Compare*, Vol. 23, No. 2, 1993.

Friedman, Edward, 'Chinese Nationalism, Taiwan Autonomy and the Prospects of a Larger War,' *Journal of Contemporary China*, Vol. 6, No. 4, 1997, pp. 5–32.

Gendian Ciren (Gendun Tsering) (ed.), '*Xizang Shuang Yu Jiaoyu de Shijian yu Tansuo*' (Exploration and Practice of Double Language Education in Tibet) [sic], *Xizang Yanjiu* (Tibet Studies), Vol. 58. No. 1, 1996 (TAR Academy of Social Sciences, Lhasa).

Goldstein, Melvyn and Cynthia Beall, 'China's Birth Control Policy in the Tibet Autonomous Region: Myths and Realities', *Asian Survey*, Fall 1990.

Gyaltsen Norbu, 'Tibet: Development Plans to Overcome Natural Enclosed Economy', interview in *Qiushi*, Beijing, 11 August 1994 (SWB 15 August 1994).

Hadfield, Jill and Charles (British Council Teachers at Tibet University 1986–87) 'Talk on Tibet for Great Britain–China Association', January 1988.

Halskov Hansen, Mette, 'Loving of Learning: Naxi Responses to Ethnic Images in Chinese State Education', in Kjeld-Erik Brodsgaard and David Strand (eds), *Twentieth Century China: Social Control, Civil Society and National Identity* (OUP, Oxford, 1997).

Halskov Hansen, Mette, 'Teaching Backwardness or Equality? Chinese State Education Among the Tai in Sipsong Panna', in Gerald A. Postiglione and Regie Stites (eds), *The Education of China's Minorities* (Garland Press, New York, 1997).

Henze, Jurgen, 'The Formal Education System and Modernisation: An Analysis of Developments Since 1978', in Ruth Hayhoe (ed.), *Education and Modernisation: The Chinese Experience* (Pergamon Press, Oxford, 1992).

Huang Wei, 'Authoritative Comments on China's Education Law', *Beijing Review*, 22–28 May 1995.

Jiang Weizhu, 'Advantages and Disadvantages and Reform Measures of the "Three Guarantees" Education Policy', *Xizang Yanjiu* (Tibet Studies), Vol. 58, No. 1, 1996 (Tar Academy of Social Sciences, Lhasa).

Kong, C. Y., 'It is Imperative to Strengthen China's Higher Education', *Ming Pao*, 29 September 1995.

Kormondy, Edward, 'Observations on Minority Education, Cultural Preservation and Economic Development in China', *Compare*, Vol. 25, 1995.

Kwong, Julia and Hong Xiao, 'Educational Equality Among China's Minorities', *Comparative Education*, Vol. 25, No. 2, 1989.

Lei Yongsheng, 'Xiandai Jiaoyu Fazhan Yuxiang Jiaoyu Gaige' (The Development of Modern Education and the Reform of Tibetan Education), *Xizang Yanjiu* (Tibet Studies), Vol. 58. No. 1, 1996 (TAR Academy of Social Sciences, Lhasa).

Lhasang Tsering, 'Some Suggested Changes', Paper at Symposium on the Education of Tibetans in India, *Tibetan Review*, February 1986.

Li Maosen, 'Moral Education in the People's Republic of China', *Journal of Moral Education*, Vol. 19, No. 3, 1990.

Ngawang Phuntsog Sipur, 'Tibetan Secular Education: a Rude Awakening', *Tibetan Review*, June 1992.

Pama Namgyal, 'Xianjieduan Xizang Zongjiao de Diwei He Zuoyong' (Lamaism in the Tibet Autonomous Region), *Xizang Yanjiu* (Tibet Studies), No. 1, 1989; trans. in J. Seymour and Eugen Werli (eds), *Chinese Sociology & Anthropology, A Journal of Translations*, Spring 1994.

Peek, Jane (VSO teacher at Tibet University 1987–89) 'Discrimination in Education in Lhasa', unpublished paper, June 1989.

Pepper, Suzanne, 'Chinese Education After Mao: Two Steps Forward, Two Steps Back and Begin Again?', *China Quarterly*, No. 81, 1980.

Postiglione, Gerard, 'Implications of Modernization for the Education of China's Minorities' in Ruth Hayhoe (ed.), *Education and Modernization – The Chinese Experience* (Pergamon Press, Oxford, 1992).

Robinson, Jean, 'Stumbling on Two Legs: Education and Reform in China', *Comparative Education Review*, Vol. 35, No. 1, February 1991.

Sautman, Barry, 'Politicization, Hyperpoliticization, and Depoliticization of Chinese Education', *Comparative Education Review*, Vol. 35, No. 4, 1991.

Save the Children Fund, *China Education Project*, Information Sheet (November 1996).

Shakya, Tsering Wangdu, 'Making of the Great Game Players: Tibetan Students in Britain between 1913–1917', *Tibetan Review*, Vol. 21, No. 1, 1986.

Shakya, Tsering Wangdu, 'The Genesis of the Sino-Tibetan Agreement of 1951', in Per Kvaerne (ed.), *Tibetan Studies. Proceedings of the 6th International Con-*

ference of Tibetan Studies, Fagernes, Norway (Institute of Comparative Research in Human Culture, Oslo, 1994).

Sharlho, Tseten Wangchuk, 'China's Reforms in Tibet: Issues and Dilemmas', *Journal of Contemporary China,* Vol. 1, No. 1, 1992.

Sherab Gyatso, 'The Crisis of Tibetan Language in Exile', *Tibetan Review,* September 1993.

State Statistical Bureau, 'Education in Present Day China', *Beijing Review,* 17 July 1989.

TAR Education Commission, 'Report by the Literacy Section', *Xizang Ribao* (Tibet Daily), 23 October 1990.

TAR Education Commission, 'Report on the Work of Experimental Teaching in Tibetan Language at Middle Schools', *Podjong Lobsu* (Tibet Education), No. 4, 1995.

Teng Xing, '*Wo guo shaoshu minzu diqu jiaoyu zhengti gaige guanjian*' (The Essence of Overall Educational Reform in China's Minority Regions), *Qiu Shi,* No. 7, April 1989.

Tenth Panchen Lama, 'Tibetan Language and Religion', *Xinhua,* 31 August 1985.

Tenzin Sangpo, 'The Case for Teaching Tibetan Children in Tibetan', *Tibetan Review,* March 1997.

Thogersen, Stig, 'China's Senior Middle Schools in a Social Perspective: A Survey of Yantai District, Shandong Province', *China Quarterly*

'Tibet Special', *Beijing Review,* 7–13 August 1995.

Tsui Kai-yuen, 'Economic Reform and Attainment in Basic Education in China', *China Quarterly,* No. 149, March 1997.

Wang, Samuel, 'Teaching Patriotism in China', *China Strategic Review,* Vol. 1, No. 3, 1997.

Wang Xiaoqiang, 'The Dispute Between the Tibetans and the Han', in Robert Barnett and Shirin Akiner (eds), *Resistance and Reform in Tibet* (Hurst and Co., London, 1994).

Wang Yao, 'Hu Yaobang's Visit to Tibet, May 22–23 1980', in Robert Barnett and Shirin Akiner (eds), *Resistance and Reform in Tibet* (Hurst and Co., London, 1994).

Xiang Xiaoli and Zhang Qing, 'Courage of Conviction Consists in Tackling the Reality of the Situation Today with a Clear Vision for the Future', *Chamdo Daily,* 15 July 1993.

Xu Hong, 'An Interview with Vice-Premier Li Lanqing: Vocational Education Can Invigorate the Country', *Tzu Ching* (Hong Kong), No. 10, 5 October 1994 (SWB 14 November 1994).

Yang Chunjing, 'A Tentative Study on the Importance of Teaching in the Tibetan Language for Developing National Education', *Xizang Yanjiu* (Tibet Studies), Vol. 59, No. 2, 1996.

Yang Jingren, '*Jianjue Guanche Zhongyang Zhishi Zuo Hao Xizang Gongzuo*' (On the Correct Implementation of the Central Committee's Directive and Carrying Out Work for Tibet Well), *Hongqi* (Red Flag), No. 15, 1980 (Nationalities Publishing House, Beijing).

Yang Jingren, 'Talk with Three Representatives of the Dalai Lama', *Nationalities Unity* (Minzu Tuanjie), No. 12, 1984.

Yang Wanli, '*Xizang Kecheng Jiaocai Yanjiu De Teshuxing Jiqi Duice*' (The Counter-measure and Particularity of Research on Teaching Materials), *Xizang Yanjiu* (Tibet Studies), Vol. 58, No. 1, 1996 (TAR Academy of Social Sciences, Lhasa).

Yang Xin and Duo Fen, 'Random Notes from Tibet University', *Beijing Review*, Vol. 31, No. 47, 21–27 November 1988.

Yin Qiping and Gordon White, 'The "Marketisation" of Chinese Higher Education: a Critical Assessment', *Comparative Education*, Vol. 30, No. 3, 1994.

Yuan Huarong, Zhang Zhiliang and Wu Yuping, 'Research on Cultural Distribution of China's National Minority Population', *Social Sciences in China*, No. 3, 1997.

Zhang Ru, 'The Starting Point of Nationality Work', *Unity of Nationalities*, No. 1, 1979.

Zhao, Simon X. B. and Christopher S. P. Tong, 'Spatial Disparity in China's Educational Development: An Assessment from the Perspective of Economic Growth', *China Information*, Vol. 11, No. 4, Spring 1997.

Zhao Sheng, 'Regulations of College Enrolment in 1980 Concerning Minority Candidates', *Unity of Nationalities*, No. 6, 1980.

Zhu Yongzhong and Kevin Stuart, *Education among the Minhe Monguor*, unpublished paper.

Government and Party documents; policy statements; local media reports

'Agreement of the Central People's Government and the Local Government of Tibet on Measures for the Peaceful Liberation of Tibet', *Xinhua*, 27 May 1951.

CCP Central Committee, 'Communique of the Third Plenary Session of the Eleventh Central Committee of the CCP', 22 December 1978, *Beijing Review*, No. 52, 29 December 1978.

CCP Central Committee, 'Decision of the CCP Central Committee on the Reform of China's Educational Structure' (Foreign Languages Press, Beijing, 1985).

CCP Central Committee and the State Council, 'Programme for China's Educational Reform and Development', 25 February 1993, *Xinhua* (SWB 5 March 1993).

Chen Kuiyuan, 'Speech on Education in Tibet', Fifth Regional Meeting on Education in the TAR, 26 October 1994, *Xizang Ribao* (Tibet Daily), 28 October 1994.

Chen Kuiyuan, 'Actively Guide Religion to Accommodate Itself to Socialist Society', *Xizang Ribao* (Tibet Daily; in Chinese), 4 November 1996 (SWB 16 November 1996).

Chen Kuiyuan, 'Speech on Literature and Art', *Xizang Ribao* (Tibet Daily), 11 July 1997.

'Chen Kuiyuan in Chamdo Says Prosperity Will Drive Out Religion', Tibet People's Broadcasting Station, Lhasa, 28 November 1994 (SWB 5 December 1994).

Constitution of the People's Republic of China (Foreign Languages Press, Beijing, 1987).

Deng Xiaoping, 'Speech to the Opening Ceremony of National Conference on Science', 18th March 1978, in Deng Xiaoping, *Speeches and Writings* (Pergamon Press, London, 1984).

Deng Xiaoping, 'Speech to National Conference on Education', 22 April 1978, in Deng Xiaoping, *Speeches and Writings* (Pergamon Press, London, 1984).

Dorje Tsering, 'Report on Economic Problems and Policies in Tibet', Lhasa Radio, 31 March 1986 (SWB 7 April 1986).

'Education Law', 18 March 1995, *Xinhua*, 20 March 1995 (SWB 19 March 1995).

Fei Xiaotong (Vice Chairman of the Eighth NPC Standing Committee), 'Report to the Committee's 22nd Session', *Xinhua*, 26 October 1996 (SWB 28 October 1996).

Gyaltsen Norbu, 'Education in Tibet', Speech to Fifth Regional Meeting on Education in the TAR on 26 October 1994, *Xizang Ribao* (Tibet Daily), 30 October 1994, pp. 1–4).

Gyaltsen Norbu, Work Report on the 'Outline of the TAR's Ninth Five-Year Plan for Economic and Social Development and its Long-Term Target for 2010', *Xizang Ribao* (Tibet Daily), 5 June 1996.

Hu Yaobang, 'Tibetan leaders set six requirements for Tibet', *Xinhua*, 30 May 1980.

Hu Yaobang, 'Report to TAR Regional Party Committee Cadres', Lhasa Radio, 1430 gmt, 30 May 1980 (SWB 4 June 1980).

'Law on Compulsory Education of the People's Republic of China' (Foreign Languages Press, Beijing, 1987).

'Law on Regional Autonomy for "Minority" Nationalities of the People's Republic of China', 1984.

'Law on Teachers', *Xinhua*, 2 November 1993 (SWB 20 November 1993).

'Law on Vocational Education of the People's Republic of China', *Xinhua*, 16 May 1996 (SWB 8 June 1996).

Lhasa Daily, 'To Further the Study, Use and Development of the Tibetan Language – Supplementary Comments by the Lhasa Municipal Education and Sports Committee', *Lhasa Wanbao* (Lhasa Evening News), 25 August 1990.

Lhasa Radio, 'Report of Regional Meeting on Education Work', 1100 gmt, 10 December 1974 (SWB 13 December 1974).

Lhasa Radio, 'Tibet Education Conference', 1100 gmt, 27 December 1974 (SWB 17 January 1975).

Lhasa Radio, 'Struggle against Revisionists in TAR Teacher's College', 1100 gmt, 4 March 1976 (SWB 9 March 1976).

Lhasa Radio, 'Looking Back at 1994 and Looking Forward to 1995: Raising High the Banner of Development', 1100 gmt, 19 January 1995 (FBIS 27 January 1995).

Li Peng, 'Speech on 20th Anniversary of the Founding of the TAR', *Xinhua*, 31 August 1985 (SWB 4 September 1985).

Ngapo Ngawang Jigme, 'Increasing Official Use of the Tibetan Language', Lhasa Radio, 12 July 1987.

Ngapo Ngawang Jigme and Tenth Panchen Lama, 'Proposal on the Study, Use and Development of the Tibetan Language', delivered at Fifth Session of Fourth TAR People's Congress, 9 July 1987, Lhasa Radio 12 July 1987.

'Opinions on Carrying out Work Across the Nation in 1996 to Remedy the Practice of Collecting Unwarranted Fees in Primary and Middle Schools', *Xinhua*, 7 June 1996.

'Outline of the TAR Child Development Programme for the 1990s', *Xizang Ribao* (Tibet Daily), 11 July 1996.

'Outline of the TAR's Five-Year Plan for Economic and Social Development and Its Long-term Target for 2010, Approved by the Fourth Session of the Sixth Regional People's Congress on 24th May 1996', *Xizang Ribao* (Tibet Daily), 7 June 1996.

Phunstok Tsering, TAR CPPCC, Eleventh Bulletin of the Second Plenary Session, May 1994.

'Procedures for the Management of Educational Fund Pooling in Rural Areas', *Xinhua*, 11 March 1994.

'Programme for China's Educational Reform and Development issued by the CCP Central Committee and the State Council,' *Xinhua*, 25 February 1993 (SWB 5 March 1993).

'Raidi and Gyaltsen Norbu Summarize Third Tibet Work Forum Conclusions', *Xizang Ribao* (Tibet Daily; in Chinese), 2 August 1994.

'Report on First Regional Conference on Tibetan Language Teaching', 16–21 July 1991, *Xizang Ribao* (Tibet Daily), 23 July 1991.

'Report to the TAR Party Committee and Government of "Investigation into Unhealthy Tendencies in Pricing, Industries and Exorbitant Fees"', 4 July 1993.

State Education Commission of the PRC, 'Ninth Five-Year Plan for Educational Development Toward the Year 2010' [sic], Beijing, 1996.

State Education Commission of the PRC, Report on the 'Circular on firmly correcting the practice of random collection of fees at secondary and primary schools', *Xinhua*, 27 August 1993 (SWB 20 September 1993).

State Education Commission of the PRC, 'Circular on Managing Funds Raised for Building New Schools, and Regulating Fees Collected in Primary and Secondary Schools', *Xinhua*, 20 December 1994 (SWB 5 January 1995).

TAR CCP, 'Document No. 5 of the Sixth Enlarged Plenary Session of the Standing Committee of the Fourth Congress of the TAR Branch of the CCP', 5 September 1994.

TAR CCP, 'Circular on Patriotic Education', *Xizang Ribao* (Tibet Daily), 22 December 1994.

TAR CPPCC, 'Thirteenth Bulletin of the Second Plenary Session of the Sixth TAR CPPCC', Secretariat of the Conference, 17 May 1994.

TAR CPPCC, 'Report of Second Committee Meeting of the Sixth Session of the TAR CPPCC', CPPCC News Bulletin, 18 May 1994.

TAR CPPCC, 'Report of the Fourth Plenary Session of the Sixth CPPCC of the TAR', 5 May 1996.

TAR CPPCC, 'Summary Report of the Fourth Plenary Session of the Sixth TAR CPPCC', Secretariat of the Conference, 15 May 1996.

TAR Education Commission and Guiding Committee on Spoken and Written Tibetan, 'Report on Tibet Medium Secondary Education', *Podjong Lobsu* (Tibet Education), No. 4, 1995.

Tenzin (TAR Deputy Party Secretary), 'Report of Speech to First Regional Conference on Tibetan Language Teaching', 16–21 July 1991, *Xizang Ribao* (Tibet Daily), 23 July 1991.

Tenzin (TAR Deputy Party Secretary), 'Speech to Meeting of TAR Guiding Committee on Spoken and Written Tibetan', 16 March 1993, *Dakpo* (The Owner), No. 2, 1993 (TAR General Trade Union).

Tenzin (TAR Deputy Party Secretary), 'Speech to TAR Education Conference' *Tibet Education*, No. 2, 1997.

Tibet Radio, 'Report of a Ceremony in Lhasa on 16th July to Mark the Foundation of the TAR Teachers' College', 1100 gmt, 17 July 1975 (SWB 23 July 1975).

Upton, Janet, 'Home on the Grasslands? Tradition, Modernity, and the Negotiation of Identity by Tibetan Intellectuals in the PRC', in Melissa J. Brown (ed.), *Negotiating Ethnicities in China and Taiwan,* China Research Monograph 46 (Center for Chinese Studies, University of California, 1996).

Yat Ming Leung, 'The People's Republic of China', in *Education and Development in East Asia* (Garland Press, London, 1995).

Zhu Kaixuan, 'Report to Fourth Session of Eighth National People's Congress Standing Committee on Educational Work', *Xinhua*, 28 October 1993 (SWB 10 November 1993).

Unpublished documents

Specialized Plan for the TAR Territory (internal government document), 1993 (Document reference: 47VH).

Teacher Training in Agricultural and Pastoral Areas (internal TAR government document), December 1995 (Document reference: 43VE).

Paper on Education Development in Tibet, by Tibetan scholar, 1995.

Internal government education planning document, November 1995 (Document reference: CB1).

Internal Party discussion paper, 1995 (Document reference: 12VJ).

Internal Party discussion paper, 1996.

Research document on education in Tibet, by Tibetan scholar, 1996 (Document reference: CBprop).

Internal TAR government planning document, October 1996 (Document reference: CBD10).

Research Paper on Education in the TAR, 1995 (Document reference: CB6).

Patriotic Education: Test Paper from a Lhasa Secondary School, 1990 (Document reference: 4ZQ).

Circular from Secondary School in Lhasa, 3 January 1989 (Document reference: 7R).

Interviews

A Lhasa primary school teacher, April 1993 (Document reference: 7YK).

Education official, October 1994 (Document reference: 3wz.doc).

Education official, 10 November 1996 (Document reference: CB14).

Educationalist, 2 February 1997 (Document reference: CB3).

Former educationalist in the TAR, January 1996 (Document reference: Dr-List).

Former TAR government cadre, 28 July 1997 (Document reference: CB13).

Former teacher at Tibet University, 2 February 1997.

Gongkar Gyatso, teacher at Tibet University 1985–1992, 2 February 1997.

Graduate of Tibet University, 2 February 1997 (Document reference: CB12).

Interview, 1993 (Document reference: 8YC).

Interview, 17 January 1993 (Document reference: 4YB).

Interview, 5 March 1993 (Document reference: 8YE).

Interview, 18 August 1993 (Document reference: 2YS).

Lhasa government official, 8 August 1996 (Document reference: 28VG).

Palden Gyal, 20 October 1996 (Document reference: CB5).

Rural county secondary school, Gannan Tibetan prefecture, Gansu province, 1995 (Document reference: 14VH).

Secondary school teacher, 1995 (Document reference: R66).

Senior Tibetan religious leader, 17 February 1997 (Document reference CB2).

Tibetan educationalist, 7 August 1996 (Document reference CB11).

Tibetan historian, August 1996 (Document reference CB10).

Tibetan parent, 1990 (Document reference: T10BB).

Tibetan parent, 7 August 1996 (Document reference: CB4).

Tibetan student, 23 October 1994 (Document reference: RV-FV2).

Tibetan teacher, 10 October 1996 (Document reference: CB9).

Tsering Shakya, Tibetan historian, 4 January and 24 July 1997.

Index

Zed Titles in its Politics in Contemporary Asia Series

Asia has come to prominence in recent years because of its economic dynamism, despite the dramatic financial collapse of 1997–98. But the decade-long economic success of this highly diverse continent has been dependent on the maintenance of effective government. It can also lead, as the Zed Books Series on Politics in Contemporary Asia shows, to the downplaying of the region's many political problems in the areas of ethnicity, religious identity, democratic control and human rights.

C. Beyrer, *War in the Blood: Sex, Politics and AIDS in Southeast Asia*

L. Chorbajian, P. Donabedian and C. Mutafian, *The Caucasian Knot: The History and Geopolitics of Nagorno-Karabagh*

P. Donnet, *Tibet: Survival in Question*

S. Goldenberg, *Pride of Small Nations: The Caucasus and Post-Soviet Disorder*

J. Goodno, *The Philippines: Land of Broken Promises*

S. Gopal (ed.), *Anatomy of a Confrontation: Ayodhya and the Rise of Communal Politics in India*

P. Marsden, *The Taliban: War, Religion and the New Order in Afghanistan*

G. Ogle, *South Korea: Dissent within the Economic Miracle*

J. Pettigrew, *The Sikhs of the Punjab: Unheard Voices of State and Guerrilla Violence*

A. Rashid, *The Resurgence of Central Asia: Islam or Nationalism?*

W. Courtland Robinson, *Terms of Refuge: The Indochinese Exodus and the International Response*

M. Smith, *Burma: Insurgency and the Politics of Ethnicity* (rev. edn. 1998)

J. Taylor, *Indonesia's Forgotten War: The Hidden History of East Timor*

For full details of this list and Zed's other Asia titles, as well as our subject catalogues, please write to:

The Marketing Department, Zed Books, 7 Cynthia Street, London N1 9JF, UK or email: sales@zedbooks.demon.co.uk

Visit our website at: http://www.zedbooks.demon.co.uk